Hearing Voices, Demonic and Divine

CW00801306

Experiences of hearing the voice of God (or angels, demons, or other spiritual beings) have generally been understood either as religious experiences or else as a feature of mental illness. Some critics of traditional religious faith have dismissed the visions and voices attributed to biblical characters and saints as evidence of mental disorder. However, it is now known that many ordinary people, with no other evidence of mental disorder, also hear voices and that these voices not infrequently include spiritual or religious content. Psychological and interdisciplinary research has shed a revealing light on these experiences in recent years, so that we now know much more about the phenomenon of "hearing voices" than ever before.

The present work considers biblical, historical, and scientific accounts of spiritual and mystical experiences of voice hearing in the Christian tradition in order to explore how some voices may be understood theologically as revelatory. It is proposed that in the incarnation, Christian faith finds both an understanding of what it is to be fully human (a theological anthropology), and God's perfect self-disclosure (revelation). Within such an understanding, revelatory voices represent a key point of interpersonal encounter between human beings and God.

Christopher C. H. Cook is Professor of Spirituality, Theology and Health in the Department of Theology and Religion at Durham University, an Honorary Minor Canon at Durham Cathedral, and an Honorary Chaplain with Tees, Esk and Wear Valleys NHS Foundation Trust (TEWV). He trained in medicine, at St George's Hospital Medical School, London, and then undertook postgraduate training in psychiatry at Guys Hospital, London. He was an Honorary Consultant Psychiatrist with TEWV until 2017. Christopher was ordained as an Anglican priest in 2001. He has research doctorates in psychiatry and in theology and is Director of the Centre for Spirituality, Theology and Health at Durham University. He is the author of *The Philokalia and the Inner Life* (James Clarke, 2011) and co-editor of *Spirituality and Narrative in Psychiatric Practice* (with Andrew Powell and Andrew Sims, RCPsych Press, 2016) and *Spirituality, Theology & Mental Health* (SCM Press, 2013). He is a member of the core research team for the Hearing the Voice project at Durham University.

"With expertise in both theology and psychiatry, Professor Christopher Cook is ideally placed to examine the complexities around the hearing of voices in spiritual and religious contexts. His book is an authoritative and comprehensive guide to the scientific and theological research in the area. It is also a delightfully engaging read."

Charles Fernyhough, Director and Principle Investigator, Hearing the Voice, Durham University, UK

"*Hearing Voices, Demonic and Divine*, is a careful and comprehensive account of the voice-hearing phenomenon. Unlike other such surveys, Cook takes seriously the possibility that voices communicate divine intention. Cook explores the vexed problem of discerning whether and when spirit speaks with thoughtfulness, empathy and wise caution."

Tanya Marie Luhrmann, Howard H. and Jessie T. Watkins University Professor of Anthropology, Stanford University, USA

"The experience of hearing voices is something that is common to religious experiences and to those experiences that some determine as unusual or pathological. Untangling the complex origins and meanings of voice hearing is not an easy task, especially if we take into consideration issues around religion and theology. The dual temptation to under or over spiritualise voice hearing is alluring and difficult to avoid. Christopher Cook recognises this difficult tension, but also realises that it is not enough simply to partition voices with some assumed to be the responsibility of psychiatrists and others open to the discernment of religion and theology. The phenomenon of voice hearing requires an integrated approach that takes seriously the insights that can be gleaned from disciplines such as psychiatry, psychology, biology and neurology, whilst at the same time taking equally as seriously the insights that theology and Christian tradition brings to the conversation. All of these perspectives in turn require to take cognisance of the profound importance of listening to the personal narratives of voice hearers. Voices do not occur apart from people. If we forget that we risk losing the soul of our therapeutic and scientific endeavours. It is within this crucial hospitable conversation that new insights and fresh possibilities emerge. This powerful and well-argued interdisciplinary reflection on hearing voices opens up vital space for re-thinking the phenomenon of voice hearing and opening up new possibilities for understanding and responding. This is a helpful and important book."

John Swinton, Professor in Practical Theology and Pastoral Care and Chair in Divinity and Religious Studies, University of Aberdeen, UK

Hearing Voices, Demonic and Divine

Scientific and Theological Perspectives

Christopher C. H. Cook

Routledge
Taylor & Francis Group
LONDON AND NEW YORK

First published 2019
by Routledge
2 Park Square, Milton Park, Abingdon, Oxon OX14 4RN

and by Routledge
52 Vanderbilt Avenue, New York, NY 10017

First issued in paperback 2020

Routledge is an imprint of the Taylor & Francis Group, an informa business

British Library Cataloguing-in-Publication Data
A catalogue record for this book is available from the British Library

Library of Congress Cataloging-in-Publication Data
Names: Cook, Chris (Christopher C.H.), author.
Title: Hearing voices, demonic and divine : scientific and theological
    perspectives / Christopher C.H. Cook.
Description: New York : Routledge, 2018. | Includes bibliographical references
    and index.
Identifiers: LCCN 2018032892| ISBN 9781472453983 (hardback : alk. paper) |
    ISBN 9780429750953 (pdf) | ISBN 9780429750946 (epub) |
    ISBN 9780429750939 (mobi)
Subjects: LCSH: Hearing—Religious aspects—Christianity. | Spirits. |
    Experience (Religion) | Auditory hallucinations.
Classification: LCC BV4509.5 .C6596 2018 | DDC 248.2/9—dc23
LC record available at https://lccn.loc.gov/2018032892

ISBN 13: 978-0-367-58243-2 (pbk)
ISBN 13: 978-1-4724-5398-3 (hbk)

Typeset in Sabon
by Swales & Willis Ltd, Exeter, Devon, UK

This book is dedicated to Andrew and Bibs, Beth and James, Rachel and Milo, Jonathan and Sarah, and to all our grandchildren.

Contents

Acknowledgements

I would like to acknowledge the help of many colleagues who have helped to shape my thinking as I have been writing this book, as well as many who have written to me, and talked with me, about their own experiences of hearing voices. I am particularly grateful to all of my colleagues in the Hearing the Voice project at Durham University, and especially Charles Fernyhough, Ben Alderson-Day, Corinne Saunders, Pat Waugh, and Angela Woods. I have learned so much from them, and from the wider team, especially at Friday afternoon meetings of Voice Club, but also in collegial conversations over coffee and in the many conferences and events on which we have worked together. Charles and Angela have kindly also read and commented on draft chapters of the book.

This book has touched on a variety of areas of scholarship that are not my primary area of expertise. I have learned a lot along the way from my colleagues in the Department of Theology and Religion at Durham University. Especial thanks go to Stephen Barton, Douglas Davies, Jane Heath, Karen Kilby, and Walter Moberly, all of whom read draft chapters and provided me with helpful comments and feedback. Collaborators and friends from far afield have also helped in a variety of ways. Thanks go to all my colleagues in the Spirituality and Psychiatry Special Interest Group at the Royal College of Psychiatrists, and especially to Andrew Powell. Mike Schuck at Loyola University in Chicago helped me in thinking through some of the foundational issues in theology and epistemology.

I am glad to acknowledge support from generous funding provided by the Wellcome Trust (grant numbers WT098455MA and 108720/Z/15/Z). It was this funding that made the writing of the book possible. Wellcome have also provided funding to make the book available on an open access basis.

Finally, as always, my thanks go to my family, and especially my wife Joy, for patient support during the writing of yet another book. I am grateful to them for so much more than can be said here.

Introduction

Voices are important to human beings. Spoken voices enable us to use language socially as a means of communication with one another. Inner voices play an important part in our stream of consciousness, assisting the self-reflection and internal dialogue which enable us to know ourselves. In prayer, both spoken and inner voices become a means of communication with God. Voices, employing words and language to convey meaning, shape our understanding of ourselves as persons and enable us to construct narratives that identify us as individuals in relation to the world around us. Voices are meaningful and significant to human creatures.[1]

The existence of a voice implies the presence of a speaker and the hearing of a voice invites the possibility of listening to what has been said. Listening to our inner voices, we become self-aware. Listening to the voices of others, we become socially aware. Having a "voice" is a crucial part of the fabric of human community. The fact that people sometimes hear voices in the absence of any visibly present speaker is therefore highly paradoxical and begs explanation. Voices are not random sounds that arise by chance. They are created, spoken, by intentional agents. The experience of hearing of a voice therefore necessitates that there must – somewhere – be a speaker. That speaker may be the unconscious self, or it may be that the voice is recorded or transmitted by means of technology from some remote time or place, but somewhere, sometime, the presumption is that someone must have spoken.

Theology is fundamentally concerned with listening to voices. This is most obviously the case in the domain of practical theology, where, for example, Jane Leach (2007) has explicitly emphasised the importance of giving careful attention to voices – both human and divine – as a core pastoral concern. It is also true more widely, however, in that theology is usually understood to be concerned with a certain kind of discourse – a process of speaking and listening – in relation to God. As will be discussed in later chapters, this may be especially evident in relation to the Abrahamic faiths, where the voice of God – directly or indirectly – plays a significant part in the creation and content of holy scripture. It is true also, however, in the other monotheistic traditions and in Eastern religion – with the possible exception of Buddhism.

Where a voice is heard in the absence of any visible speaker, within most faith traditions, the possibility therefore arises that it might be the voice of God, or at least of an angelic or spiritual being. As a part of a multimodal visionary experience, voices may also be heard as spoken by a visible – but not material – spiritual presence. According to some attempts to chart the history of such phenomena, visions and voices up until the 19th century were generally understood as spiritual or mystical experiences and thus veridical (Aleman and Larøi, 2009, p.10). Now, they are more likely to be understood as erroneous perceptions and are generally referred to in the scientific literature as hallucinations. In the minds of many, including many mental health professionals, they are indicative of mental disorder and yet – as will become clear later in this book – they are very often experienced by people who demonstrate no evidence of mental disorder.

This book will be concerned primarily with theological and spiritual understandings of voices (auditory verbal hallucinations) in the Christian tradition. Brief consideration will also be given to the occurrence of such experiences in some other faith traditions, and to the experiences of those who would define themselves as "spiritual but not religious". This general area of interest is important for a number of reasons. First, it is important within the Christian churches (and other faith communities) in relation to the spiritual and pastoral task of discerning whether – if ever – such voices convey spiritual truth. How may "erroneous perceptions" be distinguished from genuine spiritual experience in the lives of those who report experiences of seeing visions and hearing voices? When someone claims to have heard the voice of God, should they be encouraged to treat this voice as divine, or should they be encouraged to question it as coming from somewhere else, perhaps from their own unconscious? And if the voice claims to speak for the benefit of others, or for the wider community or congregation, how should others respond? Second, and similarly, it is important for mental health professionals to have some way of distinguishing between "normal" religious experience and phenomena which are symptomatic of mental disorder. Is there a difference between religious hallucinations as a symptom of mental disorder and hearing the voice of God as a religious experience? Third, however, it raises important theological questions of a wider kind. Are the voices heard by biblical figures such as Moses, Jesus, or Paul of a similar kind to those reported by voice hearers today? How have voices featured, and been understood, within the subsequent tradition? What part do voices play in Christian religious experience? How may the growing scientific account of how such experiences come about be reconciled with a theology of revelation? What does it mean to say that a voice was God's voice? May God ever be understood as speaking to people through experiences of voice hearing?

Before moving on to any attempt to respond to these questions, it is necessary to define some terms and, in particular, to be clear about exactly what is meant in this book by "hearing voices".

Hallucinations

There seems to be general agreement that hallucinations have been a part of human experience since ancient times. Most famously, Socrates (469–399 BCE) heard a voice, which he understood to be divine (Smith, 2007, pp.141–164).[2] In Latin, the term "*alucinari*", or "*hallucinari*", appears in classical literature. It is not, however, commonly employed and has more of a sense of "raving", mind wandering, or dreaming than of what we would now think of as hallucinations. The physician Aretaeus of Cappadocia (Kotsopoulos, 1986), who lived in perhaps the 1st or 3rd century CE, described hallucinations as a feature of phrenitis (delirium) in terms recognisably similar to modern usage: "the senses are perverted, so that they see things not present as if they were present, and objects which do not appear to others, manifest themselves to them" (Adams, 1856, p.303).

The term "hallucination" first appears in English medical usage in 1798 (Rojcewicz and Rojcewicz, 1997). In the late 19th century the term was introduced into psychiatry, initially in France, by Jean-Etienne Esquirol (1772–1840). Esquirol understood hallucinations, which he recognised as occurring in any sensory modality, and which he distinguished from illusions, invariably to have pathological significance. Others, such as Brierre de Boismont (1797–1881), recognised both pathological and physiological (normal) forms of hallucination. The essential characteristic of hallucinations, however, was generally recognised to be a perception-like experience in the absence of an object of sensation.[3]

Recent attempts to define hallucinations with precision have met with difficulties of avoiding ambiguity around such matters as exactly what it means to say that an experience is "perception-like", what kinds of stimulus must be absent, and the extent to which the experience is beyond voluntary control. A good recent definition, which addresses all of these matters as far as is reasonably possible, is that provided by Anthony David:

> A sensory experience which occurs in the absence of corresponding external stimulation of the relevant sense organ, has a sufficient sense of reality to resemble a veridical perception, over which the subject does not feel s/he has direct and voluntary control, and which occurs in the awake state.
>
> (David, 2004, p.110)

Following Esquirol, hallucinations are still generally distinguished from illusions, the latter arising from a misperception of a stimulus, rather than a perception in the absence of a stimulus. The distinction between the two is, however, not always clear, as hallucinations may be triggered by environmental stimuli (Aleman and Larøi, 2009, pp.18–19).

It has also long been popular to distinguish between pseudohallucinations, defined by Karl Jaspers (1883–1969) as occuring in subjective inner space, and true hallucinations, located in objective external space. The latter have generally been understood as assuming greater diagnostic significance. The proper definition of a pseudohallucination has, however, been contested and the distinction is now not generally thought to be helpful (Slade and Bentall, 1988, pp.18–19, Aleman and Larøi, 2009, pp.19–20).

Fundamentally, hallucinations are phenomena that occur in the waking state – or at least in the hinterland between sleep and wakefulness – and so voices that are heard in dreams will not be considered in the present book. However, it is recognised that there are some similarities between dreams and hallucinations and that, possibly, some similar mechanisms are involved in generating them.[4]

Whilst traditionally considered as categorical phenomena, being either present or absent, it was suggested by Strauss (1969), almost 50 years ago, that in fact hallucinations might more accurately be understood as measurable on a number of continua. The tentative criteria proposed were: degree of conviction of objective reality of the experience, degree of absence of direct cultural determinants, degree of preoccupation, and implausibility of the experience. Strauss's proposal is particularly important in respect of religious hallucinations. In particular, the cultural, religious, determinants for hearing the voice of God in prayer render this a very different experience for the Christian person than that of hearing bizarre voices, such as (for example) voices that are believed to have been broadcast by aliens.

Hallucinations may occur in any sensory modality – visual, auditory, olfactory, gustatory, or somatic/tactile. It has also been proposed that a sense of felt presence should be considered as an hallucinatory phenomenon (Critchley, 1979, pp.1–12, Nielsen, 2007, Alderson-Day, 2016). Whilst not (necessarily) associated with any sensory perceptual phenomenology, such experiences are yet associated with a sense of awareness of the presence of a person or other external object (Sato and Berrios, 2003). They thus have a perception-like quality to them. They are sometimes associated with the hearing of a voice. They are experienced as a common feature of sleep paralysis, in bereavement, in extreme survival situations, in Parkinson's disease, in Lewy body dementia, following traumatic brain injury, and in association with other brain lesions and epileptic foci (Cheyne, 2012, Alderson-Day, 2016).

Multimodal hallucinations

Unimodal hallucinations are experienced in only one modality, but hallucinations are not uncommonly experienced in multiple modalities, even if not at the same time. Terminology here is confusing and inconsistent, but multimodal hallucinations are most broadly and simply defined as hallucinations experienced by a person in two or more sensory modalities, and more narrowly defined as "[H]allucinations occuring simultaneously in more than one modality that are experienced as emanating from a single source" (Chesterman, 1994, p.275).

Unfortunately, the narrower definition does not adequately distinguish between all of the permutations and possibilities. Hallucinations in multiple modalities do not necessarily occur simultaneously and, even if they do, are not necessarily experienced as emanating from a single source. Even if they are experienced as emanating from a single source, they may not be coherent or integrated. For example, auditory verbal hallucinations might be perceived as emanating from a visual hallucination of a chair, rather than from a human speaker. In order to clarify the multiple possibilities for future research, Lim et al. (2016) have proposed first that a distinction should be made between serial and simultaneous multimodal hallucinations:

a) Serial multimodal hallucinations are experienced in two or more sensory modalities at different moments in time.
b) Simultaneous multimodal hallucinations are experienced in two or more sensory modalities simultaneously.

Lim further propose a distinction between incongruent and congruent simultaneous hallucinations:[5]

i   Incongruent multimodal hallucinations are experienced in two or more sensory modalities simultaneously, but do not add up to a coherent whole.
ii Congruent multimodal hallucination (also known as compound hallucinations) are experienced in two or more sensory modalities simultaneously and do add up to a coherent whole.

Multimodal hallucinations may not be as rare as is often assumed, but relatively little is known about their prevalence or phenomenology. Lim et al. (2016) found that in a study of 750 patients with schizophrenia spectrum disorder, 27 per cent reported only unimodal hallucinations, but 53 per cent reported multimodal hallucinations. Unfortunately, they were not able to distinguish in this study between serial or simultaneous multimodal hallucinations, let alone congruent or incongruent simultaneous multimodal hallucinations.

Daniel Dennett, approaching the matter from a rather different perspective, has proposed a category of "strong hallucinations", by which he means:

A hallucination of an apparently concrete and persisting three-dimensional object in the real world – as contrasted to flashes, geometric distortions, auras, afterimages, fleeting phantom-limb experiences, and other anomalous sensations. A strong hallucination would be, say, a ghost that talked back, that permitted you to touch it, that resisted with a sense of solidarity, that cast a shadow, that was visible from any angle so that you might walk around it and see what its back looked like.

(Dennett, 1991, p.7)

Dennett suggests that strong hallucinations are "simply impossible". He proposes, however, that hallucinations might be ranked by the number of features of strong hallucinations that they have and that "Reports of *very* strong hallucinations are rare", so that "the credibility of such reports seems, intuitively, to be inversely proportional to the strength of the hallucination reported" (p.7). Dennett therefore distinguishes between "really strong hallucinations" and "convincing, multi-modal hallucinations". Whereas the former – according to Dennett – do not occur, the latter are not infrequent.

Auditory verbal hallucinations (AVHs)

Auditory hallucinations may take the form of a variety of non-verbal sounds, such as music, whispers, cries, clicks and bangs (Nayani and David, 1996). Where voices are involved, they are referred to as auditory verbal hallucinations (AVHs),[6] and this will be the preferred term throughout the present book. However, the definition proposed above allows for hallucinations that might be identified as arising within inner subjective space, as well as externally, and some voices that people report hearing are more "thought-like" than auditory (Woods et al., 2015). There is therefore a place for talking about verbal hallucinations, as distinct from auditory verbal hallucinations, in order to emphasise that a voice is not "out loud". Where it is helpful to do so, this terminology will be adopted accordingly in the present book. However, in one recent survey, more than a third of subjects either experienced a mixture of auditory and thought-like voices, or else experienced voices that were somewhere between auditory and thought-like (Woods et al., 2015). It may therefore be more helpful to think of a spectrum of voices ranging between those that are more "thought-like" and those that are more auditory.

People who hear voices tend not to use the word "hallucination" in reference to their voices (Karlsson, 2008). Similarly, people who hear a voice as a part of a religious experience do not typically identify themselves either as voice hearers or as having experienced an hallucination. Whilst the term "hallucination" would still seem to be the most appropriate, accurate, and critical term for academic usage – whether in scientific or theological work – the definition in terms of an absence of "external stimulation" might be taken by some to deny the "reality" of the experience. It is easily understood as carrying a sense of being mistaken, or deceived, and is popularly associated with mental illness.

Religious experiences involving visual hallucinations, many of which may also include voices (and are thus multimodal), are usually referred to as visionary.[7] In the context of Christian mystical experience, voices are often referred to as "locutions", but this term does not have the same popularity of contemporary usage, and so there is no widely accepted equivalent term to "visionary" for the auditory verbal component of a religious experience. However, many people reporting their religious experiences of hearing a voice, whilst not seeing themselves as "voice hearers", do still refer to "the voice".[8]

The preferred critical terminology in the present book will therefore generally be that of (auditory) verbal hallucinations. However, it is also important to adopt where possible the preferred vocabulary of the author when discussing first person accounts of religious experience in order to avoid prematurely imposing a (privileged) external interpretation of their experience. This is especially important in relation to premodern texts. It is anachronistic to refer to "hallucinations" in synchronic accounts of historical contexts which long predated modern understandings of the term, and the term will therefore be reserved largely for discussion of the modern literature and the diachronic perspective.

Voices in the population at large

Surveys of the normal population have revealed a wide variety of estimates of the prevalence of voice hearing, from as low as 0.6 per cent (Ohayon, 2000) to as high as 84 per cent (Millham and Easton, 1998) but with figures in the range of 3 to 20 per cent commonly reported (Eaton et al., 1991, Verdoux et al., 1998, Johns et al., 2002, Beavan et al., 2011). It is clear that age, gender, and ethnicity are important variables, with voice hearing being reported more commonly amongst some ethnic minority groups (Schwab, 1977, Johns et al., 2002), women (Tien, 1991), and – less consistently – younger adults (Tien, 1991). It is clearly also important to define carefully exactly what constitutes "hearing a voice", with criteria for frequency, nature, and content of the experience making quite a difference to estimated prevalence (Posey and Losch, 1983, Barrett and Etheridge, 1992).

There does not appear to have been much (or any) scientific research on the experience of voices that lack a perceptual quality, although this depends to some extent on how one understands the validity and nature of the distinction between true hallucinations and pseudohallucinations. "Imaginal dialogues", as characterised by Watkins (2000),[9] which may or may not have perceptual qualities, may be a near-universal feature of childhood, but as adults (at least in the Western world) we are strongly predisposed to identifying imaginal voices as aspects of the self, and thus as experiences that do not occur outside of the realms of artistic creativity, mental illness, or spiritual/religious experience.

Hallucinations in various modalities – including AVHs – are commonly experienced in bereavement. In an early study in the *British Medical Journal* (Rees, 1971), almost half of a group of nearly 300 widows and widowers reported some kind of experience of the presence of their spouse after they had died: 14 per cent had actually seen their dead husband or wife, 13 per cent had heard him/her, and 3 per cent had experienced being touched by him/her. In a more recent study in Sweden (Grimby, 1993), 89 per cent of a sample of 14 men and 36 women in their early 70s reported hallucinations and/or illusions 1 month after bereavement. AVHs were reported by 30 per cent at 1 month, by 19 per cent at 3 months, and by 6 per cent at 12 months.[10]

Voices as symptoms of mental disorder

AVHs are commonly encountered amongst those diagnosed as suffering from psychotic disorders. However, as with surveys of the normal population, there appears to be a wide range of estimates as to actual prevalence, varying from under 30 per cent to over 80 per cent (Mueser et al., 1990, Verdoux et al., 1998, Ndetei and Singh, 1983, Bauer et al., 2011). There would appear to be significant cultural variation, and it has been suggested that prevalence is higher in African, West Indian, and Asian groups, and lower in Austria and Georgia (Ndetei and Vadher, 1984, Bauer et al., 2011). There is also significant diagnostic variation, with prevalence much higher in schizophrenia than in bipolar disorder or psychotic depression (Baethge et al., 2005).

It is clear that hallucinations are transdiagnostic phenomena, occuring in non-psychotic as well as psychotic disorders (Van Os and Reininghaus, 2016). Given that hallucinations also occur in people who are not diagnosed with any psychiatric disorder, the question arises as to the relationship between hallucinations occuring in the (undiagnosed) general population and in those receiving treatment from mental health services. Traditionally, psychiatry regarded schizophrenia and other diagnositic categories of psychosis as categorically and qualitatively different from normality. Increasingly, in recent years, this view has been questioned and there is now evidence to understand psychotic-like experiences observed in individuals in the general population as being on a quantitative continuum with those observed in mental illness (Johns and Os, 2001, Van Os et al., 2009). According to this view, those who have such experiences (for example, delusions or hallucinations), most of which are transitory, may be at higher risk of development of psychosis. However, this view is controversial and is argued against both on scientific grounds, and on the clinical utility of the categorical approach (Lawrie, 2016, Parnas and Henriksen, 2016, Tandon, 2016).

In a comparison of 18 patients diagnosed with schizophrenia, 15 patients diagnosed with dissociative disorder, and 15 non-patient voice hearers, the form of the hallucinations in each group was found to be similar, but the non-patient group perceived their voices in a much more positive way in comparison with the neutral/negative experiences of the patient groups (Honig et al., 1998). Stanghellini et al. (2012), in a comparison of patients with schizophrenia and healthy university students, found that, whilst both groups gave positive responses to standard questions about hallucinations (from the Revised Hallucination Scale), they gave very different descriptions of their experiences. Whereas for patients the experiences were concerned with their sense of identity, and their relationship to the world around them, for students the experiences tended to be circumstantial (for example, related to bereavement) or isolated experiences.

Spiritual and religious voices

Religious hallucinations are not uncommon, but there is no widely accepted definition of exactly what a "religious" hallucination is (Cook, 2015). Clearly, if someone reports a vision of Christ, as a result of which they are converted to Christianity, this might be described as a religious hallucination, or at least a religious visionary experience. But suppose someone reports experiencing visions of Christ and yet does not wish to renounce their atheistic beliefs?[11] To ascribe this as a religious experience when it is not understood as such by the subject would seem to be presumptuous. Voices understood to be those of disembodied "spirits", deceased relatives, or arising as a result of magic, are also more difficult to classify.

In the healthcare context, in inter-faith dialogue, and in other areas of discourse, it has become popular in recent years to distinguish between spirituality and religion (Cook, 2012b). Whilst the concept of spirituality is generally intended to be more inclusive, people (including people who hear voices) may now see themselves as spiritual and religious, spiritual but not religious, religious but not spiritual, or neither spiritual nor religious. Both spirituality and religion are contested concepts which have proved elusive of any universally accepted and unambiguous definition. If it is difficult to clearly distinguish between religious and non-religious voices, it would seem even more difficult to know how to objectively classify some voices as "spiritual" and others not.

One definition of spirituality, designed to gain as wide acceptance as possible for clinical use, is:

> Spirituality is a distinctive, potentially creative and universal dimension of human experience arising both within the inner subjective awareness of individuals and within communities, social groups and traditions. It may be experienced as relationship with that which is intimately "inner", immanent and personal, within the self and others, and/or as relationship with that which is wholly "other", transcendent and beyond the self. It is experienced as being of fundamental or ultimate importance and is thus concerned with matters of meaning and purpose in life, truth and values.
>
> (Cook, 2004)

Such an understanding of spirituality draws attention to the multifaceted nature of all voices. They have an inner, subjective, dimension as well as a social dimension. They may variously impact upon understanding of relationships with self, others, and a wider (perhaps transcendent) reality. They are understood as more or less important (usually more), perhaps fundamentally important, and they impact upon self-understanding of meaning and purpose in life. The definition asserts that spirituality is a "potentially creative and universal dimension of human experience". Whilst respecting that some people choose to self-define as neither spiritual nor religious, it might still be asserted that all voices are potentially spiritually significant. To acknowledge that for some people voices are not spiritual is thus a matter of self-identification on the part of the person hearing the voice.

The same might be said of religious voices. If the person who hears the voice is not religious, and does not understand their hearing of a voice as being a religious experience, it would generally seem unnecessary and unhelpful to impose any religious label upon them. However, for the purposes of research, it might still be important to distinguish between the hearer of the voice, the voice, and what is said by the voice. Thus the identity of the voice hearer, the identity of the voice, and the content of what is said might each be considered religious or not religious, and various possible combinations and kinds of religious voices might be envisaged accordingly.

Further attention will be given to voice hearing in contemporary spiritual and religious context (including the experiences of those who identify themselves as spiritual but not religious) in Chapter 1. The relationship between voice hearing and religion will be considered more carefully in Chapter 2.

Christians and voices

Chapters 4 to 8 of the present volume will focus almost entirely upon the Christian tradition. It is necessary to begin this study, in Chapter 3, with a focus on Hebrew scripture, such has been the impact of what Christians refer to as the Old Testament upon the subsequent tradition. However, it will not be possible here to give any detailed attention to subsequent Hebrew tradition, or to contemporary Jewish experience.

It might easily be argued that there are more examples of voices that look like the contemporary phenomenon of "voice hearing", or AVHs, in the Old Testament than in the New Testament. Conversations wth God and angels abound, especially in the earlier books of the canon, and it might well be argued that the early and later prophets must have all had some kind of experience of hearing the "voice" of God, even though we are given much more information about what they believed God had said than about their experiences of hearing it. Whether or not these arguments are critically sustainable will be the subject matter of Chapter 3.

In Chapter 4, attention will turn to the New Testament. Whilst there are relatively few accounts of the hearing of voices in Christian scripture, those that are identifiable are significant. Thus, for example, Jesus hears a heavenly voice at his baptism in the synoptic gospels, and Saul hears a voice at his conversion – as narrated in the book of Acts. The New Testament concludes with an apocalyptic visionary panorama, which includes many voices, in the book of Revelation.

In Chapter 5, attention will turn to experiences of voice hearing in the Christian tradition, and in Chapter 6 the focus will be on voice hearing as Christian religious experience. I have been very aware that this distinction is somewhat contrived, but I think that it is necessary for a number of reasons. First, it is important to consider ways in which voice hearing has become established within the tradition, because tradition is itself a significant theological resource. The fact that Christians have, over many centuries, reported hearing the voice of God, as well as voices of angels and demons, influences both Christian theology and the expectations that help to shape contemporary religious experience. Second, the study of ancient texts is necessarily a different task than the study of modern texts. The older a text is, and the more separated from us by time, culture, and language, the more cautious we need to be about our assertions as to its relationship with any underlying experience of either the author or other persons about whom it makes particular claims. Chapter 5 therefore focuses more on older texts, and Chapter 6 draws mainly on recently published texts, and on publications from the social sciences. However, some older texts provide important insights into Christian experience, and some recent texts may tell us more about the expectations and beliefs of living traditions (evangelical, catholic, etc.) than about any underlying "experience". Third, there is increasingly unanimous recognition that there is no such thing as pure experience separated from culture, tradition, or other beliefs. We must therefore be wary about any implication that tradition and experience can be separated, and the division of material between these two chapters in no way implies that they can.

Interdisciplinary perspectives on voice hearing

The present volume arises from the involvement of the author as a Co-Investigator in the Hearing the Voice project at Durham University.[12] The project team is multidisciplinary, drawing on the insights of the humanities as well as the social and medical sciences. It has worked closely with both voice hearers and clinicians, and has sought to give careful attention to an understanding of the phenomenology of the experience that prioritises first person accounts at a number of different contextual levels (Woods et al., 2014). Within this approach, theology has had an important part to play. Theology and the humanities perhaps most especially seek to balance an understanding of how we may understand the causes and mechanisms of voice hearing with an understanding of what it means to the individual and to wider society. In the clinical context, voices have for too long been generally understood as meaningless, except insofar as they represent signs and symptoms of diagnosable disorder.

This lack of interest in the meaning of the experience is now changing, as it is increasingly recognised that the content of what voices say can be spiritually, culturally, and biographically highly meaningful. Classics of English literature, such as the *Revelations of Divine Love* by Julian of Norwich and the *Book of Margery Kempe*, give every appearance of having resulted from experiences of the hearing of voices in religious and cultural context.

That such books are still read with interest in itself is significant testimony to the potential meaningfulness of experiences of voice hearing. At an individual level, the biographical significance of what voices say is now recognised as clinically, personally, and spiritually important to those who hear them.

On the other hand, the increasing body of scientific knowledge about the nature of AVHs sheds a new theological light upon the voices that have been passed down from earliest Christian times. That the "voices" of the Old and New Testaments have not previously been examined in the light of this research seems a surprising omission, given the enormous impact that social scientific methods are now making in biblical studies. Biblical scholarship is not my primary area of academic expertise, and so the present volume represents only some preliminary thoughts of an interested observer as to where this field of endeavour might take us in the future. I am, however, interested as a theologian and scientist at first hand in the ongoing debate as to the relationship between theology and science. In Chapter 7, some first steps will be taken in terms of exploring how a dialogue between science and theology might illuminate our understanding of what it means – within the Christian tradition – to assert that people hear the voice of God.

This book therefore works with "data" from a variety of different sources – historical, scriptural, empirical/scientific, and narratival. Whilst it is important to recognise the different contributions that these different sources of information bring to the topic at hand, and the different ways in which they should be properly analysed and interpreted, they are each valuable in their own way. A fundamental assumption of this book is that a purely scientific account of voice hearing is just as unsatisfactory as a purely spiritual, theological, or religious account. It is in the integration of disciplinary perspectives that a fuller understanding of the phenomenon is to be gained.

Theological anthropology

The understanding of human nature adopted in this book is firmly theological and, more specifically, Christological. However, it is also inherently multidisciplinary, recognising that both the social and biological sciences, as well as the humanities, significantly inform our understanding of what it is to be human.

Following the methodology outlined by Marc Cortez (2015), and recognising that there are significant counterarguments, it is nonetheless proposed here that Jesus Christ offers the fundamental theological starting point for a Christian anthropology appropriate to the topic at hand. As Cortez acknowledges, there are problems associated with any assumption that a universal understanding of what it is to be human should be located in the life of a particular, 1st-century, Jewish man. Nor is this concern in any way alleviated by traditional Christian doctrines that assert both the humanity and the divinity of Jesus. Even if sharing in our humanity, surely Jesus is, in important ways, different than the rest of us? Nonetheless, voices are heard at significant points in the gospel narratives by Jesus' mother, by Jesus himself, and by his disciples.[13] To what extent we can assert the similarity of these experiences to those of contemporary voice hearers will be a critical question to be addressed later in this book. However, a Christological starting point, asserting that a life lived most fully in harmony with God, amidst all its particularities of gender, culture, and history should be marked by experiences of this kind, at least avoids the usual assumptions surrounding voice hearing as pathology and the absence of voices as normative. Rather, it is asserted here, there is a receptivity within the human soul/mind to God which, at least sometimes, might take the form of "hearing" a voice.

In the prologue to John's gospel, Jesus is introduced as the "Word made flesh". This particular man is – according to traditional Christian understanding – the unique means by which God's voice is heard in human history.[14] To adopt a Christological perspective is therefore also a self-consciously Christian choice. It is to assert that our understanding of what it means to be human is most fully revealed in the life of the man whom Christians look to as the unique exemplar of life lived according to divine purpose.

The anthropology adopted will also be thoroughly multidisciplinary, although inevitably drawing upon some scientific disciplines more than others. Studies of the Cognitive Science of Religion, generally speaking, suggest that it is natural for human beings to develop religious beliefs and adopt religious patterns of behaviour (Visala, 2015, p.69). Human thinking about such things will inevitably draw upon the same cognitive processes and mechanisms that we use to think about non-religious things. Similarly, an account of human consciousness may be developed which leads most psychologists to reject dualistic notions of a soul as an ontologically separate entity to the body (including the brain). This is not fundamentally problematic for Christian anthropology. Dualism has not been categorically disproved, nor is it likely that it ever could be, and a range of alternative, monist, models of understanding are available, including such approaches as non-reductive physicalism and emergence.[15] However, whilst many ordinary Christians may continue to adopt a dualistic understanding of an eternal soul in relation to a mortal body, most scientists and medical professionals adopt monistic models of mind (soul) and body as an integral unity. This gap in understanding can cause significant misunderstanding in the clinical or research context.

Research suggests that states of mind are all associated with corresponding brain states, and all human experience, including religious experience and religious states of mind, may therefore be said to be based in the brain (Saver and Rabin, 1997, Robinson, 2015). Again, this is not problematic for Christian anthropology and neither proves nor disproves anything about the existence of God or spiritual/religious realities. However, just as the noetic and ineffable quality of many religious experiences can be located in the limbic system, so now we can identify brain structures associated with visionary and voice-hearing experiences. A better understanding of the anatomy and physiology of such experiences may have something to teach us about the nature of the human encounter with the divine.

The reader may detect that I show something of a sympathy to dualistic anthropologies when discussing the Christian mystical tradition (Chapter 5) and more of a sympathy to monistic anthropologies when discussing the debate between science and theology (Chapter 7). If I am guilty of inconsistency, then I simply plead that a fully worked-out position on this debate is not essential to the topic at hand. However, if I am forced to choose, then I would argue that an emergent dualism offers a theological anthropology which is consistent with all of the sources handled in this book, theological, philosophical, and scientific (Hasker, 2015).

Theological epistemology

I am aware that this book draws on knowledge from a variety of sources, and that it raises significant and various epistemological questions. Take, for example, the case of a person who says (or it is said that they say) that they have heard God telling them to do something – to offer a sacrifice, to visit someone in hospital, or simply to "follow me".[16] Such accounts are encountered within the pages of scripture, in Christian history, and in contemporary experience. What are we to make of them? What might the person hearing the voice reasonably make of their experience?

First, we confront the epistemological question as to whether or not there is any God who might in such a way "speak" to human beings.[17] There are far-reaching questions concerning the basis of (Christian) belief in God which are well beyond the scope of this book. I am aware, for example, that questions might be asked as to whether or not it is possible (assuming that there is a God) to know anything about God at all, or about whether there is warrant for believing in God. If negative answers to such questions are thought to be sufficiently persuasive, then accounts of having "heard" God speak will necessarily be studied and interpreted as mistaken, even if perhaps also sincere. It would be meaningless to ask what the voice conveyed in terms of divine revelation, for how could it be possible to speak meaningfully of the voice of a God who cannot be known, or in whom belief is not warranted? Without attempting to argue any detailed case in support of a contrary epistemological stance, I will simply state at the outset that this book is written within an epistemological framework that asserts not only the existence of God, but both the possibility and the rationality of knowledge of God.

Even assuming that belief in God is accepted, and also the possibility that the God believed in is one who in some sense sometimes "speaks" to people, questions might be raised about the historicity of the alleged experience. In the case of many biblical characters (especially in the Old Testament), or figures from early Christian history, this may be in doubt. An historical critical stance will therefore be adopted (particularly in Chapters 3 to 5), drawing on the resources of historical and biblical scholarship as an aid to the detective work involved in the quest for what might be said to have "really" happened. Such a quest will be pursued mindful of the impossibility of gaining any reliable firsthand evidence about psychological experiences that may or may not have happened many centuries ago. On the one hand, there is the possibility that the texts handed down to us have their origins in some actual human experience (of voice hearing or otherwise). On the other hand, biblical narratives may still have revelatory significance even if they are fictional, or (which is not the same thing) are based on myth.[18]

Whether originating in scripture, or in subsequent Christian history, there are accounts of the hearing of voices which have become a significant part of Christian tradition. The baptism of Jesus, the conversion of St Paul, or the battle of St Antony of Egypt with the demons, are amongst many examples that could be cited. There is thus a Christian tradition within which God (and sometimes a demon, angel, or other being) is said to speak to human beings. Tradition is an important epistemic concept within theology. As Mark Wynn has noted (Wynn, 2017), tradition is closely related to revelation, and is an important vehicle for conservation of revelation, but it is more than this. Tradition plays a part in elaborating upon revelation, and in reinterpreting revelation in the light of changing world views. It presents a challenge to each new generation as to how, in present experience, the tradition handed on will be appropriated and lived. The present challenge in terms of voice hearing is therefore to reinterpret, and to find new ways of living out, an understanding of divine revelation by way of voices within a radically different (scientific) world view of how voices arise.

In the case of those who have heard voices more recently, especially those who are still alive and available for interview, or those for whom extensive autograph accounts of the experience are available, much more might confidently be said than for figures such as Abraham, Jesus, St Paul, or St Antony. However, there are still significant phenomenological issues concerning the difficulty of gaining access to private, subjective, experiences. Recent scientific research, which seeks to characterise the phenomenology of voice hearing more precisely, and to elucidate the underlying psychological and neurobiological mechanisms that lay behind the experience, is an important part of the epistemic quest, and will be considered in Chapter 7. Implicit in the attention being given here to such empirical research is a belief that science does provide access to knowledge about a world created by God. We must "read" the book of nature carefully, alongside the book of scripture. Each helps us to interpret the other.

The hearing of a voice is thus (at least potentially) an experience, specifically a perceptual or perception-like experience, about which we might know quite a lot in empirical scientific terms. In the present case, as we are considering examples of hearing the voice of God (and similar phenomena, such as demonic or angelic voices) it is a religious experience. There has been much work on the epistemic significance of religious experience, and I shall draw especially on the work of William Alston (1991) in Chapter 8. For now, it simply needs to be said that (like Alston) I understand a sense in which it might be said that God has been "perceived", although I will want to qualify this somewhat in terms of just how directly we might consider a voice to be a perception "of God".

Any Christian account of the possible epistemic significance of a claim to have heard (or a report of someone having heard) God's voice must thus be set within the context of other such voices as encountered in scripture, tradition, and experience. I take it as needing no further justification here that such an account should also be subject to the critical light of reason (scientifically and philosophically as well as theologically). If we cannot proceed rationally, then I do not see how we can say anything meaningful about the topic at all. Theology proceeds on the basis that it is possible to talk rationally about God.[19]

Let us assume for a moment that, given proper attention to scripture, tradition, experience, and reason, some such voices might be considered to be "God's voice". What would this mean? It might imply that God has been in some way present, as the speaker, with those who heard the voice. However, the voice might not directly be "God's". It might be angelic, or otherwise indirectly conveyed, and so it might not reflect God's immediate presence as speaker so much as God's interest in communicating with the person concerned. Presumably, in the examples given at the outset of this section, it would imply that the voice should be obeyed – the sacrifice offered, the person visited, etc. In a certain sense, this might be considered "revelatory" – and certainly personally significant – for the hearer of the voice. However, if "revelation" is taken to mean an unveiling or disclosing of something otherwise hidden,[20] it is not clear that such voices are revelatory of God in any wider sense.

What if the voice that is heard, and is understood to be God's voice, issues not a command (to offer a sacrifice, or visit someone, or "follow me") but rather articulates a propositional statement? For example, perhaps it makes an assertion concerning the future prosperity and wellbeing of the descendents of the hearer, or asserts that things previously prohibited according to religious law have now been "made clean", or asserts that "all will be well".[21] Voices that convey propositional statements of this kind are more obviously, and explicitly, asserting that certain things should be believed, not only by the hearer of the voice, but also by others who follow in the same faith tradition. Such voices are potentially "revelatory" in a wider sense and may be significant for many people other than the original hearer of the voice.

The theme of revelation will be further explored in Chapter 8. Corresponding to the Christological emphasis adopted in terms of theological anthropology (see above), it is proposed here that a Christological emphasis is appropriate in relation to epistemology. This is partly because of the centrality of the incarnation to Christian theology, and in particular to the Johannine understanding of Christ as the Word, or Logos, of God. However, it also reflects the need to avoid unhelpful distortions of what it might mean to hear God's voice. Hearing the voice of God is not (or – it will be argued – should not be) understood as primarily concerned with special or private experiences, texts, or forms of words. It is about the creative and transformative impact of divine speech in the world through the receptivity and responsiveness of human agents.[22]

Notes

1 It might be argued that words and language are the primary consideration here (see, for example, Green, 2008, p.42, Brown and Strawn, 2015, pp.97–98, Davies, 2017, pp.11–12). I am also aware that voices may be non-verbal (as, for example, when singing a musical note or giving out a wordless cry of despair). However, for the purposes of the present study, it is voices conveying verbal utterance that are the primary consideration. It is generally difficult to imagine words and language without any kind of voice (either spoken or internalised) and silent reading is closely linked to inner speech for most people (Alderson-Day et al., 2017). Voices and language are therefore – at least generally speaking – inextricably linked.

2 Much more controversially, Julian Jaynes argued in *The Origin of Consciousness in the Breakdown of the Bicameral Mind*, originally published in 1976, that in an even earlier period of history – which he refers to as the "bicameral period" – all human beings heard voices (Jaynes, 2000). This theory has not received widespread acceptance, and textual evidence prior to the Classical period simply does not allow us to draw any confident conclusions concerning experiences of voice hearing at this time.

3 For further discussion, see Sarbin and Juhasz (1967), Rojcewicz and Rojcewicz (1997), and Aleman and Larøi (2009, pp.12–14). Sarbin and Juhasz provide a detailed account of the etymology and historical emergence of the term "hallucination" with which Rojcewicz & Rojcewicz take issue at certain points. The account provided here reflects the view taken by Rojcewicz & Rojcewicz.

4 See Watkins (2008, pp.136–137), McCarthy-Jones (2012, p.224), Fernyhough (2016, p.239).

5 It is not entirely clear that this addresses all the possibilities; nor do Lim et al. (2016) offer a definition of what is meant by "congruent" or "coherent". For example, is it congruent or incongruent to experience an auditory verbal hallucination from one corner of a room at the same time as a visual hallucination of a dog in another part of the room? Whereas Chesterman's definition is precise in terms of the source/location of multimodal hallucinations, but lacks any reference to congruence/coherence, the definitions proposed by Lim et al. include an imprecise reference to coherence, but lack any reference to spatial location. A part of the problem here is that unimodal auditory verbal hallucinations are arguably almost always incongruent, as it is not coherent to refer to a voice in the absence of a speaker, but Lim et al. confine their notions of congruence/coherence only to multimodal hallucinations.

6 The abbreviation is employed from here on in the present chapter, and in Chapters 1, 6, 7 and 8, where frequent reference is made to the term, primarily in the course of discussing the scientific literature. Elsewhere, the term is written out in full.

7 See, for example, Wiebe (1997). Even this terminology causes concern to some, and this has led to adoption of qualifying adjectives such as "objective" or "veridical" in

relation to some visionary experiences, to reinforce the assertion that such experiences do not represent false or erroneous perceptions (see Chapter 4).

8 Florence Nightingale and Teresa of Calcutta, for example, both refer to "the voice" in reporting their respective experiences.

9 Watkins takes the term "imaginal" from the work of Henry Corbin, who finds the term "imaginary" unsatisfactory, due to its sense of unreality and non-existence. The imaginal world is understood by Corbin as "an intermediary between the sensible world and the intelligible world" (Corbin, 1972, p.17). Imaginal dialogues thus include the domain of AVHs, but are not necessarily hallucinatory and are by definition not merely imaginary.

10 For a fuller review of this literature, see Castelnovo et al. (2015).

11 As a clinician, many years ago, I encountered exactly this scenario, where a woman reported repeated hypnopompic hallucinations of a golden figure, whom she understood to be Christ. She described herself as an atheist, and found the experience troubling, at least in part, because she expressly did not want to become a Christian.

12 http://hearingthevoice.org/

13 I would emphasise that the "experiences" in question are firmly located within the gospel narratives. I am making no statement at this point as to whether or not they were historical, psychological, experiences of Jesus, Mary, or the disciples. This question will be addressed in Chapter 4.

14 There must, of course, be more fundamental grounds than this for asserting that Christology is the proper starting point for all Christian theological anthropology. Like Cortez, I have reservations about Barth's grounding of a Christological anthropology in the doctrine of election. However, whilst the question might remain open as to why this should be the starting point, there are a variety of other grounds (beyond the scope of this book) on which one could argue that it should be the proper starting point. The reader is directed to Cortez (2015) for further discussion.

15 A good example of such an approach, worked out in some detail, is *Complex Emergent Developmental Linguistic Relational Neurophysiologicalism* (Brown and Strawn, 2015). Peoples (2015) further shows that a coherent Christology can exist even in relation to a materialist anthropology. A detailed exploration of the merits and demerits of such anthropologies is beyond the scope of the present volume but see, for example, Farris and Taliaferro (2015).

16 Abraham, Joyce Huggett, and Hugh Montefiore respectively – all examples explored later in this book. Montefiore's experience is also significant in that the words are biblical, and thus carry a weight of meaning associated with other contexts in which they were spoken – notably Jesus' calling of the apostles as recorded in the synoptic gospels.

17 These issues are helpfully explored by Plantinga (2015).

18 These issues will be explored in Chapter 2.

19 I would broadly align myself here with the position outlined by Ratzinger (1987, p.316).

20 See, for example, Sullivan and Menssen (2009, p.201).

21 These are references to Abraham, St Peter, and Julian of Norwich respectively – all considered later in this book.

22 As William Abraham points out, it is no accident that we use the metaphor of speech when we say that "actions speak louder than words (2006, p.60).

1 Voice hearing in contemporary spiritual and religious context

The hearing of voices in the absence of a human speaker must once have had inevitably supernatural implications. In the contemporary context, in contrast, a variety of alternative scientific explanations are potentially available, including notably those of a technological or medical nature. Voices emanating from electronic sources (phones, computers, public address systems, etc.) no longer surprise us. Those attributable to drugs, illness, or otherwise disturbed physiological states may worry or intrigue us, but they will not necessarily be thought to have any spiritual or religious implications, and, when they do, there will usually be good reasons for this. Such good reasons may include the context of use, as for example in the use of peyote in Native American religion, or the explicitly spiritual/religious content of what is heard. And when such good reasons for inferring spiritual/religious significance do pertain, they may be understood within any of a diverse variety of traditional, new and emerging, cultural or individual frameworks of meaning.

For some people, in particular those who would identify themselves as atheists, the framework of belief within which voices are interpreted will inevitably exclude any spiritual or religious explanation. For others, any voice not emanating from a human or electronic source will inevitably be interpreted in spiritual terms. And, for still others, there will be an element of critical discrimination. Some voices might be perceived as more spiritual than others, or be interpreted differently (and thus more or less religiously) according to context, form, or content. We inhabit a pluralistic environment, insofar as the spiritual and religious interpretation of voice hearing is concerned. This pluralism is contributed to not only by traditional and non-traditional forms of spirituality and religion, but also by popular, professional, and scientific bases for forming possible alternative explanations. Significant amongst these are concepts of mental disorder, but groups such as the Hearing Voices Network have ensured that there are also forums within which a plurality of views is acknowledged, alongside a recognition that the experience can be normalised.

Whilst the primary consideration here is with voices which might be understood as AVHs,[1] it is not necessarily the perceptual quality of the voice, or its location in external space, which invites spiritual or religious reflection.

Rather, there is a quality of seeming autonomy about some voices, whether experienced as thoughts or perceptions (or perception-like), which characterises them as being other than aspects of the self (Watkins, 2000), and in some cases even as seeming to be external agents. This quality has been identified and described by writers, artists, children, those who are suffering from mental illness, and by other reflective adults who are not mentally ill, as well as by those who describe religious, mystical, or other spiritual experiences. For example, Carl Jung, reflecting on what he describes as his own "confrontation with the unconscious", refers to an archetype which he called Philemon:

> Philemon and other figures of my fantasies brought home to me the crucial insight that there are things in the psyche which I do not produce, but which produce themselves and have their own life. Philemon represented a force which was not myself. In my fantasies I held conversations with him, and he said things which I had not consciously thought. For I observed clearly that it was he who spoke, not I.
>
> (Jung, 1983, p.207)

It would seem that the voice of Philemon was not hallucinatory – being described here as a figure of fantasy – but, in general terms, voices with this quality of producing themselves, of having their own life, may or may not be hallucinatory. It is their autonomy, their manifesting the character of being another self that is their defining feature. So important is this to many of those who hear such voices that qualities of form, such as location in external space, or of being heard "out loud", may seem irrelevant and not be mentioned at all, or else be difficult to clarify.

Spirituality and voice hearing

Research suggests that voice hearers interpret their experiences of voice hearing from a variety of perspectives, at least one of which may be the positively spiritual or religious (Jones et al., 2003, 2016). However, spirituality[2] is a contested and complex term, and the complexity and controversy are only increased when it is brought into relationship with voice hearing and related phenomena.

For some voice hearers, all voices are spiritual:

> the voice for some reason in my case went very often to great pains to explain voice hearing as always a case of a spiritual being communicating, though for countless different reasons depending upon the person's life and by the way also their past and future lives, which I was told were all occurring at the same time in alternate realities constantly growing in number . . . well, I became convinced by the voice itself that all voices were spiritual, that not having occurred to me until it was explained, again by the voice, and I guess though it was at first explained because

I suppose I was surprised when the voice suddenly had a male tone and then a second voice a female tone and a third a male tone also shockingly sinister in its feel.[3]

The idea that all voices (or, perhaps better, "almost all" voices) are spiritual finds expression in a variety of forms, which generally blur the boundaries between experiences of different kinds and, in particular, between mystical or spiritual experience and psychopathology. Thus, for example, Thalbourne and Delin (1994) propose that the term "transliminality" be employed in relation to a permeability of the boundary between subliminal (unconscious or preconscious) and supraliminal (conscious) events. Various groups of people are understood as being high in transliminality, including those who are highly creative, those who have mystical experiences, those who experience psychic phenomena, and those who are psychotic or have psychosis-like experiences. Amongst other things, highly transliminal people report hearing voices.

At the other extreme, an over-medical approach might label all voice hearing as evidence of mental disorder, and thus exclude any spiritual quality or interpretation at all. This is not an approach that is often explicitly argued, but it seems to be implicit in attempts to diagnose religious or mystical figures according to psychiatric categories (Cook, 2012c), and it seems to be the cause of the problems experienced by patients who find that it is difficult to discuss spirituality or religion with mental health professionals for fear that such matters will inevitably be interpreted as evidence of psychopathology.

For others, somewhere in between the extremes of "all are spiritual" and "all are medical", some voices might be perceived as spiritual and others not. Amanda Waegeli provides a helpful account of this perspective:

As a voice hearer I believe I have experienced both spiritual voices and those of psychosis. They are distinctly different and experienced differently to me. My spiritual voices have been positive and helpful and bought me peace and acceptance, and therefore have aided my recovery. They have given me hope when I have needed it and reminded me that there is a greater meaning to life than what I am experiencing in the here and now, especially when in emotional pain. The difference between spiritual and non-spiritual voices for me has been that the spiritual are heard more gently and peacefully, more softly and harmoniously they are less frequent. I hear my spiritual voices from above and feel drawn to look above to the sky/roof. I hear them coming from a different place to my psychotic voices, which seem to come from around me. I am unable to talk back but just listen to a spiritual voice. It is not a conversation or invitation to talk back to the voice, but a message for me to listen to. Although I do not see a vision, I sense and feel an intense presence that almost paralyses me in the moment and a connection which

I don't experience when hearing my other voices. My spiritual voices come with a strong complete all over body feeling of freeze, trance, and paralysis almost while I am hearing it. It is intense and after hearing it I feel tired.

(McCarthy-Jones et al., 2013)

Whilst it is helpful and important to know that voice hearers such as Waegeli make such distinction, it is less clear that such distinctions are either helpful or possible when made by researchers or clinicians. For example, Myrtle Heery has studied 30 subjects[4] reporting "inner voice experiences" and has classified their interview transcripts according to three categories:

1   Inner voice experiences as fragmented part of the self
2   Inner voice experiences characterized by dialogue, providing guidance for growth of the individual,
3   Inner voice experiences where channels opened toward and beyond a higher self.

(Heery, 1989)

Whilst this is in many ways a helpful way of studying the data emerging from this study, the danger is that such categories are too easily imposed by researchers and do not necessarily reflect the understanding of the subjects themselves. Nor is it clear that any given experience of hearing an inner voice is necessarily only to be understood within just one of these categories. Why may a voice not at the same time reflect a fragmented part of the self, with which one may engage in dialogue and from which one may gain guidance, and also be a channel through which an openness to some kind of transcendent order is found? In fact, Heery does explore the possibility that her three categories each represent different reactions to a spiritual awakening, and I have not done justice to her analysis here. However, it is still not clear that the assessment of the researcher necessarily reflects the nature and quality of the spiritual experience of the voice hearer.

Menezes and Moreira-Almeida (2010) propose a series of features indicative of non-pathological spiritual experiences, so that such experiences may be distinguished from psychosis or other mental disorder:

- Absence of psychological suffering: the individual does not feel disturbed due to the experience he or she is having.
- Absence of social and occupational impediments: the experience does not compromise the individual's relationships and activities.
- The experience has a short duration and happens occasionally: it does not have an invasive character in consciousness and in the individual's daily activities.
- There is a critical attitude about the experience: the capacity to perceive the unusual nature of the experience is preserved.

- Compatibility of the experience with some religious tradition: the individual's experience may be understood within the concepts and practices of some established religious tradition.
- Absence of psychiatric comorbidities: there are no other mental disorders or other symptoms suggestive of mental disorders besides those related to spiritual experiences.
- Control over the experience: the individual is capable of directing his or her experience in the right time and place for its occurrence.
- Life becomes more meaningful: the individual reaches a more comprehensive understanding of his or her own life.
- The individual is concerned with helping others: the expanded consciousness develops a deep link with other human beings.

Again, whilst the value of considering such features of an experience (voice hearing or otherwise) should not be entirely dismissed, it is not clear that the making of such a "differential diagnosis" is either possible or helpful. Many saints and mystics could be named (e.g. John of the Cross, or Thérèse of Lisieux) whose spiritual experiences were associated with psychological suffering, and for others (e.g. Francis of Assisi) their experiences have been deeply disruptive of relationships and activities. In any case, why may experiences not be both spiritual and psychotic? Recognising this possibility, David Lukoff (1985) has proposed that there is an overlap between the otherwise separate categories of simple mystical experiences and psychotic episodes, and proposes criteria for a category of mystical experiences with psychotic features (MEPF).

McCarthy-Jones et al. (2013), using as examples the experiences of Amanda Waegeli, identify four ways in which spirituality can help people who are distressed by hearing voices. First, it may provide a more helpful, meaningful, and appealing explanation of the experience than do medical explanations. Second, spirituality may offer constructive coping strategies (e.g. meditation, yoga, prayer, etc.). Third, spirituality may enhance social support. Fourth, spirituality may help to facilitate forgiveness. Against these benefits, these authors note also that spirituality may in some circumstances increase distress, reduce a sense of control, increase social isolation, or reduce engagement with medical treatment. In other cases, voice hearers may not feel able to access spiritual beliefs or practices in any personally meaningful way.

Religion and voice hearing

Julian Jaynes proposed that religion has its origins in an evolutionary period when, in the absence of inner mental language as we know it, voices provided the basis for initiation of human action. These voices were – according to Jaynes – "recognised as gods, angels, devils, enemies, or a particular person or relative" (Jaynes, 2000, p.89). In a later period, the experience of voices diminished and human consciousness as we now know it emerged. In the course of this transition, the voices "became" gods (Rowe, 2016). Whilst this radical evolutionary theory has not generally been accepted within psychology as an academic discipline,[5] the attribution of voices to divine sources in contemporary religious experience is indisputable.

We have little information about how frequently voices heard are understood as being "religious" – whether because they are understood to emanate from a religious source (e.g. God, saints or spiritual beings such as angels and demons), or because they have explicitly religious content.[6] In one sample of college students 8.7 per cent (Barrett and Etheridge, 1992), and in another 11.5 per cent (Posey and Losch, 1983), reported hearing the voice of God. However, Barrett and Etheridge comment in their study that "several of our subjects seemed to have trouble discriminating between actually hearing a voice they thought to be God's voice and 'knowing' that God was telling them something without actually hearing a voice outside of their head".

Mary Schwab (1977), who did not ask her southern US sample to distinguish between seeing and hearing "things that other people don't think are there", reported that hallucinations were experienced more by "fundamentalist" religious denominations. She also found a higher positive response amongst black respondents. Thus 9.2 per cent of white Baptists, but 16.3 per cent of black Baptists gave a positive response. At the other end of the spectrum, no positive responses were reported amongst Episcopalians or Jews.

In a study of 100 healthy volunteers who undertook a visual word detection task (Reed and Clarke, 2014), participants who scored highly on a religiosity scale were more likely to report false perceptions of a religious kind than were participants who had a low religiosity score. However, overall, they were not more likely to report false perceptions. The authors conclude that context and individual differences influence the content of false perceptions. Assuming, as would seem reasonable, that the results of such studies can be extrapolated to auditory perceptions, and to AVHs experienced outside of the psychology laboratory, we should not be surprised if we find that religious people experiencing AVHs are more likely to report religious content.

Simon Dein and Roland Littlewood (2007), in a study of a Pentecostal church in northeast London, identified 25 individuals (out of 40 who completed questionnaires) who reported that they heard God's voice in answer to their prayers. Similar findings have been reported by Tanya Luhrmann (2012) in her more extensive studies of two charismatic churches in the USA, and in a smaller study by Cook and Dein (Dein and Cook, 2015).[7]

There seems to be a general lack of scientific research on voice hearing in religious traditions other than Christianity, and published contemporary accounts of voice hearing from within other faith traditions are relatively uncommon. However, one such example may be found from among the 50 stories collated by Marius Romme and his colleagues (Romme et al., 2009) under the title *Living With Voices*. Here, Helen describes her experience of abuse at the hands of her father, and the voices that she hears as an adult which mirror her childhood experiences – for example, the voice of her father:

> He criticises me and tells me, for example, that I am "stupid", "use-less" and "worthless", that I "deserve to be abused" and "should never have been born". He also comments on what I do, telling me that it is "not good enough" . . . The voices are there every day and so I have to develop ways of coping with them.[8]

Helen understands her voices as post-traumatic sequelae of the psychologi-cal, physical, and sexual abuse that she experienced as a child and repudiates any "pathological labels such as 'schizophrenia'". Her explanation of her experiences is thus argued at a psychological level, but her account of cop-ing and recovery is presented within the framework of her Bahá'í faith.

> The most effective coping strategy which I have discovered over the years is prayer. Prayer has saved my life on a number of occasions as well as the faith which I discovered in answer to a prayer about 22 years ago.[9]

She goes on to refer specifically to the beauty and power of the prayers and writings from which she has drawn "strength, guidance, comfort and hope", the positive vision that she has found of humanity, and the posi-tive impact on her own self-esteem. Her self-understanding within this faith tradition, as a creation of God and a servant of God, seems to provide an antidote to the "degrading and demeaning identity" that was forced upon her in her childhood.

> Prayer seems to provide strength from another dimension, which then allows me to continue with the activities of daily life. Prayer is the main factor which has allowed me not only to survive but also study, train and work as a clinical psychologist.[10]

Helen writes that the Bahá'í faith teaches that "work is worship" and that for her it is perhaps also a form of prayer. She cites examples known to her of similar benefits that she has observed others to find within the Buddhist, Islamic, and Christian traditions but also gives secular examples of the ben-efit of repeating such phrases as "I am loved".

Voices of new spiritualities

A diverse array of new spiritualities has exploded onto the secular scene over the last 50 years or more, and it has been suggested that there is now a spir-itual marketplace (Roof, 1999) within which traditional religions take their place alongside a variety of newer, more subjective, and often individualistic options which are untethered from formal institutional structures. These options arguably meet the criteria for definition as religion (Hanegraaff, 2000) but are usually contrasted with traditional religion. They are sometimes referred to as "New Age" spiritualities, although this term is a highly disputed category (without any widely accepted alternative), which may be understood in narrower or broader terms (Sutcliffe and Gilhus, 2013). Whilst it is said by some that they are more concerned with the immanent realm, in contrast to the transcendent focus of traditional religion (Heelas, 2008), the immanent and the transcendent are more appropriately understood as being in an inseparable relationship (Cook, 2013b). All spiritualities and religions, to a greater or lesser extent, have to address both the transcendent – that which is understood in some sense as above and beyond human experience – and also the immanent – that which is within the perceivable order of things.

Voice hearing is, almost by definition, an immanent experience. However, as we have already seen, it also has significant potential for interpretation within a transcendent frame of reference. Thus it should not be surprising that we encounter, outside traditional religious frames of reference, interpretations of hallucinations both, on the one hand, as the "world of spirits" (Dusen, 1970), and also, on the other hand, as "inner spiritual voices" (Scott, 1997). The former might be seen as emphasising more the personal encounter with a surrounding transcendent spiritual order, and the latter more as an inward turn to the immanent spiritual order within. However, in fact, both are attempts to articulate a complex dynamic of the immanent and transcendent in an inextricable tension. Two examples will be explored here by way of illustration. One focuses more on listening to the inner voice as a turn to "God within", and the other more on a listening to voices "out there". Both concern the stories of individual human experience, but one has also found expression in community, whereas the other remains a much more private (but by no means unique) experience.

The Findhorn community in northeast Scotland has as one of its principles a "deep inner listening" that was significantly formed by the voice-hearing experience of one of its founders, Eileen Caddy. In 1953, in the context of the crisis surrounding the breakup of her first marriage, and having fallen in love with the man who was to become her second husband, Peter Caddy, Eileen found herself separated from her children and feeling guilty about having committed adultery. Visiting a quiet sanctuary in Glastonbury, she was struck by the quiet and peacefulness of the place which somehow seemed to penetrate her distress. The experience that she had here was to change her life. In her autobiography she describes what happened:

> I began to pray in the only way I knew, talking to God as if he were a person who could hear me. I saw the face of my father, kind, strong, loving, and I wished he was with me. He would understand and tell me what to do. From the very depths of my heart I called out for help. I had no one but God to turn to.

"Be still and know that I am God."

The voice was quite clear, and I turned to see who had spoken. It couldn't have been Peter or Sheena, and there was no one else in the room. The voice was inside my head. Was I going crazy? I sat very still, rigid with fear, my eyes tight shut. The voice went on: "You have taken a very big step in your life. But if you follow my voice all will be well. I have brought you and Peter together for a very special purpose, to do a specific work for Me. You will work as one, and you will realise this more fully as time goes on. There are few who have been brought together in this way. Don't be afraid, for I am with you."

(Caddy, 1988, p.28)

On leaving the sanctuary, she describes this as a "peculiar, terrible experience"[11] and expresses fears for her own sanity, but she is reassured by Peter and his ex-wife Sheena, who are convinced that she has heard the voice of God. Eileen is not so sure about this and finds herself wondering why God would speak in this way to someone who has committed adultery and left her husband and children.

Caddy describes the period that follows as "the most frightening time of my life"[12] and the story is in many ways a very sad one. Whilst it is told with grace and humility, the reader might not always feel able to interpret events in such a positive way as its author, or to be as generous to some of its characters as she is herself. The voice that she heard in the sanctuary at Glastonbury is taken to justify a course of action that leads to the breakup of her family and to pain and suffering for her children, as well as for Eileen herself. The question must be asked as to whether or not the rest of the story is a convincing justification of this – especially when her relationship with Peter later breaks down and she is forced to reinterpret what the voice had meant in saying that they were brought "together for a very special purpose". In the short term, however, there follows a period during which Sheena takes charge of Eileen's "training", insisting that she listen frequently to the inner voice, record what it said and report back to her. Eileen is understandably resistant to this, but the doubts that she has initially do eventually fade.

Elsewhere, in what appears to be a later reflection on how her experience of voice hearing developed, Caddy states:

I had always thought of God as someone who was "out there", someone I could talk to, but who never seemed to answer me in actual words. Yet here I was hearing a voice that said it was the voice of God. What did it all mean?

I found after that first experience of hearing the voice every time I sat quietly by myself, the voice would talk to me. I discovered that when I asked it questions, it would give me the answers. I soon learned that here was a wonderful friend who was present when I needed help. I could talk to my friend at any time, and I would always get an answer.[13]

She goes on to indicate that she would do whatever the voice asked her to do. She decided that it must be very wise and she habitually turned to it for guidance. Initially, the voice addressed Eileen, as a parent would, as "My child", and later as "My beloved child", and then still later as "My beloved". She describes a deepening love for the voice, until:

> I began to feel that this wonderful voice was right here within my own being, within my own heart, and my love for it grew even deeper. I could feel a oneness with it, as if nothing could ever separate me from it, that it was always here as part of me, morning, noon, and night.
>
> Now, after listening to the voice for more than 46 years, I have come to accept it as an expression of the highest part of myself, the divinity within me.[14]

Eileen Caddy's first book, *God Spoke to Me* (1992, first edition 1975), provides a collection of the messages that the voice spoke to her over the first 10 years, and some of these are quite revealing of the nature of the experience as she interpreted it. For example, under the title "The one voice", she presents the following message:

> An animal knows its master's voice amongst many voices and obeys it. It listens for that voice and ignores all others. When training begins, it will rush from one voice to another, pulled around from pillar to post, completely muddled and confused. As training continues, that one voice becomes clearer, more distinct than all the others. That voice becomes greatly loved and no other matters.
>
> So it has been with your training. There have been severe tests and trials but the training has been invaluable. You now know My voice, no matter what is happening around you, and that is all that matters.
>
> (Caddy, 1992, p.81)

There thus appears to be an evolutionary process, perhaps akin to the learning of "absorption" as described by Luhrmann,[15] by which discernment is developed and the "one voice" is better heard and understood.

Caddy describes in her autobiography how she asked her friend David Spangler for an explanation of her voice, and the answer that she received – relayed from his "higher sensitivity" – was that it is "an amalgam of your own consciousness and the source". He continues:

> Now you yourself must expand and grow, so that your relationship with your source, a life energy inexpressible in words, can grow. Out of that relationship shall come a new voice, or perhaps a fuller communication . . .

Behind the voice, then, is a source which is your true nature, which you are seeking to grow into ever more fully.[16]

In the early years, the community gathered regularly to hear Peter read out the guidance that Eileen had received, but in 1971 Eileen was instructed by the voice to discontinue this practice in favour of allowing other members of the community to make their own contact with the divinity within and to receive their own inner direction.[17]

Findhorn is not associated with any particular spiritual or religious tradition, and welcomes members of all such traditions. However, it is a community that shares a sense of the need to discern an inner voice, a voice which is identified with that of God. The experiences of others are often more individualistic, in terms of the experience of the hearer, and more plural, in terms of the voices that are heard. An illuminating example of this kind is provided by Skye Thomas in her autobiographical *Voices: Divinity or Insanity?* Having related a painful breakup with the father of one of her two children, Thomas speaks of her distress in the context of her ex-partner's blackmail and the stresses of being a single mother of two children. Eventually, she burns a photograph of him and some letters from him whilst "seriously visualising him dead and burning in hell". She writes:

> I allowed all of my hurt and anger to call out for his suffering. I wanted him to hurt the way he had hurt me, the way that he was willing to hurt my children. I prayed, meditated, visualised, and spoke the words of intention that I wanted him stopped.
>
> (Thomas, 2004, p.15)

Immediately after doing this, she describes how silly she felt herself to be, and berated herself.

> It was then that I felt a group of people enter into my living room . . . maybe half a dozen or more. I don't know how to explain it, but I got the sense that the mystical group represented an entire civilization or race of THEM.

Looking around the room, she could see no one but had a distinct sense that they were in an upper corner of the room and shortly a conversation with them begins:

> "Who are you and what do you want?" THEY said THEY had come to let me know I wasn't really alone. THEY hadn't abandoned me. THEY reminded me that I was not of this world, not in the normal sense that everyone else is . . . THEY gave me the impression that I was some kind of beloved family member that had suffered from amnesia and didn't remember who I was. THEY just kept patting me on the

head and loving me . . . THEY were proud of me, loved me, would look after me, and THEY didn't want me to worry anymore. Then, THEY left me without saying if THEY would be back or not.[18]

THEY do not return that night, but do begin visiting Skye frequently. THEY would show her visions of the future, and are seldom wrong. THEY are, however, also in Skye's words, "tricksters", and in one example cause her to act contrary to her own better judgement in such a way as to sabotage a budding romance. Being angry with THEM, Skye pushes THEM away and experiences a period of almost a year without THEM but then, missing THEM, allows THEM back.

In the penultimate chapter of the book, Thomas explores the question of who THEY are. She likes to call THEM guardian angels, but is careful to exclude any possible traditional religious understanding of what angels might be. She admits to a wish to be able to say that God is somehow behind THEM, but she confesses that she has never found God mentioned by them, or any other single being "in charge".

THEY say THEY don't need a God in charge because THEY are all interconnected and share a common vision and have a universal love that is non-individualistic. Each is separate but part of one energy source of love and compassion. THEY don't need a God because THEY are self-directed by love. The bible verse "God is love" comes to mind. THEY say that I'm not too far off.[19]

Whilst Thomas usually speaks of the voices as THEM, named voices do appear in her narrative. MARGARET jolts her out of her hermit lifestyle and helps her to take more care of her appearance. THOMAS is a knowing old man whom Thomas first encounters in a vision and who is always pleased to see her, but from whom she is kept away by MARGARET and by THEM.

In a section of the book which Thomas indicates she did not want to include, but which THEY insisted should be included, Thomas explores the possibility that THEY are aliens. But then she concludes this reflection on who THEY are with consideration of the possibilities that her voices are a tapping into the Jungian collective unconscious, or that they are her own higher self, or that she is mentally ill. She remains seemingly open to all of these possibilities (although her reluctance to include the section on aliens seems to reflect her own insight into how bizarre this account of things might sound). What she is clear about is that "I know that THEY came *to* me not *from* me."[20]

Religious voices as symptoms of psychosis

Religious content is a not uncommon feature of the psychopathology of psychosis. However, the exact frequency of occurrence is difficult to estimate. Many more studies appear to have been published of religious delusions than of religious hallucinations (Gearing et al., 2011, Cook, 2015), and there are relatively few papers giving any detailed quantitative account of the extent to which the content of AVHs is religious. We know that delusions and hallucinations are commonly experienced together (Baethge et al., 2005, Laroi and Van Der Linden, 2005,) and there is some reason to believe that the content of delusional beliefs may often derive from that of hallucinations (Siddle et al., 2002). Studies of the prevalence of religious delusions may therefore provide some additional indication of the prevalence of religious hallucinations. However, the criteria for defining what counts as a "religious" delusion or hallucination are variable between studies and often unsatisfactory (Cook, 2015).

Overall, somewhere between 20 and 60 per cent of diagnosed subjects with delusions appear to have some religious content to their delusional thoughts. Typically, similar or slightly lower proportions of patients with AVHs either hear religious content in what the voice says, or else identify the voice as being from a religious source (God, an angel, etc.). However, the methodology of studies to date is variable and sometimes poor, and it is probably safer to say at the present time that we know very little about exactly how frequent religious voices actually are in psychosis.[21]

Culture clearly influences the religious content of delusions and hallucinations. Kent and Wahass (1996) studied 40 patients in the UK and 35 patients in Saudi Arabia, all of whom had an ICD-10[22] diagnosis of schizophrenia. The samples were collected so as to include only patients who reported auditory hallucinations. In the Saudi sample, 53 per cent of patients with second person voices, and 33 per cent of patients with third person voices, reported religious content. In the UK sample, the corresponding figures were 11 per cent and 6 per cent, suggesting a strong cultural influence on the prevalence of religious hallucinations in schizophrenia.

In a UK/Pakistan study of patients with psychosis with "organised delusions and hallucinations", 50 white British subjects were compared with 53 British Pakistani subjects and 98 Pakistani subjects (Suhail and Cochrane, 2002) – 88 per cent of white British subjects, 72 per cent of British Pakistani subjects, and 52 per cent of Pakistani subjects reported AVHs. Interestingly, the "voice of God" was reported more frequently in the white British (10 per cent) and British Pakistani (9 per cent) than in the Pakistani sample (6 per cent). The prevalence of religious delusions in the three samples was 14 per cent, 21 per cent, and 11 per cent respectively.

Given the impact of culture on religious delusions and hallucinations, one might also expect to find an influence of religiosity. In a study conducted in Pakistan, no significant difference was found in the frequency of AVHs between more and less religious patients (65 per cent vs 76 per cent respectively) with psychosis (Suhail and Ghauri, 2010). However, more religious patients were more grandiose, more likely to have religious delusions, and more likely to hear the voices of "paranormal agents". In this study, 62.3 per cent of patients reported religious delusions. In a more recent study conducted in the USA (Abdelgawad et al., 2017), increased severity of auditory and visual hallucinations was found to be significantly associated with Intrinsic Religiosity, but not with Organisational or Non-Organisational Religiosity. Another recent study, of adolescents, found a non-linear relationship between religiosity and AVHs, suggesting a more complex connection where, in some cases, religiosity may represent a coping response (Steenhuis et al., 2016).

Much of the research has been based on Western populations and thus reflects religious content associated with the Judeo-Christian tradition. However, there are also reports of AVHs with religious content reflecting Islamic (Kent and Wahass, 1996), spiritist (Guarnaccia et al., 1991), Buddhist and other Eastern (Yip, 2003) religious traditions. It has been claimed that religious delusions are less frequent in Hinduism, Far Eastern, and Jewish religious traditions (Murphy et al., 1963).

Stompe et al (2007), applying a principal components analysis to data obtained from the International Study on Psychotic Symptoms, identified a "religious grandiosity syndrome" characterised by delusions of grandeur and descent, religious delusions, and visual hallucinations (but not auditory hallucinations – which were associated with a separate syndrome of "apocalyptic guilt"). The religious grandiosity syndrome was encountered much less frequently in Pakistan, and the authors note that "no Pakistani claimed that he is God, Jesus or Mohammed".

In a very few studies, variation of religious content of hallucinations and/or delusions has been studied across time. In a study in Poland, the content of 50 per cent of patients' delusions/hallucinations in 1932 included religious topics. This fell to 46 per cent in 1952, but rose to 49 per cent in 1972 and then fell again to 42 per cent in 1992 (Krzystanek et al., 2012). In another study, in Egypt, fluctuation in "religious symptoms" (delusions, hallucinations, speech, and behaviour) across time was thought to reflect socio-political changes (Atallah et al., 2001). It has been suggested that religious delusions are now less common than they used to be, at least in some countries (Stompe et al., 2006, Skodlar et al., 2008). However, a recent review of the literature suggests that – worldwide – it is not clear that there is any overall evidence of decline in frequency of religious delusions and hallucinations (Cook, 2015).

Rieben et al. (2013) sought to understand how patients with religious delusions experienced their spirituality or religiousness. Semi-structured interviews were undertaken with 62 patients with past or present religious delusions, revealing three categories or themes of religious content: spiritual identity, meaning of the illness, and spiritual/religious figures. Open and closed structural dynamics of these beliefs were identified. In open dynamics, the beliefs in question are constantly being revised and restructured in interaction with the world around. In closed dynamics, a more complete rupture with the surrounding world was observed and the beliefs are more resistant to change. In some cases, mixed (open *and* closed) dynamics were observed.

Although it is the content of delusional belief that is the main focus of the study by Rieben et al. (2013), it is clear that AVHs play a significant part in forming the religious content and dynamics of these beliefs, at least in some cases. Thus, in one case, the meaning of the illness, understood in spiritual/religious terms, is influenced by AVHs: "I can hear voices from the dead in purgatory, it's a warning . . . It means I need to pray more." In another case, the religious figure (the Devil) identified as a significant component of the content of delusional beliefs was identifiable on the basis of the perceived identity of the associated AVH: "The Devil told me: help yourself with your medication, come on, have some, it makes everything easier! But don't tell this to your therapist." In yet another subject, the open dynamics of the reported belief structure seem to have been significantly related to the influence of the voices that he heard:

> Patient B's spiritual beliefs give meaning to the voices and help him to deal with them. He makes a distinction between voices that are related to the illness and the ones that are related to his spiritual belief. "Some voices have a psychological explanation," which allows him to "ignore them." Some voices are assigned to God, and some are assigned to demons. The ones that are from God help him to go on in his life and to heal. To deal with the ones that are from demons, he asks "God" for help, which calms his fear.

The authors of this study go on to propose various psychological functions of delusions with religious content, such as helping to deal with the adverse connotations of their diagnosis, or overcoming loneliness. They suggest that patients who hear voices are especially likely to project guilt and blame onto external beings, and that this "can lead to feelings of fear and persecution".

Even where the content of delusions and hallucinations is not explicitly religious, there is evidence that spirituality/religion provide important coping resources. For example, Mohr et al. (2011), in a study of 115 outpatients with psychotic illness, have shown that, for 71 per cent of patients, religion provided a source of hope, meaning, and purpose in life, but that for 14 per cent it was associated with spiritual despair. For most patients (54 per cent) religion reduced psychotic and general symptoms, while for 10 per cent it increased them. Similarly, it may increase social integration (28 per cent) or be associated with social isolation (3 per cent). It may reduce the risk of deliberate self-harm (33 per cent) or increase it (10 per cent). It may reduce substance use (14 per cent) or increase it (3 per cent). In terms of compliance with treatment, the risks and benefits were more evenly balanced, with 16 per cent finding it helpful, and 15 per cent seeing it as being associated with opposition to treatment.

Mohr et al. (2006) give a number of examples in which spirituality/religion specifically helped in coping with AVHs. For example, one woman with a diagnosis of schizophrenia said: "I believe that my hallucinations and delusions are due to bad spirits; this gives me an explanation that helps me to lessen my fear and distress and to stay calm." A 25-year-old man with a diagnosis of schizophrenia said: "If you tell yourself that you have an eternal life ahead of you, you know that the voices will end, that they are not eternal. Consequently, voices are nothing in fact when they will not always be there."

Whilst spirituality/religion seemed generally to be helpful at a personal level, only one third of subjects in this study for whom religion was a positive coping factor received social support from a faith community. Often, it seems, they found it difficult to go to church, or else they attend church and keep apart from others. In some cases, other members of the community or congregation were found to be positively unhelpful. However, clergy and religious leaders clearly do, at least sometimes, play a positive role:

> Two years ago, I began to hear voices of demons; I believed I was Jesus Christ. I met an exorcist priest. He told me that I could not be Jesus Christ and he taught me the gospel. I met him every week. The voices told me not to take any medication. He told me not to listen to them, that demons are liars. He told me that the medication could help me. Since then, I've agreed to take it.

Not only do subjects find it difficult to talk to members of their own faith community, but sometimes also their psychiatrist:

> My illness opened my mind to spirituality. I do not talk about it to psychiatrists since they do not believe it. Before I received medication, I heard voices. Once I took refuge in a church; I prayed to the Virgin Mary and the voices fell silent. Since that day, she has protected me. Sometimes she appears to me; it is not a hallucination.

In a three-year follow-up study of the same sample of patients, Mohr et al. (2010) have subsequently demonstrated that, whilst religion is a stable factor over time for 63 per cent of patients, for others there is a significant process of evolution and change. For 20 per cent, positive changes occurred, but for 17 per cent there were negative changes. Both positive and negative changes were seen to be indicative of suffering: lower quality of life, reduced self-esteem, or lessening of satisfaction with social activities.

Wahass and Kent (1997) found that patients diagnosed as suffering from schizophrenia in Saudi Arabia were more likely to use strategies associated with their religion as a means of coping with the voices than were similar patients in the UK.

Most of the research to date on religious/spiritual coping with AVHs and other symptoms of psychosis has been concerned with what people do spontaneously, or on their own initiative. There is, however, scope for therapeutic interventions to be developed which take into account the spiritual and religious frameworks within which people experience these phenomena. Chadwick and Birchwood (1994), in a study of a group of 26 patients with a diagnosis of schizophrenia who had drug-resistant auditory hallucinations, showed that beliefs about the identity and meaning of voices are not always linked to the content of what the voice says. Indeed, in 31 per cent of cases, the ascribed beliefs were incongruent with this content. In a subgroup of four of these patients, they showed that beliefs about the voices could be changed by cognitive therapy. In the case of one woman, this included reduction of a 100 per cent conviction at the start of therapy that God was talking to her to only a 5 per cent conviction at the conclusion of therapy and again at follow-up. Moreover, a 90 per cent conviction at the onset of therapy that she would be punished if she resisted the voice was also reduced to only 5 per cent at conclusion and follow-up.

There is also preliminary evidence to suggest that the spiritual practice of mindfulness might provide an effective way of managing unpleasant voices (Abba et al., 2008). Whilst mindfulness has its origins within the Buddhist tradition, it has parallels with spiritual practices in other traditions and has increasingly been applied in mental health services as an evidence-based therapy for a range of different disorders (Mace, 2008, Cook, 2012a). A related treatment, Acceptance and Commitment Therapy (ACT), which incorporates a number of "mindfulness functions" (Mace, 2008, pp.69–71), has been shown to halve rehospitalisation over a four-month follow-up period following discharge in a study of 80 inpatients experiencing auditory hallucinations or delusions at the time of admission (Bach and Hayes, 2002).

Comparative studies

The foregoing research demonstrates that voice hearing occurs in a variety of contexts including both those who are diagnosed as mentally ill, and those who are not, and in those who belong to particular religious or spiritual traditions, as well as in those who do not belong to any such tradition. A number of comparative studies have identified some important differences between these groups.

Davies et al. (2001), in a comparison of psychotic (n=18), evangelical (n=29), and control (n=55) groups, found that evangelical Christians reported having heard voices more than twice as frequently as the control group (58.6 per cent vs 27.3 per cent). Furthermore, the Christian group rated the experience much more positively than did the control group, with the psychotic group reporting least positive experiences of voice hearing.

In a comparative study of AVHs in 111 healthy individuals and 118 psychotic outpatients, all of whom heard voices at least once a month, Daalman et al. (2011) found that 57 per cent of the healthy subjects, but only 28 per cent of the patients, gave a "spiritual" explanation for the experience. One of the patients (2 per cent) believed their voice(s) to be from God, and five (9 per cent) from the Devil or demons, but none of the healthy subjects gave such an explanation.

A study by Cottam et al. (2011) compared the experience of three groups of voice hearers: 20 mentally healthy Christians, 15 Christians with psychosis, and 14 non-religious patients with psychosis. The three groups were reported to have similar perceptual experiences, although the patient groups reported more frequent and louder voices, but the interpretations and affective responses of the healthy Christians were more positive. Patients in both groups had mainly negative emotional responses. A religious identity was ascribed to the voice by 100 per cent of the healthy Christians and 67 per cent of Christian patients, in comparison with only 23 per cent of the non-religious group. For the healthy Christians, 87 per cent reported that they only heard the voice of God, while 16 per cent also said that they heard the voice of the Devil. For the Christian patient group, these figures were 27 per cent and 40 per cent respectively. Almost all subjects reported that the voice that they heard was powerful, but 84 per cent of the healthy Christians, compared with only 13 per cent of the Christian patients and none of the non-religious group, reported that the voice was experienced as a positive power. Overall, the authors conclude that mentally healthy Christians are able to assimilate their experience of voice hearing with their faith in such a way as to provide positive meaning and emotional response.

There is clearly much scope for further comparative studies, but research to date suggests that voice hearing can be both a healthy and positive experience within at least some religious contexts and mental states, whilst for others it can be very negative. It is not clear to what extent these differences may reflect the existence of differences in underlying pathology or neurodiversity, to what extent they may be related to difference of social/ religious context, and to what extent the particular content of hallucinatory voices is itself determinative of positive or negative concomitants and interpretations. However, the possibility exists that better understanding of these comparative differences may actually provide important information to inform treatment interventions.

Conclusions

Spirituality and religion are not the only significant contexts within which voices may be experienced or interpreted, but they clearly provide important frames of references within which many people find meaning and construct explanations for such experiences. For many individuals, whether or not the voices include spiritual or religious content, spirituality, or religion provide important resources which support, or sometimes impede, effective coping with their experience. Some voice hearers apparently experience their voices as an important part of a normative spiritual experience, which may be affirmed by their spiritual or faith community. For others, the experience may be identified (by themselves and/or others) as evidence of mental disorder. In such circumstances, there may be significant barriers to discussing the spiritual or religious aspects of such experience, either with others who share their world view, or with the mental health professionals who seek to help them.

It would seem that diagnoses of mental disorder are generally associated with voices that are more negative and derogatory. Voices that are normalised within particular faith traditions or spiritualities are generally experienced in a more positive way, although there is also evidence that such voices may often be experienced as "inner voices", rather than as AVHs with perceptual (or perception-like) qualities. Religious and spiritual voices that are experienced with "hallucinatory" quality may sometimes be infrequent and exceptional, but there are also clear examples (such as that of Skye Thomas) in which they appear to be both pervasive and enduring, albeit also under some degree of personal control.

The experience of hearing voices often seems to have spiritual and/or religious biographical significance. Several examples considered demonstrated onset during a period of significant interpersonal distress. Whether the experience is associated with diagnosis of mental disorder, or interpreted within a normative spiritual/religious frame of reference, it has important implications for self-identity, purpose in life, and relationships with significant others.

Whilst attempts are made to suggest that some voices are spiritual and others pathological, such distinctions are difficult. When made by professionals or researchers, they seem to be prone to overgeneralisation and to value judgement. When made by voice hearers themselves – as in cases where the hearer distinguishes some voices as spiritual, and others as not spiritual – the distinction must be acknowledged as an important one. However, here it is the nature of the distinction that is made by the hearer, and the perceived basis for making this distinction, that is significant in the context of the life and experience of hearer. The danger is not so much in the making of such distinctions as that the hearer develops a self-validating system of interpretation which isolates him or her from the surrounding spiritual or religious community.

The experienced, seeming, autonomy of the voices that are heard is, I believe, a significant factor that has generally been neglected in the literature. It is the basis for much spiritual and religious interpretation of the experience of voice hearing. It gives the voice – which is essentially an immanent experience – a quality which invites interpretation in terms of transcendence.

Spirituality and religion provide valuable resources to inform both clinical care and scientific research on voice hearing. However, voice hearing also presents an approach to spiritual and religious experience which has hitherto not been adequately explored and which opens up potentially important areas for theological enquiry.

Notes

1 Auditory verbal hallucinations; see Introduction.
2 See Introduction for a definition of this term as it will be understood here.
3 Personal communication from a voice hearer (female, age 48 years).
4 15 subjects were known personally to the author, and 15 subjects were randomly selected from amongst 30 respondents to a questionnaire sent to a psychological-educational mailing list of 200 people in California.
5 Iain McGilchrist, for example, argues that Jaynes' radical misunderstanding of the nature of schizophrenia has contributed to this (McGilchrist, 2009, pp. 260–262). McGilchrist argues that the relationship between the "voices of the gods" and the mental world of human beings is exactly the opposite of that proposed by Jaynes. Rather than being a problem of increasing intercommunication of the two cerebral hemispheres, as Jaynes proposed, McGilchrist suggests that the reverse has happened and that the two hemispheres now operate much more independently. Mental contents previously recognised as one's own are now objectified and experienced as voices coming from outside the self.
6 Graham Turner (Turner, 2017) provides accounts of experiences of voices in a number of different religious traditions, based upon his interviews as a journalist with a variety of people who have "learned to listen". His conversation partners include followers of Christianity, Islam, Buddhism and Hinduism. Only in conversation with a Jewish rabbi did he elicit an account of a "now silent God", and an argument against expectation of hearing God's voice.
7 For further discussion of these studies, see Chapter 6.
8 Romme et al. (2009, p.180).
9 Ibid., p.182.
10 Ibid.
11 Caddy (1988, p.29).
12 Ibid.
13 Platts (1999, pp.23–24). This is a quotation attributed to Eileen Caddy. I have not been able to find it any other published source,
14 Ibid., p.24.
15 See Chapters 6 and 7.
16 Caddy (1988, pp.194–195).
17 Ibid., p.37.
18 Thomas (2004, pp.16–17).
19 Ibid., p.76.
20 Ibid., p.83.
21 For a detailed review, see Cook (2015).
22 This refers to the tenth revision of the International Statistical Classification of Diseases and Related Health Problems, a medical classification list created by the World Health Organization.

2 Voices in religion
History, tradition, and sacred texts

Religion is notoriously difficult to define (McKinnon, 2002). William James influentially defined religion in his 1901–1902 Gifford Lectures as the: "feelings, acts, and experiences of individual men in their solitude, so far as they apprehend themselves to stand in relation to whatever they may consider the divine" (James, 1902, p.31). This definition has come under heavy critique in recent times, not least from Nicholas Lash (1988), and it is clear that there are dangers in hiving off religious experience as somehow unrelated to the rest of life. On the other hand, as Ann Taves (2011) has argued, building on the work of Durkheim, religion is concerned with "special things" – things that are "set apart" from the rest of life. Taves identifies two principle kinds of special things – ideal things,[1] and anomalous things. Amongst "anomalous things"[2] are "anomalous experiences (that is, perceptions, sensations, or feelings) that suggest the presence of an unusual agent".[3] Taves gives Bernadette Soubirous' visions of Mary as an example of an anomalous experience of this kind. She suggests that special things are the "building blocks" of religion.

Whether or not one accepts the larger scheme of Taves' argument, I think it is helpful here to think of voices "that suggest the presence of an unusual agent" as one of the potential building blocks of religion. Clearly not all voices fall within this category, and for the purpose of the present chapter it is suggested that we are primarily concerned with voices that suggest the presence (directly or indirectly) of God. Clearly voices (and visions) are not the only kind of religious experience, and religion is also concerned with other special things (other building blocks) than just religious experience. However, I would propose that accounts of voices experienced in some as an encounter with the divine are found frequently enough within religious texts and traditions to warrant that they be considered one important kind of religious building block.

Later chapters of this book will consider in detail the appearances made by such voices in Hebrew (Chapter 3) and Christian (Chapter 4) scripture, in Christian tradition (Chapter 5), and in Christian religious experience (Chapter 6). In the present chapter, consideration will be given to some of the more general issues, and also to some examples from outside the Judeo-Christian tradition.

Religious building blocks: history, texts, and psychology

At first blush, it might all seem rather simple. Thus, for example, Myrtle Heery writes:

> The history of the world's major religions makes it clear that saints, sages, prophets, and teachers (such as Moses, Mohammed, and Teresa of Avila) have relied heavily on the inner voice as their inspiration, their guidance, and their authority.
>
> (Heery, 1989, p.75)

But have they? Certainly, there are texts and traditions that associate each of these figures, in different ways, with what might be understood as the hearing of a voice. The texts tell us little specifically about whether the voices in question were experienced as "inner" or "outer", but (as we shall see in later chapters) this may not be too significant. Voices are experienced variously in each of these ways, perhaps more often as "inner" than as "outer". But how securely do the texts and traditions in question historically anchor the inspiration, guidance, and authority of Moses, Mohammed, or Teresa in actual human experiences of voice hearing?

Whilst we know that Mohammed and Teresa of Avila were historical figures who, at least potentially, may have heard an "inner voice", there is much debate as to whether Moses ever existed as an historical character at all. Furthermore, the texts that give the account of Moses' life, including his conversations with God, are at least two and half millennia old, written in a vastly different cultural context, heavily redacted, and – most importantly of all – were not written by Moses himself.[4] They therefore need to be understood –at least by historians – in the wider context of what is known about ancient near eastern literature.

Of these three religious figures, only Teresa of Avila wrote the texts that have been passed down to us with her own hand, and we cannot interview any of the three to clarify the nature of their experiences according to modern scientific criteria. We simply do not have direct access to any of the psychological experiences behind the texts.

The principal texts associated with these three figures are also very different in form and genre. For Moses, most of the material available to us is in narrative form. Some of Teresa's writings are also narrative – especially those taken from her autobiography. The Qur'an, a unique work, according to tradition is a transcript of the revelations received by Mohammed. It includes narrative, alongside other genres of literature, but does not prioritise narrative chronology.

The key texts from which we draw our knowledge of Moses, and the texts which Mohammed recited, which are now known as the Qur'an, are respectively considered by Jews and Christians, and Muslims to be Holy Scripture. They are thus interpreted within, and by, religious communities, according to certain traditions, in the context of faith. However, they are also available for academic – historical critical, and literary – study by scholars who may or may not share the presuppositions and interpretations of faith.[5] Muslims believe that the Qur'an was revealed verbally, by God to Mohammed, through the angel Gabriel, but non-Muslims may have quite another view of the processes involved.[6] Indeed, in a secular society, any discussion at all of God as an explanation for events is potentially problematic (Kaufman, 1972).

When we begin to talk about experiences of hearing voices that suggest the presence of God as building blocks of any particular religion, we must therefore acknowledge that there are at least four different accounts to be offered:

1   An historical account – which will depend upon evidence drawn from a variety of sources, including primarily various texts but potentially also archaeological evidence. It will take into account the cultural and historic assumptions of the authors and redactors of the texts.
2   A narrative account – which is constructed by an author as a device to convey theological, spiritual, or other truth, but which may or may not be historical. Some narrative accounts are also canonical for a particular tradition, and some are not.
3   A theological, or confessional, account – which will privilege evidence drawn from canonical texts (scripture) and creeds, interpreted in the context of faith. This account may rely upon tradition, metaphor, allegory, and myth.
4   A psychological account – which will usually depend upon what can be gleaned from sources available from the historical account – concerning a scientific understanding of any historic human experience(s) behind the text(s). Such accounts may vary according to the psychological theories that are brought to bear upon the historical evidence, and so there may be multiple possible psychological accounts. Lacking any opportunity to interview historical figures directly, such accounts inevitably involve a psychological-historical interdisciplinary engagement.

These four possible accounts are different and need not accord, but they usually overlap in various ways. They differently prioritise and interpret the evidence. In the case of ancient traditions such as Judaism or Christianity, or even more recent traditions such as Islam, they all lack any direct access to the experiences in question. They are therefore all to be distinguished from the actual events of history, and the actual human experiences of history, as they really occurred.[7]

Even in the case of Christianity and Islam, let alone Judaism, there is insufficient historical or scientific evidence to support any firm conclusions concerning a psychological account of any voices heard by the figures to whom Heery refers. However, as Colleen Shantz has argued (Shantz, 2009) in relation to mystical experience, a psychological account might reasonably assume that there has not been any significant change in human neurophysiology in recent history. In evolutionary terms, even the pre-monarchical history of the Hebrew people is very recent indeed and it would seem very unlikely that voice hearing – as a psychological and neurobiological phenomenon – was unknown to human beings during the historical period to which the texts in question relate. There is therefore an a priori reason for supposing that experiences of voice hearing, at least possibly, *may* lay behind ancient religious texts.

There has also been increasing interest in recent years in the application of psychological insights to the interpretation of the Bible (and – in a similar fashion – other historical and/or sacred texts). For example, Wayne Rollins has suggested that it is a "fundamental premise" that:

> From a biblical-critical perspective, the Bible is to be seen as part and product, not only of a historical, literary, and socio-anthropological process, but also of a psychological process. In this process, conscious and unconscious factors are at work in the biblical authors and their communities, in the texts they have produced, in readers and interpreters of these texts and in their communities, and in the individual, communal, and cultural effects of those interpretations.
>
> (Rollins, 1999, p.92)

Rollins suggests that from this fundamental premise follow two research objectives, concerned respectively with psychological *context* and *content*. The Bible is thus, at the same time, both a product of human psychological processes, and also a commentary upon, or interpretation of, these same processes.[8] From the point of view of our present concern with voice hearing, we might say that we are concerned both with a psychological understanding of how the phenomenon of voice hearing may have given rise to (or contributed to) the biblical texts, and also with what the Bible may have to say (if anything) about psychological experiences of voice hearing. In this way, there might be a very creative engagement between biblical scholarship and the discipline of psychology. Unfortunately, as we shall see, psychological accounts have in practice tended either to pathologise the phenomenon of voice hearing in relation to religion, or else ignore it completely.

Hearing voices in texts

Voice hearing is experienced psychologically as an auditory-perception-like phenomenon, but the historical and confessional accounts that are purported to refer to voice hearing are conveyed as textual media. Whatever the relationship between the two, it is important to recognise that they are fundamentally different.

If a text has a voice, then this is a metaphorical voice. Even if it is understood as (for example) the "word of God", it is still the written word, and not the spoken word, not a voice heard out loud. Even if it is read out loud, it is the voice of the reader that is literally heard – and not the voice of the author, far less the voice of any perceived source of inspiration (be that God or some other) which can only – of necessity – be heard indirectly. There is therefore a stark contrast between auditory voices and textual voices. The former are transient and immediate (although they can be written down, thus becoming texts) and the latter are more enduring (although they may be read out loud). The former can, potentially, be interrogated by way of conversation, whereas the latter lose their connection with their authors and can be independently read, re-read, studied, and subjected to a variety of interpretations by a variety of readers. The former are direct, and can be heard by only a few people (perhaps only one), whereas the latter are much more indirect, and can be heard by many people.

When an auditory voice (let us say, for a moment, an auditory verbal hallucination) is translated in some way into text, it changes its nature in some important ways. New possibilities emerge for meaning and significance which may be far removed from those associated with the context of the original voice as heard by the original listener. Something that was significant in a particular way for one particular person now assumes different significances, possibly in a whole variety of ways and for whole communities of readers. A process of expansion and transformation has taken place which has a momentum and trajectory quite independent of, and far larger than, the original experience of the person who first heard the voice.

Interpreting voices heard in texts

The older any text is, and the further removed from its original geographical, cultural, and historical context, the greater the potential for misunderstanding. There are thus enormous problems to be acknowledged in respect of the interpretation of ancient documents originating from diverse cultural and historical contexts. Whilst scripture may be held, according to some confessional accounts, to be "infallible" or "inerrant", and historically accurate in every way, such a view is no longer academically plausible. Over the last century or two we have become more aware than ever before of the complex processes that bequeathed scripture to us in its present form. The intention of those who originally wrote and edited the texts that we have received, whatever it may have been, was clearly not to produce what we would now understand as an historically or scientifically accurate record. Indeed, the whole idea of what we count as historical and scientific was completely unknown to ancient authors. Writing of Hebrew scripture, Keith Ward says:

The narratives seek to bring out the spiritual meaning of events which are far in the past, and have been recalled through long oral traditions and re-enacted in generations of ritual celebrations. They thus reflect the sorts of relation to God which the community of the final writers and editors felt themselves to have, inextricably intertwined with and projected back on to memories of far distant events which had been treasured as founding-events of the Israelite community.

(Ward, 2007, pp.193–194)

As Ward goes on to argue, this does not mean that history is irrelevant, or that there is absolutely no historical basis to the narratives that we find in Hebrew scripture. It does mean that the texts available to us will never allow us to disentangle completely the underlying historical events and context from the primary spiritual concerns of the tradition that has conveyed them to us.

In many, perhaps most, cases it will therefore be impossible to know exactly what the original experience of the original writer of (or character within) a text might have been. It will often be impossible to confirm beyond doubt whether or not that experience might have been similar to the phenomenon that we now know as "hearing voices". Nonetheless, the similarity of some of these experiences at least renders it fruitful to ask the question as to whether the experience might have been one of hearing voices. Mapping the similarities and dissimilarities may be a useful exercise, both for our understanding of voice hearing and for our understanding of the nature of revelation.

The fact that some experiences look similar, even if they were in fact not really similar at all, is in any case significant in itself. The appearance of things informs our understanding and interpretation of the nature and meaning of experiences, and thus our expectations. For example, if on the basis of reading their bibles Christians believe that God speaks to his faithful people by way of a voice that may be heard, this may well influence their expectation (and perhaps also their experience) of hearing his voice in response to their prayers.

Inspired voices

If a voice (assuming, for a moment, an actual experience of hearing a voice by an historical character or author) has undergone translation into textual form and is then also incorporated into scripture, its interpretation will be influenced by the context of the scriptural tradition within which it has found its adopted home. As noted above, this will usually mean that it is then understood (at least within the community of faith) as in some way inspired or revelatory. However, it might not be. Scriptures include voices that are explicitly identified as not being inspired, or else as negatively inspired, such as the voices of false prophets or demons, as well as voices that are understood as positively inspired. If we allow the possibility that some voices are "inspired", or revelatory, and others are not, the question then arises as to how the former may be distinguished from the latter. What criteria might be applied in order to aid discernment? Theological traditions usually have criteria – implicit or explicit – for making such distinctions, and especially so when the voices concerned are voices found within the pages of scripture. Thus it will be important, when considering examples from Hebrew and Christian scripture, in the next two chapters, to give consideration to how such criteria for discernment operate within these traditions. This is not to say that the criteria will always be unambiguously agreed upon, but rather that it will be important to identify them where they are to be found. Voices differ, and are interpreted and evaluated differently.

The reality of the voice

It is in the nature of human perceptual experience that we usually assume the reality in the external world of what we hear, see, feel, or smell. Sometimes such perceptual experiences occur in a context that might give us reason to doubt their reality – for example, where it is difficult to hear or see clearly, or where the experience is fleeting, or where we have cause to re-examine what we thought we heard or saw. However, we usually know when there is cause for such doubt and, conversely, convinced of the reality of what we perceive when there is no obvious reason for doubt. Thus, there are many examples of voice hearing where the person concerned has looked around to see who was speaking, only to be surprised to find that no visible speaker was present. Even if there was no one there, in an important sense the experience itself was still real.

In the ancient world, but still today in many parts of the world, the reality of the divine was taken as a part of the fabric of the way that things are. Within such a fabric of life, the possibility of atheism does not arise and the world is an enchanted place, within which spiritual realities are understood to be – at times – visible, audible, tangible. Experiences of the divine in such a context may be "appallingly real".[9] It is generally with such an understanding of the world in mind that scriptural texts have been written, and it is in this context that they are interpreted by faithful readers. On the one hand, then, this raises questions of what the reality of the psychological experience behind the text might have been. On the other hand, however, it raises questions as to the nature of reality and how the intervention of the divine within the material order might be understood. These questions will largely be left for exploration in a later chapter of this book, but for now it is important to acknowledge both the importance of beliefs and psychological expectations concerning reality, and their impact on the writing and reading of texts. Scriptures (or at least those scriptures that have their origins in an enchanted world) both affirm and assume a reality of a spiritual or divine order of things which is not necessarily shared by modern readers of the text.

Literary voices

Within scripture, and in wider religious literature, there are many different genres of writing. Hebrew scripture, for example, includes history, poetry, prophecy, and so-called "wisdom" writings, as well as hymns, or psalms. Amongst these different literary forms, many stories are told. Whilst many of these stories clearly have some historical basis, it is not clear that all of these stories are necessarily to be understood as "true" in any historical or literal sense. Thus, for example, the stories of Jonah or Job would not now be understood by many scholars as intended to provide historical biographical accounts of actual lives. Indeed, it would seem unlikely that Job was even an historical figure. Nor does the message and meaning of these books depend upon such historicity. Even if fictional, Jonah provides a true-to-life account of how human nature sometimes propels people to do the opposite of what they believe God has told them to do, and then to feel angry when God doesn't do what they think he should do. Similarly, Job provides a timeless account of the search for meaning amidst sickness and misfortune which illuminates the plight of many who struggle to reconcile their faith in God with the seeming injustice of human suffering. It does not require that a character of this name really lived in a land called Uz, or that Satan literally appeared in the court of heaven to incite God to inflict Job's suffering upon him. Within the respective narratives, both Jonah and Job hear the voice of God, but we are not required to believe that this is any more than a literary device.

Of course, it is still possible that such narratives do draw upon historical experiences of voice hearing of (or known to) the authors concerned. It is therefore important to distinguish between experiences of voice hearing attributed to a character in a text and experiences of an author of a text. The former may be inspired by the latter, or they may not.

Mythical voices

Things get much more complicated with some other scriptural narratives, where historicity is perceived as more important, and especially when such stories are referred to as myth. For some readers of scripture, the labelling of certain stories as myth appears to be a blatant assertion that these stories are not true and thus that the reliability and authority of scripture is in question. For other readers of the same stories, to say that these stories are mythical is simply a way of reconciling the text with more modern ("scientific") accounts. In the first case, then, the attribution of the label of "myth" is perceived as an assault upon the truth, whereas in the latter case it is employed as a defence of the truth. The problem is that myth is a contested and ambiguous concept which means quite different things to different people and is thus easily misunderstood.

In ordinary usage of the word, to say that something is "mythical" often simply means that something is "untrue". Such a view is also reflected in the New Testament in the Pastoral Epistles and in 2 Peter.[10] In much modern academic usage, however, and perhaps especially in anthropology, myth has quite a different connotation. Thus, according to Alan Dundes (1984), "A myth is a sacred narrative explaining how the world and man came to be in their present form." Leaving aside his use of the word "man", and allowing a more gender-inclusive understanding, Dundes' concept of myth as sacred narrative with power to explain the human situation might be understood as almost exactly the opposite of the popular view of myth as falsehood. This is an understanding of myth rich in spiritual and religious significance. According to this view, such stories tell us everything important and true about the way that things now are from the perspective of faith. Furthermore, myths may well be essential to human flourishing (Davies, 2013).

For followers of Dundes' approach, the question arises as to the relationship between the kind of truth that this understanding of myth conveys and the scientific or historical kind? Moreover, this question is vitally important within the context of any consideration of the place of voice hearing in scripture. For example, the voice of the serpent speaking to Eve in Genesis 3 might be understood as a part of a mythical narrative, and thus a mythical voice with no historical basis in human experience, or it might be taken to have its origins in an ancient account of a woman who heard the voice of a snake speaking to her. In the latter case, the story is amenable to comparison with the experiences of contemporary voice hearers, but in the former case it is completely unamenable, since there was no historical figure called Eve. This is not to say that the author(s) of the text had not encountered experiences of voice hearing (their own or other people's) upon which the story might have been based. However, mythical stories (understood in this way) are not constrained by historical reality and so may not be based on any account of real-life experience at all.

For many readers, the example that I have just chosen will seem unambiguous. The first chapters of Genesis (indeed the whole book) might appear so far removed from modern scientific and historical understandings of the world as to be obviously mythical. Such was the approach to myth taken by Rudolf Bultmann (1884–1976). According to Bultmann, writing in an essay originally published in 1941, in the "mythical world picture"

> Human beings are not their own masters; demons can possess them, and Satan can put bad ideas into their heads. But God, too, can direct their thinking and willing, send them heavenly visions, allow them to hear his commanding or comforting word, give them the supernatural power of his Spirit.
>
> (Bultmann, 1985, p.1)

For Bultmann, such "mythological talk" was "incredible to men and women today because . . . the mythical world picture is a thing of the past" (p.3). It was understood by Bultmann not only as unscientific but also as non-Christian, insofar as it simply reflected the beliefs of a pre-scientific age and was not an essential part of the Christian kerygma. In order to understand the essential truth of scripture, Bultmann believed that it is therefore necessary to demy-thologise it: "By 'demythologizing' I understand a hermeneutical procedure that enquires about the reality referred to by mythological statements or texts. This presupposes that myth indeed talks about a reality, but in an inadequate way."[11] For Bultmann, scientific understanding and mythology alike are objectifying and talk only about the visible, audible, observable world. But, unlike science, myth also talks about an existential reality that seeks to understand the meaning of human experience. Demythologising thus seeks not so much to remove the myth as to expose its true purpose: "demythologizing seeks to bring out myth's real intention to talk about our own authentic reality as human beings".[12]

Bultmann's programme of demythologisation as an hermeneutical method became notorious; heretical in the eyes of some, and widely con-troversial within the Church.[13] It is debatable whether or not myth and kerygma can be separated at all, but if they can the result seemed to many to be deeply reductionistic. This may well have been founded upon a misunder-standing of what demythologisation intended, and Bultmann acknowledged that it was "an unsatisfactory word, to be sure".[14] After all, he wanted to recover the "real intention" of myth, not to eliminate it, and the term itself is therefore somewhat self-contradictory. It has been suggested more recently that what is really needed is to "remythologize", not in order to return to mythology, but rather in order to reaffirm that God does indeed act and "speak" in human history (Vanhoozer, 2010).

Insofar as I am interpreting Hebrew and Christian scriptures through the lens of a particular phenomenon (voice hearing), and the scientific body of knowledge that has grown up in association with the study of this phe-nomenon, it might be thought by some that I am engaged in an exercise of demythologisation. If demythologisation is understood strictly according to Bultmann's purpose of finding a way of talking about our authentic reality as human beings, then perhaps this is so. I find myself less reluctant to be associated with what Bultmann actually said than with what his critics seem to have understood him as saying. What I am explicitly not doing is reducing religious experience to, or explaining it away, in psychological terms. Nor am I suggesting that the designation of a story as mythical means that it is necessarily unhistorical. To say that a story is mythical – at least in my usage of the term here – neither refutes nor confirms historicity. It is rather a state-ment about its value as containing a truth about authentic human reality.

Regardless of the likelihood that what I write is open to such misinterpre-tations, I still believe that the exercise is worthwhile. This is both because I do not believe that it is helpful to disconnect the discourse of faith from the discourse of science and because I think that both faith and science are enriched by a more critical and thoughtful engagement between different ways of looking at reality. To study scripture in relation to voice hearing thus does not deny its status as in some way inspired or revealed; rather, it enriches our understanding of the way in which the immanent and the transcendent are interrelated (Cook, 2013b).

It is also not the case that I am exploring hermeneutical territory where Jews and Christians have not previously trespassed. Such is the scope of debate within both of these traditions that there has actually already been much consideration of most possible interpretations well before now. Thus, for example, in *Contra Celsus* (1:48), Origen (184/185–253/254 CE) considered what exactly we should understand when we read that Ezekiel, Isaiah, or Jesus, is said in scripture to have had a vision of the heavens opened:

> Just as we receive an impression in a dream that we hear and that our sense of hearing has been physically affected, and that we see with our eyes, although these impressions are not experienced by our bodily eyes or made by any vibration in our ears, but are only in our mind; so also there is nothing extraordinary in such things having happened to the prophets when, as the Bible says, they saw certain marvellous visions, or heard utterances of the Lord, or saw the heavens opened. For I do not imagine that the visible heaven was opened, or its physical form divided, for Ezekiel to record such an experience. Perhaps therefore the intelligent reader of the gospels ought to give a similar interpretation also in respect of the Saviour, even if this opinion may cause offence to the simple-minded, who in their extreme naïveté move the world and rend the vast, solid mass of the entire heaven.[15]

Origen concludes that there is a "divine sense" which is superior to ordinary, corporeal, sensing: "The blessed prophets found this divine sense, and their vision and hearing were spiritual."[16] Whether or not this spiritual sensing is a variety of what we now know as voice hearing might be debated, but essentially this only returns us to the question of how we discern the difference between those voices (or visions) that are inspired and those that are not. My point here is simply that the hermeneutical questions are not fundamentally new and that the critical exploration of them has a long history. Now, as in the 3rd century, the asking of such questions might cause offence to some, and the failure to ask them will seem naïve to others, but a serious critical exploration of the topic must still risk causing offence, or else it will indeed be naïve.

Possible relationships between voice hearing and scripture

Having thus acknowledged that our understanding of scripture (and other ancient texts) in relation to voice hearing will encounter a variety of hermeneutical challenges, and recognising the limitations that these will impose upon what we can historically prove, it is possible to identify four broad kinds of connection that might be made between scripture and voice hearing.

First, the writing of the text may have been connected in some way to an experience of hearing a voice. There would seem to be two principal ways in which this might happen. The writing of scripture may have been announced or affirmed by an experience of voice hearing, or else the sacred status of a text may have been revealed by a voice. Thus, the authority and status of the text is conveyed by a voice. Alternatively, the authors of sacred texts may have written, or be thought to have written, what they heard (that is, they may themselves have been hearers of a voice or voices); or, the authors of sacred texts might have written down what other people (voice hearers) heard. In either of these cases, the text itself is conveyed by a voice. I will refer to both of these kinds of connection as one of a voice *conveying* scripture.

Whether direct or indirect, reliable or unreliable, scripture might thus be a record of what a voice has initially conveyed. This is most clearly represented to be the case in respect of Islam, where both the authority and the text of the Qur'an are understood to have been conveyed to Mohammed by a voice.

Second, sacred texts might include accounts of voice hearing, as it were, within the text. Within such narratives there may be included a record of what certain voices said, but the supportive fabric of the narrative would be that of the author, and not of the voice. The record of what the voice(s) said might claim or aspire to historical accuracy, or it might be mythical, or even fictional. Examples of the kind which claim historical accuracy (whether or not this claim is accepted) might include the voice of God as heard by Moses in the books of the Torah, or the voice heard at Jesus' baptism in the synoptic gospel narratives. Examples of a mythical kind might include God speaking to Adam and Eve in the Garden of Eden in the narrative of Genesis 3. Whether the narratives are actually historical, mythical, or fictional is not the point here. (I am well aware that for many scholars Moses is understood to be a mythical figure and that for some readers, Adam and Eve are believed to be historical characters.) Rather, the significance of all of these accounts is that the authors of scripture accord divine authority to the voices heard by those about whom they write. In all instances of this kind, the voice has become a part of the text, and is conveyed within the text, rather than the text being conveyed by the voice. I will thus refer to examples of this kind as being voices *conveyed by* scripture.

Third, sacred texts might include material which is an elaboration upon, or reflection on, experiences of voice hearing (personal or otherwise). Depending upon the exact view of authorship adopted, most of the Hebrew prophetic writings may be understood in this way, and these will be considered further in Chapter 3. We might refer to these examples as *elaborative* and/or *reflective*.

Fourth, sacred texts might include poetry and prose within which "voices" have a metaphorical or symbolic significance. Thus, for example, in Sirach 17:13–14, where all human beings are said to have heard the voice of God, this would be difficult to understand literally. It is really only amenable to a metaphorical interpretation. Human beings can "hear" the voice of God in nature, in sacred writings, and in the lives of godly men and women. Given that theological language employs metaphor extensively, not least because it is almost impossible to find words that are adequate to convey the character, nature, and actions of God, including what God has "said", we might expect that this form of voice hearing – that is, a *metaphorical* form – is likely to be encountered commonly in scripture.

In any of these cases the voices heard in scripture may be understood as either the same as, or else different from, those heard by voice hearers today. If they are the same in form, then they might still be understood as different by virtue of the interpretation of the value and inspiration of the content. (This would be similar to the way in which all people dream, but only certain dreams are identified in scripture as divinely inspired – for example, as in the case of Joseph's dreams in Genesis.) However, it will be difficult or impossible in any given case to evaluate these similarities and differences with complete confidence, since the original hearers of the voices can no longer be questioned about their experiences, and the purpose of the authors in writing was not to clarify such matters. Even if it had been, their basis for clarification would not have reflected 21st-century historical or scientific premises of evidence and argument.

Voice hearing and scriptures in different religions

Before moving to a more detailed study of Hebrew scripture (the "Old Testament") in Chapter 3, and Christian scripture (the "New Testament") in Chapter 4, it might first be helpful to look briefly at some examples from other traditions. No attempt will be made here to cover all of the world's faith traditions. However, an attempt has been made to select some examples which are significant as illustrations of different textual kinds. Similarly, some of the omissions are notable. Quite apart from the huge diversity of different traditions within Buddhism, and the different relationship of Buddhism to its sacred texts, we might not expect a tradition which is essentially atheistic, and which emphasises the emptiness of all things, to be one within which the hearing of voices would feature prominently. On the other hand, the hearing of voices is very significant within spiritualism, and spiritism, but these traditions do not have a canon of sacred texts in the same way that most other religious traditions do.[17] It is clearly not the case that voice hearing is a significant consideration in all faith traditions, and neither are scriptural texts the only means by which voice hearing becomes in some way important (or unimportant) within any particular tradition. However, the hearing of voices does seem to have been a significant theme in virtually all of the monotheistic traditions.

The 7th-/6th-century BCE Iranian prophet Zoroaster (Zarathustra) was founder of what is arguably the world's oldest monotheistic tradition. At the age of 30, according to tradition, he experienced a vision of the archangel

Vohu Mana ("Good Intention"), who brought him into the presence of God (known within the tradition as Ahura Mazda).[18] The conversation that subsequently took place between Zoroaster and Ahura Mazda is recorded in Yasna 43 of the Zoroastrian scriptures.[19] This vision, or "conference", was the first of a series of seven such experiences recorded to have taken place, including encounters both with Ahura Mazda and six archangels.[20] It is explicitly referred to as including a visual component, but may also be understood to have included auditory verbal perceptions, and a sense of the presence of Ahura Mazda.[21] In a prologue to his translation of Yasna 43, Anklesaria writes:

> To say that Zarathustra held converse with Ahura Mazdâ, does not mean that Mazdâ assumed a material form; but it means that the knowledge of spiritual existence cannot be derived from earthly teachers, but by deep meditation. This idea of meditation is plausible, because in the Pahlavi writings we are told that Zarathustra sought inspiration and divine knowledge by going to the river Dareji . . . or the river Veh-Daitya.
>
> (Anklesaria, 1953, p.67)

Ahura Mazda's voice, whether or not it was of an audible kind, may well have been one experienced by Zoroaster in meditation or prayer.

According to Islamic tradition, in the year 610 CE , at the age of 40, Mohammed (d. 632 CE) experienced a vision of the angel Gabriel and heard a voice which told him that he was God's messenger (Nigosian, 2015, pp.61–62). From this time on, he continued to hear a voice which conveyed to him words which he believed were revelations from God. It is thus usually understood that God was the speaker, and that the angel played only an intermediary role (Gilliot, 2006, p.41). Within the Qur'an, it is affirmed that God had previously spoken to the prophets of Hebrew scripture, and to Jesus:

> We have sent thee
> Inspiration, as We sent it
> To Noah and the Messengers
> After him: We sent
> Inspiration to Abraham,
> Ishmael, Isaac, Jacob
> And the Tribes, to Jesus,
> Job, Jonah, Aaron, and Solomon,
> And to David We gave
> The Psalms.
> Of some Messengers We have
> Already told thee the story;
> Of others we have not –
> And to Moses Allah spoke direct –
> (Surah 4:163–164)[22]

Given the central role of the prophet Mohammed in Islam, and the particular way in which the Qur'an is understood to have been revealed to him, it is not surprising that there has been some significant debate as to the exact nature of his experiences. For those who do not identify themselves with the tradition, this has included both the suggestion that unconscious psychological processes were at work (Moberly, 2006, pp.19–25) or else that the prophet was suffering from temporal lobe epilepsy (Freemon, 1976). Needless to say, such explanations are not generally accepted by those who identify themselves as Muslims, although it is not immediately obvious (at least to the present author, as a non-Muslim) that either case would necessarily preclude divine inspiration.

The founder of Mormonism, Joseph Smith (1805–1844), having had a vision of an encounter with God the Father and God the Son, and then three visionary encounters with an angel, according to tradition, was shown where a book written on golden plates would be found buried. He is understood to have eventually translated this book, and in 1830 the *Book of Mormon* was first published in English. The *Book of Mormon*, according to Douglas Davies, "was one form of embodiment of the ideal of revelation: it focused and manifested the belief that God had spoken through prophets in the past and was speaking again through Joseph Smith in the present" (Davies, 2003, p.48). The 15 books contained within the *Book of Mormon* are each named after a prophetic figure and they contain narratives of a variety of prophetic voices and encounters, including resurrection appearances of Jesus Christ, angelic visitations, and hearing "the voice of the Lord".

In *Epistle to the Son of the Wolf*, the founder of the Bahá'í tradition, Bahá'u'lláh (1817–1892), wrote of an experience which seems to have marked the beginning of his receiving of what he believed to be revelations from God:

> During the days I lay in the prison of Ṭihrán, though the galling weight of the chains and the stench-filled air allowed Me but little sleep, still in those infrequent moments of slumber I felt as if something flowed from the crown of My head over My breast, even as a mighty torrent that precipitated itself upon the earth from the summit of a lofty mountain. Every limb of my body would, as a result, be set afire. At such moments My tongue recited what no man could bear to hear.
>
> (Bahá'u'lláh, 1986, p.314)

When Bahá'u'lláh spoke, as Bahá'ís believe, direct utterances of God, his human personality is understood as having been bypassed altogether.[23] If this was strictly the case, we may wonder whether the experiences were really voice hearing at all, or whether Bahá'u'lláh was inspired to speak words that he had not previously heard? However, in places, he writes as though he clearly has himself heard a voice which he is reporting. For example:

At this moment a Voice was raised from the right hand of the Luminous Spot: "God! There is none other God but Him, the Ordainer, the All-Wise! Recite Thou unto the Shaykh the remaining passages of the Lawḥ-i-Burhán (Tablet of the Proof) that they may draw him unto the horizon of the Revelation of his Lord."[24]

There thus seems to be some kind of scriptural tradition of voice hearing within all of the Western monotheistic traditions. It seems to be a little more difficult to identify scriptural examples of voice hearing within the Eastern religious traditions, but this is not to say that clear examples may not be found. In particular, it seems to be in evidence in Hinduism.

Hinduism is an ancient tradition which has a great variety of expression and is difficult to define. Amongst other things, the authority of the Veda (Hindu scriptures) may be the closest to a universal criterion of Hindu identity.[25] The Vedas are said to be sruti – "that which is heard" – revealed by the gods to ancient seers.[26] As far as I can tell, voices do not appear to be a common theme within the text. However, examples of interest may be found. Book 9 of the *Rig Veda* comprises a series of hymns in praise of soma, an hallucinogenic plant of uncertain identity. The properties of soma most in evidence here are entheogenic and mood-altering effects which generally do not seem to include auditory hallucinations, but there are occasional references to voices. (For example, in Hymns 12 and 95 there are references to the voice of Indu.) In chapter XI of the *Bhagavad Gita* Arjuna is granted a theophanic vision, within which he is addressed by Krishna, an incarnation of the supreme deity. However, Hinduism does not seem to be a religion within which scriptural voices feature prominently and the practice of yoga according to the Yoga-sutras of Patanjali involves withdrawal of the senses and culminates in a state of trance, or ecstasy characterised by a unitive state of consciousness.[27]

Voice hearing and scripture

The picture that begins to emerge from this very preliminary and general exploration of the possible relationships between voice hearing and scripture is one of the inspired voice as conveying, and conveyed by, divine authority. Whether this voice conveys the text, or is conveyed by the text, or if the text is elaborative or reflective upon it, or even if it is a voice heard metaphorically rather than literally, in each case the scriptural voice is understood to be authoritative. The possible relationships between the voice and the source of authority are complex and various. The voice may be that of a messenger (or angel), rather than the divine voice heard directly. It may even be a false or demonic voice, identified as such by the scriptural text and context within which it is located. (We might say that in such cases the voice conveyed by the text has negative authority.) The voice may be mythical, in which case the interpretive task is one of seeking out its inner account of authentic human experience. There is thus a need for criteria for discernment by means of which false voices may be distinguished from true voices, and positive sources of inspiration from negative sources.

Voice hearing as a building block of religion

The proposition here is that, in a variety of ways, voices experienced as an encounter with the divine constitute a kind of religious building block, with which (and upon which), along with building blocks of other kinds, a religion may be constructed. However, this proposition is not of the naïve kind that jumps directly from an ancient text providing a narrative account of Moses holding conversation with God, to the assumption that Moses was a voice hearer. Rather, it is a more complex proposition. Different accounts and interpretations may be given of voice hearing as an encounter with the divine, and the possible relationships between texts and psychological experiences are complex and varied.

Notes

1 Ideal things are special because they seem "ideal, perfect, or complete" (p.69). This specialness may be relative or absolute. When the relative qualities of ideal things are turned into absolutes, Taves proposes that they be given initial capitals. Such absolutes thus include Beauty, Transcendence, Infinite, Reality, Truth, Good, Evil, Purity, Perfection, Nature, and Ground of Being (p.70).
2 Anomalous things are identified by Taves as such on the grounds of being strange or unusual, or because they violate ordinary expectations (2011, p.72). She distinguishes between anomalous experiences that suggest the presence of an unusual agent – which form the group with which we are primarily concerned here – and those that do not. The latter group includes event, places, objects, and experiences, whereas the former are all considered to be experiential.
3 Taves (2011, p.73).
4 For further discussion, see Chapter 3.
5 See Davies (2004) for a discussion of the issues in relation to Judeo-Christian scripture.
6 See, for example, Freemon (1976).
7 Thus, for example, James Charlesworth draws attention to the need to distinguish between the Jesus of History, the Historical Jesus and the Christ of Faith (Charlesworth, 2004, p.22). Charlesworth does not separate the psychological account from the historical account in the way that I have done. Taves and Asprem (2017) show how narratives may be constructed from psychological experiences taking into account complex cultural concepts such as religion.
8 See Rollins' discussion (1999, pp.93–94).
9 Kuntz (1967, p.31).
10 For example: "For the time is coming when people will not put up with sound doctrine, but having itching ears, they will accumulate for themselves teachers to suit their own desires, and will turn away from listening to the truth and wander away to myths." (2 Timothy 4:3–4; see also 1 Timothy 1:4, 4:7, Titus 1:14, and 2 Peter 1:16).
11 Bultmann (1985, p.155).
12 Ibid., p.161.

13 Fergusson (1992, pp.107–108, 113–118).
14 Bultmann (1960, p.18).
15 Chadwick (1980, p.44).
16 Ibid.
17 Voices also play an interesting part in Native American religion. See, for example, Lame Deer's account of the voices that he heard in the vision pit, as a part of his rite of passage into adulthood (Lame Deer and Erdoes, 2009, pp.1–7). Black Elk tells of voices that he heard from the age of 4 years, and of a series of visionary experiences, commencing with the "great vision" that he experienced during a serious illness when he was only 9 years old (Neihardt and Deloria, 1979).
18 Anklesaria (1953, p.64), Nigosian (2015, pp.78–81).
19 Anklesaria (1953, pp.64–89).
20 A helpful account is provided by Jackson (1965, pp.36–55).
21 Nigosian (2015, p.79).
22 Translation: Ali (2000).
23 Esslemont (2006, pp.47–53).
24 Bahá'u'lláh (1986, p.347).
25 Brockington (1996, p.5).
26 Bowker (1999, pp.920, 1018; Parrinder, 1974, p.39).
27 Brockington (1996, pp.102–103).

3 Hearing voices in Hebrew scripture

God appears frequently as a conversation partner in the Hebrew scriptures that form the Christian Old Testament, especially in the earlier texts. In the Pentateuch (the first five books of the Old Testament) conversation between God and the Patriarchs, and between God and Moses, is generally a very direct affair and is narrated much as any other conversation between two people. God is not usually reported as being visibly present,[1] and the gravity of divine speech is of an altogether higher order of significance than human speech, but the literary presentation is nonetheless very much that of regular conversation. Later, the divine voice is conveyed mainly via the prophets and is a much more indirect affair. In other cases, messages from God are conveyed by an angel, or within a dream or vision. In Proverbs it is the "voice" of wisdom personified that is heard by those who are wise. In various places within the Psalms the voice of God interjects, and in some places (e.g. Psalm 50) there is extended divine discourse. In Psalm 115 Yahweh is contrasted with idols which do not speak.[2]

Voices other than the voice of God are also encountered in various places, notably the voice of a serpent in Genesis 3, a donkey in Numbers 22, and the spirit of the deceased prophet Samuel, conjured by a medium in 1 Samuel 28. In each case, as with angelic messengers elsewhere, there is a clearly identified speaker present within the narrative. In Genesis, Adam and Eve both converse with the serpent, just as they do with God, albeit the serpent serves as a counterpoint to the divine voice, encouraging disobedience to what God has previously said. In the case of the donkey in Numbers, we might consider that it is really God who is speaking (indirectly), as the narrator tells us "the Lord opened the mouth of the donkey" (verse 28). And when Samuel is summoned up by the medium, he speaks, as he did in life, as a prophet on behalf of God. In each case, the voice functions as a narrative device to move the plot forward and, indirectly, to make clear the truth of what God has previously said.

All of these texts are more than 2,000 years old, and were written according to literary and cultural conventions which are far removed from those of the modern world. Might it yet be reasonable to refer to the direct and indirect speech of God within these texts as a voice heard – and to those who heard it as "voice hearers"? Some people clearly think so. For example, Gerda de Bruijn, a psychologist, writing in one of the seminal texts of the Hearing Voices movement, says without qualification: "The originators of the Western monotheistic religions (Moses, Jesus and Mohammed) all heard voices not apparent to others" (de Bruijn, 1993, p.30).

Similarly, Richard Bentall (2004, p.349) writes that "it is certainly true that hallucinatory experiences have been recorded since biblical times". A recent journal article by a distinguished group of researchers, asserts that "unusual sensory experiences" have been spiritually foundational throughout the world – and the first example given is "Moses and his burning bush" (Laroi et al., 2014, p.S214). Simon McCarthy Jones, in his monograph work *Hearing Voices*, writes: "The inclusion of a range of voice hearing experiences in the books of the Old Testament firmly established hearing voices as a potentially divine experience, and validated it as a way that God could contact humanity" (McCarthy-Jones, 2012, p.22). In a footnote, McCarthy-Jones indicates that he is "not concerned here with the veracity of these stories, but rather the influence they had on how people understood hearing voices". The clear assumption is that, questions of "veracity" aside, these stories may be understood as examples of "hearing voices".[3] But are they?

First, it is important to note that in Hebrew scripture God is said to have spoken even before the first human beings appeared on earth. In the first Genesis creation narrative, it is through God's speech that things are brought into being. Thereafter, the word of God is understood as powerful and effective in sustaining creation and in bringing about the divine purpose in diverse ways, many of which do not involve human hearing at all.[4] This ancient Near Eastern understanding of the power of the voice of God was not exclusive to Israel. Psalm 29 is a hymn in praise of "the voice of the Lord", which may well have its origins as a Phoenician hymn to Baal, modified for the worship of Yahweh.[5] Within this psalm there is both a recognition of the power of the voice of God in nature and also, at least in the version in the Hebrew psalter, a praise of God for his power in bringing victory in war. The voice of God, as understood in Hebrew scripture, is thus much more than words heard in human hearing.

Second, there would appear to be within Hebrew scripture a genre or form of text that we might describe as theophanic (Kuntz, 1967). A simple definition of theophany might be that it is "a temporal manifestation of the deity to man involving visible and audible elements that signal God's real presence".[6] Kuntz points out that, within the Hebrew tradition, hearing seems to have been a particularly important component of the theophany.[7] It is thus not adequate to define a theophany merely as the "appearance" of a divinity.[8] However, it would also seem that the hearing of God alone does not constitute a theophany. This is not a perceptual matter, or an assertion that a theophany has to be multimodal in some way, so much as an observation on the way in which Kuntz identifies the theophany as a form within the canon of Hebrew scripture. Thus he outlines a core of six formal elements of the theophanic genre[9] within which the "hieros logos", or special word, of the deity is but one.[10] Whilst he notes that these do not all need to be present, it is also clear that there are places where the divine voice is heard and is not, on its own, considered to be theophanic.[11] This may reflect his primary concern with form criticism of the text. He does not explore theophany as a psychological phenomenon, but only as a textual form. Nonetheless, we are left with theophany as a key genre, or form, within Hebrew scripture, within which the "hearing of the voice" of God is central but not necessarily definitive.

If Hebrew scripture has anything at all to do with the hearing of voices, it is thus immediately clear that it is going to be much more complex than a simple extrapolation from "the Lord said to Moses" to an assumption that Moses heard voices. In order to test the nature of the relationship further, we will need to look a little more closely at some specific examples. It will not be possible to study all of the "voices" of Hebrew scripture in detail here, but some earlier and later examples will be considered. Attention will also be given to the nature of prophecy as a means by which a voice heard – the voice of God – becomes significant as a voice proclaimed.

Genesis

According to Genesis, direct conversations were had with God by Adam and Eve, Cain, Noah, Abraham, Isaac, Rebekah, and Jacob. In the story of Adam and Eve, a dialogue is also had with the serpent. In Genesis 16 and 21, Hagar has conversations with an angel. In Genesis 18, Abraham and Sarah receive three visitors who are often said to be angels, although in fact the text refers to them as men, and the encounter is referred to as being with God. In Chapter 19, it is angels who rescue Lot and his family from Sodom.

Amongst these narratives, is an account of God's command to Abraham to sacrifice his son Isaac.

> God tested Abraham. He said to him, "Abraham!" And he said, "Here I am." He said, "Take your son, your only son Isaac, whom you love, and go to the land of Moriah, and offer him there as a burnt offering on one of the mountains that I shall show you."[12]

Abraham proceeds in obedience to the divine command, but then – at the very last minute – an angel intervenes:

> Then Abraham reached out his hand and took the knife to kill his son. But the angel of the LORD called to him from heaven, and said, "Abraham, Abraham!" And he said, "Here I am." He said, "Do not lay your hand on the boy or do anything to him; for now I know that you fear God, since you have not withheld your son, your only son, from me."[13]

Abraham, again obedient to the voice, offers a ram in sacrifice instead of his son, and then he hears the angelic voice again:

> By myself I have sworn, says the LORD: Because you have done this, and have not withheld your son, your only son, I will indeed bless you, and I will make your offspring as numerous as the stars of heaven and as the sand that is on the seashore. And your offspring shall possess the gate of their enemies, and by your offspring shall all the nations of the earth gain blessing for themselves, because you have obeyed my voice.[14]

What are we to make of such conversations? According to George Graham, Abraham was clearly delusional, and the voices hallucinatory.[15] But do these texts tell us anything about the psychological experiences of historical characters?

Genesis probably has its origins in a number of sources, drawing on oral traditions which may have been quite ancient, which were then written down and gathered together by later authors or redactors. Recent scholarship has suggested that the composition of Genesis may thus have taken place as late as the 6th century BCE (Dozeman, 2016). For all its theological significance, which is enormous for both Judaism and Christianity, it is now clear that its historical and scientific significance (which have both been the subjects of considerable attention) require critical and careful consideration. Whether or not any of the characters portrayed in this book were historical figures is open to considerable debate. Even if they were, the purposes of the unknown author(s) in writing about them were far removed from our present purpose. Genesis adopts a narrative mode of portrayal, within which voices – divine, angelic, animal, and human – play a significant part. However, the narration of a voice is not the same thing as the hearing of a voice – as the first creation narrative, and the later divine soliloquies[16] in Genesis clearly show.

This means that we should not jump to naïve or overly literal conclusions about the relationship between the hearing of divine or angelic voices in these texts and the phenomenon of voice hearing as we encounter it today. The authors of Genesis were not phenomenologists or psychologists. Indeed, the whole notion of phenomenology is anachronistic to a 6th-/5th-century understanding of human experience.[17]

Genesis does, however, introduce the notion of a God who speaks, and the significance of this (for Judaism and Christianity, perhaps also for Islam) is huge. Theologically, it portrays a God in intimate relationship with the natural order that he has created, and particularly with people in it. The world as portrayed in Genesis is not some kind of deistic desert, from which God keeps himself far removed, but rather a living – if now also flawed – paradise within which God reveals himself and thus is encountered by human beings. This is a world within which the voice of God may be heard. The implications of this have echoed down the centuries since and have been important to all three of the world's major monotheistic traditions.

Moses

As Walter Moberly[18] has suggested, Moses is presented in Deuteronomy as the prophet *par excellence*. Moses occupies a hugely significant place in the biblical account of the early origins of the worship of Yahweh.[19] There is no historical evidence either to confirm or refute the assertion that an historical character identifiable as Moses ever existed, but it would appear that he might be located in or around the 13th century BCE.[20]

Early in Exodus, a story of a theophany experienced by Moses provides the basis for an account of his calling as a prophet.

> Moses was keeping the flock of his father-in-law Jethro, the priest of Midian; he led his flock beyond the wilderness, and came to Horeb, the mountain of God. There the angel of the LORD appeared to him in a flame of fire out of a bush; he looked, and the bush was blazing, yet it was not consumed. Then Moses said, "I must turn aside and look at this great sight, and see why the bush is not burned up." When the LORD saw that he had turned aside to see, God called to him out of the bush, "Moses, Moses!" And he said, "Here I am." Then he said, "Come no closer! Remove the sandals from your feet, for the place on which you are standing is holy ground." He said further, "I am the God of your father, the God of Abraham, the God of Isaac, and the God of Jacob." And Moses hid his face, for he was afraid to look at God. Then the LORD said, "I have observed the misery of my people who are in Egypt."
>
> (Exodus 3:1–8)

This theophany is almost immediately followed (in verses 7ff.) by a story of the calling of Moses as a prophet and leader of the Hebrew people.[21] The pattern that is established is thus one of the interrelatedness of an experience of the presence of God and the response that such an experience elicits.[22]

The perceptual phenomenon that initially attracts Moses' attention is that of the fire. This in itself was not an unusual experience in a hot desert where dry vegetation could easily ignite. Rather, it attracted attention because it continued to burn when it should have burned itself out. This does not appear to be presented as a visionary experience, so much as a normal perception (albeit perhaps of a miraculous event), in a mundane context, which nonetheless has important symbolic significance.[23] Moses, his attention thus engaged, then finds himself in an encounter with the God who speaks. God identifies himself as holy, as *his* God (the God of his father and of the patriarchs), and as concerned with the suffering of his people.

This encounter marks the beginning of a new phase in the life of Moses, and a turning point in the story of the oppressed people of Israel. From this point on in the narrative, dialogue between God and Moses is a frequent occurrence. Describing Moses' regular meetings with God in the "tent of meeting", the narrator of Exodus says: "Thus the LORD used to speak to Moses face to face, as one speaks to a friend" (33:11).

Not all of the subsequent encounters between Moses and God are as dramatic as the one described in Chapter 3. Much later (33:18–34:8) Moses experiences another theophany in which it becomes clear that his more usual exchanges with God were of a different (much more mundane) order. However, the narrator of Deuteronomy draws attention to Moses as being unique among the prophets for the directness of his communication with God: "Never since has there arisen a prophet in Israel like Moses, whom the Lord knew face to face" (34:10).

The indirect voice: dreams, angels, diviners, prophets, and seers

Somewhere after the end of Genesis and before the beginning of the era marked by Judges, things change. Whilst Moses clearly belongs to the earlier era of directly hearing the voice of God (and Joshua is represented as following him in this tradition, albeit to perhaps a lesser degree), the later prophets seem to have a different experience. Before turning to the later prophetic tradition, it is important to give some further consideration to this transition, and to various experiences of more indirectly hearing the voice of God.

Westermann[24] identifies a number of transitional forms, beginning with a key initial transition point in the Genesis narrative in the story of Joseph, to whom God reveals himself in dreams, but not in direct speech. A further transitional form is that of the angelic messenger. Between the times of the Patriarchs and the Judges, Westermann says, angels appear to proclaim a message from God to a recipient, but then disappear again. Thus, for example, angels appear and speak to Gideon (Judges 6–8) and to Manoah and his wife (Judges 13). In fact, at the beginning of Judges, an angel apparently addresses "all the Israelites" (2:1–5). During the later prophetic era – another transition point according to Westermann – God's revelations are also delivered indirectly – but by means of human messengers, the prophets. After this era, he argues, both direct and indirect revelations by God are understood to have ceased. It is now the inherited text which is revelatory.

Westermann clearly draws attention to an important point. There do seem to be transitions. Given the lack of narrative clarity as to exactly what the experiences of Moses and the later prophets were supposed to have been, I don't think we can say that these were actually transitions in the mode of revelation, or the phenomenology of voices. However, there do appear to be literary transitions, and perhaps theological transitions, in the ways in which God's voice is understood to be heard. We might debate exactly where these transition points fall, historically or canonically. For example, Wieseltier locates the key transition point – from direct revelation to inherited text and tradition – much earlier than the later prophetic era:

The rabbis in the midrash comment: "The voice makes its way to Moses and all of Israel does not hear it." Moses, of course, reported what he heard. It was precisely when the report of the voice did the work of the voice that tradition was born.

(Wieseltier, 1987, p.37)

Whether or not Westermann's exact account of things is accepted, it is clear that there is an important transition from the direct speech, reported as being heard by the patriarchs and by Moses, to the more indirect forms of communication found in the later biblical literature.

Richard Friedman has an altogether more radical account of this transition. For Friedman, "God disappears in the Bible":

Gradually through the course of the Hebrew Bible . . . the deity appears less and less to humans, speaks less and less. Miracles, angels, and all other signs of divine presence become rarer and finally cease. In the last portions of the Hebrew Bible, God is not present in the well-known apparent ways of the earlier books.

(Friedman, 1995, p.7)

The wider argument that Friedman constructs is beyond the scope of the present work, and it is interesting to note that he refers to absence of God primarily through visual language – "disappearance". However, a theme of the diminishing audibility of God is also charted through his book.

In the early chapters of Genesis, Friedman notes, "God speaks familiarly to the humans in conversation (3:9–19)".[25] In later chapters (as in stories about Hagar and Abraham), the words of God are spoken by an angel.[26] At Mount Sinai, the voice of God is heard by all of the Israelite people,[27] but is such a terrifying experience that they say to Moses, "You speak with us, and we will listen; but let not God speak with us lest we die."[28] For Friedman, this point in the biblical narrative marks the birth of prophecy. "After this scene in the Bible, Yahweh never again speaks directly to an entire community Himself. All communication from the deity is directed only to individuals, prophets, who then deliver the message to whomever they are told."[29] The personal experience of Moses is declared to be unique, and never to be repeated.[30] Prophecy subsequent to Moses is less direct, and inferior to that of Moses.[31]

Friedman identifies Samuel as the last person in Hebrew scripture to whom God is said to be "revealed" and David and Solomon as the last kings of Israel to whom God "speaks".[32] In Elijah's encounter with God on Mount Sinai, in contrast to the revelation to Moses on the same site, God is present not in the noisy phenomena of earthquake, wind, and fire, but in silence.[33] In the books of Ezra and Nehemiah, God speaks to no one, and, in the book of Esther, God is not even mentioned.[34]

The consistency of this gradual process of the "disappearance" of God across so many books, written at different times by different authors, is remarkable. Its course appears to follow the internal chronology of the Bible, and not the order in which the books were written. Friedman accounts for this on the basis of a variety of considerations – notably by a move of emphasis from experience of God in nature to knowing God in the events of history, psychological processes which make it easier to imagine extraordinary divine communication in earliest times, and processes of literary composition which, as a "fortuitous side effect", make it appear that God was more involved in human affairs in earlier times. Friedman does not – and should not be expected to – appeal to actually changing frequencies of visionary and voice-hearing experiences through history. Even if we assume that such experiences were commonly occurring in the ancient world as they are now, we have no way of knowing what the relationship between such experiences and the writing of the texts might have been. As a biblical scholar Friedman appeals simply to influences upon authors and editors which create an impression of the disappearance of visions and voices within the biblical narratives.

Prophecy after Moses thus represents an important transitional phase in divine communication in Hebrew scripture. Before we turn our attention to a more detailed consideration of Hebrew prophecy, we need to clarify some differences in terminology and practice.

Two words are encountered in Hebrew scripture which are usually translated as "seer".[35] There is some debate about how these terms might best be distinguished from each other, and from the more usual Hebrew word for "prophet".[36] However, a seer might be understood as someone having a gift for exercising clairvoyance, soothsaying, or divination,[37] by means of which things concealed to ordinary people are revealed. The seer enquires of a spirit or divinity on behalf of a supplicant and, by various means,[38] provides a response, thus acting as a mediator between that person and the divinity or spirit. The utterance that constitutes the response is usually referred to as an oracle.[39] The seer might thus be said, at least in some cases, to have heard the "word of God", or else, perhaps, to have heard a "voice" (literal or otherwise) from a sacred source.[40]

Whilst the roles of seer and prophet seem largely to have overlapped, there were also seers whose activities and practices were deemed illegitimate insofar as the Yahwistic tradition was concerned. Thus, for example, the King of Babylon is portrayed in one of the prophecies of Ezekiel as using methods of divination to determine that he should pursue his military campaign against Jerusalem.[41] In general, such methods were forbidden to the faithful Hebrew people,[42] but exceptions may be found. For example, Joseph is presented by the author of Genesis as practising cup divination,[43] and the Urim and Thummim are presented in various places as having been used by the priests.[44] In each case, there is no explicit approbation. In 2 Samuel 5:24, an example of divination may be found which employed the sound of the wind in trees. Generally speaking, however, such practices seem to have been subject to disapproval. In Deuteronomy 18:9–14, various practices, including divination, soothsaying, reading of omens, and mediumship, are proscribed and are contrasted in verses 15–19 with the role of the true prophet who both hears the voice of Yahweh and speaks his words.[45]

The Hebrew prophets

The biblical record of the earlier prophets (11th to 9th century BCE) is provided mainly in the books of I & II Samuel and I & II Kings.[46] These notably include Samuel, Nathan, Elijah, and Elisha, but also Ahijah, Ahithophel, Deborah, Gad, Huldah, Jehu, and Michaiah. Saul and David, both kings of Israel, also act as prophets.

By the time of the "earlier" prophets, things have already changed in comparison with the prophet *par excellence*, Moses. By way of examining this transition, it is worth pausing, in passing, to contrast the encounters of Moses and Elijah with God on Mount Sinai, narrated respectively in Exodus 19 and 1 Kings 19.[47] The former encounter is associated with thunder and lightning, thick cloud, a "blast of a trumpet", smoke and fire, and an earthquake. When Moses speaks, God answers "in thunder". The people are permitted to hear God from a distance, but not to approach the mountain. When God has finished speaking, Moses is given two stone tablets, on which the law that God has spoken is written "with the finger of God" (31:18). Elijah's encounter is of an altogether different order. He is completely alone with God. He experiences a wind so strong that it splits mountains and breaks rocks, an earthquake, and a fire, but God is "not in" any of these events. He then hears a "sound of sheer silence", at which he emerges from the cave in which he has been sheltering and his dialogue with God resumes. In contrast to Moses, Elijah comes to Sinai in a state of exhaustion and fear, overwhelmed by his victorious encounter with the prophets of Baal and the threats made against him by Jezebel. The message that he is given there is primarily for his own encouragement, albeit he is commissioned to anoint a king over Israel and a prophet to succeed him in his own work. Between the time of Moses and the time of Elijah, in the biblical narrative, prophecy has changed dramatically. The early prophet (here Elijah)[48] still hears God speak, but it is a much more private affair, and God is heard not so much in the context of dramatic theophanies as in silence.

The later, or classical,[49] prophets of the 8th to 6th centuries BCE include the major prophets – Isaiah, Jeremiah, and Ezekiel – as well as the 12 minor prophets.[50] In contrast to the earlier prophets, we are left mainly with a written record of the prophecies of these figures, and little or no historical or biographical information about their lives. In many cases it is not clear whether these individuals were the authors of the books attributed to them, and these books may well have been edited or added to. The book of Isaiah, for example, is thought to represent three distinct collections of prophecies, those of "first" Isaiah dating to the 8th century BCE, of "second" Isaiah dating to the 6th century BCE at the time of the Babylonian exile, and of "third" Isaiah dating to a post-exilic 6th-century context.

Prophecy

Prophecy might most simply be characterised as "human speech on behalf of God".[51] This presumes that the prophet knows what to say on behalf of God, and thus we can identify at least a two-stage process of reception and transmission. Where a prophecy is transmitted to its recipient by an intermediary, where it is written down, and (especially) where it is thought to be worthy of preservation and wider dissemination, there may be additional stages in the process, potentially involving multiple messengers, scribes, and editors.[52] Given also that the texts which concern us here are all more than two millennia old, we must clearly be cautious about what is asserted about any underlying human experience behind the text.

Lindblom, in his classic work *Prophecy in Ancient Israel*, characterises the prophet as:

> a person who, because he is conscious of having been specially chosen and called, feels forced to perform actions and proclaim ideas which, in a mental state of intense inspiration or real ecstasy, have been indicated to him in the form of divine revelation.
>
> (Lindblom, 1967, p.46)

We might debate whether the consciousness of a special calling, the sense of compulsion, or the unusual mental state are essential elements of the concept or the role. It is not difficult to imagine prophecy in which one or more of these elements might be lacking.[53] Biblical terminology is more that of being "sent"[54] than compelled or inspired. Neither is there any reason to suppose here, or in many examples from Hebrew scripture, that an unusual mental state is a necessary concomitant. Indeed, Old Testament writers usually show no interest in such things.

Lindblom later[55] suggests that revelation is the central feature of the experience and work of the Hebrew prophet. Within his understanding of the concept of revelation, are included visions, auditions, thoughts and ideas. He thus understands the prophet as regarding their proclamation as "words"[56], received from God and passed on to those who listen. God is understood as speaking by or through the prophet. Thus, in Deuteronomy (5:27, 31), the people ask Moses to "hear all that the Lord our God will say" and then to relay back to them what God has said.

This process of reception and transmission may be, precisely, by way of words that are received by the prophet and then spoken verbatim: "The word that the LORD spoke concerning Babylon, concerning the land of the Chaldeans, by the prophet Jeremiah" (Jeremiah 50:1).[57] In other cases, the words received may then be proclaimed by way of action, rather than speech. Thus, for example, in Isaiah: "at that time the LORD had spoken to Isaiah son of Amoz, saying, 'Go, and loose the sackcloth from your loins and take your sandals off your feet,' and he had done so, walking naked and barefoot" (Isaiah 20:2).

In either case, the receptive part of this process is regarded as an act of speech on the part of God, and thus it may be said that God "has spoken". For example: "The earth shall be utterly laid waste and utterly despoiled; for the LORD has spoken this word" (Isaiah 24:3).[58] In some places, this spoken word is explicitly described as being the voice of God: "Jeremiah said, 'That will not happen. Just obey the voice of the LORD in what I say to you, and it shall go well with you, and your life shall be spared'" (Jeremiah 38:20).[59] And, in at least some instances, it is explicitly stated that this is a voice that is *heard*: "Mortal, I have made you a sentinel for the house of Israel; whenever you hear a word from my mouth, you shall give them warning from me" (Ezekiel 3:17)[60]

As with the proclamation, the receptive part of the process may not literally, or solely, be in the form of speech. Thus, for example, Samuel's initial prophetic experience appears to have taken the form of an auditory verbal hypnagogic hallucination,[61] but Samuel is also referred to in the text as having experienced a "vision" (1 Samuel 3:15). Amos receives a series of visions[62] that are in mixed modality, including both visual and auditory elements. Perhaps one of the most famous visionary experiences of Hebrew prophecy is that reported in Isaiah 6:

> In the year that King Uzziah died, I saw the Lord sitting on a throne, high and lofty; and the hem of his robe filled the temple. Seraphs were in attendance above him; each had six wings: with two they covered their faces, and with two they covered their feet, and with two they flew. And one called to another and said: "Holy, holy, holy is the LORD of hosts; the whole earth is full of his glory." The pivots on the thresholds shook at the voices of those who called, and the house filled with smoke. And I said: "Woe is me! I am lost, for I am a man of unclean lips, and I live among a people of unclean lips; yet my eyes have seen the King, the LORD of hosts!" Then one of the seraphs flew to me, holding a live coal that had been taken from the altar with a pair of tongs. The seraph touched my mouth with it and said: "Now that this has touched your lips, your guilt has departed and your sin is blotted out." Then I heard the voice of the Lord saying, "Whom shall I send, and who will go for us?" And I said, "Here am I; send me!" And he said, "Go and say to this people: 'Keep listening, but do not comprehend; keep looking, but do not understand.' Make the mind of this people dull, and stop their ears, and shut their eyes, so that they may not look with their eyes, and listen with their ears, and comprehend with their minds, and turn and be healed." Then I said, "How long, O Lord?" And he said: "Until cities lie waste without inhabitant, and houses without people, and the land is utterly desolate."
>
> (6:1–11)

This account is the more compelling for its first person perspective of what the prophet sees and hears.[63] The setting in the heavenly court is evocative of a prophetic claim to stand in the council of God.[64] It has been suggested (and also disputed) that this passage is a "call narrative", descriptive of the prophet's first calling and vocation to a prophetic ministry.[65] Watts (2005, pp.108–109) draws attention to the pervasive themes of hearing, seeing, and understanding. Ironically, although the prophet hears, sees, and understands, the people to whom he takes the divine message fail to hear, or see or understand.

Is it plausible that a prophet could understand his mission in these terms from the outset or, as much scholarship asserts, is it really the case that this record concerns his subsequent reflection upon a mission that has failed – in which he tried in vain to get people to look and listen and understand, but failed?[66] Is this in fact the prophet's retrospective attempt to make sense of God's purpose in it all from the beginning? But then again, is it really credible, as Otto Kaiser asks, that, if this were the case, a prophet should retrospectively present this as the word of God which he received from the beginning: "Are we in any way on the right course if we are concerned to interpret this story in psychological and biographical terms; in the end is it not meant to be understood theologically?" (Kaiser, 1983, p.119). It is not entirely clear what it might mean to understand this story "theologically". Eventually, Kaiser concludes that we should "give up the notion, still prevalent today, that in this chapter we can hear directly the voice of the prophet Isaiah".[67] This seems a very pessimistic conclusion, but Kaiser does well to draw our attention to the complex layers of meaning within this story. Yes, it is a story of a visionary experience within which the hearing of voices plays an important part. But, no, we cannot know exactly what the biographical or psychological experiences of the prophet actually were. It was surely never the author's purpose[68] that we should be focussed on such experiences, but rather that we should continue to reflect theologically on what it means to hear and see and understand.[69]

It is not necessarily the case that the receptive part of the prophetic process need be perception like at all. Lindblom[70] suggests that what is received may, rather, be inspiration of a more general kind, or even a purely literary creation. McKane goes even further, suggesting that "God does not speak Hebrew."[71] That is, the prophet may be understood to have "filtered" a more or less mysterious experience of encounter with God, which is then "translated" and expressed in human language (in this case, Hebrew).

Wilson also draws attention to the role of the prophet in interpreting the message that he or she receives:

> Thus when a prophet receives a divine message, he "translates" it into human terms and communicates it using traditional speech forms and actions which indicate that he is functioning as a prophet and that the message which he brings comes from the divine realm.
>
> (Wilson, 1980, p.9)

Abraham Heschel goes even further than this and suggests that the fundamental content of the prophetic experience is not one of receiving and relaying words (or visual or other perceptual experiences) but rather one of a profound and all-consuming sympathy with God:

> the fundamental experience of the prophet is a fellowship with the feelings of God, a sympathy with the divine pathos, a communion with the divine consciousness which comes about through the prophet's reflection of, or participation in, the divine pathos.
>
> (Heschel, 2010, p.26)

In this way, the receptive part of the prophetic experience is not so much about hearing "voices", as about discerning divine "feelings", or perhaps (better) developing a sympathy with divine concerns and priorities.[72] Mordecai Schreiber (2013) similarly argues that it was not hearing voices that made the Hebrew prophets prophets, but rather a moral compulsion to proclaim the divine message.

It has been argued that prophecy in ancient Israel fulfilled an important social function in confronting injustice and maintaining social order (Wilson, 1980). Marvin Sweeney has suggested that the prophets' "basic function is to persuade people to follow the divine will" (Sweeney, 2016, p.233). The prophet, in the pre-exilic period, both occupied an institutional position within the Temple cult, and also exercised a more spontaneous oppositional role, critical of the monarchy and institution. Whilst this role was valued, and prophets were consulted by kings, and interceded on behalf of others, at the same time they were also objects of mockery and contempt,[73] sometimes hated, or even feared.

False prophecy

Prophecy might be comforting or disconcerting – depending upon one's point of view. Faced with a difficult moral dilemma, or an irresolvable dispute, it might be very nice to receive prophetic clarification about what God wants you (or others) to do. On the other hand, when set on a particular course of action that seems attractive, it might be very disconcerting to be told emphatically that this is *not* what God wants you to do. Presumably this is why prophets were hated and feared, as well as valued. But this question of perspective also conceals another problem. Claims to speak for God can evoke emotive responses, and may or may not accord with reasoned argument. How can they be validated? And what happens when different prophets say different things?[74]

Within the broad category of those who were considered to be prophets, distinctions came to be made between true prophets and false prophets. Thus, for example, in Deuteronomy 18, following a discussion of the contrast between divination, soothsaying, etc. with true prophecy (see above), there is a condemnation of the false prophet:

"But any prophet who speaks in the name of other gods, or who presumes to speak in my name a word that I have not commanded the prophet to speak – that prophet shall die." You may say to yourself, "How can we recognize a word that the LORD has not spoken?" If a prophet speaks in the name of the LORD but the thing does not take place or prove true, it is a word that the LORD has not spoken. The prophet has spoken it presumptuously; do not be frightened by it.

(Deuteronomy 18:20–22)

According to this passage, the marks of a false prophet are that he or she speaks in the name of gods other than Yahweh, or else proclaims things which do not come true. More fundamentally, the false prophet presumes to speak words that God has not given to them. But, as Moberly[75] has pointed out, the "wait and see" part of this test is not much help at the time of first hearing the prophecy – which is exactly when the ability to discern true from false prophecy is most needed. And how are we otherwise to know whether the prophet is truly speaking words given by God or not?

Lindblom notes that those who are condemned as false prophets are frequently found to prophecy peace and prosperity, whereas the true prophet usually brings words of judgement.[76] The fundamental distinction, according to Lindblom, is concerned with an authentic experience of hearing the voice of God:

> The divine voice which they heard with the inward ear, their insight into the religious and moral situation of the people, the lessons they learned from the events of history – by all these they were infallibly led. They were not in the service of a religious dogma or a national ideal, they were in contact with the living God of history. Out of this experience came their prophetic message, the content of which was Yahweh's word and nothing else.[77]

Of course, the true prophet is in contact with the true God – and nothing less – but how are we to know the truth of the matter? How were authentic prophets to be distinguished from false prophets in practice? And how do we know that true prophets were "infallibly" led? Perhaps – sometimes – they simply got it wrong?

Micah condemns those who prophesy for financial gain,[78] Isaiah condemns the prophet who is drunk,[79] and Zephaniah condemns prophets who profane what is sacred and do not respect the law.[80] Jeremiah bluntly condemns those who are simply liars.[81] Whilst most cases of false prophecy do not obviously seem to be associated with drunkenness or profanity, and while it is not always easy to tell who is lying, the moral character of the prophet is clearly a crucial issue – to which we shall return. But what about the moral character of the message? Samuel, amongst the most respected and moral of "true" Hebrew prophets, nonetheless is not averse to conveying a message to the man whom he is about to make king which, by modern Western standards, would be considered deeply immoral:

> Samuel said to Saul, "The Lord sent me to anoint you king over his people Israel; now therefore listen to the words of the Lord. Thus says the Lord of hosts, 'I will punish the Amalekites for what they did in opposing the Israelites when they came up out of Egypt. Now go and attack Amalek, and utterly destroy all that they have; do not spare them, but kill both man and woman, child and infant, ox and sheep, camel and donkey.'"[82]

A voice – if voice there was – that incited to genocide, including the murder of innocent infants and children, would by modern standards immediately appear to be an obvious case of "false" prophecy – and yet is not identified as such within the pages of Judeo-Christian scripture.

Prophetic ecstasy

There has been considerable debate concerning the state of consciousness of the prophet when prophesying. On the one hand it has been asserted that prophecies were delivered in a state of ecstasy. Theodore Robinson, for example, provides a colourful account of what (he says) ecstasy might have looked like:

> It consisted of a fit or attack which affected the whole body. Sometimes the limbs were stimulated to violent action, and wild leaping and contortions resulted. These might be more or less rhythmical, and the phenomenon would present the appearance of a wild and frantic dance. At other times there was more or less complete constriction of the muscles, and the condition became almost cataleptic. The vocal organs were sometimes involved, noises and sounds were poured out which might be unrecognisable as human speech. If definite words were uttered they were often unintelligible. Face and aspect were changed, and to all outward appearance the Ecstatic "became another man".[83] An additional feature was insensibility to pain, and the extravagant activities of the Ecstatic frequently included violent slashing and cutting of his own body and limbs.
> (Robinson, 1953, p.31)

According to Robinson, such phenomena were common throughout the Mediterranean and were associated at different times with various cults, including the Baals, the Delphic oracle, and the Dionysians, as well as the Hebrew prophets. Ecstasy was understood by Robinson as being a key point of distinction between the seer and the prophet. Whilst often spontaneous, it might also be induced by music, alcohol, or focused staring at a visual point of reference. It might easily be confused with insanity. Whole groups of prophets, and not simply individuals, could be seized by ecstasy.[84] But does Robinson's description – based upon prophetic ecstasy observed in other cultural contexts – have anything at all to do with ancient Hebrew prophecy?

The earliest references to ecstatic frenzy in the Hebrew Bible appear to be at the time of Saul. In particular, in 1 Samuel 19:23–24 we read:

> [Saul] went there, toward Naioth in Ramah; and the spirit of God came upon him. As he was going, he fell into a prophetic frenzy, until he came to Naioth in Ramah. He too stripped off his clothes, and he too fell into a frenzy before Samuel. He lay naked all that day and all that night. Therefore it is said, "Is Saul also among the prophets?"
>
> (1 Samuel 19:23–24)[85]

This, widely cited, episode appears to be exceptional and very uncharacteristic of the wider canonical accounts of prophecy. Nonetheless, it has formed the basis for much speculation. According to Lindblom, it would have been within ecstatic experiences[86] that the prophets (or, at least, some prophets some of the time) would have heard the divine voice speaking to them.[87] Westermann, in his tracing of the history of the study of prophetic forms of speech, suggests that it was a process of reflection and elaboration upon ecstatic experiences that would have led to the production of the written records that include the prophetic books included within Hebrew scripture.[88] In this way, a distinction is made between the ecstatic experience and the later texts that are referred to as prophetic.

The view of Israel's prophets as ecstatic is not, however, without its critics. Leon Wood (1979), for example, argues that the scriptural evidence is not as strong as is commonly asserted, and that virtually the whole case rests upon arguments from comparative religion which only provide indirect evidence from other historic and contemporary religious practices, and not from within the Hebrew prophetic tradition itself.

Sigmund Mowinckel (1935, p.268) distinguishes between the great 8th-/7th-century BCE prophets whose texts are included in Hebrew scripture and what he calls "the ordinary type" of prophet, or professional prophet, whose frenzy

> is not – say the prophets – due to a holy possession by the deity; he is a "fool," an intellectually and morally inferior individual who only falls into this frenzy from lack of intelligence.[89] Such men are possessed by Baal and have seduced the people to worship idols.[90]

According to this view, the prophets known for their ecstatic frenzy were, in fact, the false prophets. Not that there is not an ecstatic element to the experience of the true prophet, but rather that this is inessential and it is not the means of prophetic insight: "It is through concentration, prayer and listening that the 'word' comes to the prophet".[91] Mowinckel thus emphasises much more the rational element of the prophetic experience, not the ecstasy, visions, or auditions,[92] but rather inward perception, wisdom, and moral judgement.[93]

In between these two extremes of seeing prophecy, on the one hand, as more or less inevitably associated with a state of ecstasy and, on the other hand, as more or less a rational affair, rarely associated with ecstasy, there are a variety of typologies, variations, combinations and intermediate views.

For example, Obbink (1939) distinguishes between different forms of revelation. In the "half-psychical" form of prophetism revelation comes through dreams or perceptual experiences (visions, etc.). In the "technical" method, revelation comes through the methods of divination. In the "full-psychical" method, revelation comes in clear consciousness. Whatever the method, Obbink concludes: "the prophet does not pass on the divine revelation in the way a postman delivers a letter without knowing what it contains. Rather he has an active part in the formulation of the divine message."[94]

McKane (1995) draws attention to the impossibility of knowing from the textual evidence exactly what the experience of the biblical prophets was. Inevitably, their written records, even if of an originally visionary or ecstatic experience, must reflect processes of subsequent recollection and reflection which are distinguishable from the original experience itself. These processes, we may assume, must have taken place in non-ecstatic mental states.[95] Conversely, some of the experiences described in the Hebrew texts would appear to represent normal perceptual phenomena which are subsequently (allegedly) processed in unusual ecstatic or revelatory states.[96] For example, Jeremiah's "vision" of the branch of an almond tree (1:11) or Amos's "vision" of a bowl of summer fruit (8:1–2) might fall into this category.[97]

There is no reason to assume that the stereotypical behaviour of the Hebrew prophets remained constant through history, or that it was exactly the same in every geographical and cultural location. As Wilson has rightly observed, in view of these considerations, "the question of prophecy and ecstasy is far more complex than earlier scholars . . . supposed".[98] However, the normative canonical portrayal of prophecy does not appear to be one in which ecstatic or visionary experience predominates.

Madness

Elisha (2 Kings 9:11), Hosea (9:7), and Jeremiah (29:26) all seem to have been accused of madness by their contemporaries, although it is not entirely clear that these were serious allegations as opposed to dismissive contempt or abuse. John Gray (1980, pp.541–542) understands the reference to the madness of Elisha in 2 Kings as being merely an allusion to prophetic frenzy.

Various scholars have asserted that prophecy in ancient Israel must have been associated with mental disorder.[99] Ezekiel seems to have come under particular scrutiny in this regard (Cook, 2012c), perhaps as a result of the intense and unusual visionary experiences related in the book attributed to him, and the associated narratives of strange behaviour. A wide range of psychiatric diagnoses have been proposed, from schizophrenia to temporal lobe epilepsy, substance misuse, bipolar disorder, and post-traumatic stress disorder, and yet there is little or no hard evidence to support any diagnosis of Ezekiel at all. Saul has been diagnosed as possibly suffering from bipolar affective disorder. Andrew Sims (2010, pp.258–259) speculates that his episodes of prophetic frenzy may have been associated with the periods of ecstatic elation associated with this condition.

Perhaps it is most surprising that in fact most of the Hebrew prophets appear not to have been accused of mental illness at all, either by their contemporaries or by later scholars. When madness is invoked, within the text or by later scholars, it is only ever in a dismissive fashion. Yet, often, it is simply not considered at all. In his meta-commentary on Amos, speaking from within a secular, post-Christian culture David Clines reflects on just how astonishing this is:

> The book of Amos is founded on the belief that Amos the prophet had actually been spoken to by God. This is what he claims when he says, "Thus says Yahweh". It is an amazing claim, and a shocking one. Most of our acquaintances, we ought to recall, think that people who claim to hear voices from the sky should be locked up. Commentators are hardy souls, however, not easily alarmed, and generous of spirit. How else to explain the fact that almost every textbook on Amos accepts Amos's claim, the book's ideology?
>
> (Clines, 1995, p.85)

Discerning voices

The existence of a canon of scripture – within whichever tradition it might have been defined – already implies a process of discernment, by which canonical texts have been distinguished as authoritative, inspired, or revelatory. This is not to say that non-canonical texts are completely lacking in these qualities, but rather that the canon has been affirmed and distinguished as particularly demonstrating them. One would hope and expect that this process of including and excluding texts from a canon suggests some kind of process of evaluation and discrimination whereby the value of things has been sifted and distinguished according to their value.

It was suggested in Chapter 2 that scripture – or at least some scriptures – might be related to a kind of experience of voice hearing in various ways. Within the foregoing study of Hebrew scripture, various examples of this have been considered. In particular, Hebrew prophecy would seem to be an experience of the hearing (and relaying) of a voice. However, it is also clear that not all Hebrew prophecy has been affirmed by the tradition as being authoritative or inspired. There were false prophets as well as true prophets, and this implies that distinctions have been made. In some cases, the false prophets were simply considered to be liars, motivated by gain, or else simply saying what people wanted to hear. However, in other cases, it would seem possible (if not even likely) that they too were hearing voices, and so the question arises as to whether some voices are more inspired than others – more authoritative, more revelatory? If this is the case, then how may they be distinguished?

In *Prophecy and Discernment*, Walter Moberly writes:

> if there were no rational and disciplined way of discriminating between claims to speak for God, or of knowing when human speech should and should not appropriately be recognized as being in some way a word from God, the consequences would be far reaching . . . If such were indeed the case, then one could hardly deny that the characteristic modern approach would indeed be the best approach: the redescription of such voices in social scientific categories, especially those of psychology and sociology, that bracket out God and theology, and the marginalizing of such voices so that they no longer trouble the public sphere and can be confined to what consenting adults say and do in private (or, in some cases, in the wards of psychiatric hospitals).
>
> (Moberly, 2006, p.222)

In his search for a "rational and disciplined way of discriminating", Moberly notes that sincerity is beside the point. Prophets – and, we might add, others who hear voices – can be completely sincere and convinced of what they have heard, and yet the message that they proclaim, or the words that they report the voice as saying, might not be from God. Similarly, the presence or absence of unusual mental states proves nothing. Whether one views ecstatic states as characteristic of true or false prophecy, it is not the ecstatic state in itself that makes the prophecy true, and in the case of almost all of the Hebrew texts concerned we have no access to the associated original experiences anyway. Similarly, with mental illness, evidence for which is in most cases all but completely lacking, it is not clear in principle that there is any reason to believe that someone who is mentally ill could not be a prophet.

Moberly contends, I think correctly, that the key discriminating factor must be the moral character of the one who speaks and of the message that they convey. He is not naïve as to the difficulty of using such discrimination in ways that are not facile or bland, or which employ religious language so as to obscure rather than facilitate discernment. He draws on Christian concepts of grace and self-giving in order to examine more carefully how discernment may be applied in practice, but also notes the value of engagement between different faith traditions and the importance of valuing integrity wherever it may be found – even (or perhaps especially) if it is found in someone else's tradition. He notes also that the prophets did not often appear successful within their own society. It is subsequent reflection within the tradition that has discerned the value of their message and that has bestowed the authority associated with inclusion in the canon of scripture.

Hearing voices in Hebrew scripture

The voice of God is conveyed, directly and indirectly, within Hebrew scripture, from the earliest to the latest texts. It is conveyed as an ostensibly historical voice, heard by the patriarchs, by Moses and the prophets, and it is conveyed in metaphor, and in myth. In the later prophetic books, it is conveyed in an elaborated and reflective form. The processes of elaboration and reflection dedicated to these prophecies represent both the necessity of elaboration and reflection in order to convert an experience of voice hearing into the medium of a written text, and also the value of these texts as worthy of being reflected on.

Whilst we cannot be absolutely certain that the underlying experiences behind any of these texts are in any way similar to those of contemporary voice hearers, it would seem to be going against the evidence to rule this possibility out entirely. That some kind of human experience of hearing a voice – even if that voice was more like a thought than a sound, or more metaphorical than literal – lay behind these texts would seem highly probable. The prophetic process – as evidenced within the Hebrew texts that we have considered – clearly included an element of reception, as well as one of proclamation. Prophets were sometimes subject to allegations of madness, but not always do so. Wisdom and value have been discerned within the voices that they heard, whatever those voices might have been, and this has been reflected upon and passed on for the benefit of future generations.

I have referred at some length to the conclusions of Moberly's *Prophecy and Discernment* because it is almost unique in addressing the central question of how we may discern whether or not it is actually God who is speaking through a purportedly prophetic voice in scripture – or elsewhere. Or, to put things differently for the purposes of the present book, it addresses the question of how we may discern whether or not a voice heard in the absence of any objective speaker may be from God, or an angel or spirit or other sacred source. Further discussion of this will have to await a later chapter of the present book, but this chapter concludes simply with the assertion that the scriptures of the Hebrew tradition provide – alongside critical reflection on other scriptural traditions – a valuable resource for reflecting on what meaning might be found, not just by an individual, but by whole communities, in at least some experiences of hearing voices.

Notes

1 But see Genesis 18, where "The Lord appeared to Abraham".
2 Julian Jaynes (2000, pp.165–175), proposed the interesting idea that in fact some idols did speak. The possibility that some ancient near eastern idols were in fact "aids to hallucinated voices" is further discussed in a review of this aspect of Jaynes' work by Rowe (2016). However, the "bicameral period" of history to which this work relates (roughly 9000 BCE to 1000 BCE) is largely pre-biblical.
3 See also Murray et al. (2012), who further go on to offer psychiatric diagnoses for Abraham, Moses, Jesus and St Paul on the basis of their supposed hallucinatory and other symptoms.

4 See, for example, Isaiah 55:10–11; cf. Isaiah 30:30.

5 Gaster (1946), Cross (1950), Dahood (1966, pp.174–180), Craigie (1983, pp.241–249).

6 Kuntz (1967, p.17). Kuntz goes on to develop a fuller definition of theophany as a literary form within Hebrew scripture (pp.28–45). Amongst other things, this fuller description includes the divine initiative, temporality, the necessarily partial nature of the self-revelation of the deity, the involvement of visual and auditory components, location in place, and the evoking of human fear.

7 Cf. Lindblom (1961), who asserts that "In most cases what was heard in the theophany was regarded as more important than what was seen" (p.106). Westermann (1961, pp.99–100) distinguishes between theophanies, in which God appears in order to reveal himself, and to communicate, and epiphanies, in which God appears in order to bring aid. He further identifies two kinds of theophany. The first kind, the model exemplar of which is the Sinai theophany (Exodus 19 and 34), is distinguished by the cultic context, in which God appears to an individual as mediator of a communication to the people. The second kind, examples of which include 1 Kings 19 and Isaiah 6, are distinguished by the calling or commissioning of the individual prophet.

8 Kuntz (1967, pp.17–18).

9 Using the technical language of biblical scholarship, Kuntz refers to this as a *Gattung*, a type or form of text which follows a particular pattern.

10 Kuntz (1967, p.59).

11 Kuntz does not seem to consider dialogue with God prior to Genesis 12 as theophanic – although he is not explicit about this. Interestingly, he identifies Exodus 24:1–2, 9–11 as the only theophany in which there is no divine voice (1967, p.40) – and yet the voice of God is clearly spoken in verses 1– 2 and 12, and referred to in verses 3–4 and 7. The theophany is thus separated out from the surrounding narrative, including the words spoken by God. Later, Kuntz refers to the frequency of theophany as a vehicle for prophetic calling (1967, p.134) but does not seem to expect that the prophets then received every subsequent word of God in this form.

12 All biblical quotations are from the New Revised Standard Version (NRSV) 22:1–2.

13 22:10–12.

14 22:16–18.

15 Graham (2015). Graham does acknowledge that not all scholars agree that Abraham was an historical figure, but he does not take into account the genre of literature or the impossibility of knowing what Abraham's actual psychological experience, in historical and cultural context, might actually have been.

16 As, for example, in Genesis 2:18, 3:22, 6:3, 6:7, 8:21–22, 11:6–7, 18:20–21.

17 This has not prevented Lindblom (1961), for example, from asserting that the theophanies of Hebrew scripture, including those of Genesis, were "hallucinatory experiences" and that even though some of the biblical accounts may be "legendary", yet "experiences of this kind may really have occurred" (p.106).

18 Moberly (2006, p.4).

19 Yet, this account is confined almost entirely to the books of Exodus, Leviticus, Numbers and Deuteronomy. As with Genesis, scholarship concerning the origins and history of composition of these texts has suggested increasing recent origins – perhaps as late as the 6th century BCE (Dozeman, 2016).

20 Coats (1988, p.11).

21 According to some accounts, these might originally have been two separate stories which were later combined (Childs, 1974, pp.52–53, Durham, 1987, p.29). This has been disputed, for example by Buber (1946, p.39), who points out the fundamental homogeneity of the text. Childs suggests that, whatever the original sources, the combined text as we have received it invites, indeed requires, reflection on the interplay of the different elements comprised within it.

22 Durham (1987, pp.29–30).
23 Ibid., pp.30–31.
24 Westermann (1967, pp.99–100).
25 Friedman (1995, p.8).
26 Ibid., p.9.
27 Exodus 19:19, 20:1, 22.
28 Exodus 20:19.
29 Friedman (1995, p.17).
30 By implication in Numbers 12:6–8, and more explicitly in Deuteronomy 34:10.
31 Friedman (1995, p.17).
32 Ibid., p.20.
33 Ibid., pp.22–24.
34 Ibid., p.27.
35 Koch (1982, p.15), Zucker (1994, pp.15–17).
36 According to 1 Samuel 9:9, the terminology changed during the course of Israelite history. Various prophets – including Samuel and Gad – are referred to as both prophets and seers. Wilson (1980, p.7) notes that the term seer was used primarily in circles associated with Jerusalem, and considers that there is a basic continuity between the terms.
37 Lindblom (1967, pp.83–95).
38 For example, dreams, signs, omens, premonitions, visions, and auditions.
39 Tucker (1978, p.34), Sawyer (1993, pp.27–30).
40 For most purposes, in the present context, we might simply assume that these represent the same thing – that is, that hearing "the word of God" is hearing the *voice* of God. However, it is not absolutely clear that this can be taken for granted, and the word of God might conceivably be received in a variety of ways other than that of hearing a voice.
41 Ezekiel 21:21. In this example, the methods used are shaking of arrows from a quiver (belomancy), consulting the teraphim (objects of uncertain identity that were used for divination), and inspecting an animal liver (hepatoscopy). In 1 Samuel 28, Saul consults a medium who engages in necromancy. Reference to the use of dreams for divination may also be found in Hebrew scripture, including Jeremiah 27:9 and Zechariah 10:2. A useful review of divinatory practices in ancient Israel has been provided by Porter (1981).
42 For example, Deuteronomy 18:10, 1 Samuel 15:23, Ezekiel 13:23.
43 Genesis 44:5.
44 For example, Deuteronomy 33:8, Ezra 2:63. Little is known about exactly what the Urim and Thumim were like, but they seem to have been a means of casting lots – rather like dice (Cross and Livingstone, 2005).
45 Christensen (2001, pp.398–413). Interestingly, verses 17–20 are given as God's reply to Moses – and thus are represented as divine speech.
46 These books are generally classed as "historical" within the Christian canon, but as the "former" prophets within Judaism (where they are grouped together with Joshua and Judges).
47 Elijah's encounter with God in 1 Kings 19 is said to take place on Mount Horeb, now generally considered to be an alternative name for Mount Sinai.
48 We know much less about the encounters of the other early prophets with God, but they resemble Elijah much more closely than they do Moses. The era of dramatic theophanies – including dramatic voices – appears to have passed.
49 These would generally be referred to as the "latter" prophets of Judaism.
50 Hosea, Joel, Amos, Obadiah, Jonah, Micah, Nahum, Habakkuk, Zephaniah, Haggai, Zechariah, Malachi. In the Christian canon Daniel is also included as prophetic literature, whereas in Judaism this book features within the "writings" or wisdom literature. Written in the 2nd century BCE, Daniel ostensibly refers to events taking place four centuries earlier. (See, for example, Porteous, 1979.)

51 Moberly (2006, p.1).
52 See Nissinen (2000).
53 For example, in John's gospel in the New Testament, it is said of Caiaphas, a Jewish high priest, after he has said that it is better for one person to die on behalf of the whole nation of Israel: "He did not say this on his own, but being high priest that year he prophesied that Jesus was about to die for the nation" (11:50–51). This might be taken to represent an "unconscious prophecy". Brown (1966, p.442), Barrett (1978, p.407). However, this would appear to be an atypical occurrence, and not characteristic of Hebrew prophecy.
54 See, for example, Jeremiah 7:25, 27:15, Ezekiel 3:5.
55 Lindblom (1967, pp.108–122).
56 In the Hebrew texts, it is usually the "word" (singular) that is said to be received from God – as opposed to human "words" (plural).
57 Cf. Jeremiah 37:2, Haggai 1:1, Zechariah 7:7, Malachi 1:1.
58 Cf. Isaiah 40:5, Ezekiel 5:15.
59 Cf. Jeremiah 11:7, 42:6, Haggai 1:12.
60 Cf. Isaiah 5:9, 22:14. However, elsewhere, the word is "seen" rather than heard. See, for example, Isaiah 2:1, 13:1.
61 Cook (2013a).
62 Amos 7–9; cf. Ezekiel 1–3, where there is also a gustatory element to the vision. The prophets are also said to have "seen" as well as "heard" God's word. See, for example, Amos 1:1, Isaiah 2:1, Jeremiah 38:21.
63 Cf. Micaiah in 1 Kings 22, and Amos 7. Watts (2005, p.104).
64 Ibid., p.105. Deuteronomy 5:27 is suggestive of a similar courtly image.
65 Kaiser (1983, pp.121–123), Watts (2005, p.104).
66 Kaiser (1983, p.119).
67 Ibid., p.121.
68 I do not presume to suggest that we can ever fully fathom authorial intention. Rather, I am suggesting that this text does not seem to be written so as to encourage the seeking after experiences such as those that Isaiah may have had, but rather that the vision underlines the authority and importance of the message that emerged from it, and which the prophet subsequently proclaimed.
69 Themes which the prophet Jesus was later to return to in the course of his teaching. See, for example, Matthew 13:16, Mark 8:18, Luke 8:8.
70 Lindblom (1967, p.121).
71 McKane (1995, pp.x, 145–146).
72 "Feelings" may not be a helpful term here – although it is clearly the word that Heschel uses. Given that the attribution of "feelings" to God is an anthropomorphism, we might question the directionality of this process. Are the (human) feelings of the prophet attributed to God – or do they arise in response to God in some way? Or perhaps prophet and God simply both "feel" the same way about things? But what, exactly, are divine "feelings" anyway?
73 Koch (1982, pp.19–32).
74 As, for example, in 1 Kings 22.
75 Moberly (2006, p.102).
76 Ibid., pp.210–215. But this also is not a reliable practical test of true prophecy, as there are clearly exceptions – see ibid.
77 Lindblom (1967, pp.214–215).
78 Micah 3:11.
79 Isaiah 4:5.
80 Zephaniah 3:4.
81 Jeremiah 14:14, cf. 23:25, 27:10, 14–16 and elsewhere. Jeremiah further asserts that they commit adultery (23:14) and prophecy "visions of their own minds" which do not come from God (23:16).
82 1 Samuel 15:1–3.

83 Robinson may have intended a reference here to 1 Samuel 10:6.
84 For example, 1 Samuel 10:5.
85 See also 1 Samuel 10:9–13.
86 Lindblom (1967), however, distinguished between "orgiastic" and "lethargic" forms of ecstasy, the former being essentially akin to that described by Robinson, and the latter being a milder and more passive form, lacking the excitatory features of orgiastic ecstasy.
87 Ibid., p.55.
88 Westermann (1967).
89 Hosea 9:7.
90 Jeremiah 23:13.
91 Mowinckel (1935, p.276).
92 Mowinckel considers that true hallucinations occur only rarely in the great prophets.
93 Similarly, Abraham Kuenen (1969), in his classic work *The Prophets and Prophecy in Israel*, writes "The ecstatic state is not the rule, but the exception, in the life of the Israelitish prophet" (p.84). And, again: "The difference between the prophetical literature and the revelation to the prophets, would certainly have been very great, if the revelation was communicated to them while they were in a state of trance. Where we discover clear marks of reflection, deliberation and study, may we not confidently infer there the absence of ecstasy?" (p.84).
94 Obbink (1939, p.26).
95 McKane (1995, p.138).
96 Ibid., pp.140–141.
97 But then again, as McKane (1995, pp.142–143) shows, by reference to the work of Schökel, there is no need to invoke any abnormal mental state in such cases at all.
98 Wilson (1979, p.337).
99 See, for example, Heschel (2010, pp.175–177).

4   Hearing voices in Christian scripture
The New Testament

In contrast to the Old Testament, the New Testament seems to offer many fewer examples of what might be understood as "voice hearing". However, the voices that are identifiable are very significant and, as with the Old Testament, there have again been those who are quick and unhesitating in their identification of examples of voice hearing within its pages. For example, Jesus and St Paul are listed by John Watkins in his book *Hearing Voices* (2008, p.30) amongst other "famous voice hearers",[1] and Kauffman (2016) also lists them both as founders of religion who had "verifiable persistent non-drug-assisted hallucinations". Laroi et al. (2014, p.5214) list "Paul on the road to Damascus", amongst foundational religious figures, as having had "Culturally Meaningful" hallucinations.[2] And, as will be discussed later in this chapter, there have been various attempts to "explain" the resurrection appearances of Jesus on the basis of bereavement-related hallucinations. There is thus an important case to answer. Does voice hearing "explain" some of the most significant spiritual and religious experiences of the New Testament?

As previously argued in Chapter 2, the complexities incurred by the existence of overlapping and diverse accounts of the phenomenon that might be offered are significant. The primary concern here is with the search for a psychological account, but it will not be possible to explore this in any detail without also giving consideration to historical, theological, and narrative accounts.[3]

The "voices" that are heard in the New Testament mostly appear within narratives that are presented as historical.[4] The four figures who might most readily be identified as putative voice hearers within these narratives are Jesus, Peter, Paul, and John (the author of Revelation). This is not to suggest at the outset that any of these figures necessarily were voice hearers (although this possibility will be explored). Nor is it the case, as will also become clear, that these are the only figures in the New Testament who might be considered to have heard voices. However, I propose that the most theologically and psychologically significant narratives that might be understood as examples of voice hearing in the New Testament may usefully be grouped together in this way.

The canonical gospels mark a significant change of understanding of how God speaks to people in comparison with the preceding Hebrew tradition. In the synoptic gospels, God's voice is heard primarily through the life, teaching, death, and resurrection of Jesus. In the prologue to John's gospel, Jesus is introduced as the "Word" that was in the beginning with God, and was God, and which has now lived among us. This richly imbued language, implicitly appealing both to Hebrew tradition and Greek philosophy, is illustrative of the important changes in understanding of divine–human communication that were taking place in Christian communities in the wake of the Jesus "event".

Referring to this more explicitly, the author of the letter to the Hebrews wrote: "Long ago God spoke to our ancestors in many and various ways by the prophets, but in these last days he has spoken to us by a Son" (1:1–2). In continuity with Hebrew tradition, the writer quotes extensively from Hebrew scripture, and especially from prophecy, but in a significant development from the preceding tradition he outlines a case for the uniqueness of Jesus in the history of divine–human relationships. This might be characterised as a move away from expecting to hear God speak through prophets, and a greater emphasis on reflecting on how God has spoken through Jesus of Nazareth. This is not to say that prophecy[5] and voice hearing find no place in the Christian New Testament, but they are made relative and subordinate to God's revelation of himself in the person of Jesus.

Jesus

Voices that might be religious "building blocks"[6] – that is, voices experienced as an encounter with the divine – are important in the gospel narratives at four key points. First, angelic voices play a part in the infancy narratives in Luke.[7] Second, according to the synoptic gospels, a voice from heaven is heard at Jesus' baptism.[8] Immediately after this, Jesus is tempted in the wilderness and hears the voice of Satan. Third, a voice is heard by Peter, James, and John at the transfiguration. Finally, there are various encounters with angels, and with the risen Jesus, in the resurrection narratives, most of which involve some kind of dialogue.[9]

The annunciations

According to Luke, the conceptions of John the Baptist and of Jesus are respectively announced to Zechariah and to Mary by the angel Gabriel,[10] and the birth of Jesus is announced to the shepherds, also by an angel.[11] The angel "appears" to Zechariah, is "sent" to Mary, and "stood" before the shepherds. In each case the angel speaks, and implicitly a voice is heard. Zechariah and Mary converse with the angel. But these narratives are introducing important births at the outset of the gospel. Are they psychological accounts – or more importantly to be understood as narrative devices?

Raymond Brown, in *The Birth of the Messiah*, draws attention to a stereotyped pattern of biblical annunciations of birth which may be identified in relation to Ishmael, Isaac, Samson, John the Baptist and Jesus (Brown, 1993, pp.155–159).[12] There are clear parallels between the circumstances of the parents of John the Baptist as recorded in Luke – that is, Zechariah and Elizabeth – and the parents of Isaac (Abraham and Sarah) and Samuel (Elkanah and Hannah).[13] Within the Lukan narrative, John the Baptist is thus set both within the context of the patriarchal tradition recorded in Genesis (Brown, 1993, p.269) and in the prophetic tradition of Samuel. The only previous biblical appearance of the angel Gabriel had been in Daniel, one of the last books of Hebrew scripture to be written. Thus, John is set in the tradition of Hebrew scripture (p.270), as it were, from beginning to end. The words that the angel speaks to Zechariah draw on passages of Hebrew scripture that further reinforce these parallels, and also link John with Elijah.[14]

Similarly, the message of the angel to Mary also evokes reference to Hebrew scripture. Brown has shown that the words of the angel in Luke 1:32–33 parallel those of Nathan to David in 2 Samuel 7:8–16 (Brown, 1993, pp.310–311). They also (in verse 35) possibly reflect a Christological formulation of the early Christian church (Brown, 1993, pp.311–316). Again, in the annunciation to the shepherds (2:9–12) there may be implicit references to passages from Isaiah and elsewhere, including incorporation of a theophany-like experience evocative of Isaiah 6 (Brown, 1993, pp.424–427).

Luke, as an author, thus appears to have been incorporating a rich array of allusions within his narrative, but does any of this reflect actual human experience of the characters involved, or does it tell us more about the author than about any of the historical participants in the narrative? There would not appear to be sufficient evidence to settle this question one way or the other[15] but, whether in the narrative or in human experience (or both), an important point is established by Luke early in his gospel. As Caird observes:

> The message came to [Zechariah] through the angel Gabriel. It is inevitable that our religious experiences clothe themselves in garments provided by our habitual cast of thought. All those who have had any vivid sense of God's presence have wanted to speak of it in terms of seeing and hearing, though well aware that God himself can be neither heard nor seen. In early times the Israelites overcame this difficulty by speaking of God's presence as his 'angel' [Gen 22:11; Exod. 23:20; cf. Isa. 63:9] and this reverential manner of speech later developed into a belief that God communicates with men through a host of messengers, among whom Gabriel was especially the angel of revelation.
>
> (Caird, 1985, p.51)

Even if the information that Luke gives us about Zechariah and Mary is not historically reliable, so that it is not Zechariah or Mary who are trying to convey their religious experience in terms of seeing and hearing, but rather Luke himself, the voice of the angel as a narrative device is still significant. In the Lukan narrative God communicates with human beings. In this sense, at least, his voice is heard.

The Baptism and Temptation

At Jesus' baptism the heavens are torn apart and Jesus sees the Spirit descending on him like a dove. Then comes a voice from heaven, which says: "You are my Son, the Beloved; with you I am well pleased" (Mark 1:10, Luke 3:22). The story is very similar in Mark and Luke, and the words of the voice are exactly the same, although Luke seems to allow us to read the story in such a way that the voice might have been heard by others, as well as by Jesus (Michaels, 1981, pp.27–28, 30–31). In Matthew (3:17) the voice is addressed to all who are present, and not just to Jesus:[16] "This is my Son, the Beloved, with whom I am well pleased."

In all three gospels, the words seem to be a combination of Psalm 2 and (less certainly) Isaiah 42. In Psalm 2 (verse 7) we read: "I will tell of the decree of the Lord: He said to me, 'You are my son; today I have begotten you.'" In Isaiah 42 (verse 1) we read: "Here is my servant, whom I uphold, my chosen, in whom my soul delights; I have put my spirit upon him; he will bring forth justice to the nations." The link with Isaiah is perhaps more tenuous, but the words are reminiscent of various passages in Isaiah where a chosen – and suffering – servant of God fulfils a divinely appointed mission. The voice thus may be taken to imply that Jesus is the suffering servant called by God.[17]

Some commentators[18] understand the voice as that of the "bath-qol", referred to in various passages by rabbis of the time. The bath-qol, literally the "daughter of the voice", or the echo of a heavenly voice, is a kind of inferior substitute for the word of God as given directly to the prophets. It is likened by the rabbis to the chirping of a bird, or the moaning of a dove. According to this view, when the last Hebrew prophets – Haggai, Zechariah, and Malachi – died, the Holy Spirit then vanished from Israel, and God could no longer be heard directly. But the bath-qol could still be heard – as it were indirectly, an echo of God's voice. In fact, most recent commentators do not think that this was what the gospel writers had in mind. On the contrary, they were emphasising that the heavens have been opened – that, theologically speaking, God's voice was being heard directly.[19] But how might we now understand this speaking of God "directly" to Jesus?

For centuries, the baptism narratives were understood primarily from a devotional point of view. Serious critical scholarship on the baptism narratives came on the scene only in the 19th century. David Strauss (1808–1874), in *The Life of Jesus Critically Examined* (1973; originally published in 1835)[20] – having examined the conflicting gospel accounts of the events at Jesus' baptism, and having considered the difficulties inherent in considering them to be either supernatural or natural occurrences – eventually concluded that these phenomena "have merely a mythical value" (p.245). In his view, the texts follow a Hebrew prophetic tradition that put Messianic declarations "into the mouth of Jehovah, as real, audible voices from heaven" (p.243). He noted that the dove referred to by the gospel writers has rich symbolic significance within the Hebrew and other Eastern traditions. He therefore proposed that the heavenly voice and the hovering dove were gathered from contemporary sources and then incorporated into Christian legend, but that they had no historical basis in the experiences of Jesus or of those who were present at his baptism.[21]

In the early 20th century, based upon their reading (or misreading) of the gospels, a number of psychiatrists – taking a completely opposite approach to Strauss – argued that Jesus had such extraordinary beliefs about himself, combined with voices and visions, that a psychiatric diagnosis was indicated. Jesus, they said, was clearly psychotic. Amongst the pieces of evidence used to support this conclusion, the accounts of Jesus' baptism featured significantly. It was argued that people who have hallucinations of the voice of God, and who believe that they are sent by God, must be mad.[22]

Even a century ago, such arguments were patently crude and contentious. In a dissertation entitled *The Psychiatric Study of Jesus*, published in 1913, Albert Schweitzer (Schweitzer, 1948) – the biblical scholar and medical missionary – convincingly demonstrated that the proponents of such a diagnosis were both ignorant of research on the gospel texts, and also arrogantly over-confident about the ability of psychiatry to make reliable diagnoses on the basis of those texts. Much of the evidence for asserting that Jesus was suffering from such conditions as megalomania, or religious paranoia, arose from dubious speculation. Taking the voice at Jesus' baptism as a starting point, one psychiatrist immediately proposed that Jesus must have experienced hallucinations at other times, too – such as at the transfiguration. Yet it is the disciples (and not Jesus) to whom the heavenly voice is addressed on that occasion. Schweitzer's rebuttal of these crude arguments remains convincing on its own terms, although it should also be said that psychiatry has moved on and now operates by rather different criteria.[23]

Serious psychological studies of Jesus entered a lull after Schweitzer's *Psychiatric Study*,[24] but a series of psychological analyses and psychobiographies have appeared over the last 30 to 40 years.[25] Most have paid little or no attention to the voices that Jesus is said to have heard. Amongst these, John Miller's *Jesus at Thirty* is worthy of comment as offering a more positive psychological approach. Miller does not eschew attribution of inner disharmony to Jesus, but does so without employing diagnostic categories (Miller, 1997, pp.19–29). Miller understands Jesus as having been attracted to John the Baptist's movement as a result of inner conflicts, possibly concerning the death of Joseph, which were then resolved through a

86 Hearing voices in Christian scripture

"conversion" experience at the point of his baptism. Evidence for this is largely speculative, but Miller portrays a very human Jesus, who must have been drawn to John out of some sense of inner conviction, and who struggled with thoughts and feelings about vocation and family and priorities in life, just as other human beings do. The approach taken is firmly psychological rather than psychiatric. Whilst Miller's account of Jesus' "conversion" at his baptism is in many ways an attractive one, within which the humanity of Jesus is affirmed, and naïve diagnoses of mental disorder are avoided, it still lacks a critical positive account of the voices that Jesus hears. William James, whose account of conversion experiences is cited by Miller, proposed that voices may be a common concomitant of such experiences (p.228) but (even now) we know little about how common they may be in this context, or what their significance is.

More recent scholarship has generally affirmed the historicity of the baptism of Jesus,[26] but has been much more cautious about what can or cannot be asserted about the experiences of Jesus himself. John Meier, for example, sees the theophanic component of the baptism narratives as clearly being a later Christian composition: "a psychological interpretation of the baptismal story as a path to Jesus' inner experience ignores the basic insights of close to a century of tradition, form, and redaction criticism" (Meier, 1994, p.108). James Dunn[27] is a little less pessimistic, leaving open at least the possibility that Jesus in some way experienced some sense of commissioning at his baptism, but this is a far cry from finding evidence in the text to support any constructive account of Jesus' mental state at the time of his baptism, far less any evidence of mental illness.

We should therefore be cautious about asserting too confidently that we know exactly what experiences Jesus had at his baptism. After all, each of the evangelists gives us a differing account. In John's gospel (1:32–34), it is John the Baptist who sees the Spirit descend on Jesus from heaven, like a dove, and who testifies that Jesus is the Son of God, but neither Jesus nor the crowd hears a voice.[28]

Following the baptism, in Mark (1:12–13) we are told very briefly that Jesus went into the wilderness and was tempted by Satan and waited on by angels. No voices are mentioned. In Matthew (4:1–11) and Luke (4:1–13) a longer account is provided in which the Devil (or "the tempter") speaks to Jesus three times. In two of the utterances, the heavenly voice heard by Jesus at his baptism – "You are my Son"[29] – is reflected back as a question: "If you are the son of God ..."

Bultmann (1963, pp.253–257) identified the temptation narratives as legendary, being drawn from an uncertain mythological tradition such as, possibly, a nature myth (e.g. Marduk's combat with the chaos of nature) or a story of temptation as commonly found in mythological and hagiographical accounts of saints and holy men. The dialogue with the voice of Satan he understood to be modelled upon a Hebrew pattern of Rabbinic disputation. Thus, the voice is mythical but shaped by Hebrew tradition.

Caird, acknowledging that the account is coloured by language that many will understand as mythological, also offered some interesting reflections on how this voice might be understood in terms of Jesus' experience:

> Conscious of a unique vocation and endowed with exceptional powers, he must set aside all unworthy interpretations of his recent experience. He has heard a voice saying, "Thou art my Son"; now he hears another voice, "If you are the Son of God … ", and he must decide whether or not it comes from the same source. Three times he makes up his mind that the voice which prompts him to take action is that of the Devil.
>
> (Caird, 1985, p.79)

Consciousness of a unique vocation, and "exceptional powers", might appear to contrast strongly with Miller's account of inner struggle, but the latter also acknowledges a positive sense of messianic vocation. It is the understanding of vocation as bringing fame, power, and esteem that presents temptation (pp.55–64). Rather than being evidence of delusional grandiosity, the temptation reflects a conscious decision on Jesus' part to relinquish such ideas.

As with the baptism narratives, contemporary scholarship remains sceptical as to what the temptation narratives tell us – if anything – abut the psychological experiences of the historical Jesus. Dunn points out that both the baptism narratives and the temptation narratives are clearly stories told by others about Jesus, rather than stories told by Jesus about himself.[30] We simply do not have the first person account upon which to base any judgement concerning whether or not Jesus heard voices. We do have important gospel narratives within which heavenly and Satanic voices play an important part in conveying to the reader significant information about the identity and calling of Jesus – but this is a very different thing.

The transfiguration

In each of the synoptic gospels there is an account of an episode in which Jesus goes up a mountain with Peter, John and James.[31] On the mountain, Jesus' appearance is changed or "transfigured". His clothes become "dazzling white", his face "shone like the sun",[32] and he is seen and heard talking with Moses and Elijah.[33] Following some remarks by Peter, who is terrified and does not know what to say, a cloud overshadows the group. From the cloud a voice is heard: "This is my Son, the Beloved; listen to him!" (Mark 9:7), "This is my Son, the Beloved; with him I am well pleased; listen to him!" (Matthew 17:5), and "This is my Son, my Chosen; listen to him!" (Luke 9:35) After the voice has spoken, the disciples find themselves alone with Jesus.

There has been a variety of interesting accounts of this episode by commentators.[34] Some say that it is a legendary development of a resurrection story[35], and some that it is a completely symbolic[36] narrative. Cranfield, who distinguishes what might be considered a vision and an audition from what might be considered "factual", ends up concluding that it is both.[37] Caird draws attention to research on mystical experiences in which intense devotions are allegedly associated with changed physical appearance.[38] Fenton, noting the parallels with the account of Jesus' baptism, considers this to be an epiphany story of a kind common in ancient writings.[39] I. Howard Marshall suggests that there must have been some historical event to "trigger off" the formulation of the narrative, but that "the nature of the event is such as to almost defy historical investigation".[40]

We are therefore left with a polyphony of views, but France (commenting on Matthew's account) is right to draw attention to the fact that the experience "is narrated in vivid terms of the disciples' visual and auditory sensations".[41] We are left with a narrative of a voice heard by Peter, James and John that does not really fit the expected pattern of modern accounts of mental disorder, voice hearing or mystical/religious experience. Whilst its theological and narrative significance is clear, as confirming divine affirmation of Jesus to the three disciples and to the reader of the gospel, its historical, psychological and biographical[42] fabric is not.

The Resurrection Narratives

The most distinctive and remarkable of Christian beliefs is that of the resurrection from the dead of Jesus of Nazareth.[43] The resurrection narratives as recorded in the four canonical gospels[44] comprise a series of different accounts of men and women who are variously said to encounter in some places angels announcing the resurrection of Jesus, and in other places the risen Jesus himself.

In Matthew 28:1–8, Mark 16:1–7, and Luke 24:1–11 Mary Magdalene, accompanied by one or more other women,[45] is recorded as encountering one or more angels, at or near the empty tomb, who tell her of the resurrection. In John 20:12, Mary alone encounters two angels who ask her why she is weeping. The variety of different accounts of angelic encounters has been taken by some as evidence that this was a literary device, developed to emphasise the significance of the discovery of the empty tomb.[46] It is impossible to know exactly what actually happened.[47]

In Matthew (28:9–20), Mary Magdalene and another Mary, and later the 11 disciples, all have encounters with the risen Jesus in which he speaks to them. In the longer ending to Mark (16:9–20), Mary Magdalene, then two unnamed disciples, see Jesus, but we are not explicitly told that they speak with him (or hear him speaking to them). Later the 11 all encounter Jesus and hear him speaking to them. In Luke (24:13–53), two disciples on the road to Emmaus encounter Jesus and speak with him. When they eventually recognise him, he mysteriously vanishes out of their sight. Subsequently, the 11 disciples and their companions also see and hear Jesus. Reference is also made to an earlier, and separate, appearance to Peter.

In John (20), Mary Magdalene is the first to see and speak with the risen Jesus and subsequently the other disciples also see and speak with him on two separate occasions. Finally, Jesus appears to, and speaks with, Peter and six other disciples by the Sea of Tiberius.

What are we to make of these resurrection appearances and auditions? First, it is important to note that – according to the canonical narratives – they do primarily appear to be visual in nature – although there are communications (with Jesus and with angels) that take an auditory verbal form.[48] There are no voices here in the absence of visual phenomena. Second, Reginald Fuller[49] has argued that the verb used to characterise these appearances – ὤφθη – taking into account its use in the Septuaguint and elsewhere – emphasises a revelatory initiative on the part of God, rather than a sensory experience on the part of those to whom Jesus appeared. Third, we receive accounts of these experiences in narrative form. They come to us as an innovative genre of literature from a particular time and place in history, and must be interpreted as such.[50] We do not have any accounts that could be considered scientific in any modern sense – historical or psychological. For some scholars, at least, they make sense only as "creative storytelling".[51] At best, they are late and retrospective accounts of what happened, being written more than half a century after the events to which they relate.[52]

A broader evaluation of the traditional Christian belief in the resurrection of Jesus is beyond the scope of the present work. The critical literature on the resurrection of Jesus is now vast.[53] Within this literature, visionary and voice-hearing experiences have found a place as "naturalistic" explanations for the historical events that are presumed to underlie the texts, and were especially popular in the 19th and early 20th centuries. There has recently been something of a resurgence of interest in such theories. Although they do not currently appear to have widespread support as "explanations",[54] there is, in contrast, widespread agreement that "something" happened. That is, there seems to be a consensus that the early Christians had experiences of some kind or another that account for both the historical rise of Christianity and also the central and distinctive Christian belief that Jesus had risen from the dead. Whilst the nature of the experiences is debated hotly, it seems to be almost unanimously agreed that "the early followers of Jesus thought that they had seen the risen Jesus".[55]

The traditional Christian conviction, argued strongly in recent years by Tom Wright (2003), is that Jesus literally and bodily came back to life. According to this account, the experiences of the early Christians were therefore neither visions nor hallucinations, but rather veridical perceptions of the bodily presence of Jesus. It is beyond the scope of the present work to debate this assertion per se. However, if the traditional account is not accepted, then the alternative comprises a relatively small number of possibilities.[56] Visions/hallucinations do not play any part at all according to some of these accounts (that is, the "something" that happened did not take the form of visionary or hallucinatory experiences). Where they are appealed to, they are taken up in one of three ways:

1   Belief in the resurrection is taken to be premised on an empty tomb.[57] Subsequently, this conviction was confirmed by visionary/hallucinatory experiences.
2   Certain disciples, in the context of their grief at Jesus' death, might have had visionary/hallucinatory experiences. These experiences then generated similar experiences in the wider community (usually explained fairly crudely on the basis of "mass hysteria" or similar allegedly social psychological processes). These experiences in turn begot a (fictional) story that the tomb was empty.
3   Visionary experiences of the risen Jesus are said not to be due to hallucinations, but rather to some psychical or spiritual mechanism. This category – of "veridical visions"[58] – will not be discussed further here, as it is not clear how it can be distinguished from other perception-like experiences in which an object of perception is not actually present. However, if this is accepted, the tomb was not empty and Jesus did not bodily rise from the dead. Beliefs of this kind only arose secondary to the visions.

Essentially, then, the proposal is that the resurrection appearances of Jesus, as attested to in the New Testament, were mixed modality (auditory and visual) hallucinatory experiences of the early Christians. This possibility seems to have been considered from very early times. Celsus, writing in the 2nd century CE, suggested that the supposed witnesses to the resurrection of Jesus "through wishful thinking had a hallucination due to some mistaken notion".[59] David Strauss (1865), in *A New Life of Jesus*, seems to have been the first modern scholar to popularise the view that the experiences in question may in fact have been visions arising from "instrumentality of the mind, the power of imagination, and nervous excitement".[60] Arguing first for a psychological account of the experiences of Paul on the road to Damascus (see below), he proceeded to propose that the accounts of the disciples' experiences in encountering the risen Jesus were of an essentially similar kind. In each case he identified preceding beliefs and psychological states which he understood to have predisposed to these experiences.

As historical evidence of what Strauss considered to be a similar kind of phenomenon, he cited an example that now seems very strange – the reported 15th-century sightings of Duke Ulrich of Württemberg in his home country following his exile. Much of Strauss's argument was concerned with textual arguments around the timing and location of biblical encounters with the risen Jesus, all of which might also appear to a contemporary reader to be of little relevance. It is noticeable that Strauss goes beyond what we might consider to be reliable historical evidence and demonstrates significant gender prejudice, on the basis of which the reliability of female testimony is dismissed out of hand. Thus, for example, he says of Mary Magdalene that "In a woman of such a constitution of body and mind it was no great step from inward excitement to ocular vision."[61]

One of the best recent exponents of a hallucination theory of the resurrection is Michael Goulder. In an essay entitled "The Baseless Fabric of a Vision" (1996), he argues that there are other, essentially similar, psychological circumstances in which people are known to experience hallucinations – specifically, religious conversion experiences, grief reactions, and collective delusions.

Amongst the examples of conversion experiences that Goulder considers, two (Isaiah and Paul) are in fact other biblical accounts, and one (Arthur Koestler) is neither religious nor associated with any kind of hallucinations. Only the story of Susan Atkins might be considered strictly relevant. Atkins was a controversial figure who professed a conversion experience in prison following her conviction for her part in the murders committed by Charles Manson. In court she was found to be a highly unreliable witness, and her story is arguably completely unlike the Easter visions and auditions of the disciples as recorded in the gospels. Nonetheless, according to her own account of her conversion, Atkins saw and heard Jesus speaking to her, and Goulder argues that such hallucinations are typical of many religious experiences.[62]

Goulder is not alone in arguing that the resurrection appearances were in fact hallucinations experienced in the context of a grief reaction.[63] In a book entitled *Psychological Origins of the Resurrection Myth*, Jack Kent (1999), a Unitarian minister, explores the possibility at greater length. However, there are some serious problems with this view. The individual experiences of a grieving widow or widower would seem to be far removed from a group of 11 disciples and their companions all seeing and hearing Jesus at the same time. Hearing or seeing the person who has been lost as a result of bereavement is usually comforting, but almost never associated with a belief that they have come back to life and are no longer dead. It is usually fleeting or short-lived, and yet some of the resurrection narratives are concerned with relatively long interactions and conversations. Furthermore, this theory does not account for the tradition of the empty tomb.[64] This would generally, therefore, not appear to be a very plausible hypothesis on its own – although, of course, such occurrences could have been the basis for subsequent elaboration and exaggeration within the tradition.

Finally, Goulder refers to the phenomenon of collective delusion, for which his primary example is a series of reported sightings of the "Bigfoot" monster in rural South Dakota in the autumn of 1977. Essentially the proposition is that, with the right psychological circumstances – including such things as a close-knit community, poor education, and anxiety – an initial visionary ("conversion") experience can lead to a collective sharing of mistaken, false or delusional beliefs within a community. There are undoubtedly group experiences of this kind that might be used to support the contention that social processes following the crucifixion fostered something similar amongst the disciples. However, Goulder's case is not helped by his choice of such a bizarre and dissimilar example, and it is further undermined by his prejudicial grouping of women with "poorly educated people" as those who are more vulnerable to such phenomena.

Goulder's essay is an important example – argued at greater length and with better cited evidence than some others – of the recent resurgence of interest in hallucination theories as explanations for the biblical accounts of the resurrection of Jesus.[65] This resurgence of interest does not generally seem to have kept pace with the literature on voice hearing, and is not very convincing on purely scientific grounds. A different example of this resurgence of interest in hallucination theories is provided by Gerd Lüdemann (1994) in *The Resurrection of Jesus*. Lüdemann presents an extended argument for the "vision hypothesis" on critically argued historical grounds. Importantly, he argues that the biblical account does not present a primary theological statement (e.g. "God has raised Jesus from the dead") but rather an account of the disciples' experiences of the risen Jesus, which then find expression in such statements. However, he does not follow this critical historical analysis with a similarly extended and critical psychological analysis. Where he does refer to the importance of psychological considerations he demonstrates both a naïveté as to the ability of the historical-critical method to provide the necessary scientific basis for this, and also a reliance on "depth psychology" which would be seen by many today as highly subjective and unscientific.[66]

More recent biblical scholarship has generally been much more cautious about what can be said, and especially about the designation of resurrection appearances as hallucinatory. James Dunn concludes that it is not possible from the texts to say other than that witnesses to the resurrection "saw" Jesus. Whilst the emphasis seems to be on "normal" seeing, rather than on visionary experiences, he concludes that "A more refined psychological analysis has no real basis in the data examined."[67] Maurice Casey similarly argues that it is most appropriate to refer to the resurrection "appearances" of Jesus "because that is how those people who saw them interpreted them, and so did the early tradition about them".[68] Whilst he is willing to concede that "visions" might also be an appropriate term, Casey eschews the use of the word "hallucination" "because it belongs to our culture, not theirs, and its pejorative implications have been almost invariably used to confuse the major issues".[69]

Others are a little more confident about what can be said, arguing on the basis of what is known about 1st-century Jewish and Christian beliefs about resurrection and visionary experience. For example, David Catchpole, based upon an analysis of the understanding of the concept of resurrection within the early "Jesus movement", concludes that

In accordance with the through-and-through Jewish context of that movement, resurrection belongs to an *earthly* setting, presupposes the final divine judgement, and almost certainly involves the removal of bodies from tombs. The experience of seeing and hearing a recently deceased person who has returned from the post-mortem world to this world would definitely not count as resurrection. Nor would some internal experience, explicable in depth psychological terms, generate talk of resurrection.

(Catchpole, 2000, p.195)

Similarly, Tom Wright argues that "the ancient world as well as the modern knew the difference between visions and things that happen in the 'real' world".[70] Against this, Pieter Craffert argues that such approaches fail to understand the ways in which reality and consciousness are constructed differently in different cultures. In particular, visions (to be distinguished here from modern Western notions of "hallucination") might well have been taken to be experiences of reality in the ancient Mediterranean world: "in a world where visionary perceptions are as real as other sensory perceptions, there is no doubt that what is seen, heard and felt in the visions are as real as what is experienced in waking consciousness" (Craffert, 2009, pp.146–147). It is not clear that Craffert's argument finally succeeds. The "reality" of visions is one thing, but an empty tomb is quite another. The inclusion in the gospel narratives of references both to an empty tomb and to resurrection appearances suggests a more sophisticated argument than is explicable on the basis of a visionary "reality" alone.

Licona reviews six different hypotheses for the resurrection, including those of Goulder and Lüdemann, and finds the hypothesis of a bodily resurrection most convincing – thus eliminating all those hypotheses based upon hallucinations. Amongst his reasons for considering hallucinatory experiences as unlikely bases for the resurrection narratives, he gives more attention to the recent scientific literature on hallucinations than most other authors (albeit largely in footnotes, and relying on very few sources).[71] In particular, he notes the rarity of multimodal hallucinations, and the extreme rarity of reliable accounts of group hallucinations.

On the former point, it is not clear that such experiences are so rare. Biblical narratives, later Christian mystical literature, and recent accounts of visionary experience are replete with multimodal experiences.[72] On the latter point, however, it is clear that there is an important argument to be considered. Whilst collective hallucinations seem to be rare, they do apparently occur. Jake O'Connell (2009) describes a series of more or less well-documented cases in which groups of people appear to have shared visual religious experiences of an unusual (arguably hallucinatory) kind. However, he identifies a number of features of these experiences that appear to put them in a different category to the New Testament resurrection narratives. Amongst other things, people who shared these visions each saw them differently, and not everyone present reported seeing the vision. More importantly for the present purpose, O'Connell was able to identify no other examples of collective visions where the vision carried on a conversation with those present. He goes on to argue that an apparition that could carry on a group conversation "would thereby prove itself to be no hallucination".[73] Whether or not this is true would appear to depend upon the nature of the evidence available but, as we have seen, the nature of the New Testament resurrection narratives is such that we cannot confidently make such a refined analysis.

Perhaps a better and more critical psychological account of the resurrection appearances of Jesus to his disciples can still be written. However, it is also clear that the historical-critical method will never be able to produce the evidence that would be needed for such an account to be completely convincing in the light of modern psychological and phenomenological criteria. Firsthand accounts of the phenomenology are simply not available, and modern scientific criteria are anachronistic to the texts. Lüdemann is right to emphasise that it is the experience – and not the theology – that is presented as the primary evidence in the gospels, but it is presented on 1st-century, and not 21st-century, terms. Similarly, we might note, it is presented as narrative, and so must be interpreted in the first instance by literary and socio-rhetorical means.[74]

Kent may therefore be right to draw attention to the importance of myth. As discussed in Chapter 2, it does rather depend upon how one understands the concept of myth. Kent and Bultmann, amongst others, have in mind a view of myth as something which "didn't happen" in some historical sense. However, such an understanding is neither necessary nor sufficient to an understanding of the essential nature of myth. If we take, for example, Dundes' (1984) notion that myths are "sacred narratives", explaining how things in the world came to be as they are, then I think that this is exactly what the gospel accounts of the resurrection of Jesus are.[75] The resurrection of Jesus of Nazareth makes sense of the world and, in particular, of the "Good Friday" experiences that Christians encounter. It provides hope. It does this through narratives that portray God as visible, audible, and tangible in the risen Jesus.

Voice hearing in the gospels

We can only speculate on what actual experiences of voice hearing, if any, lie behind the gospel texts. As narratives, they include accounts of a variety of events, some of which might be construed as incorporating voice hearing experiences. The voices – angelic, divine, and demonic – are heard at key junctures in the narrative, affirming and announcing the significance of the birth of Jesus, his identity as Son of God, and his resurrection from the dead. They are heard by Jesus himself, by the disciples, and (in some cases) by others too. Whilst John the Baptist appears at the outset as a prophet in the Hebrew tradition, and angelic messengers appear at various points to speak on behalf of God, the emphasis is not on God's voice as heard through such messengers, but rather on Jesus himself as God's son, towards whom these messengers point. The central voice – that of Jesus – is therefore not that of a disembodied or visionary voice, but rather that of a visible human speaker, who is bodily present. This voice, conveyed by the text, takes centre stage. Even the heavenly voice – at the baptism and transfiguration – serves primarily to affirm the identity of Jesus as Son of God. In an inverse fashion, the voice of Satan serves a similar function within the narrative. Questioning what has been said by the divine voice at Jesus' baptism, but being out-manoeuvred by Jesus, it is eventually silenced and shown to be false.

The appearances of Jesus after the resurrection, where he speaks to the disciples, are uniquely ambiguous in form and uniquely important to theology. If they are taken to be historical manifestations of a bodily resurrection, then they are not psychological instances of "voice hearing", in the sense with which we are presently concerned. In this case they are voices like any other human voices, spoken by an embodied human speaker. On the other hand, if they are understood to be manifestations of a visionary kind, they still affirm the central place of Jesus within the gospel narratives. In a very real sense, it might be said, Jesus has the last word in the gospel narratives.[76]

Peter and Cornelius

In Acts 10, a narrative account is given of visionary experiences of a pious Roman centurion called Cornelius and the apostle Peter.[77] Cornelius has a vision of an angel who calls his name and then tells him that his prayers have been heard by God and that he is to send for Peter. The following day, as the centurion's slaves are approaching with the message that they have to convey to Peter, Peter has a vision of heaven being opened and a large sheet lowered which contains all kinds of animals. He hears a voice which says "Get up, Peter; kill and eat",[78] to which he responds, in accordance with his Jewish tradition: "By no means, Lord; for I have never eaten anything that is profane or unclean."[79] The voice then says to him again: "What God has made clean, you must not call profane."[80] All of this is repeated three times before the centurion's messengers arrive, asking Peter to accompany them to their master's house.[81]

The events as narrated subsequently have some significance within Acts in regard to the place of gentiles within the early Christian community. As scripture, this passage has influenced the Christian tradition regarding non-observance of traditional Jewish customs concerning which foods may or may not be eaten.[82] By extrapolation it has also influenced Christian attitudes more widely towards Judaism and Jewish traditions in (what Christians would call) the Old Testament. However, there has been a critical view that the narrative is not historical, and in particular that Peter's vision was devised by the author of Acts (generally thought to be Luke) in support of his contention of the legitimacy of the Christian mission to the gentiles.[83] If this is correct, it reveals an interesting understanding of the significance of the visions and auditions that the story includes. Thus, for example, Haenchen comments:

> Luke virtually excludes all human decision. Instead of the realization of the divine will *in* human decisions, *through* human decisions, he shows us a series of supernatural interventions in the dealings of men: the appearance of the angel, the vision of the animals, the prompting of the Spirit, the pouring out of the ecstatic pneum/a. As Luke presents them, these divine incursions have such compelling force that all doubt in the face of them *must* be stilled. They compellingly prove that God, not man, is at work. The presence of God may be directly ascertained.
> (Haenchen, 1971, p.362)

Haenchen does not see this tendency as a good thing, and goes on to argue that it undermines the nature of true faith and makes human beings into mere puppets. It demonstrates a point of view – whether in the context of the 1st or the 21st century of the Common Era – that visions and voices must be miraculous events attributable to divine intervention. As Haenchen argues, this is problematic, and especially so (we might add) in the light of contemporary scientific awareness of the nature of the experience of hearing voices.

Peter is said to hear voices in two other places in the narrative of Acts (5:19–20 and 12:7–9), both in the context of miraculous escapes from prison facilitated by an angel. In the first instance he is not mentioned by name, but is implicitly included as one of the apostles, all of whom hear the voice. In the second instance, it is Peter alone who hears (and sees) the angel.

Luke has groups of people hearing an angelic or divine voice on at least six occasions in his gospel and Acts – the annunciation to the shepherds, the baptism of Jesus, the transfiguration, the encounter of the women with the angels in the resurrection narrative, the angelic freeing of the apostles from prison, and the conversion of Saul (see below).[84] If the various resurrection encounters with Jesus are also to be included, then this would add two more instances.

Voices heard by individuals, where only one person hears the voice, are in comparison rare in Luke's writings. Peter's vision of the sheet lowered from heaven and Cornelius's corresponding vision, although each representing a voice heard individually, still comprise parts of a story within which the narrative asserts that more than one person heard a voice, and that these voices were apparently from the same source. Similarly, the annunciations to Zechariah and to Mary (and to the shepherds) are all part of a larger story within which the narrative is constructed around the notion that the voice speaks to multiple people on the same topic in a coordinated way over a period of time. In contrast, an angel (or the devil) speaks to an individual, and no voice is heard by others, on only two occasions: the temptation of Jesus, and Peter's second experience of release from prison by an angel.

The hearing of voices is not primarily an individual phenomenon in the Lukan narratives,[85] and is usually associated with visionary experiences (that is, it is multimodal). However, it serves in the narrative of Acts to demonstrate that God "speaks" in the lives of individuals, groups of Christians, and the wider Christian community. In each case the voice serves to effect (or play a part in effecting) a change in direction – a change of understanding of Jewish food laws, a change of understanding of the relationship between Jewish and Gentile Christians, and (in Peter's case) a change from imprisonment to freedom. All of these changes are, I think, indirectly, sequelae of the resurrection. Whilst visions and angelic appearances are not unknown in the Old Testament, they take on a new significance, a new authority, when embedded here in Luke's account of what happens after the resurrection of Jesus.

Paul

According to Luke, Saul, a Pharisee known for his persecution of the early Christian church, was on his way to Damascus with a view to arresting anyone found following "the Way" and then bringing them back to Jerusalem.

> Now as he was going along and approaching Damascus, suddenly a light from heaven flashed around him. He fell to the ground and heard a voice saying to him, "Saul, Saul, why do you persecute me?" He asked, "Who are you, Lord?" The reply came, "I am Jesus, whom you are persecuting. But get up and enter the city, and you will be told what you are to do." The men who were travelling with him stood speechless because they heard the voice but saw no one. Saul got up from the ground, and though his eyes were open, he could see nothing; so they led him by the hand and brought him into Damascus. For three days he was without sight, and neither ate nor drank.
>
> Now there was a disciple in Damascus named Ananias. The Lord said to him in a vision, "Ananias." He answered, "Here I am, Lord." The Lord said to him, "Get up and go to the street called Straight, and at the house of Judas look for a man of Tarsus named Saul. At this moment he is praying, and he has seen in a vision a man named Ananias come in and lay his hands on him so that he might regain his sight." But Ananias answered, "Lord, I have heard from many about this man, how much evil he has done to your saints in Jerusalem; and here he has authority from the chief priests to bind all who invoke your name." But the Lord said to him, "Go, for he is an instrument whom I have chosen to bring my name before Gentiles and kings and before the people of Israel; I myself will show him how much he must suffer for the sake of my name." So Ananias went and entered the house. He laid his hands on Saul and said, "Brother Saul, the Lord Jesus, who appeared to you on your way here, has sent me so that you may regain your sight and

> be filled with the Holy Spirit." And immediately something like scales
> fell from his eyes, and his sight was restored. Then he got up and was
> baptized, and after taking some food he regained his strength.
>
> (Acts 9:3–19)

This story[86] must be one of the most famous conversion stories in the history of religious experience – and it revolves not around a sudden change
of thought, but rather around the impact of a blinding light and an accompanying voice. It is arguably a call narrative rather than a conversion story,
and it shows some similarities with the theophany in Isaiah 6 and other
similar accounts of the call of the Hebrew prophets.[87] The biographical
and historical reliability of the account provided in Acts have been much
debated.[88] However, this has not inhibited speculation about the possible
medical diagnoses – both of the eye condition (Bullock, 1978), and also of
the possible cause of the visions and voices (Landsborough, 1987).[89]

In his correspondence with the Corinthian church, Paul refers to "visions
and revelations" and to having heard things "that are not to be told, that
no mortal is permitted to repeat".[90] In his letter to the Galatians, he says in
passing that he did not receive knowledge of the gospel through a human
source, but through a "revelation of Jesus Christ".[91] Exactly how all of this
relates to Luke's account in Acts is not clear.

For Luke, who relates many conversion narratives in his gospel and in
Acts, it would seem that it was important to include the conversion experience of a person who played a key part in establishing the mission of the
early church to the Gentiles. Voice hearing plays a part in this story – but
not so crucial a part that he is worried about changing the details between
the three versions of the story that he tells. And, as is typical elsewhere in his
writings, it is not only Paul who hears a voice.

For Paul himself, "visions and revelations", which certainly do seem to
include voices, and which draw upon his Jewish inheritance,[92] have also
been important. However, they are not so important that he feels happy to
boast about them.[93] He seems, rather, to fear that all of this might give the
wrong impression. He knows that such things will gain the attention and
respect of his readers, but he thinks that the key to understanding the nature
of Christian faith is to be found elsewhere:

> But if I wish to boast, I will not be a fool, for I will be speaking the truth.
> But I refrain from it, so that no one may think better of me than what is
> seen in me or heard from me, even considering the exceptional character
> of the revelations. Therefore, to keep me from being too elated, a thorn
> was given me in the flesh, a messenger of Satan to torment me, to keep
> me from being too elated. Three times I appealed to the Lord about this,
> that it would leave me, but he said to me, "My grace is sufficient for you,
> for power is made perfect in weakness." So, I will boast all the more
> gladly of my weaknesses, so that the power of Christ may dwell in me.
>
> (2 Corinthians 12:6–9)

It will be no surprise that the exact nature of the "thorn in the flesh" has also been the subject of much discussion, including various proposed medical diagnoses. And yet, this (along with voices and visions) is exactly the kind of thing that Paul is trying to take the focus away from. It is Christ's power "made perfect in weakness" that he wishes attention to be devoted to. Voices (and visions) for Paul are of secondary importance, but where they are of importance they affirm the identity of Jesus, they affirm and effect a radical change in Paul's understanding of his faith in God, and they affirm Paul's relationship with Jesus.

The revelation to John

Revelation was probably written in or around the 95 CE.[94] It is generally considered to be an example of apocalyptic literature, similar in genre to that of Daniel and Ezekiel in Hebrew scripture. It is the only extended apocalyptic writing included in the New Testament, although there is also a so called "synoptic apocalypse" included in Mark 13 (cf. Matthew 24 and Luke 21). Revelation shares important links with Daniel, with allusions being made to the latter within Revelation, and with a broadly similar use of symbolic language to interpret current political events.[95] However, Revelation also incorporates elements of the genres of prophetic and epistolary literature.[96] Beale has defined the apocalyptic-prophetic nature of Revelation as:

> God's revelatory interpretation (through visions and auditions) of his mysterious counsel about past, present, and future redemptive-eschatological history, and how the nature and operation of heaven relate to this. This revelation irrupts from the hidden, outer, heavenly dimension into the earthly and is given to a prophet (John), who is to write it down so that it will be communicated to the churches.
>
> (Beale, 1999, p.38)

Although the book is traditionally ascribed to John the apostle, in fact we know very little about the author.[97] The book may have been edited by more than one person, it might have been pseudonymous, or it may have been another John who actually wrote it. We do not know.[98] The author, whoever he is, presents the book as an account of a visionary experience which begins with the hearing of a voice:

> I was in the spirit on the Lord's day, and I heard behind me a loud voice like a trumpet saying, "Write in a book what you see and send it to the seven churches, to Ephesus, to Smyrna, to Pergamum, to Thyatira, to Sardis, to Philadelphia, and to Laodicea." Then I turned to see whose voice it was that spoke to me, and on turning I saw seven golden lampstands, and in the midst of the lampstands I saw one like the Son of Man,[99] clothed with a long robe and with a golden sash across his chest.
>
> (Revelation 1:11–13)

Some scholars believe that the book may in fact have been written down as a considered and planned attempt to write an apocalyptic work, and it does show at least some attempt to organise and structure the material in a coherent way.[100] However, there is no good reason not to take the text for what it purports to be – a written account of a visionary experience. Christopher Rowland[101] notes that actual visions may well have arisen as a result of meditation on scripture, and also be the subject of continued subsequent reflection. There is therefore good reason to believe that at least some of the visions in Revelation – but probably not all – are based upon authentic visionary experience.

Rowland[102] also notes that an appeal to revelation received directly in this way can reflect a desire to eliminate uncertainty in the face of life's complexity.

> Apocalyptic may seem to pander to the desire for certainty and the unambiguous divine directive. Here after all is the voice from beyond which bursts like a flash of lightning into the greyness of our world and shows things up in their true colours. Temporising and uncertainty seem out of the question in the face of the crisis provoked by this irruption of clarity.
>
> (Rowland, 1993, p.43)

Whether or not such appeals are actually made, Revelation hardly indulges them. As Rowland points out[103] it offers unambiguous convictions about some things – notably about the central place of Jesus Christ in Christian faith – and it urges suspicion of the values of secular culture. It expects Christians to live distinctively in the light of these convictions. However, it does not prescribe the answers and its rich symbolism leaves plenty of scope for uncertainty and debate about interpretation.[104]

After the opening vision of the Son of Man, John is told what to write to each of the seven churches. In effect a letter appears to be dictated to each of them, and it is interesting to reflect on what has happened here. If we allow for a moment that John heard each of these letters dictated to him in his vision, word for word, it is hard to imagine (short of miraculous intervention) that he was able to remember each of them perfectly afterwards. But the words of the letters are presented very specifically as "the words of him who holds the seven stars in his right hand, who walks among the seven golden lampstands".[105] Understood simply as a literal account of a visionary experience, this is hard to reconcile.

As Beale indicates, the formula in Revelation 2:1 is recognisable as a form of words frequently used to introduce prophetic writings in Hebrew scripture.[106] Similarly, when a warning is issued at the end of the book[107] against adding to, or subtracting from, the words of the book, this might be understood to be not so much concerned with affirming an authoritative text word for word, as it is with warning against false teaching.[108] In this respect, Revelation belongs to the genre of prophecy and emerges from a similar process of "translating" prophetic experience into prophetic writing as is observed in the books of written prophecy in Hebrew scripture. It is more concerned with the authentic prophetic message, we might say, than with either the original experience or the precise wording of the text.

Following the narrative of the dictation (if we may still call it that) of the seven letters, the focus of Revelation turns to heavenly events and becomes somewhat surreal. From this point on there has been much discussion and little agreement concerning the exact structure and subdivisions of the book. There is rich imagery and symbolism, drawing on Hebrew scripture[109] and a series of events unfold in multiples of seven.[110] Notably, there are seven seals which are broken by the Lamb,[111] seven trumpets which are blown by angels, and seven bowls of the wrath of God which are poured out upon the earth by angels. There are thunder and lighting, earthquakes, huge hailstones, fire in a bottomless pit, plagues, a dragon, strange beasts, a great whore, a sea of glass and fire, and a lake of fire. There are angels in abundance, there are the armies of earth and heaven, and there are "those who have conquered the beast". All in all, the imagery is vivid, colourful, and arresting, and the action is dramatic. Whilst there is much that is inappropriately referred to in our day as "awesome", the acts and scenery of this book are indeed truly awesome.

Eventually, in chapter 21, a new heaven and a new earth emerge in the wake of the destruction of all things, and a holy city, a new Jerusalem, comes down from heaven. John hears a loud voice from heaven, which says:

> See, the home of God is among mortals. He will dwell with them; they will be his peoples, and God himself will be with them; he will wipe every tear from their eyes. Death will be no more; mourning and crying and pain will be no more, for the first things have passed away.[112]

In Revelation, John presents a narrative in which he is involved in rich visual, auditory, olfactory, gustatory, and somatic perceptual experiences. This narrative is of a truly multimodal visionary experience, on a cosmic and heavenly stage. Insofar as voices are concerned, John is directly addressed in the narrative by the Son of Man and by angels, who command or question him, or explain what is happening. He is also, as it were, in the audience listening to a variety of heavenly voices. For example, in the theophany in chapter 4, he hears the four living creatures around the throne of God who without ceasing sing: "Holy, holy, holy, the Lord God the Almighty, who was and is and is to come."[113] And, in the same scene, he hears the 24 elders who sing: "You are worthy, our Lord and God, to receive glory and honour and power, for you created all things, and by your will they existed and were created."[114] At one point, later in this theophany, John hears the singing of "every creature in heaven and on earth and under the earth and in the sea, and all that is in them".[115] Elsewhere, he hears the voices of the souls of the martyrs,[116] a great multitude robed in white,[117] an eagle,[118] a voice from the altar,[119] a voice from heaven,[120] and the voice of a beast like a leopard speaking blasphemous words.[121] He hears a voice from heaven that is at once like the sound of many waters, like the sound of loud thunder and like the sound of harpists playing.[122] He hears the voices of many and various angels, he hears the kings of the earth lamenting the fall of Babylon,[123] and he hears the voice of a great multitude praising God.[124]

John Sweet has suggested that the logic of Revelation is in fact more auditory than visual:

> What John sees is again and again interpreted by what he hears; for example, the meaning of *the Lamb standing, as though it had been slain*, is given by the new song of the living creatures and elders [5:6–10]. The refrain of the letters to the churches is *He who has an ear, let him hear*. 'Hearing' opens up the whole realm of scripture, the words of God which demand man's immediate response. 'Blessed is he who reads aloud the words of the prophecy, and blessed are those who hear, and who keep what is written therein; for the time is near' [1:3].
>
> (Sweet, 1990, p.17)

In the vein of this logic, Revelation, the last book of Christian scripture, brings the voice of the promise of Jesus to the final pages of the Bible, just as Genesis opens it with the creative voice of Elohim (God). The voice of Jesus in Revelation, no less than the voice of Elohim in Genesis, is a heavenly voice.

Voice hearing in the New Testament

So varied are the examples surveyed in this chapter that it is impossible to make any generalisations about the place of voice hearing in the New Testament. In most places the historical and psychological basis of the texts is open to question, and we do not have any direct access to the human experiences underlying the texts. There is considerable variation as to the amount and quality of the evidence that we do have. It is clear that authors have used various literary devices appropriate to their theological purpose, and in some cases these may well involve metaphorical or reconstructed (or perhaps even fictional) "voices"; in others, they clearly purport to present historical voices verbatim.

On the one hand, then, unqualified and confident listing of Jesus and St Paul amongst "famous voice hearers" is both premature and naïve. There is every reason to emphasise doubt as to whether Jesus, Paul, Peter, or any other New Testament character, "heard voices" in any historical or psychological sense. We simply cannot know beyond doubt what their experiences actually were. The evidence does not allow scientific certainty. On the other hand, confident assertions that none of these figures heard voices – in the sense of the contemporary phenomenon that we now identify as voice hearing – would also be going beyond the evidence. The experiences of Paul – and even of Jesus – could reasonably be construed as psychologically very similar to those of contemporary voice hearers.

Notwithstanding the attention of this chapter to some texts within which voices play a very significant part, it might be argued that the hearing of voices is not overall an important theme in the New Testament according to any of the accounts in which we are interested – historically, theologically, psychologically, or narratively. Leaving aside the unique place of the voices associated with the resurrection appearances of Jesus, most of the central teaching of the gospels is to be found on the lips of Jesus himself, a very visible and bodily present human speaker. It is the authorial (or at least editorial) voice of the evangelists which bequeaths to us the passion narratives. Most of the action in Acts does not depend upon the hearing of voices. Voices do not play a major part in the Pauline epistles. In the prologue to John's gospel, as set out in the introduction to this chapter, a strong theological case is presented for Jesus himself as taking on the identity of the divine "Word". The phenomenon of voice hearing – if it is in evidence at all – is thus, at best, marginal.

On the other hand, voice hearing in the New Testament, if and where it may be identified, usually carries Christological content.[125] Voices, directly or indirectly, affirm the unique status of Jesus and thus preclude equivalent or greater revelatory significance to other voices or persons. "Voice hearing" (if it may be called that) in the New Testament is not insignificant. Whereas the voice of God might be said to fade out in Hebrew scripture, the New Testament concludes with an apocalyptic narrative within which divine and angelic voices play a highly significant part. Voices reappear in the New Testament in a significant, dramatic, and eventually apocalyptic, fashion.

Whilst the voice of Jesus, especially as it is heard in the gospel texts, is central to the New Testament (and to Christian tradition), other voices – mostly in a visionary context – are not insignificant within the narratives of the gospels and Acts. Historical-critical scholarship may well raise doubt about how these voices should be understood psychobiographically, but their presence in the canon, and in tradition, is theologically significant and, as we shall see in the next two chapters, sets the scene for later Christian voice-hearing experiences.

Notes

1 Elsewhere Watkins refers also to voices heard by Mary, the mother of Jesus, Joseph, and Mary Magdalene (2008, p.36).
2 See also Murray et al. (2012), who further go on to offer psychiatric diagnoses for Abraham, Moses, Jesus, and St Paul on the basis of their supposed hallucinatory and other symptoms.
3 See Chapter 2.
4 Whether or not they may be considered historical according to modern criteria is of course another matter – and beyond the scope of the present book.

5 For example, in Acts 21:9 there is reference to four daughters of Philip who "had the gift of prophecy"; Paul refers to the gift of prophecy in his letters to the Romans (12:6), and to the Corinthians (1 Corinthians 11, 12, 14) and there are references to prophecy in the pastoral epistles (1 Titus 4:14) and the second letter of Peter (1:20–21). We should not assume that this was either exactly the same phenomenon as, or completely different from, prophecy as understood in the Old Testament. The interested reader is referred to Aune (1983).

6 See Chapter 2.

7 Also in Matthew – but there only in dreams. In Luke (3:3) we are also told that "the word of God came to John [the Baptist]" in a manner very reminiscent of the Hebrew prophets.

8 This voice is not recorded in the fourth gospel, but in John 12:28–30 both Jesus and the crowd hear a voice in response to Jesus' prayer that God the Father would glorify his name. The voice says "I have glorified it, and I will glorify it again." Some of the crowd claim that it was not a voice – but only thunder.

9 This organisation of the material is not entirely comprehensive. For example, in the "Johannine Gethsemane", in John 12:28–30 both Jesus and the crowd hear a voice in response to Jesus' prayer that God the Father would glorify his name. The voice says "I have glorified it, and I will glorify it again." Some of the crowd claim that it was not a voice – but only thunder.

10 Luke 1:11–20 and 1:26–38 respectively.

11 Luke 2:9–15.

12 An account of the annunciation of the birth of Jesus is also provided in Matthew, albeit Brown notes that it fits the standard pattern somewhat less well. In the Matthean account, the angel appears to Joseph, not to Mary. Significantly for our present purpose, the angel also appears to Joseph in a dream, rather than in waking consciousness, and would therefore not represent an instance of voice hearing in the sense previously defined in the Introduction.

13 John the Baptist and Samuel were both set apart to be Nazirites. All three sets of parents were seeking a child together which they had previously been unable to have. In the case of John the Baptist and Isaac, both parents were also elderly. See Brown (1993, pp.268–269).

14 Ibid., pp.272–279.

15 Marshall (1998, p.51).

16 Michaels (1981, pp.29–30) nonetheless understands the voice as addressed to "the reader of the Gospel". He argues that no bystanders are mentioned and that too much should not be made of small changes to the wording of the voice as compared with the Markan text. He eventually concludes (p.36) that "Jesus and Jesus alone saw the Spirit in the form of a dove at his baptism, and only Jesus heard the voice of God saying, 'You are my beloved Son, with you I am well pleased.'"

17 This is made more explicit in Matthew 12:17ff.

18 For example, Cranfield (1959, p.54), Nineham (1963, p.58), Gundry (1994, p.53).

19 See, for example, France (2007, p.122).

20 See English translation: Strauss (1973, pp.239–246).

21 Similarly, writing in the 20th century, Bultmann understood the baptism story as legend, with the dove symbolism drawn from either Persian or Hebrew tradition (Bultmann, 1963, pp.247–253).

22 Miller (1997, pp.103–119) and Capps (2004) provide helpful reviews of this literature.

23 In his 1952 paper "What Did Jesus Think of Himself?" Anton Boisen (1952), drawing on Schweitzer's work, focused on Jesus' messianic beliefs and completely ignored the possible significance of perceptual phenomena. In 1970–1971, a

debate on the matter in *Faith and Freedom* also completely neglected hallu-cinations as possible evidence that Jesus was suffering from a psychosis, and focussed instead on evidence of mood disorder and abnormal beliefs (Lloyd, 1970, 1971, Robinson, 1972, ibid.). Since the publication of DSM-III in 1980, psychiatric diagnosis has become much more concerned with issues of reliability and validity, and has been less influenced by psychodynamic thinking. Studies of the historical Jesus have also emphasised the lack of reliable evidence as to Jesus' actual (historical and psychological) experiences.

24 The history of psychological studies, and psychobiographies, of Jesus is charted by Charlesworth (2004), Meggitt (2007), and Os (2011). The recent renewal of interest in such studies appears to coincide with the so-called "Third Quest" for the historical Jesus – beginning in the early 1980s. There is of course a significant distinction to be made between "psychiatric" studies, such as those that Schweitzer so effectively critiqued in the early 20th century, and "psycho-logical" studies, such as those that emerged in the latter part of the century. Whilst the two disciplinary approaches have much in common, and to a large extent overlap, more recent studies seem to have been much more cautious about identifying diagnosable psychiatric disorder. Indeed, most seem to remain completely silent on the topic.

25 See, for example, Dominian (1998), Ellens and Rollins (2004), Os (2011), Watts (2007).

26 See, for example, Meier (1994, pp.106–116), Dunn (2003, pp.371–377). Meier suggests that "Jesus being baptised by John is one of the most historically cer-tain events ascertainable by any reconstruction of the historical Jesus" (1994, p.129).

27 Dunn (2003, p.377).

28 The emphasis here is on seeing – but it would appear, from verse 33, that the fourth evangelist may also have intended us to understand that John did hear a voice.

29 So in Luke – in Matthew: "This is my son…"

30 Dunn (2003, pp.374–375, 380–381).

31 Matthew 17:1–9, Mark 9:2–9, Luke 9:28–36.

32 Thus, Matthew. In Mark there is no specific reference to Jesus' face. In Luke we are told only that "his face changed".

33 In Luke (verse 31) we are told that the conversation was about Jesus "depar-ture, which he was about to accomplish at Jerusalem".

34 In addition to other sources cited here, see Hooker (1991, pp.213–214), Hagner (1995, pp.491–492).

35 See, for example, Bultmann (1963, pp.259–261).

36 However else it might be understood, the narrative certainly is rich with sym-bolism. Moses and Elijah represent, respectively, the law and the prophets. The shining of Jesus' face is an allusion to the similar transformation of Moses' appearance when receiving the law. The mountain may represent Mount Sinai. The cloud was understood as the medium in and through which God revealed himself Nineham (1963, pp.232–237), Caird (1985, pp.131–133), Hooker (1991, pp.213–218), France (2007, p.644).

37 Cranfield (1959, pp.292–294). This is an interesting distinction to make, which seems to imply that visions and auditions are not factual. Thus, the "transfigu-ration" element in verses 2–3 is historical and factual, and the appearance of Moses and Elijah, and the voice from the cloud, in verses 4–7 are both visionary and miraculous.

38 Caird (1985, p.132).

39 Fenton (1980, p.275).

40 Marshall (1998, p.381).

41 France (2007, p.643).
42 Interestingly, Miller (1997) does not refer to the transfiguration narratives in his account of *Jesus at Thirty*, presumably because he considers that they lack biographical significance?
43 See, for example, James Dunn's discussion of this. That God raised Jesus from the dead seems to have been "the earliest distinctively Christian affirmation and confession" (Dunn, 2003, p.826).
44 Other encounters with the risen Jesus are also reported in 1 Corinthians 15:6–7. This Pauline account represents the earliest historical reference to the resurrection appearances of Jesus. See, for example, Casey (2010, pp.456–461).
45 In the Matthean account, Mary is accompanied by "the other Mary". In Mark she is accompanied by Mary the Mother of James and Salome. In Luke she is accompanied by Joanna, Mary the mother of James, and other women. In Matthew and Mark there is only one angel, and in Luke there are two.
46 Marshall (1998, p.883).
47 Thus, for example, Cranfield (p.465).
48 Dunn (2003, pp.859, 861).
49 Fuller (1972, pp.30–32).
50 Kermode (1997).
51 Crossley (2005, p.186).
52 John Hick (1993) points out that the earliest account that we have is actually that of Paul's experience on the Damascus Road (see below). Whilst this might appear to be of a different category, occuring two or three years after the crucifixion, it is equated by Paul with the appearances to Peter and the other apostles (p.24). The gospel accounts of resurrection appearances to Peter and the other apostles are, according to Hick, all "later elaborations" (p.25).
53 Habermas has identified well over 2000 scholarly publications during the 30-year period from 1975 to 2005 alone (Habermas, 2005).
54 Habermas suggests that the "vast majority of scholars … still reject such proposals" (2005, p.140). See also Habermas (2001).
55 Habermas (2005, p.151).
56 See, for example, Cranfield (1990), Barclay (1996), Allison (2005).
57 Various theories are asserted to explain why a tomb might have been found empty. See, for example, Allison (2005, p.118).
58 Also referred to as "objective visions" (Fuller, 1972, p.33, Carnley, 1987, pp.69–72).
59 Chadwick (1980, pp.112–113).
60 Strauss (1865, p.440).
61 Ibid., p.427.
62 Atkins' account of her conversion is considered further in Chapter 6.
63 See Introduction for a brief account of the scientific literature pertaining to hallucinations experienced in bereavement. The proposal that the New Testament resurrection narratives were experiences of this kind has also been taken up by Dewi Rees (2010). Responding to Rees, O'Collins (2011) concludes that, although there are some basic similarities, there are too many dissimilarities for the analogy to be considered "close and illuminating".
64 Craig (1981). Cranfield (1990) also points out that there is no reason to believe that the disciples were expecting anything of this kind. This raises the interesting question as to whether normal bereavement hallucinations are in any sense "expected". On the one hand, they are clearly not, as most people do not expect to see or hear the person whom they know (at a rational level) has died. On the other hand, after years of familiar and daily interaction with a close friend or family member, there is inevitably an expectation or seeing and hearing them that arises out of habit and forgetfulness. The normal pattern, however, would

seem to be that perceptions arising in this context are immediately subject to disconfirmation the moment that the death of the person concerned is called to mind. Other than in exceptional circumstances (for example, psychosis) I am not aware of accounts of continuing hallucinations that persist despite such conscious disconfirmation.

65 Habermas (2001).

66 Lüdemann (1994, pp.6–7).

67 Dunn (2003, pp.873–874).

68 Casey (2010, p.488).

69 Ibid.

70 Wright (2003, p.690).

71 Licona (2010, pp.483–491).

72 See, for example, Wiebe (1997).

73 O'Connell (2009, p.87).

74 Gowler (2010).

75 Lest there should be any doubt, I am referring to the use of term "myth" here in its technical sense, as defined by Dundes, and thus I am categorically not saying that the event of the resurrection did not happen. My belief in the resurrection represents a faith commitment which the reader may not share. What I am therefore suggesting is that the resurrection narratives are mythically true, whatever else may be believed to have happened – or not happened – in an historical sense. However, I am aware that the nature and definition of "myth" are contested, and that this assertion also hangs on the choice of definition. Dundes represents an anthropological and comparative tradition. Definitions drawn from other disciplines may lead to correspondingly different conclusions.

76 I would argue this to be implicitly the case even in the original shorter ending of Mark's gospel, where the witnesses to the empty tomb are silenced by fear and it is left only to the angel to announce that Jesus has gone ahead to Galilee. The reader is left to imagine what happens next, but it is hardly a silent Jesus whom we are to imagine awaits the disciples in Galilee.

77 The experiences are related again in chapter 11, when Peter gives an account to the Christians in Jerusalem about what has happened.

78 Verse 13.

79 Verse 14.

80 Verse 15.

81 When they arrive, Peter is still caught up with the vision and in verses 19–20 we are told "While Peter was still thinking about the vision, the Spirit said to him, 'Look, three men are searching for you. Now get up, go down, and go with them without hesitation; for I have sent them.'" It is not clear whether this is a similar voice to the one that he has already heard (referred to simply as "a voice", or perhaps different and to be distinguished in some way.

82 This influence, however, has not been accepted without any dissent. Interesting questions arise, for example, as to why continuing distinctions are made between clean and unclean foods and related matters in Acts 15 if the authority of Peter's vision was historically accepted.

83 Haenchen (1971, pp.355–363).

84 In 9:7 we are told that the men travelling with Saul heard the voice, but in 22:9 we are told that they did not hear the voice. This could therefore be understood as a voice heard by Saul alone if the latter text is taken to be correct and the former incorrect. However, this is still a story within which voices heard individually by Saul and by Ananias together comprise a story which is not one of private voice hearing but rather of multiple people (in this case, two) hearing a voice which, on different occasions, speaks to each of them.

85 Nor indeed would the other gospels lead us to any fundamentally different conclusion. In Mark, the voice from heaven at Jesus' baptism is addressed to him
alone. In John 20, Mary Magdalene is the first to encounter the risen Jesus, and
this is a one to one meeting between the two of them, and no one else is present
to see or hear what takes place, but Jesus is subsequently seen and heard by all
of the disciples.

86 The story is related again in Acts 22:6–16 and 26:12–18. There are differences
in the various accounts, which should perhaps urge caution about placing too
much weight on details of the narrative. For example, in 26:14, the initial words
of Jesus to Paul are expanded by a second sentence: "'Saul, Saul, why are you
persecuting me? It hurts you to kick against the goads." In this version the part
played by Ananias is also omitted. There is a helpful verse by verse comparison
in Barrett (2002, pp.130–131). See also Hedrick (1981).

87 Barrett (2002, p.131).

88 See, for example, Shantz (2009, pp.47–50).

89 Interestingly, I have not seen any discussion of possible diagnoses for Ananias.
All the attention focuses on Paul. Admittedly he is more famous, but the implausibility of two characters in the story developing similar diagnoses, with similar
voices, content of which relates each to the other, is (as far as I can see) nowhere
considered.

90 2 Corinthians 12:1–4.

91 Galatians 1:12.

92 Bockmuehl (1990).

93 2 Corinthians 12.

94 Beale (1999, pp.4–27), Sweet (1990, pp.21–27). There is a view that it may have
been written before this – perhaps around 68 CE.

95 Sweet (1990, pp.17–21).

96 Beale (1999, pp.37–43).

97 Sweet (1990, pp.35–47).

98 The author will be referred to here as "John" without prejudice to this debate.

99 "Son of Man" is a title found also in Daniel, and is used by Jesus in the synoptic
gospels as a form of self-reference. John's vision is therefore to be understood as
a vision of Jesus.

100 Rowland (1993, p.23).

101 Rowland (1982, pp.214–247).

102 Rowland (1993, pp.42–45).

103 Ibid., p.44.

104 Beale identifies four major approaches to the interpretation of Revelation, and
he outlines his own approach, which might most simply be described as eclectic
(1999, pp.44–49).

105 Revelation 2:1

106 Beale (1999, p.229). See also Chapter 3.

107 Revelation 22:10.

108 Beale (1999, p.1151).

109 Sweet (1990, pp.13–17).

110 Seven is itself a significant number – representing completeness. Sweet (1990,
pp.14–15) provides a helpful summary of the numerical symbolism of
Revelation.

111 The Lamb is symbolic of Christ.

112 Revelation 21:3–4.

113 Revelation 4:8.

114 Revelation 4:11.

115 Revelation 5:13.

116 Revelation 6:9–10.
117 Revelation 7:9–10.
118 Revelation 8:13.
119 Revelation 9:13.
120 Revelation 10:4, 8, 11:12, and elsewhere.
121 Revelation 13:5–6.
122 Revelation 14:3.
123 Revelation 18:9–10.
124 Revelation 19:1ff.
125 For example, the voices of 2 Corinthians 12 are arguably exceptions to what I am saying here, being responses to Paul's suffering. In verse 3 Paul hears things that are "not to be told" and so we do not know the content of what was said. In verse 9 the voice ("the Lord") is concerned with God's grace and power in Paul's weakness. However, the context is still Christological. Paul concludes in verse 10 that he is content with weakness, insults, etc. "for the sake of Christ". He is clearly affirmed in this view, amongst other things, by the voices of verses 3 and 9.

5 Hearing voices in the Christian tradition

Given the part that conversations with God, angelic messengers, and heavenly voices play in the Bible, it is hardly surprising that voices and visions play a significant part in subsequent Christian tradition. Whilst there are some significant accounts of voices in early Christianity, notably in the visions of some early martyrs and in the *Life of Antony*, there are many fewer examples during the first millennium than in the second. From the 12th century onwards, accounts of voices and visions flourish.

The *Life of Antony*

Athanasius' *Life of Antony* was probably written soon after the death of Antony of Egypt in 356.[1] Before the end of the 4th century, it had become a hugely popular Christian classic.

As a young man, having lost both his parents, Antony found himself responsible for the family home and his young sister. Reflecting on how the apostles had forsaken everything to follow Jesus, he went into church one day as a passage from Matthew's gospel was being read:

> *If you would be perfect, go, sell what you possess and give to the poor, and you will have treasure in heaven.*[2] It was as if by God's design he held the saints in his recollection, and as if the passage were read on his account.
>
> (Gregg, 1980, p.31, italics in original)

He promptly gave the family land to the townspeople, sold all his possessions, and gave the rest of the money to the poor.[3] Devoting himself to manual work and to prayer, and taking as his example a holy hermit from a local village, he grew in love and respect in the eyes of all. Eventually, he lived as a hermit in the Egyptian desert, pursuing a life of ascetical discipline and prayer. He attracted increasing numbers of followers and a reputation for great spiritual authority.

The *Life of Antony* became the first significant post-biblical biography of a Christian saint and set the tone for all subsequent hagiography. It presents Antony's experiences in the desert after the model of the synoptic gospel accounts of Jesus' temptation in the wilderness. However, the *Life* is marked by a much more colourful demonology than is found in the gospels. It is easy for the modern reader to misinterpret this. The narratives are psychologically sophisticated and any purely literal interpretation is in danger of missing the subtle and complex ways in which they reveal Antony's[4] awareness of the challenging nature of the spiritual life.

Soon after Antony embarked on his life of prayer and self-discipline, Athanasius tells us:

> The devil, who despises and envies good, could not bear seeing such purpose in a youth, but the sort of things he had busied himself in doing in the past, he set to work to do against this person as well.
>
> (Gregg, 1980, p.33)

Initially, demonic assaults on Antony are all related in purely cognitive terms. He is assailed by memories of a more comfortable life, concern for family obligations, and thoughts of the difficulties of his new life in the desert. Then follow "foul thoughts" and sexual dreams. Antony responds with prayerful resolve, turning his thoughts to Christ and to "the threat of the fire of judgement". Eventually, when the devil is unable to defeat Antony by these means, he changes his strategy:

> And as if succumbing, he no longer attacked by means of thoughts (for the crafty one had been cast out), but using now a human voice, said, "I tricked many, and I vanquished many, but just now, waging my attack on you and your labors, as I have upon many others, I was too weak."[5]

Antony asks who has spoken, and the devil responds again: "I am the friend of fornication. I set its ambushes and I worked its seductions against the young – I have even been called the spirit of fornication."[6] Like Christ in the wilderness, Antony quotes scripture against the devil and he flees. Thus ends Antony's "first contest against the devil".[7] In his next encounter, Antony is assailed by a multitude of demons who whip him, leaving him "as if dead". In a third encounter, the demons make "such a crashing noise that that whole place seemed to be shaken by a quake". They are then transformed into the appearance of "beasts and reptiles".[8] These beasts assault and wound Antony, so that he is in great pain, but "being in control of his thoughts" Antony responds by mocking the demons and reaffirming his faith. Eventually Antony has a vision of light, the demons vanish, and he is no longer in pain. When Antony asks why he was not thus rescued earlier,

> a voice came to him: "I was here, Antony, but I waited to watch your struggle. And now, since you persevered and were not defeated, I will be your helper forever, and I will make you famous everywhere."[9]

Antony goes on to endure more temptations, which take both visual and auditory (verbal and non-verbal) forms, and he is supported by "visions from above" (p.40). As a result of his experiences he is able to teach others how to combat temptation. Whilst Antony was not averse to answering back when he heard the voice of the devil, his later instruction suggests also a technique of not paying attention to the voices and visions:

> Therefore let us not pay attention to what [the devil] might say – for he lies – nor let us be frightened by his apparitions, which themselves are also deceptions. What appears in them is not true light . . . They do, without doubt, appear, but they disappear again at once, harming none of the faithful, but carrying with themselves the likeness of the fire that is about to receive them. So here it is not necessary to fear them, for by the grace of Christ all their pursuits come to nothing.[10]

He goes on to indicate that the devils are treacherous and multiform. They do not always become visible. They sing sacred songs and recite scripture. They repeat a text that is being read "as if in echo".[11] They simulate prophesy[12] and take on the appearance of light.[13] He encounters one demon who calls himself "the Power of God"[14] and another who identifies himself as Satan.[15] He generally responds to the demonic voices and visions with prayer, chanting of Psalms, and invocations of the name of Christ.

Antony also hears a divine voice. In addition to the voice that promised to make him famous, he hears a voice "from above" telling him where he may better seek solitude.[16] On another occasion, a voice from above accompanies a vision of souls passing to heaven (and of other souls being prevented from doing so) after their death.[17]

Antony was not the only desert father to hear voices.[18] Thus, for example, in the *Apophthegmata*, Abba Arsenius tells a story of a hermit sitting in his cell who heard a voice that said "Come here, and I will show you the works of the children of men."[19] The voice shows the hermit various men, working in different ways, and then interprets their actions as a kind of parable. Abba Macarius, like Antony, has conversations with the devil,[20] and Abba Piterion hears the voice of an angel.[21] On the other hand, Evagrius and Cassian both emphasised the importance of imageless or pure prayer, beyond words.[22] Alongside the tradition of voices, there is thus also a tradition within which hearing the voice of God represents something less than the height of spiritual experience.[23]

The *Life of Antony* gives an account of a life lived in imitation of Christ, of the overcoming of temptation, of Christian holiness, self-discipline, and prayer. Antony condems the Arian heresy and supports doctrine affirmed at the First Council of Nicaea (325 CE). The *Life* was clearly not provided as an account of voice hearing and – even if it had been – it was written according to pre-scientific norms and expectations. However, given

its seminal influence upon subsequent Christian hagiography and spirituality, the fact that it accords a significant place to Antony's ability to hear
demonic and divine voices is significant.

Augustine of Hippo

Augustine of Hippo[24] (354–430 CE) was born to a pagan father and a
Christian mother. Raised initially as a Christian, he took a mistress at
the age of 17 and became a Manichaean. Increasingly dissatisfied with
Manichaeism, he grew in admiration for the sermons of Bishop Ambrose.
He also read the *Life of Antony*.

In 386, events came to a crisis in a garden in Milan. Hearing the voice of
a child in a neighbouring house chanting a refrain "Take it and read, take it
and read", he remembered how Antony had happened to go into a church
when the gospel was being read and had taken the words of Matthew 19:21
as being addressed by God to him. Accordingly, he took the words of the
child as a divine command, addressed to him, to open the Christian scriptures and read the first passage on which his eyes should fall. When he did
this, the passage that he read was from St Paul's Letter to the Romans:
"Not in revelling and drunkenness, not in lust and wantonness, not in quar-
rels and rivalries. Rather, arm yourselves with the Lord Jesus Christ; spend
no more thought on nature and nature's appetites."[25] The impact of this
experience on Augustine was immense: "it was as though the light of confidence flooded into my heart and all the darkness of doubt was dispelled."[26]
Augustine went on to become Bishop of Hippo and one of the most significant theologians of the Christian Church.

Augustine's mystical experiences are a subject of some interest.[27] In
Confessions he records his discovery of a transcendent order hidden in God:
"And so, in an instant of awe, my mind attained to the sight of the God
who IS. Then, at last, *I caught sight of your invisible nature, as it is known
through your creatures*."[28] In another experience, shared with his mother
Monica just before she died, he records:

> And while we spoke of the eternal Wisdom, longing for it and strain-
> ing for it with all the strength of our hearts, for one fleeting instant we
> reached out and touched it. Then with a sigh, leaving *our spiritual har-
> vest* bound to it, we returned to the sound of our own speech, in which
> each word has a beginning and an ending – far, far different from your
> Word, our Lord, who abides in himself for ever, yet never grows old
> and gives new life to all things.[29]

Augustine's mystical experiences do not include the hearing of voices.[30]
However, Augustine and Antony (as portrayed by Athanasius) shared a
sense that God addresses the human soul through the voice of scripture.

Augustine also understood the voice of the child who chanted "take it and read" as conveying a divine command. Simple though these observations are, they are enormously important. If God can speak to human beings through the reading of scripture, or through the voice of a child in a neighbouring garden, then why not also through a voice heard in the absence of any visible speaker?

In *The Literal Meaning of Genesis*[31] Augustine distinguishes between corporeal visions, spiritual visions, and intellectual visions.[32] Corporeal visions are perceived through the body, spiritual (or imaginative) visions are perceived through the mind, and intellectual visions (understood by Augustine as being the highest form) are perceived by the intellect, without images. Applied initially to visions, this taxonomy can equally be applied to voices and to other perceptual phenomena. It had enduring influence, being adopted by Thomas Aquinas,[33] Teresa of Avila, John of the Cross, and many other later theologians and spiritual writers.

Early medieval voices

It is difficult to find clear Christian examples of the hearing of voices between the 5th and 10th centuries CE, and during this period McGinn[34] notes also the relative lack of significant mystical authors.

Where visionary experiences were reported during the early Middle Ages, they appear to have taken a particular form, usually a once-in-a-lifetime experience effecting a personal conversion of some kind.[35] St Symeon the New Theologian (949–1022) describes simply (and yet in great depth) an experience of light unaccompanied by any voice:

> One day, as he stood repeating more in his intellect than with his mouth the words, "God, have mercy upon me, a sinner" (Luke 18:13), suddenly a profuse flood of divine light appeared above him and filled the whole room. As this happened the young man lost his bearings, forgetting whether he was in a house or under a roof; for he saw nothing but light around him and did not even know that he stood upon the earth. He had no fear of falling, or awareness of the world, nor did any of those things that beset men and bodily beings enter his mind. Instead he was wholly united to non-material light, so much so that it seemed to him that he himself had been transformed into light. Oblivious of all else, he was filled with tears and with inexpressible joy and gladness. Then his intellect ascended to heaven and beheld another light, more lucid than the first. Miraculously there appeared to him, standing close to that light, the holy, angelic elder of whom we have spoken and who had given him the short rule and the book.
>
> (Palmer et al., 1995, p.18)

Symeon had many more such visions before eventually he heard the voice of Jesus. This voice was a significant turning point for him,[36] but his theology is still dominated by visual imagery.

High medieval voices

From the 12th century onwards, visionary experiences of a different kind begin to emerge, exemplified in such figures as Hildegard of Bingen (1098–1179) and Elisabeth of Schönau (1129–1165), and a "new mysticism" emerges. This is characterised by a shift of focus away from cloistered religious communities, a much more prominent role being taken by women, and a sudden flourishing of biographical and autobiographical accounts of mystical experience. At the forefront of this new mysticism were figures such as Mary of Oignies (1177–1213) and Frances of Assisi (c.1181–1226).[37] Within the visionary experiences reported by mystics of this period, voices play a significant and varied part, but the visual element almost always predominates.

In Hildegard of Bingen's *Scivias*, the visions are complex and extended. The texts that Hildegard left were accompanied by miniature paintings, thought to have been produced under her supervision and, in the case of the last vision, by music composed by Hildegard herself. In these visions, voices play a small part. However, they are preceded in the manuscript by an account of hearing a voice:

> And behold! In the forty-third year of my earthly course, as I was gazing with great fear and trembling attention at a heavenly vision, I saw a great splendour in which resounded a voice from Heaven, saying to me, "O fragile human, ashes of ashes, and filth of filth! Say and write what you see and hear."
>
> (Hart et al., 1990, p.59)

The voice continues to emphasise that Hildegard should write down her visions, and yet she does not do so for some time, until encouraged by others to do so. Thus the voice supports the authority of the visions and excuses any apparent lack of humility in sharing them with others.

Elisabeth of Schönau provides an example of the variety of forms that voices might take within a vision.[38] Elisabeth's visions began when she was 23 years old, and were recorded by her brother Ekbert. They soon assumed a strongly liturgical pattern within which she typically experienced visions corresponding with saints, feasts, and festivals of the liturgical year. Contrary to this later pattern, her initial visions in May 1152 – in the context of low mood and suicidal ideation – were of a "phantom in a monks cowl" which she heard laughing, threatening her, and swearing.[39] On 31 May 1152 she had a vision of the Virgin Mary, in which she reports that Mary:

> implanted – I don't know how – these words in my mind, "Do not fear, because these things will not harm you at all." In truth I did not hear the sound of her voice; rather I only clearly saw the movement of her lips.
>
> (Clark and Newman, 2000, p.47)

On 7 June 1152, in a vision which she re-experienced every Saturday on Marian festivals, she reports that, "Looking at [Mary], I carefully watched the movement of her lips, and I understood that she was calling me by my name, Elisabeth, and then she said no more."[40] On other occasions, she seems more straightforwardly to "hear" the voice of the visionary figure, as on 14 August 1152: "at noon, my heart was struck by a sudden shock and I heard these words, 'Do not be afraid, daughter, because the Lord your comforter chastises every child He takes to Himself.'"[41] On 15 March 1153, in another vision, she poses a question to St Gregory and receives what appears to have been an audible reply.[42] At yet other times, the distinction between words that she has heard and spoken in her prayers is blurred. For example, on 14 August 1153 she reports that she "unexpectedly turned over these words in my mouth" and "this suddenly rushed into my mouth".[43]

Hadewijch (mid-13th century) provides a further example of complex visionary experience, within which voices play a part. Her vision of "The Perfect Bride", experienced on the festival of the Epiphany during celebration of the Mass, involves a vision of a large city, in the midst of which a figure is seated upon a round disk:

> And he who sat there above the disk was sitting in constant stillness; but in the disk his Being circled about in unspeakable swiftness without stopping. And the abyss in which the disk ran as it circled about was of such unheard-of depth and so dark that no horror can be compared to it.
>
> (Hart and Mommaers, 1980, p.293)

After further description of the disc and the figure, Hadewijch falls down in adoration. Four eagles then appear in turn, each crying out with words which Hadewijch records.

> At that moment I was taken up, through the voice of [the fourth] eagle who spoke to me. And then there came into the city a great crowd in festive apparel, and each one rich in her own works. They were all virtues; and they were conducting a bride to her Beloved. They had served her nobly and had looked after her so proudly that they could present her as worthy to be received by the mighty great God as his bride.[44]

There then follows a description of each of 12 virtues that comprise the bridal robe, and the bride is led into the city. At the end, Hadewijch comes to see herself as the bride and is "received in union by the One who sat there in the abyss upon the circling disk, and there I became one with him in the certainty of unity".[45] Finally, after further words spoken by the eagle, Hadewijch sees herself swallowed up in the abyss: "Then I received the certainty of being received, in this form, in my Beloved, and my Beloved also in me.[46]

Gertrude of Helfta (1256–c.1302) provides a different example of vision-ary experience from this period. At the age of 26, standing in the dormitory after night prayers had been said she bowed, as custom dictated, at the approach of an older nun. When she looked up, she saw:

> a youth of about sixteen years of age, handsome and gracious. Young as I then was, the beauty of his form was all that I could have desired, entirely pleasing to the outward eye. Courteously and in a gentle voice (cf. Gen. 50:21) he said to me: "Soon will come your salvation; why are you so sad? Is it because you have no one to confide in that you are sorrowful?"
> (Winkworth et al., 1993, p.95)

The youth takes Gertrude's hand, "as though to plight a troth", and quotes verses from Psalm 71 and Psalm 35 before being separated from her by a hedge with sharp thorns which appears to have no end:

> As I hesitated, burning with desire and almost fainting, suddenly he seized me and, lifting me up with the greatest ease, placed me beside him. But on the hand with which he had just given me his promise I recognised those bright jewels, his wounds, which have canceled all our debts (Co. 2:14).[47]

Gertrude goes on to experience further visions, but inevitably also peri-ods of not having such experiences. When she asks God about this in her prayers, he replies:

> Too great a proximity sometimes prevents friends from seeing each other clearly. For instance, if they are very near one another, as some-times happens in embracing and kissing, it is not possible for them to have the pleasure of seeing each other clearly at the same time."[48]

Just as she is thus encouraged to find growing intimacy with God without see-ing, she is also encouraged to find intimacy without hearing God speak to her:

> Formerly I used to instruct you with responses which you could use to show my pleasure to others. Now I let you feel in your spirit my inspira-tion in your prayers, because it would be very difficult to translate them into words . . . You will be like a bride who knows all the secrets of her spouse, and who, after having lived a long time with him, knows how to interpret his wishes.[49]

The Franciscan tradition

The earliest of many biographies of Francis, written by Thomas of Celano in 1228–1229, was commissioned by Pope Gregory. It records that Francis was born into a rich merchant family and that, as a young man, he was vain and arrogant. When recovering from a long illness, he began to undergo a far-reaching change of heart. Selling his possessions, and seeking to give his money away, he alienated his father and was cast out of his family home. He then devoted himself to restoring a small ruined church, dedicated to San Damiano, in which he had previously sought refuge. According to this account, Francis receives inspiration in a dream (which he initially misinterprets as foretelling worldly wealth and honour), and in conversations with a holy friend and with a priest, but there is no reference to any hearing of voices. Subsequent biographies by Julian of Speyer (written in 1232–1235) and Henri d'Avranches (written in 1232–1239, in verse) offer a similar account.[50]

An anonymous manuscript found in Perugia in 1671, thought to have been written in 1240–1241, adds an additional episode following Francis' dream. In this account, when half asleep (and perhaps therefore also in a dream), Francis hears a voice. The voice asks him where he is travelling to and then poses a question that clarifies for Francis the true meaning of his earlier dream:

> "Who can do more for you, the Lord or the servant?" "The Lord" [Francis] answered. "Then why are you abandoning the Lord for the servant, and the patron for the client?" To which Francis responded: "Lord, what do you want me to do?" "Go back," it said, "to your own land to do what the Lord will tell you."
>
> (Armstrong et al., 1999, p.36)

In the *Legend of Three Companions*, written in 1241–1247 by Brothers Angelo, Leo, and Rufino, drawing on the accounts provided previously by Thomas of Celano and the anonymous manuscript found in Perugia, further additions to the narrative are incorporated. Notably, and most famously, when Francis first visits the church of San Damiano, he hears a voice:

> while he was walking by the church of San Damiano, he was told in the Spirit to go inside for a prayer. Once he entered, he began to pray intensely before an image of the Crucified, which spoke to him in a tender and kind voice: "Francis, don't you see that my house is being destroyed?" Go, then, and rebuild it for me." Stunned and trembling, he said: "I will do so gladly, Lord." . . . He was filled with such joy and became so radiant with light over that message, that he knew in his soul that it was truly Christ crucified who spoke to him.
>
> (Armstrong et al., 2000, p.76)

In *The Remembrance of the Desire of a Soul*, written in 1245–1247, Thomas of Celano drew on additional material in order to write a fuller account of the life of Francis. This now incorporated an account of the voice at San Damiano.[51] In 1260, the General Chapter gave to Bonaventure of Bagnoregio the task of compiling a new account of the life of Francis, taking into account all of the information provided in the earlier accounts. This resulted in the *Major Legend of St Francis* (written 1260–1263).

The *Major Legend* includes a variety of ecstatic experiences, beginning with a vision of Christ crucified which is inserted into the narrative after the two initial dreams and before Francis hears the voice from the cross at San Damiano. In the account of the events at San Damiano, Bonaventure has Francis hearing the words of the voice repeated three times:

> While his tear filled eyes were gazing at the Lord's cross, he heard with his bodily ears a voice coming from that cross, telling him three times: "Francis, go and repair my house which, as you see, is all being destroyed."
>
> (Armstrong et al., 2000, p.536)

This repetition of the voice is interpreted in Bonaventure's *Minor Legend* (1260–1263) as referring to the three Franciscan Orders.[52]

There is no evidence to suggest that Francis heard voices on a regular basis, and the episode at San Damiano – assuming that it has an historical basis – appears to have been unique. A number of ecstatic experiences may be identified within the *Major Legend*,[53] including (in addition to the vision of Christ crucified, and the episode at San Damiano) a vision of light, various experiences of contemplative prayer, and the exercise of prophetic gifts. He is reported as having had encounters with demons,[54] which are reminiscent of the *Life of Antony*. The famous vision of the seraph,[55] following which Francis received the stigmata, appears to have been a primarily visual experience. Insofar as voices are a feature of the story of Francis's life, they are very much associated with conversion and transformation of life.

According to the *Legend of St Clare* (13th century), Clare of Assisi (1193/4–1253), founder of the second Franciscan order, also heard voices.[56] These included both the voice of an "angel of darkness", whom she saw in a vision, and the voice of a child – taken to be Christ. Rather like St Antony, Clare rebuffs the demon and he flees. The Christ child grants her request for protection of her land/city. According to the *Legend*, her mother also heard a voice from a crucifix whilst pregnant with Clare.

In 1288, Angela of Foligno (c.1248–1309), in a short space of time, suffered the death of her mother, her husband, and all her sons. In 1291, she was professed as a Franciscan tertiary and went on pilgrimage to Assisi. At this time, she had a significant visionary experience and then went on to have increasingly intense visions of Christ. In her *Book* she describes the stages of her inner journey, her visions, and a culminating experience of ineffable darkness. Within these experiences, voices again have a part to play. For example:

while I was asking God what I could do to please him more, in his mercy, he appeared to me many times, both while I was asleep and awake, crucified on the cross. He told me that I should look at his wounds. In a wonderful manner, he showed me how he had endured all these wounds for me; and he did this many times. As he was showing me the sufferings he had endured for me from each of these wounds, one after the other, he told me: "What then can you do that would seem to you to be enough?"

(Lachance and Guarniari, 1993, pp.126–127)

At a later stage of her spiritual journey, she describes an experience of a voice in the absence of visual experiences:

[O]ne day while I was in prayer and wanted to say the Our Father, suddenly my soul heard a voice which said: "You are full of God." I truly felt all the members of my body filled with the delights of God. And I wanted to die, just as before, when I went to Assisi, and again, when I had returned and was lying down in my cell . . . The voice then told me, and I felt it, that God was embracing my soul. I truly did feel that this was what was happening. But now it seems to me that everything we are trying to say about this experience reduces it to a mere trifle, because what took place is so different from what can be said about it. I myself am very ashamed that I cannot find better words to describe it.[57]

Towards the end of her *Book*, Angela outlines seven ways in which God reveals his presence within the soul. It is in the second way that the soul "mysteriously hears divine words which make it secure in the knowledge that God is present".[58] Voice hearing is therefore only one of the ways in which Angela understands herself as having encountered God, and it is not the pinnacle of her experiences but, when it occurs, it is inseparable from her experience of the presence of God.

Late medieval voices

Amongst the many examples of voice hearing that might be drawn from the late medieval period, three – all women living amidst the turmoil and conflict of the Hundred Years' War – will be considered briefly here. Julian of Norwich (c.1342–c.1416) and Margery Kempe (c.1373–1438) were both English, and Joan of Arc (c.1412–1431) was French. Julian was an anchoress, Margery a married woman with 14 children, who travelled extensively on pilgrimage, and Joan a single woman who managed to engage herself in the military campaign against the English forces in France. Julian's experiences were all focused around the events of a few days in 1373, upon which she reflected deeply for a further 20 years, whereas Margery describes daily experiences lasting over many years. Julian's *Revelations*, the earliest book to be written in English by a woman, continues to be a source of spiritual and theological interest down to the present day. Margery's *Book*, the first autobiography of an Englishwoman, was written by an amanuensis as she was herself illiterate. Joan, the only one of these three women to be canonised by the Roman Catholic Church, significantly influenced the course of the history of her nation, yet was burned at the stake as a heretic at the age of only 21 years, unwilling to deny her honest account of her experiences. Our only record of these experiences, albeit a uniquely detailed one, is that of the trials that led to her execution and later her posthumous exoneration.

The voices that Julian heard were all associated with visionary experiences of the passion of Christ, occurring in the context of a near-fatal illness. Medically, it would appear that she was suffering from a delirium – or toxic confusional state – associated with her illness.[59] This does not invalidate the significant content of the visions, especially given Julian's careful and thoughtful reflections upon what they might mean both for her and for the wider Christian Church. *Revelations* attends to the nature of divine love, human shame, and suffering, and the feminine aspects of the Godhead in a deeply engaging, provocative, and challenging way.

All but one of Julian's 16 visions were associated with the hearing of a voice. One is verbal with no visual element. Julian distinguishes between three modes of revelation – similar to, but different from, Augustine's typology of visionary experience. It is not always clear exactly which of these experiences Julian is referring to, but only in one place is a voice clearly and unambiguously heard with the bodily sense of hearing, and this is the voice of the devil (following the 16th revelation). Many of Julian's experiences have a conversational quality about them. For example, in the first revelation, Julian experiences a spiritual vision of Mary, the mother of Christ. She also sees

> something small, no bigger than a hazelnut, lying in the palm of my hand, as it seemed to me, and it was as round as a ball. I looked at it with the eye of my understanding and thought: What can this be? I was amazed that it could last, for I thought that because of its littleness it would suddenly have fallen into nothing. And I was answered in my understanding: It lasts and always will, because God loves it; and thus everything has being through the love of God.[60]

The voice comes in response to a question that Julian poses in her thoughts, rather as one person might ask a question of another person, and then she receives an answer in response. In a similar way, Julian receives answers to some of the deep questions with which she is struggling – as when she cannot understand why God allowed sin in the world: "Jesus. . . . answered with these words and said, Sin is necessary, but all will be well, and all will be well, and every kind of thing will be well."[61]

Margery Kempe, in her *Book*, hears the voices of devils, of a variety of saints, and – most notably – of Jesus. In one place she hears the voices of both the first and second persons of the Trinity. She never hears the Holy Spirit as a voice. Rather, she hears a sound like bellows, the sound of a dove, and the sound of a robin.[62] It is not always clear whether these voices and sounds are heard as if with her bodily sense of hearing, or whether they are more imaginative, but in many instances it would appear that the voices have a more inner, imaginative or mental, quality to them. She has a variety of conversational exchanges.

> Sometimes our Lady spoke to her mind; sometimes St Peter, sometimes St Paul, sometimes St Katherine, or whatever saint in heaven she was devoted to, appeared to her soul and taught her how she should love our Lord and how she should please him. These conversations were so sweet, so holy and so devout, that often this creature could not bear it, but fell down and twisted and wrenched her body about, and made remarkable faces and gestures, with vehement sobbings and great abundance of tears, sometimes saying "Jesus, mercy," and sometimes "I die."[63]

Margery is not slow to tell others about her experiences. Combined with her loud and frequent weeping, this has a propensity to annoy those around her, and opinion seems to have been divided between those who were sympathetic and supportive of her and those who found her irritating. She has been diagnosed by recent commentators as either hysterical (Drucker, 1972) or psychotic (Craun, 2005). Yet, her strength of character, her sincerity, and her devotion speak to her integrity of heart and mind.

Joan of Arc's voices seems to have begun at an earlier age, and to have been of a different quality, than either Julian or Margery. On the second day of her trial (22 February 1431), the record states:

> she declared that at the age of thirteen she had a voice from God to help her and guide her. And the first time she was much afraid. And this voice came towards noon, in summer, in her father's garden: and the said Jeanne had [not] fasted on the preceding day. She heard the voice on her right, in the direction of the church; and she seldom heard it without a light. This light came from the same side as the voice, and generally there was a great light. When she came to France she often heard the voice.
>
> Asked how she could see the light of which she spoke, since it was at the side, she made no reply, and went on to other things. She said that if she was in a wood she easily heard the voices come to her. It seemed to her a worthy voice, and she believed it was sent from God; when she heard the voice a third time she knew that it was the voice of an angel. She said also that this voice always protected her well and that she understood it well.
>
> (Barrett, 1931, pp.54–55)

Joan lived at close proximity to war, in an area loyal to France against England and Burgundy, an uneducated girl, the daughter of farmers. Yet, when her voices told her that she would raise the siege of Orleans, and bring about the coronation of the Dauphin in Rheims, in 1429 she some-how managed to get an audience with the Dauphin and to persuade him, and his advisers, that she should have a part in the military campaign. Even in an age when the significance of divine revelation was taken more seriously and literally in political debate than now, this was an impressive achievement. She participated in the military action which led to the rais-ing of the siege, and the Dauphin was duly crowned. However, in subse-quent fighting, at Compiègne on 23 May 1430, Joan was captured by the Burgundians and handed over to the English. She was tried on a series of charges, ranging from heresy to witchcraft and dressing in men's clothes. At the trial, much attention was paid to the nature of her voices. Initially she abjured, and was sentenced to life imprisonment, but the voices taunted Joan "that she had damned herself in order to save her life".[64] On the grounds that she had relapsed – due to the resuming of wearing men's clothes – Joan was tried again, found guilty, and executed as a relapsed heretic on 14 May 1431.

At her trial, Joan identified her voices as being those of St Katherine of Alexandria, St Margaret of Antioch, and St Michael (the archangel). St Katherine, whose voice was heard by both Margery and Joan, spoke to Margery in English and to Joan in French. It is almost certain that Katherine never existed, but a cult developed across medieval Europe based on a leg-end of her martyrdom written in the late 8th century. The legend appears to have been based upon a collective memory of one or more unknown early Christian women who were martyred for their faith.[65]

As with Margery, modern scholars have not hesitated to attribute psy-chiatric diagnoses to Joan, varying from multiple personality disorder (Jacobson, 1917) to psychopathy (Henderson, 1939) and schizophrenia (Allen, 1975). Yet others have defended her mental health, taking into account religious and cultural context (Henker, 1984). By McGinn's crite-ria, whereby "presence of God" is the defining feature of mysticism, Joan cannot be considered a mystic. Her voices may – as she herself said – have been "from" God, but they were never "of" God. They spoke primarily to patriotic concerns rather than theological or spiritual matters – although such were inseparable in the thinking of the time. But they were transforma-tive. Joan's conviction of the rightness of her cause, based upon what her voices told her, and her courage to act in accordance with what she heard, remain impressive and she continues to offered an inspiring role model, especially for women.[66]

Notwithstanding the significance of the voices heard by all three of these women, there were those in the late medieval period who expressed con-cerns about such phenomena. For example, Walter Hilton (c.1340–1396), an Augustinian canon writing in England, distinguished between "true contemplation", by which he understood inner spiritual virtues and "a true knowledge and perception of God and spiritual things", and almost any kind of voice or vision:

> From what I have said you may understand that visions or revelations by spirits, whether seen in bodily form or in the imagination, and whether in sleeping or waking, do not constitute true contemplation. This applies equally to any other sensible experiences of seemingly spiritual origin, whether of sound, taste, smell, or of warmth felt like a glowing fire in the breast or in other parts of the body; anything, indeed, that can be experienced by the physical senses.
>
> (Sherley-Price, 1988, p.10)

For Hilton, it was "spiritual feeling" that is to be sought, a kind of awareness of God that operates within soul and mind and not in bodily perception. Spiritual feelings both of the presence and of the absence of God are alike intended to increase the soul's desire for God.[67] Echoing this silent reception of God, Hilton understands prayer as being expressed in its highest form also in silence, rather than in words spoken out loud.[68] Hilton's mystical journey is one of loving desire for God, expressed in a life of virtue, ascending eventually to a place of both "seeing" Jesus (with the inner spiritual eye) and "hearing" the "hidden voice of Jesus" within.[69]

Voices of the early modern period

The early modern period saw the birth of major new traditions of Christian spirituality. In Spain, Ignatius Loyola developed a programme of *Spiritual Exercises*, within which attention focused on the human desires expressed in inner voices and visions. The reformation of the Carmelite order by Teresa of Avila and John of the Cross was associated with the writing of some of the great classics of Christian spiritual literature, within which phenomena such as visions and voices were both well recognised, but also subject to critical attention. Whereas the Protestant Reformation was generally much more cautious about – or even overtly critical of – mystical experiences, it too acknowledged that faith had an experiential dimension, within which voices sometimes played a significant part.

The Ignatian tradition

Ignatius Loyola (1491–1556) suffered a serious wound at the siege of Pamplona in 1521, following which he spent a prolonged convalescence with limited reading material and ample time to reflect and meditate on what he read about the lives of the saints. He underwent a profound spiritual experience at Manresa during 1522–1523, arising from which he gained many of the insights later incorporated in his *Spiritual Exercises*.

The *Exercises*, traditionally undertaken during a 30-day silent retreat, form the basis for a process of discernment concerning vocation and life choices. First published in 1548, the *Exercises* became a seminal text of Christian spirituality, and the basis for spiritual formation and retreat direction in the Society of Jesus (which Ignatius founded) and more widely.

In late 1537, on a journey to Rome, in a small church at La Storta, Ignatius had a visionary and locutionary experience which was to mark a turning point in his life. One of his companions, Diego Laínez, reported that Ignatius heard both God the Father and God the Son speaking to him "in his heart".[70] Later, in his *Spiritual Diary* for 13 March 1544 to 27 February 1545, Ignatius refers frequently to "loquelas", or words from God. Loquelas could be internal or external, and were associated with musical tone. Whilst Ignatius seems to have understood these words as primarily emanating from God, he was also concerned with the possibility of diabolical deception.[71]

The *Exercises* are divided into four "weeks"[72], respectively devoted to themes of sin and repentance, discipleship, the passion of Jesus, and the resurrection of Jesus. They do not refer specifically to any hearing of "voices", but the *Exercises* do encourage various modes of listening in prayer. In the meditations which form the core of the *Exercises*, most of which are based on passages of scripture, there are repeated instructions to imagine what is seen and heard. For example, in respect of a meditation on Christ's Last Supper with his disciples prior to his crucifixion – a meditation undertaken in the 3rd week of the Exercises – following various preludes:

> The first point is to see the persons at the supper and by reflecting within myself to try and draw some profit from them.
> The second point. To hear what they are saying, and in the same way to draw some profit from this.
> The third point is to watch what they are doing, and draw some profit.[73]

This imaginative process is distinguished from a further element within the *Exercises*, initially introduced to exercitants in the second week, usually undertaken at the end of each day. Generally referred to as "application of the senses",[74] this form of contemplative prayer involves systematic application of the five "senses" to previously undertaken meditations. There has been much debate about exactly how this process – including the component that gives attention to listening – should be distinguished from what has already taken place in the imaginative process of the meditations themselves.[75] The question was already being asked in the official *Directory* of 1599,[76] and has been variously articulated as concerning a difference between meditation and contemplation, or perhaps between a prayer that does involve rational analysis, and one that does not. However, at an early stage within the tradition that emerged from the *Exercises*, it was clear that reference was definitely not being made to "ordinary" physical perception.[77]

There are also frequent injunctions within the *Exercises* to engage in a form of prayer referred to as "colloquy". Ignatius explains:

> A colloquy, properly so called, means speaking as one friend speaks with another, or a servant with a master, at times asking for some favour, at other times accusing oneself of something badly done, or sharing personal concerns and asking for advice about them.
>
> (Ivens and Hughes, 2004, p.21)

A colloquy is thus a form of prayer that is usually addressed to God, but potentially also to a saint or to a character in a biblical meditation. The two-way nature of this prayer – both speaking and listening – is attested to in early Jesuit sources. Thus, for example, Duarte Pereyra (1527–1587), a Jesuit novice-master, encouraged those giving the exercises to ask those taking them about "What our Lord has communicated".[78] However, it is also clear that colloquy is initiated by the excercitant, even if this is something that occurs spontaneously outside of the formally set pattern for the exercises.[79] It is not initiated (in any text that I have found) by the hearing of a voice. Nor is the receptive part of the process of colloquy frequently, if ever, referred to as the hearing of a voice.

At an early point in the *Exercises*, Ignatius states an important presupposition about the nature of thoughts:

> I presuppose that there are three kinds of thought processes in me, one sort which are properly mine and arise simply from liberty and will, and two other sorts which come from outside, one from the good spirit and the other from the bad.[80]

Again, Ignatius rarely (if ever) refers to the "voices" of the good and bad spirits, but it is significant that, as thoughts, they are identified as coming from outside the self. They are not "out loud" voices, but they are significant inner voices that Ignatius believes it is important to identify accurately, and respond to appropriately.

The *Exercises* include two sets of rules for discernment of the "various movements produced in the soul" by these spirits. The first set, proposed as more suitable for the first week of the exercises comprises 14 rules. The second set, offering a more advanced "discernment of spirits" and proposed as more suitable for the second week of the exercises, comprises a further eight rules. Together, these rules include attention to the course of inner thoughts and feelings with a view to identifying and distinguishing those which draw the soul closer to God and those which have the opposite effect, referred to respectively as consolation and desolation. Despite the reference to "spirits", the rules are (as we might judge from a modern perspective) psychologically perceptive and sophisticated. For example, they recognise that the person beginning the spiritual life should be wary of sensual pleasures, and should expect that it will be God who provokes pangs of conscience and remorse, whereas for the Christian making more progress in the spiritual life things may appear to be the other way around. They recognise the complexity and deceptiveness of the place of human thoughts and emotions in the spiritual life and encourage a reflective self-awareness. They are also theologically discriminating, placing emphasis on growth in virtues such as faith, hope, patience, humility, and love.

The Carmelite tradition

The great Carmelite reformers of the early modern period, Teresa of Avila (1515–1582) and John of the Cross (1542–1591), are amongst those within the Christian tradition who have expressed most concern at placing too much weight upon experiences of voices and visions. However, this should not be taken to imply that voices have played no part in the Carmelite tradition. Teresa herself heard voices, and so did others within the tradition. It is perhaps this familiarity with the experience that led Teresa and John to be so aware of its dangers.

Teresa's first experience of hearing a voice ("locution") took place in about 1557 whilst she was reciting her daily prayers.[81] Having reached Psalm 119, verse 137, she reflected on God's goodness and power:

> Thus, while I was thinking that You justly permit that there be many, as I have mentioned, who are very good servants of Yours and yet do not receive these gifts and favors You grant me because of what I am, You answered me, Lord: "Serve me, and don't bother about such things." This was the first locution I heard You speak to me, and so I was very frightened.[82]

Subsequently, such experiences became very common for Teresa. She is clear that the voices she heard were not out loud. In fact, she considered that she understood them much more clearly than they would have been if heard in that way. It was also to no avail to try to resist them or turn attention elsewhere.[83] Teresa also – on only a few occasions – heard what she believed to be the voice of the devil, a voice that she learned to distinguish from the voice of God.[84] She distinguishes all such phenomena from her ecstatic mystical experiences:

> It should be understood that, in my opinion, visions are never seen nor words understood while the soul is united in the rapture itself. For during this time . . . all the faculties are completely lost and, in my opinion, one can neither see nor understand nor hear.[85]

Teresa considered that it was eminently possible to be deceived by such phenomena. Like Evagrius, she distinguished between voices that come from the "good spirit" (or God) and those that come from the "bad spirit", and also those that came from her own thoughts.[86] Voices that are in reality one's own thoughts are "composed" and, as such, are distinguishable from those that are "listened to". The former are as though "muffled" and the latter come with greater clarity. It is possible to distract attention from one's own thoughts – but not from words that come from God. The effect of the voice of God is also very different from other thoughts or voices. Even if the voice brings a rebuke, if it is from God it brings peace and takes away agitation and worry.[87] It is not easily forgotten.[88] It brings fortitude of soul.[89] In the case of divine locutions of the "intellectual" kind, Teresa also identifies a depth of meaning within single words, and a depth of understanding which goes beyond the words themselves.[90]

Teresa also experienced a sense of the presence of Christ that she associated with the voice that she heard:

> I felt Christ beside me. I saw nothing with my bodily eyes or with my soul, but it seemed to me that Christ was at my side – I saw that it was He, in my opinion, who was speaking to me.[91]

Ana de San Bartolomé (1549–1626) seems not only to have heard voices of various kinds on a frequent basis, but also to have experienced much less hesitation than her famous mentor in accepting their veracity.[92] Ana was born to a pious peasant family, orphaned at the age of 10, and entered the convent of St Joseph in Avila in 1570. She became a close and trusted companion of Teresa of Avila. In her autobiography, Ana reports numerous visions, usually brief and intense. She frequently hears voices – of God, of saints, of Teresa after her death, and of supernatural beings – with which she sometimes engages in conversation.

Ana is a very different personality than Teresa and clearly had far fewer educational opportunities. Her voices respond to her requests for help and are usually affirming of her. She generally seems to accept them without question or comment, all of which can sometimes seem to be in stark contrast to the teachings of Teresa and John. However, she clearly assimilated both the terminology and the spirit of her spiritual mother in relation to visions and voices. Thus, for example, when afraid that God might be calling her to something painful and difficult, she writes of both the nature of the experience and its effects upon her:

> Since the flesh was fearful, one day the Lord appeared in an intellectual vision, for I felt him but did not see him, and he told me, "Olives and the grape must pass through the winepress of martyrdom to give their liquid; all my friends have gone down this road," and the vision disappeared, telling me, "That's how I want you." This awoke a new courage in me, for I had been downhearted, and taking heart I offered myself anew for whatever God wanted of me.
>
> (Donahue, 2008, p.78)

John of the Cross did not write of his own experiences of hearing voices in the way that Teresa or Ana did. However, according to a number of manuscripts, John related to his brother Francesco an experience of hearing a voice speak to him when he was praying in front of a crucifix.[93] The voice said:

> "Fray John, ask me what you like, for I will grant it you for this service you have done me." I said to him: "Lord, what I should like you to give me is trials to suffer for you, and to be despised and esteemed of little worth."[94]

Whatever his own experiences of voices, through his work as a priest and confessor John was clearly familiar with the phenomenon as experienced by others and produced a systematic taxonomy of locutions, embedded within the large complex analysis of supernatural experiences that he provides in Book II of *The Ascent of Mount Carmel*.[95] He is particularly wary of voices heard by way of bodily hearing. He considers the risks of deception and vanity associated with such voices to be very great. Even if they come from God, he considers it best not to rely on them and not to spend time examining them: "The more exterior and corporeal these things are, the less certain is their divine origin."[96] Indeed, he considers that the best response is to reject such voices.[97] Failure to reject them may lead to six kinds of harm:[98]

a   diminishing of faith
b   impeding of the spirit
c   possessiveness
d   loss of spiritual benefit conferred by the voice
e   loss of God's favour
f   deception by the devil.

Even when it comes to intellectual (spiritual) locutions, John expresses concern about the possibility of deception. Only with regard to a particular kind of intellectual voice – which he refers to as "substantial" – does John express positive regard. Such voices effect in the soul what they signify. Thus the voice that says "love me" would be associated with an increase in love for God. John considers this kind of voice to be of great value, but the soul has nothing to do, as all is done by God, and the only appropriate response is one of humility and resignation.

John's teaching on voices can seem very negative, self-distrustful, and even paranoid. Only in the case of substantial spiritual locutions is there no need to fear deception by the devil. Voice hearing is thus a minefield of deception and pride. However, it is important to locate this work in context. In Book I John has already addressed the dark night of the senses – in which appetites and sensory satisfaction are left behind. Books II and III deal with the dark night of the spirit, in which faith seeks to proceed without the benefits of knowledge and certainty. Elsewhere (e.g. in the *Spiritual Canticle* and *The Living Flame of Love*) John deals with the love that motivates such an undertaking. There is thus a very positive dimension to John's spirituality which balances his teaching on the dark nights of sense and spirit. The *Ascent of Mount Carmel* was written when he had only recently suffered cruel imprisonment by other members of his own order, an experience from which he only narrowly escaped with his life. John is forging a spirituality which reconciles the depths of human suffering with the love of God. Acknowledgement of the existence of voices that deceive the human mind about what is right and good is a key part of this theodicy.

A final, and much less well-known, example from this tradition is illustrative of voices of a much more negative kind. Maria Maddalena de' Pazzi (1566–1607) joined the rigorous Carmelite convent of Santa Maria degli Angeli at the age of 16. During the period 1585–1590 she experienced severe spiritual temptations, including visions and voices of the devil, but following this enjoyed daily ecstatic experiences including visions and conversation with Christ and the Trinity. Her experiences were taken down verbatim by her sisters, who also enquired afterwards concerning the nature of the experiences. Maria herself was initially resistant to this, and on one occasion burned some of their writings, but was then ordered by her superior not to do this. In one of her later experiences (*Dialogue* 39), immediately prior to her mystical "marriage" to Jesus, the sisters write of the following episode:

> [Maria] moaned and shook so vehemently that we could neither look at her nor listen to her. And this lasted from the twenty-fourth hour to the first hour sharp, when all of a sudden she calmed down and was rapt in spirit again.
>
> Later, during our conversation we asked her what she had been experiencing when she was shaking so intensely and crying so much that we feared that the devil himself was hitting her like St. Anthony, for she kept saying: "Oh good Jesus," screaming, crying, shaking as if someone were hitting her.
>
> She told us that no, she was not being hit; she was rather hearing voices swearing in her ears so that she was compelled to shake as she did each time that she heard those swears because those swearers' voices terrified her . . . And we think that the Lord let her experience this to purge her because that night he wanted to give her the great present of his wedding ring in order to marry her, as he had done to St Catherine of Siena.
>
> (Maggi and Matter, 2000, p.127)

Although Maria reported that she was not being hit by demons, the demonic voices paradoxically demonstrated her sanctity, placing her in a tradition established by Antony as one who is both valiant and faithful in the face of evil.

Protestant tradition

John Bunyan (1628–1688), author of *Pilgrim's Progress*, records in his autobiography *Grace Abounding to the Chief of Sinners* an episode that took place during a game of cat:[99]

> But the same day, as I was in the midst of a game at cat, and having struck it one blow from the hole, just as I was about to strike it the second time, a voice did suddenly dart from heaven into my soul, which said, Wilt thou leave thy sins and go to heaven, or have thy sins and go to hell? At this I was put to an exceeding maze; wherefore, leaving my cat upon the ground, I looked up to heaven, and was, as if I had, with the eyes of my understanding, seen the Lord Jesus looking down upon me, as being very hotly displeased with me, and as if he did severely threaten me with some grievous punishment for these and other my ungodly practices.[100]

Bunyan continued in a period of spiritual struggle for some years after this episode but subsequently became a dissenting preacher and spent the period 1660–1672 in jail for his beliefs.

Emanuel Swedenborg (1688–1771) was born to a Lutheran family but underwent a spiritual crisis during the period 1743–1745, within which he experienced a vision of Christ:

> I sat in his bosom, and saw him face to face; it was a face of holy mien, and in all it was indescribable, and he smiled so that I believe that his face had indeed been like this when he lived on earth. He spoke to me and asked if I had a clean bill of health. I answered "Lord thou knowest better than I."[101]

Subsequent to this, he kept a spiritual journal of his insights and experiences, and reported daily encounters with a spirit world mediated through dreams, visions, and voices. Henry Maudsley (1869a, 1869b) published a case study asserting that Swedenborg's experiences arose from a psychotic illness.

William Blake (1757–1827) had visionary experiences from an early age[102] and attributed some of his poems to dictation by spirits.[103] In *The Marriage of Heaven and Hell* he reported a visionary conversation with the biblical prophets Isaiah and Ezekiel, in which the whole notion of the experience of hearing the voice of God is ironically brought into question:

> The Prophets Isaiah and Ezekiel dined with me, and I asked them how they dared so roundly to assert. that God spake to them; and whether they did not think at the time, that they would be misunderstood, & so be the cause of imposition.

Isaiah answer'd. I saw no God. nor heard any, in a finite organical perception; but my senses discover'd the infinite in every thing, and as I was then perswaded. & remain confirm'd; that the voice of honest indignation is the voice of God, I cared not for consequences but wrote.

Then I asked: does a firm persuasion that a thing is so, make it so? He replied. All poets believe that it does, & in ages of imagination this firm perswasion removed mountains; but many are not capable of a firm perswasion of any thing.

(Erdman and Bloom, 1982, pp.38–39)

The Society of Friends (the "Quakers")

Quakerism is distinctive amongst the traditions that emerged from the Protestant Reformation in its experiential and mystical emphasis and a corresponding de-emphasise on creedal and written tradition (Spencer, 2015). The inner experience to which it appeals was initially referred to, by way of visual metaphors, as "The Light Within" or "the Inward Light of Christ". In the late 19th century the term "Inner Light" came into use, and this term is now employed alongside the equivalent term, "Inward Light" (Angell and Dandelion, 2013, p.7).[104] However, there are hints that this metaphor includes, rather than excludes, the possibility of an inner voice. For example, William Penn (1644–1718), founder of Pennsylvania and a leading early Quaker theologian, wrote:

> If you would know God and worship and serve God as you should do, you must come to the means he has ordained and given for that purpose. Some seek it in books, some in learned men, but what they look for is in themselves, yet they overlook it. The voice is too still, the Seed too small and the Light shineth in the darkness.[105]

George Fox (1624–1691), founder of the Society of Friends, records in his *Journal* various experiences of hearing a voice, or of having visions. These experiences appear to have begun, in 1647, at a point when he felt disillusioned with the clergy of the day, none of whom, he felt, were able to speak to his condition:

> And when all my hopes in them and in all men were gone, so that I had nothing outwardly to help me, nor could tell what to do, Oh then, I heard a voice which said, "There is one, even Christ Jesus, that can speak to thy condition", and when I heard it my heart did leap for joy.
> (Nickalls, 1975, p.11)

James Nayler (1616–1660) emerged as one of the leading preachers and theologians of the Quaker movement. Like Fox, he wrote of hearing a voice that effected a significant turning point in his life:

I was at the Plow, meditating on the things of God, and suddenly I heard a Voice, saying unto me, *Get thee out from thy kindred, and from thy Father's House* . . . Whereupon I did exceedingly rejoice, that I had heard the Voice of that God which I had professed from a Child, but had never known him.

(Nayler, 1716, p.12)

John Woolman (1720–1772) another prominent Quaker, and anti-slavery campaigner in colonial America, also kept a journal (published in 1774) which became a popular classic. Like Fox, Woolman writes in his journal of his experience of hearing a voice. On one occasion, he was woken in the night and saw a light:

As I lay still without any surprise looking upon it, words were spoken to my inward ear which filled my whole inward man. They were not the effect of thought or any conclusion in relation to the appearance, but as the language of the Holy One spoken in my mind. The words were, "Certain Evidence of Divine Truth," and were again repeated exactly in the same manner, where-upon the light disappeared.

(Moulton, 1989, p.58)

Another example from Woolman's journal occurs in the context of sickness, possibly involving delirium. Woolman indicates that he could not remember his name, and wanted to know who he was:

I then heard a soft melodious voice, more pure and harmonious than any I had heard before. I believed it was the voice of an angel, who spake to the other angels, and the words were these, "John Woolman is dead." I soon remembered that I was once John Woolman; and being assured that I was alive in the body, I greatly wondered what that heavenly voice could mean.

(Fremantle and Auden, 1964, pp.171–172)

Following this, Woolman is "carried in spirit to the mines" where he sees Christ blasphemed by slaves who are told that they are digging for treasure for followers of Christ.

Voices of late modernity

There are numerous figures of the late modern period whose voices and visions might profitably be the subject of study here. Three examples are offered. Bernadette Soubirous is illustrative of a Catholic tradition of Marian visions,[106] and also of the way in which visionary and voice hearing experiences can establish an ongoing devotional tradition. Maria Kowalska recorded in her journal accounts of an ongoing interior dialogue with Christ over a long period of time. Within Protestant Christianity, visions and voices seem more commonly to be reported in association with conversion experiences. An interesting example of this kind in a non-Western cultural context is provided by Sundar Singh.[107]

Bernadette Soubirous

Bernadette Soubirous (1844–1897) was born to a poor family in Lourdes, France, one of six children. When out collecting bones and firewood on 11 February 1858, at a grotto at Massabielle, she unexpectedly experienced the first of a series of 18 visions. Initially, in her own accounts, she refers to the vision simply as "aquero", a Bigourdanian word meaning "that". Subsequently, the apparition was understood by Bernadette and others to be of the Virgin Mary.[108] One is left with the impression of a young woman and a local community trying to make sense of an initially ambiguous or uncertain experience, with the eventual outcome that everyone settled on Mary as the best explanation. In a series of subsequent visions, Bernadette is accompanied first by a group of children, then by a small number of adults, but eventually by groups of up to 10,000 people. Amongst those who attended were those who were sceptical, as well as the devout and the curious.

Bernadette returned to the grotto on 14 February, and was seen to go into a trance. On 18 February, someone asked her to ask the vision what she wanted, and to write it down. In response, Bernadette stated:

> For the first time, I heard her voice which said to me: "It is not necessary that I write anything down. I do not promise to make you happy in this world, but in the next. Have the goodness to come here each day for a fortnight and I will be very pleased."
>
> (Taylor, 2003, p.68)

Bernadette was obedient to the vision. She experienced no vision at the grotto on 22 February, the day after being interrogated by the police, or again on 26 February, the day after being interrogated by the Imperial Prosecutor. On 24 February (the eighth vision), she heard aquero say:

> "Penitenço . . . Penitenço . . . Penitenço . . ." (penance . . . penance . . . penance . . .) and she also heard an exhortation to kiss the ground and pray for the conversion of sinners.[109]

On 2 February (the ninth vision), aquero told her to "Go and drink at the spring and wash yourself in it."[110] On 2 March (the 13th vision), she was told, "Go and tell the priests that people are to come here in procession and to build a chapel here."[111] On 26 March (the Feast of the Annunciation, and the occasion of the 16th vision) Bernadette asked, four times, "What is your name?" On the fourth time of asking, the vision replied, "I am the Immaculate Conception."[112]

On 8 April, Bernadette experienced her 18th and final vision, but by the beginning of July 50 or more others claimed to have experienced visions at the site – even despite the revelation that a white stalactite some 10 metres inside the cave might have formed the basis for what Bernadette saw.[113] In 1866, Bernadette entered the convent of the Sisters of Charity at Nevers, where she remained until her death. She was canonised in 1933. The site on which she experienced her visions remains a place of pilgrimage.

Sundar Singh

Sundar Singh (1889–c.1929), known as "the Sadhu",[114] was born to a wealthy Sikh family in North India in 1889.[115] As a young person he took an interest in various religions, reading the Qur'an, and the Upanishads as well as the Sikh scriptures. However, whilst he sometimes read the Bible, he found himself antipathetic towards Christianity. He later confessed to throwing stones at Christian preachers and to tearing and burning copies of the Bible. Whilst not so aversive towards Islam, Hinduism, or Sikhism, he did not find fulfilment in them and at the age of only 15 years, on 18 December 1904, he found himself on the verge of suicide:

> I was faithful to my own religion, but could not get any satisfaction or peace, though I performed all the ceremonies and rites of that religion. So I thought of leaving it all and committing suicide. Three days after I had burnt the Bible, I woke up about three o'clock in the morning, had my usual bath, and prayed, "O God, if there is a God, wilt thou show me the right way or I will kill myself." My intention was that, if I got no satisfaction, I would place my head on upon the railway line when the 5 o'clock train passed by and kill myself. If I got no satisfaction in this life, I thought I would get it in the next. I was praying and praying but got no answer; and I prayed for half-an-hour longer hoping to get peace. At 4.30 A.M. I saw something of which I had no idea at all previously. In the room where I was praying I saw a great light. I thought the place was on fire. I looked round, but could find nothing. Then the thought came to me that this might be an answer that God had sent me. Then as I prayed and looked into the light, I saw the form of the Lord Jesus Christ. It had such an appearance of glory and love. If it had been some Hindu incarnation I would have prostrated myself before it. But it was the Lord Jesus Christ whom I had been insulting a few days before. I felt that a vision like this could not come out of my own imagination. I heard a voice saying in Hindustani, "How long will you persecute me? I have come to save you; you were praying to know the right way. Why do you not take it?" The thought then came to me, "Jesus Christ is not dead but living and it must be He Himself." So I fell at His feet and got this

wonderful Peace which I could not get anywhere else. This is the joy I was wishing to get. This was heaven itself. When I got up, the vision had all disappeared; but although the vision disappeared the Peace and Joy have remained with me ever since.

(Streeter and Appasamy, 1926, pp.5–7)

The story shows a remarkable similarity to the conversion of St Paul, although Singh later said that he did not think that he knew of that story at the time. Like St Paul, Singh went on to become a Christian missionary, but he adopted the mode of life and dress of a Hindu Sadhu. Occupying a social position that crossed boundaries and transgressed against expectations he was a controversial – or, perhaps better, discomforting – figure both within the Anglican Church into which he was ordained deacon and amongst Hindus. Whilst he expressed hesitation at referring to himself as a mystic, perhaps out of a sense of humility, others have not hesitated to see him in this vein and he left written accounts of the visionary experiences that he had subsequent to his conversion.[116]

Maria Kowalska

Maria Faustina Kowalska (1905–1938) was born in Glogowiec, Poland, to a poor family who baptised her under the name of Helen. She received only three years of schooling and, at the age of only 7 years, experienced an inner voice calling her to religious life:

From the age of seven, I experienced the definite call of God, the grace of a vocation to the religious life. It was in the seventh year of my life that, for the first time, I heard God's voice in my soul; that is, an invitation to a more perfect life.

(Drabik, 2007, p.6)

Aged 18, despite the disapproval of her parents, Maria entered a convent.

Once I was at a dance [probably in Lodz] with one of my sisters. While everybody was having a good time, my soul was experiencing deep torments. As I began to dance, I suddenly saw Jesus at my side, Jesus racked with pain, stripped of his clothing, all covered with wounds, who spoke these words to me: How long shall I put up with you and how long will you keep putting Me off? At that moment the charming music stopped, [and] the company I was with vanished from my sight; there remained Jesus and I.[117]

She slipped out to pray in the Cathedral of St Stanislaus Kostka: "Then I heard these words: Go at once to Warsaw; you will enter a convent there."[118] Leaving home, telling only her sister and taking only the dress that she wore, she travelled to Warsaw. As she was getting off the train, the enormity of what she had done struck home:

> I was overcome with fear. What am I to do? To whom should I turn, as I know no one? So I said to the Mother of God, "Mary, lead me, guide me." Immediately I heard these words within me telling me to leave the town and to go to a certain nearby village where I would find a safe lodging for the night. I did so and found, in fact, that everything was just as the Mother of God told me.[119]

Next day she went back into Warsaw and entered the church of St James in Grojecka Street:

> There I began to pray to know further the will of God. Holy Masses were being celebrated one after another. During one of them I heard the words: Go to that priest [Father James Dabrowski, pastor of St James' Parish] and tell him everything; he will tell you what to do next.[120]

The priest directed her to someone with whom she could stay and Maria then approached various convents, all of which turned her away. Eventually, she knocked on the door of the convent of the Congregation of the Sisters of Our Lady of Mercy. The Mother Superior told her to go to "the Lord of the house" and ask whether he would accept her:

> I understood at once that I was to ask this of the Lord Jesus. With great joy, I went to the chapel and asked Jesus: "Lord of this house, do You accept me? This is how one of these sisters told me to put the question to You."
> Immediately I heard this voice: I do accept; you are in My Heart.[121]

On 1 August 1925 she formally entered the convent but within three weeks had doubts about whether this was the right place for her. Praying about this in her cell, she had a vision:

> Brightness filled my cell, and on my curtain I saw the very sorrowful Face of Jesus. There were open wounds on His Face, and large tears were falling on my bedspread. Not knowing what all this meant, I asked Jesus, "Jesus, who has hurt you so?" And Jesus said to me, It is you who will cause Me this pain if you leave this convent. It is to this place that I called you and nowhere else; and I have prepared many graces for you. I begged pardon of Jesus and immediately changed my decision.[122]

Maria continued to have an interior dialogue – mainly with Jesus – on a more or less frequent basis. On 22 February 1931, Maria wrote (retrospectively) in her diary of another visionary experience:

> In the evening, when I was in my cell, I saw the Lord Jesus clothed in a white garment. One hand [was] raised in the gesture of blessing, the other was touching the garment at the breast. From beneath the garment, slightly drawn aside at the breast, there were emanating two large rays, one red, the other pale. In silence I kept my gaze fixed on the Lord; my soul was struck with awe, but also with great joy. After a while, Jesus said to me, Paint an image according to the pattern you see, with the signature: Jesus, I trust in You. I desire that this image be venerated, first in your chapel, and [then] throughout the world.[123]

Maria further received instructions for the image that was painted to be blessed on the first Sunday after Easter, and for this to become the "Feast of Mercy" – on which would be granted "complete remission of sins and punishment" to "whoever approaches the Fount of Life".[124] Much later (1934), Maria asked Jesus about the meaning of the two rays in the image: "During prayer I heard these words within me: The two rays denote Blood and Water. The pale ray stands for Water which makes souls righteous. The red ray stands for the Blood which is the life of souls."[125] The image was eventually painted, in 1934, not by Maria herself, but under Maria's guidance by the artist E. Kazimirowski.[126]

From 28 July 1934, at the instruction of her confessor, Maria began writing down her inner experiences on a more contemporaneous basis. On Friday 13 September 1935, she had a vision of an angel – "the executor of divine wrath" – and then found herself "snatched up before the Throne of God". Maria pleaded with the Angel, and then with God, on behalf of the world.[127]

> The words with which I entreated God are these: Eternal Father, I offer You the Body and Blood, Soul and Divinity of your dearly beloved Son, Our Lord Jesus Christ for our sins and those of the whole world; for the sake of His sorrowful passion, have mercy on us.
>
> The next morning, when I entered the chapel, I heard these words interiorly: Every time you enter the chapel, immediately recite the prayer which I taught you yesterday.[128]

Maria was told by the voice that this prayer would appease the divine wrath, and was given further instructions concerning its use with the rosary. To the image, the feast day and the prayer have been added various other elements of 'devotion to the Divine Mercy', all drawn from Maria's diary and the voices recorded in it.[129] Maria died of tuberculosis at the age of 33, on 5 October 1938.

Often, Maria's diary simply records that she heard the words,[130] or the voice,[131] or that Jesus spoke to her.[132] At other times she says that she heard words or a voice "in [her] soul"[133] or that she heard an "interior voice"[134] or a "voice within me".[135] Sometimes (e.g. as above) the words are spoken to her by the figure that she sees in a vision. On certain occasions, Maria refers to the voice as coming from external space in the absence of any visionary experience (e.g. the tabernacle in the chapel,[136] or the Eucharistic host[137]).

Conclusions

This brief survey of voices in the Christian tradition reveals a broad diversity of texts, located within a wide spectrum of cultural, spiritual, and theological traditions, across many centuries. However, some consistent themes emerge.

First, and most important, there is a Christian tradition that God (and sometimes the devil, or saints, or angels) may be encountered in the hearing of a voice. The Augustinian distinction between corporeal, spiritual, and intellectual visions/voices has had a particularly deep influence upon this tradition, with many authors at pains to stress that the particular vision or voice that they describe is of the more significant spiritual/intellectual kind, and thus less open to deception. Some other early accounts – notably the *Life of Antony* – have also been influential upon, and have informed and reinforced, the later tradition. Thus, for example, the account of the experiences of Maria Maddalena de' Pazzi is coloured by her sisters' expectations based upon what they know of Antony of Egypt. Antony's temptations would in turn appear to be modelled on the biblical narrative of the temptations of Christ.

Some other biblical themes also appear to carry through directly from scripture into the subsequent tradition. For example, Christians have continued to report hearing the voices of angels, relay as prophecy what they believe they have heard from God, and describe visionary encounters with Jesus within which they hear his voice. However, other themes are more discontinuous. Prolonged, frequent, and mundane conversational encounters with a divine voice are not evident in scripture, at least certainly not in the New Testament, but examples of voices of this kind are not difficult to find in diverse later contexts (as with Margery Kempe, Ana de San Bartolomé, and Maria Kowalska).

Second, many accounts of voice hearing have occurred as accompaniments of visionary phenomena. Voices on their own seem to be less common. Both the visual and auditory modes of perception are thus understood as being potential vehicles for divine encounter, but with preference apparently (in general) given to the former. Neither of these perceptual modes of experience is necessary to validate an experience as being genuinely one of an encounter with God. However, divine visions and voices – when they occur – usually are experienced as manifestations of the presence of God.[138] Elsewhere, as with Elisabeth of Schönau, Joan of Arc, and Bernadette Soubirous, the encounter with God is mediated by visions and voices of angels and saints.

Third, various spiritual traditions within Christianity have either de-emphasised voices and visions, or else have been actively hostile toward them. Rather than being a way in to the presence of God, voices (and similarly the corresponding phenomena in other perceptual modalities, notably visions) have thus been understood as a snare and a potential cause of distancing from God. This is perhaps most fully elaborated in the Carmelite tradition, but it is implicit in the hierarchy of the Augustinian typology of visions, in the Ignatian rules for discernment of spirits, in Protestant wariness of mystical experiences, and in diverse other places.[139]

Finally, the meaning, significance, and interpretations of voices have been various. For Antony of Egypt voices were a direct source of demonic temptation, and for John of the Cross they presented a temptation even when coming from God. For Elisabeth of Schönau they reflected devotion to the saints. For Francis of Assisi and Joan of Arc – in very different ways – they conveyed a vocational calling.

The more ancient the text, especially where it is not clearly autobiographical, the more difficult it is to know with confidence what the underlying human experience might have been. In the next chapter, we shall therefore turn to more recent accounts of voices and to an analysis of the different kinds of experience to which they attest.

Notes

1 Robert Gregg (1980) provides a helpful introduction to the importance of this *Life*.
2 Chapter 19, verse 21.
3 Initially he kept some things back for his sister, but then – on going to church again – he heard read "Do not be anxious about tomorrow". He then sold all that remained and entrusted his sister to the care of a convent (Gregg, 1980, pp.31–32).
4 I am assuming here that the *Life* is anchored in an account of Antony's understanding of his experiences. It may, of course, reflect Athanasius' psychological awareness as much, or more, than Antony's.
5 Gregg (1980, p.35).
6 Ibid.
7 Ibid.
8 Ibid., p.38.
9 Ibid., p.39.
10 Ibid., p.50.
11 Ibid.
12 Ibid., pp.54–57.
13 Ibid., p.60.
14 Ibid., p.61.
15 Ibid., p.62.
16 Ibid., p.68.
17 Ibid., p.80.
18 As discussed in Chapter 2 in more general terms, and in Chapters 3 and 4 in relation to the biblical material, it is not strictly possible to know that Antony "heard voices". We only have Athanasius' account of his life. However, having

acknowledged these limitations on what we can know, it is cumbersome and repetitive to keep drawing attention to them. I trust that the reader will therefore interpret these words throughout the present chapter as implicitly including all relevant reservations and qualifications.

19 Ward (2003, p.184).
20 Ibid., pp.188–189.
21 Ibid., pp.192–193.
22 See, for example, the relevant respective discussions of this in Cook (2011) and Stewart (2013).
23 The account presented in this chapter is focused largely on Western Christianity. The negative influence deriving from the Desert Fathers has perhaps been more pervasive in the Eastern Christian traditions. This illustration is taken from the *Paraphrase of the Homilies of St Makarios of Egypt*, included in the *Philokalia*: "The saint is he who is sanctified and totally purified in his inner being. One of the brethren was praying with others when he was seized and taken captive by the divine power, and he saw the heavenly Jerusalem and the resplendent dwelling-places there and the boundless and ineffable light. Then he heard a voice saying that this was the place of repose for the righteous. After this, he became very conceited and full of presumption, and fell deeply into sin and was overcome by many evils. If such a man fell, how can anyone say that because he fasts, lives in voluntary exile, gives away all his property and desists from all outward sins, there is nothing wanting for him to be a saint? For perfection consists not in abstention from outward sins but in the total cleansing of the mind" (IV.82; Palmer et al., 1984, p.321).
24 For further biographical information, see Cross and Livingstone (1997, pp.128–129).
25 *Confessions*, VIII.12. Pine-Coffin (1961, pp.177–178). The passage is from *Romans* 13, 13–14.
26 Ibid., p.178.
27 See Kenney (2013).
28 *Confessions*, VII.17. Pine-Coffin (1961, pp.151–152).
29 *Confessions*, IX.10. Ibid., pp.197–198.
30 It is generally assumed that Augustine's conversion experience involved an actual child in the neighbouring garden, whose voice was therefore heard as a normal perception. However, it is also possible to speculate that this voice might have been an auditory verbal hallucination.
31 Book 12, Chapters 6–12. For an English translation, see Taylor (1982, pp.185–195).
32 Respectively, in Latin, *corporale*, *spirituale*, and *intellectuale*.
33 McCarthy-Jones (2011a).
34 McGinn (1994, p.119).
35 Ibid, p.325.
36 Maloney (1975, p.104).
37 McGinn (1998).
38 Agnes Blannbekin (Wiethaus, 2002) provices another example. Her initial experiences seem to be entirely visionary. Later, when voices accompany the visions, they are variously said to be "a word of the Savior [that] came into [her] memory" (p.29), "a serene voice, mild and sweet" that she "felt and she heard within her chest" (p.32), "sweet and diverse voices of those who praised with a sonorous sound to be sure, not in words, yet nonetheless meaningful to the intellect of the listeners" (p.47), "a strong voice speaking in words and with joy" (p.48). More often, she simply refers to the "voice within".
39 Clark and Newman (2000, pp.44–46).

40 Ibid., p.50.
41 Ibid., p.57.
42 Ibid., p.69.
43 Ibid., pp.57–58.
44 Hart and Mommaers (1980, p.294).
45 Ibid., p.296.
46 Ibid.
47 Winkworth et al. (1993, p.95).
48 Ibid., p.86.
49 Ibid., p.87.
50 See Armstrong et al. (1999).
51 In this account Thomas writes that "with the lips of the painting, the image of Christ crucified spoke to him." The words spoken are slightly different than in the *Legend of Three Companions*: "Francis, . . . go rebuild My house; as you see, it is all being destroyed" (p.249). Thomas attributes the same words to the voice in *The Treatise on the Miracles of St Francis*, written in 1250–1252 (Armstrong et al., 2000, p.401).
52 The Friars Minor, the Poor Clares, and the Third Order.
53 See Armstrong et al. (2000, p.534n).
54 For example, ibid., pp.224–225, 326, 606–607.
55 See *The Life* by Thomas, Book II, chapter 3; *The Life* by Speyer, chapter 11; *The Versified Life*, 12th Book; *The Legend of the Three Companions*, chapter 12; *The Treatise on the Miracles of St Francis*, chapter 2, *The Major Legend*, chapter 13, *The Minor Legend*, chapter 6.
56 Armstrong (2006).
57 Lachance and Guarniari (1993, pp.147–148).
58 Ibid., p.188.
59 McIlwain (1984) considers the various possible diagnoses, and concludes that Julian may have been suffering from Botulism.
60 Colledge et al. (1977, p.183).
61 Ibid., pp.224–225.
62 Windeatt (1994, p.127).
63 Ibid., p.75.
64 Barrett (1931, p.319).
65 Walsh (2007).
66 Barstow (2003).
67 For a discussion of Hilton's concept of *goostli feelynges*, see McGinn (2012, pp.389–391).
68 Ibid., p.389.
69 Ibid., p.395.
70 McGinn (2017, pp.67–68).
71 Ibid., pp.96–97.
72 The weeks are not equal divisions of time, with seven days allocated to each, but rather represent four thematic divisions of the exercises. Typically, excercitants will spend longer on some weeks than on others, and one exercitant may spend less or more time on a particular week than another exercitant.
73 *Exercises*, 194, Ivens and Hughes (2004, p.57).
74 This term does not appear in the original Spanish text of the *Exercises*.
75 For a helpful and critical essay exploring this conundrum, see Endean (1990).
76 Palmer (1996, p.322).
77 See the comments of Gil González Dávila (16th century), who also acknowledges the influence here of Bonaventure (ibid., p.236).
78 Ibid., p.59.
79 Ivens and Munitiz (2007, p.67).
80 *Exercises*, 32. Ivens and Hughes (2004, p.14).

81 Kavanaugh and Rodriguez (1976, Intro p.37; chapter 24, p.212n7).
82 *The Life*, 19.9, ibid., p.76.
83 *The Life*, 25.1.
84 *The Life*, 25.10–13.
85 *The Life*, 25.5, Kavanaugh and Rodriguez (1976, p.215).
86 *The Life*, 25.2. In *The Interior Castle*, Teresa distinguishes between voices that come from God, those that come from the devil, and those that are merely the product of a "lively imagination" (6th Mansion, chapter 3).
87 *The Life*, 25.3. Teresa contradicts herself in 25.6, where she says that words of reproof – if from God – "make one tremble".
88 *The Life*, 25.7.
89 *The Life*, 25.13. cf. *The Interior Castle*, 6th Mansion, chapter 3, 7–11.
90 *The Interior Castle*, 6th Mansion, chapter 3, 23–24.
91 *The Life* 27.2, Kavanaugh and Rodriguez (1976).
92 Donahue (2008).
93 It would appear that Francesco was incorrect about this, and that it was actually a painting of Christ carrying the cross (Crisógono de Jesús, 1958, p.269), Ruiz et al. (1991, p.338).
94 Crisógono de Jesús (1958, p.268).
95 Kavanaugh and Rodriguez (1991, pp.152–349). For a helpful summary and analysis of this taxonomy, see Jones (2010).
96 *The Ascent of Mount Carmel*, 11.2.
97 *The Ascent of Mount Carmel*, 11.5.
98 *The Ascent of Mount Carmel*, 11.7.
99 A game involving a small piece of wood, called a "cat", which is flipped up into the air and hit with a bat, similar to a baseball bat.
100 Bunyan (1666, p.10, para 22).
101 Dole et al. (1984, p.11).
102 The detail of these experiences is somewhat unclear, and subject to multiple and conflicting accounts, but most famously seems to have included a vision of angels (Churton, 2014, pp.27–36).
103 Erdman and Bloom (1982, pp.60, 728, 730).
104 See also Frost (2015, p.81), Spencer (2015, p.141).
105 This quotation is taken from a Preface by Penn to an 1831 edition of the journals of George Fox (Fox, 1831, p.xlvii).
106 Marian visions have a long history, dating back at least to the Middle Ages, but they seem to have become relatively more frequent in modern times. Catherine Labouré had visions and locutions of the Blessed Virgin Mary commencing in 1830, 14 years before Bernadette was born. Subsequently numerous visions of Mary have been reported across Europe and around the world (Englebert, 1958, Carroll, 1986).
107 Another interesting example is that of John Sung (1901–1944), a missionary to China. Sung initially studied chemistry, even gaining a PhD, but then went to study theology after hearing a voice that said "What shall it profit a man if he gain the whole world and lose his own soul?" (Lyall, 1965, p.27). Later, following an intense period of bible study and prayer, he again heard a voice, this time saying, "Son, thy sins are forgiven" (p.34), following which his shouting and praising in the corridors of the dormitory at midnight caused some disturbance. The episode clearly concerned the authorities and he was admitted compulsorily to a mental hospital. Whilst a patient there, according to Lyall's biography, he read the entire Bible, from beginning to end, 40 times. A more critical account of his hospital stay suggests that he was probably experiencing significant religious delusions and hallucinations (Ireland, 2016).
108 Taylor (2003, p.60).
109 Ibid., p.88.

110 Laurentin (1998, p.60).
111 Ibid., p.67.
112 Taylor (2003, pp.104–105).
113 Laurentin (1998, p.88).
114 A Hindu term for a religious ascetic or holy person.
115 Streeter and Appasamy (1926).
116 Ibid., pp.109–156, Singh (1922).
117 Drabik (2007, p.7).
118 Ibid.
119 Ibid., pp.7–8.
120 Ibid., p.8.
121 Ibid.
122 Ibid., p.10.
123 Ibid., p.24.
124 Ibid., p.139.
125 Ibid.
126 Ibid., p.xxxiv.
127 Ibid., p.207.
128 Ibid.
129 Ibid., pp.viii–xxv.
130 For example, ibid., p.262.
131 For example, ibid., p.108.
132 For example, ibid., p.157.
133 Ibid., pp.262, 390.
134 For example, ibid., p.25.
135 For example, ibid., p.38.
136 Ibid., p.86.
137 Ibid., p.89.
138 Usually this seems to be in the form of the presence of Jesus – as with Gertrude of Helfta, Julian of Norwich, Teresa of Avila, and Maria Kowalska. However, Augustine and Monica felt as though they could reach out and touch divine wisdom, and for Angela of Foligno it was simply "God" that embraced her soul.
139 Other examples might include Marguerite Porete, who, although she does not explicitly mention voices, takes miracles, martyrdom, and the visionary experience of St Paul as examples of things that are worthless in comparison with subservience of the soul to the will of God (Babinsky and Lerner, 1993, p.130). Mechthild of Magdeburg offers a taxonomy of three "places" in which God speaks to the soul. The first place, that of the senses, is equally open to the voices of other people and of the devil. Indeed, she warns that the devil often speaks to people in this place. In the second and third places, respectively the soul and heaven, the devil cannot speak, but here words are not heard with the bodily sense of hearing (Andersen, 2003, p.114). Gertrude of Helfta relates a growing intimacy with God within which she finds herself sometimes "deprived of the Lord's visit". She is given to understand that sometimes greater proximity "prevents friends from seeing each other clearly . . . as sometimes happens in embracing and kissing" and that some things are very difficult to translate into words (Winkworth et al., 1993, pp.86–87).

6   Hearing voices in Christian experience

Whilst scripture and tradition are bequeathed to us primarily as texts, the hearing of a voice is in essence a perceptual experience. In Chapter 2, we explored some of the ways in which texts about voices and experiences of voices might be interrelated. In Chapters 3, 4, and 5, we have been concerned primarily with texts. We now turn to voice hearing as Christian experience.

Experience

Experience is a complex and multifaceted concept. On the one hand, as Nicholas Lash has pointed out, we talk of experience in most contexts as "whatever it is we have undergone and done" (Lash, 1988, p.91). Thus experience is something from which we learn. We become "experienced". In this sense, it is concerned both with things that we actively do, and also with things to which we might be relatively passive respondents or observers. It is concerned with our interaction with our environment – the external world – as embodied observers and agents of an objective reality. On the other hand, experience also implies something about our subjective consciousness of things – an inner world of how things seem to us.

Wayne Proudfoot takes as an example a perceptual experience: "I may have been frightened by the bear that I saw up ahead on the trail. My friend points out to me that it is not a bear but a log, and my fear subsides" (Proudfoot, 1985, p.217). There is thus an ambiguity. On the one hand, the experience was of seeing a bear – because that was the subjective reality, and this accounted for the experience being one of fear. On the other hand, the experience was one of seeing a log. As Proudfoot says, "I was wrong about what I experienced." But he was not actually "wrong" about what he experienced unless the external account of experience is privileged. The subjective reality was one of seeing what was thought to be a bear, and only this accounts for the fear that was an integral and important part of the experience. He was wrong merely in the sense that there was no bear – only a log – but the experience was still one of seeing a bear.

It is also possible to privilege the inner account over the external. Lash objects to Richard Swinburne's definition of experience as "a conscious mental going on", on the grounds that, "For *human beings*, experience, at least in the vast majority of its forms, includes a great deal more than mental goings-on" (Lash, 1988, p.92). For Lash, Swinburne's approach reflects a kind of dualism between the mental and material worlds. It privileges the inner (mental) reality over the external (physical) reality. Swinburne acknowledges this. In the second edition of *The Existence of God*, he defines an experience as "a conscious mental event", but then goes on to say:

> It may be described in such a way as to entail the existence of some particular external thing apart from the subject, beyond the stream of his consciousness, normally the thing of which it is an experience; or it may be described in such a way as to carry no such entailment.
>
> (Swinburne, 2004, pp.294–295)

Swinburne, like Proudfoot, takes a perceptual experience as an example. However, Swinburne's example is of a veridical perception. Thus, he is able to offer two accounts of an experience of hearing – in the example in question, "hearing the coach outside the window". To say that one heard the coach outside the window is what Swinburne refers to as an external description. However, an internal description is also possible: "having an auditory sensation that seemed to come from a coach outside the window". This would normally seem a strange and cumbersome way of describing our experiences, and so we normally tend to assume that the statement of the external description implies a corresponding internal description.

Things get more complicated when we are mistaken. Thus, taking Proudfoot's example, an immediate exclamation of "There is a bear on the trail!" might later be followed by a retrospective statement such as "It really looked like there was a bear on the trail!" The external description is replaced by an internal description, and the internal description implies the discrepancy between the external reality and the internal experience.

Our sense of interiority is clearly deeply embedded in Western culture (Taylor, 1989), and to some extent I suspect that we do privilege this way of talking about experience. However, I think that it is also significant that we normally expect a correspondence between internal experience and external reality, and that we use the external account to imply that there is correspondence. I'm therefore not convinced by Lash's allegations of dualism. In normal practice, we assume that the internal and external accounts correspond – we have one account, not two. We use the internal description either to correct ourselves, when we realise that there is or was a discrepancy between our internal experience and external reality, or else to be more precise. For example, we might have great difficulty explaining how we feel following a bereavement. In an attempt to explain, and fully aware of the reality of our loss, we might say, "It really feels as though he is still here. I could have been sure I saw him in town yesterday, but then he was gone." It does not imply dualism to recognise that our language of experience acknowledges both that we can be wrong about the external world, and that other people's experiences sometimes differ from ours.

As Proudfoot, Lash, and others have cogently argued, our experiences incorporate all kinds of assumptions about the world. An experience and our interpretation of that experience cannot easily be separated – although Proudfoot's example of the bear on the trail does show that we are capable both of incorporating our interpretation of what we perceive into the experience of perceiving, and also later of separating our evolving retrospective interpretation from what we actually thought we perceived at the time. Regardless of this, there is no such thing as uninterpreted experience: "All observation is theory-laden. We can design procedures in which certain hypotheses can be tested, but any perception or experience is already shaped by the concepts and implicit judgements we bring to it" (Proudfoot, 1985, p.43). Contrary to our Western proclivity for privileging interiority, it is therefore possible to argue that religious experience is, in fact, socially constructed (Dein, 2011). However, assertions of the integral union between interpretation and experience can easily still sound univocal. That is, it is assumed that the conscious mental events (to use Swinburne's language) which define the internal dimension of experience are to be understood as a single unified consciousness of any given experience. However, consciousness research has cast significant doubt upon such assumptions.

Dennett's (1991) pandemonium model has been particularly influential. It proposes that there is no single stream of consciousness and no place in the mind where it all "comes together". Rather, there are "multiple drafts" of what is going on which are held in parallel and which are under constant editorial revision. According to this model, there is something of a mental pandemonium (although this is not necessarily always obvious at the conscious level) as various fragmentary drafts of the narrative of what is going on are created, promoted, assembled, or abandoned. Consciousness thus becomes not something that is intentionally constructed by a single author (a "central meaner"), nor viewed as though in a mental theatre by a single spectator, but rather a product of simultaneous mental processes each paying attention to different aspects of our experience.[1]

Dennett gives a variety of names to the contributors to the pandemonium. They are variously referred to as channels, units, drafts, agents, specialists, words (or phrases or sentences), homunculi, or (most often) demons. Seager (2016, p.182) proposes that it is best understood as a cognitive pandemonium, dealing as it does primarily with mental content (or thoughts).

Within this pandemonium, Dennett has the interesting idea that some words "want to get themselves said".[2] It is as though mental contents are vying for attention, some more successfully than others. Such a model offers potentially rich and hitherto unexplored possibilities for understanding how the content of AVHs[3] – what the voices actually "say" – can be at once both a thought of the person hearing the voice, and yet also experienced as some-how coming from outside the self. Perhaps the voices that we call AVHs are simply word-demons who shout loudly enough amidst the pandemonium to get heard?[4]

Religious experience

If the concept of experience is itself complex, then things do not become any easier when we start talking about religious experience, spiritual experience, or mystical experience. Religion, spirituality, and mysticism are all complex and contested concepts and it is often debatable as to whether any particular experience is "religious", "spiritual", "mystical", or some combination of the three. However, we must take seriously the attribution of experience to one of these categories by the person who has had that experience – even if we disagree. If two people on a walk through a beautiful sunlit pasture have differing experiences – the one saying it was mystical, and the other simply that it was beautiful – we do well to find out why they describe their experiences as they do.

Swinburne defines religious experience essentially at this level – at the level of individual, subjective, attribution: "an experience that seems (epis-temically) to the subject to be an experience of God (either of his just being there, or of his saying or bringing about something) or of some other super-natural thing" (Swinburne, 2004, p.296). Leaving aside the question of how ordinary folks self-identify their experiences as religious, spiritual, or mystical, any critical academic definition of religious experience is difficult to agree. Whilst Stark affirms categorically that religious experiences are concerned with "some sense of contact with a supernatural being",[5] Alston finds the term "obfuscating" and Proudfoot goes so far as to suggest that it is "futile" to search for any definition of religious experience.[6] Lash, going further still, objects to the inherent dualism in the notion of religious experi-ence, and prefers to explore Christian experience in terms of the encounter with God in all things, within the ordinary and not just the extraordinary.[7]

Gwen Griffith-Dickson particularly objects to the idea of any kind of perception as a basis for understanding the nature of religious experience:

> Sense perception is a relatively simple affair; religious experience is ter-ribly complex. Perhaps then our interpretative model for religious expe-rience should not be sense experience or other kinds of "perception". Experiencing God may not be at all like perceiving a chair. This I sug-gest is not merely because of the phenomenal or emotional content (few report feelings of ecstasy and union when looking at a chair). Nor is it simply that God is not an object to experience like a chair . . . I am not convinced that *any* sense is proper, not even the sense in which another human being can be the object of my perception.
>
> (Griffith-Dickson, 2000, p.143)

Griffith-Dickson goes on to take relationships as her model for understanding spiritual/religious experience, noting that even here the transcendent nature of God renders the analogy imperfect. The transcendent is not amenable to perception in the way that, for example, a human lover is. Whilst the model of spiritual/religious experience as relationship is, I think, a helpful one, Griffith-Dickson does rather over-simplify things by taking as her example a perception of a chair. A chair (except perhaps in psychosis) is not normally perceived as speaking. A voice is necessarily relational and implies the presence of a speaker. The inherent paradox of a disembodied voice might even get closer to the nature of religious experience, perhaps hinting in some way at a transcendent source of the voice, more than an ordinary perception of a voice spoken by a human conversation partner. Voices are more complex than Griffith-Dickson portrays perceptions in general as being, and this may make them a better model of religious experience than she allows.

Perceptions of God may, however, take different forms and, within the Christian tradition, there is a further complication in that God may be perceived in human form – visually or audibly – as Jesus. David Brown has suggested that "on the whole Protestants, Jews and Mohammedans hear voices while Catholics and Hindus see visions" (Brown, 1985, p.39).

In fact, it is not so clear that Protestants are more likely to hear voices and Catholics to see visions. Much voice hearing seems to occur within the context of visionary experience (or at least in people who have at other times seen visions) and so it is difficult to separate the two phenomena. Visionary experiences clearly do occur amongst Protestants. Chester and Lucile Huyssen's (1992) collection of accounts of experiences of visions of Jesus includes mainly Protestant examples. In Phillip Wiebe's (1997) study of contemporary accounts of visionary experiences of Jesus, at least half of the 28 subjects are identifiable as having been Protestant at the time of the experience. Voice-hearing experiences – in the absence of visionary experiences – do also occur amongst Catholics.[8]

Whether or not there are differences between Catholics and Protestants in the ways in which religious experience takes a perceptual form, the fact is simply that many Christian religious experiences do seem to be perceptual.

Taxonomies of religious experience

There have been many different proposals as to the best way to classify religious experience. A seminal work in this field has been Stark's (1965) taxonomy, within which four main categories are identifed: the confirming experience, the responsive experience, the ecstatic experience, and the revelational experience. In this taxonomy, voices fall primarily within the revelational category, which Stark believed to be the least common. Notably, this taxonomy may be applied to experiences of evil, as well as to experiences of the divine.

Caroline Franks Davis (1989, pp.32–65) identifies six categories of religious experience:

1 interpretive
2 quasi-sensory
3 revelatory
4 regenerative
5 numinous
6 mystical.

This taxonomy is understood as reflecting categories into which religious experiences "naturally" fall, and is explicitly not intended to identify mutually exclusive categories. Franks Davis suggests that the six categories might be understood rather as "aspects" of religious experience – but that few religious experiences show evidence of all six aspects. Whilst the quasi-sensory category is the one that explicity identifies voices, visions, and phenomena involving other sensory modalities, it is not at all implied that the other categories necessarily do not include such phenomena.

Within the quasi-sensory category, Franks Davis distinguishes between three types: those in which a spiritual entity is "actually present", those which are "hallucinatory", and those in which "the quasi-sensory elements have no religious significance themselves and convey no religious insight". The New Testament resurrection appearances of Jesus would be of the first type, the visions of Julian of Norwich are given as an example of the second type, and the lights and (non-verbal) sounds sometimes associated with the other categories of religious experience are given as examples of the third type.

Swinburne[9] identifies five types of religious experience which he considers to be both exclusive and exhaustive. These are, respectively, experiences of God or the supernatural in

1 an ordinary, publicly perceived, non-religious, object or objects (e.g. looking at the night sky and suddenly "seeing it as" God's handiwork)
2 unusual, but publicly perceived, objects (e.g. the light seen by Paul and his companions on the road to Damascus)
3 private perceptions describable using normal sensory vocabulary (Swinburne includes dreams within this category, as well as perceptual experiences)
4 private perceptions not describable in such terms
5 private, non-sensory, awareness.

Swinburne locates the New Testament accounts of encounters with the risen Jesus as being of the second type, and mystical experiences as belonging to the fourth and fifth types. The inclusion of the fifth type of experience – the non-sensory – recognises that religious experience may or may not be mediated by "something sensory". However, it is notable that four out of the five types include perceptual, or perception-like, phenomena.

John Hick (2010, p.29) identifies four different "modes" of religious experience:

1   "a distinctive way of experiencing aspects of the natural world, or the natural world as a whole"
2   "the sense of presence, whether of God or of an angelic being or of a surrounding and indwelling more ultimate supra-natural reality"
3   "religious visions and auditions, both inner and outer"
4   "the experience of unity with God or with the Ultimate reported by mystics within each of the great traditions".

Hick does not consider this classification to be exhaustive and refers also to other rarer forms of religious experience, including near-death experiences (NDE), out-of-body experiences, mediumship, and reported memories of past lives. Elsewhere, Hick suggests that the resurrection appearances to Peter and Paul,[10] and perhaps a few others, were similar in form to an NDE. He also asserts – somewhat contradictorily – that "the original happening is more likely to have been in the realm of inner spiritual experience than in that of outer sense experience".[11] In either case, he eschews classification of the resurrection appearances as belonging to either the "sense of presence" or "religious visions" modes of religious experience.

Whilst the present focus is on perceptual, and perception-like, experiences it is not clear that it is helpful either to make this the overarching framework (as Swinburne has done) or to separate out visions and auditions (as Hick has done). Some kind of perceptual (or perception-like) component is likely to be a part – even if only a small part – of any religious experience. However, classification on other grounds is far from reaching widespread agreement.

Many religious experiences are significant, amongst other things, because of their transformational nature. Traditionally, transformative religious experiences might be referred to as "conversion" experiences. Joshua Iyadurai, for example, prefers the term "transformative religious experience", but treats this as more or less synonymous with "religious conversion" (Iyadurai, 2015, p.3). Franks Davis understands conversion experiences as falling within both the revelatory and regenerative categories of her taxonomy (Franks Davis, 1989, p.45), the former emphasising the transformative nature of the "mystical vision" or of sudden insights and convictions (p.39) and the latter a kind of change more concerned with a (non-mystical) renewal of spiritual, moral, psychological,, or physical well-being (p.44). Miller and C'de Baca, in their study of sudden and dramatic life changes, adopted the term "quantum change" to refer to "vivid, surprising, benevolent, and enduring personal transformation", but they consider this to be a larger phenomenon, of which religious conversion is but one example

(Miller and C'de Baca, 2001, pp.4, 7). They subdivide quantum change into two major forms – mystical and insightful.

Mental illness is usually either ignored in discussions of religious experience, or else distinguished from it as a mutually exclusive category. That is, if someone is mentally ill, it is determined that they are not having a genuine religious experience.[12] It is not clear, however, that this is a helpful distinction, or that it is free from prejudicial assumptions about people with mental illness. Why should someone not have a positive (genuine) spiritual experience amidst the context of an otherwise negative (pathological) experience of illness? Quite apart from this, mental illness in which psychopathology takes on religious content is, surely, still a "religious" experience? Even if delusions and hallucinations demonstrate religious content which others determine to be in some way "false", it is not clear why this should not still be considered a religious experience for the person concerned.[13] That person may themselves interpret the experience differently when they have recovered from the episode of illness, and they may then no longer evaluate their experiences as genuine "experiences of God". Thus they may reinterpret their experience as a negative one – but it would still be a "religious" experience.

The problem, then – rather like Proudfoot's example of the person who was mistaken in thinking that they saw a bear – is one of the discrepancies between the internal and the external account of the experience. However, in this case we are dealing with a presumed external theological reality, about which Christians and others have different views. The category "religious experience" should therefore not rely for its definition on value judgements made by others concerning the nature of the presumed external theological reality, or by changes in evaluation of the experience by the person themselves, or by prejudicial assumptions that a person with mental disorder cannot – by definition – have a religious experience.

The purpose here is not to classify all religious experiences – or to imply that all religious experiences necessarily involve perceptual, or perception-like, phenomena such as voices. Rather, the aim is to map out some of the Christian religious experiences within which voices (AVHs and verbal hallucinations) seem most commonly to have played a part. The categories of Christian experience to be considered here will therefore be:

1   mystical
2   crisis and transformation
3   mental illness
4   prayer.

Mystical experience

The variety of mystical experiences – even within the Christian tradition – is very marked and it is clearly not the case that mystical experiences that include voice hearing are a unitary phenomenon. Quite apart from differences in phenomenology, cultural, religious, and historical context are likely to play a significant role in varying description and interpretation of experiences of voice hearing. Literary style, genre, and use of metaphor are also significant in written accounts. Thus, the "voices" in Catherine of Genoa's *Spiritual Dialogue,* or in Marguerite Porete's *The Mirror of Simple Souls,* follow in a classical tradition of the use of personification to construct a metaphorical dialogue such as that employed by Boethius in *Consolation of Philosophy.*[14] Whilst this does not make these texts any less mystical, their "voices" would seem to be more clearly a literary device than a perceptual (or perception-like) phenomenon. It is not always possible to assert such distinctions with confidence, but the examples taken for further consideration in the present chapter will be ones which, at face value, would seem more likely to reflect perceptual experience behind the text than the literary genre of the text.

Mysticism is notoriously difficult to define.[15] It is usually understood as being concerned with certain kinds of experience, or consciousness, of the presence of God. It is identified by some as a common feature of diverse religious traditions. However, there is much debate and numerous different definitions are on offer. Furthermore, there are difficult cases to address. Notably, Buddhism does not acknowledge any transcendent reality which may be experienced, some mystics have been very much concerned with experience of absence rather than presence, and some writers usually understood as mystics (e.g. Meister Eckhart) are not acknowledged by other scholars as being mystics at all.[16]

According to some authorities, notably William James (1902) in *The Varieties of Religious Experience,* one of the defining characteristics of mystical experience is its ineffability.[17] This feature is disputed by others,[18] but is worthy of mention here given its particular significance for the experience of voice hearing. Whatever else there is about an experience that might be described as ineffable, surely a voice – by definition – cannot be ineffable? If we take this view, then a voice in itself cannot be a defining feature of a mystical experience. However, I think that this view is wrong for at least two reasons. First, if ineffability is a defining mark of mystical experience (and this is clearly debatable), then it is presumably definitive of the experience as a whole. This does not mean that every part of the experience is ineffable, or that the experience is totally beyond words, or else nothing at all could meaningfully be said about any mystical experience, whereas in fact many mystics have had much to say about their experiences. Second, whilst those who have heard voices as a part of their mystical experience have often reported the words that they heard, this clearly does not mean that the experience of the voice has been totally and adequately conveyed. There may be much that remains ineffable about the voice – such as its quality, its source, its impact upon the hearer, its significance and its meaning.

Leaving aside issues of definition, ineffability, and the difficult cases, it is clearly not true to say that all mystics hear voices. Hearing the voice of God – or other transcendent voices – has never been a core component of any definition of mystical experience of which I am aware. In some historical cases, where we only have textual evidence, and in some cases little biographical information, we cannot take lack of reference to experiences of voice hearing as evidence that the mystical experiences of the person concerned never included voices. However, in other cases (e.g. Augustine of Hippo)[19] we have extensive biographical and/or other textual information and it would seem clear that voice hearing was simply not a part of the spectrum of mystical phenomena experienced by that person. It seems pretty clear that not all mystical experiences include voices (or, indeed, any other hallucinatory experience).

Even where the phenomenology of mystical experience does include voices, these voices are often a small part of a bigger mystical picture, within which the voice takes only a subsidiary role. Thus, for example, the mystical experiences of Symeon the New Theologian and Hildegard of Bingen might be characterised as largely visual, but both also reported hearing a voice. This is not to say that such voices are insignificant, but rather that they are not the most prominent phenomenon within the overall mystical experience taken as a whole.

But what about the person whose reported experience of the presence of God is mediated by the hearing of a voice? Are they necessarily a mystic? There seems to be a general reluctance to concede any definition of mystical experience on grounds of perceptual phenomena, and the voice of God might clearly be heard in many different ways, some of which might be considered mystical and some not. Nonetheless, it is not immediately obvious why a divine voice should be any less a mark of the presence of God than other experiences which are proposed with less hesitation.

Perhaps the most obvious circumstances within which it is asserted that such voices are not a feature of mystical experience is when they are understood to be due to mental illness. Thus, for example, authors who identify Margery Kempe as suffering from major mental disorder generally seem not to consider her experiences to be mystical. It is not clear why this should necessarily be so. Why may a mystical experience not be had by a person suffering from a mental disorder? Even if we allow for the moment that people who are mentally ill do not have mystical experiences (a supposition which is both doubtful and prejudicial), it is clear from contemporary research that there are hard cases where it is extremely difficult to disentangle mystical experience from mental disorder (Lukoff, 1985, Jackson and Fulford, 1997). The possibility of making such distinctions reliably, especially where based solely upon texts that are centuries old, must therefore be highly questionable.

A second context within which voices are often not considered to be mystical experiences is traditional. Protestants have generally been less likely to describe unusual experiences as "mystical". For example, after the model of St Paul, some evangelical accounts of conversion to Christianity are associated with the hearing of a voice,[20] but are not usually referred to as mystical experiences (even if perhaps they should be). In fact, examples of Protestant mysticism are not difficult to find,[21] but they are simply not usually labelled as such within Protestant traditions. This is not so much a question of when hearing a divine voice might not constitute a mystical experience as it is a question concerning the willingness to identify any religious experience at all as "mystical".

Others, however, assert more boldly that visions and voices simply are not mystical phenomena under any circumstances. Thus, for example, Walter Stace (1973) asserts that this is not only his view, but the view of "most competent scholars" and of "the great mystics themselves".[22] He goes on to argue that this view is justified because the most typical and important mystical states are devoid of imagery. This argument further rests upon his prioritisation of introvertive over extrovertive mystical states (as he classifies them) – the latter being more sensuous, and the former lacking in sensual experiences. However, he acknowledges that

> although visions and voices are clearly distinguished by mystics from the higher states which they attain, there is a certain correlation between the types of persons who have mystical experiences and those who see visions and hear voices. That is why they themselves are so careful to distinguish them.[23]

Stace places a lot of weight upon what others say – and upon his own evaluation of extrovertive (more sensuous) experience as merely a "stepping stone" to something better (introvertive experience). However, it is not clear that this is anything more than a matter of making value judgements. Even if sensory experiences are only a "stepping stone", then perhaps they are a very important one? Even if they are not the defining feature of mystical union, yet perhaps they are still significant concomitants?

A more sophisticated argument concerning voices that might not be mystical is articulated, primarily in regard to visionary experience, by Bernard McGinn (1994, pp.326–328). McGinn distinguishes (as – he argues – many mystics have done) between the *visio Dei* as "visualisable perception of God" and the *visio Dei* as "conscious experience of God's immediate presence". These, as he suggests the mystics have "insisted", are related but distinguishable and independent phenomena. He also points out that the visions of many mystics have been of saints or angels, but that they do not always include visions of Christ or of God. Thus, "visions may or may not be mystical in content" and – even where they are visions of God – "do not constitute the essence of mysticism". Whilst McGinn is talking here primarily about visionary experience, it is clear that the argument works equally well in relation to experiences of voice hearing. Indeed, examples given by McGinn not infrequently include both visions and voices.

McGinn suggests that mystical experience

> tends to place emphasis on special altered states – visions, locutions, raptures, and the like – which admittedly have played a large part in mysticism but which many mystics have insisted do not constitute the essence of the encounter with God. Many of the greatest Christian mystics (think of Origen, Meister Eckhart, and John of the Cross) have been downright hostile to such experiences, emphasizing rather the new level of awareness, the special and heightened consciousness involving both loving and knowing that is given in the mystical meeting.[24]

It is therefore not visions or voices, but rather awareness, or "heightened consciousness", that are definitive of the direct (mystical) encounter with God.

McGinn makes a persuasive point.[25] However, I think that it presents a number of problems. First, sense of presence, like the hearing of a voice, is an hallucinatory experience of a kind (Alderson-Day, 2016). Voices, at least often, and perhaps usually, are associated with some kind of a sense of presence, and where the voices are religious – or divine – it is likely that the associated sense of presence will also be religious or divine. It is not at all clear that a "conscious experience of God's immediate presence" is ever lacking when someone reports that they hear the voice of God, although this is clearly a question that could be addressed – at least in the contemporary context – by empirical research. If divine voices are experienced devoid of divine presence they are, at least to a degree, inherently self-contradictory phenomena. Such experiences would need careful empirical study in order to understand what it means to someone to hear the voice of God in association with a conscious experience of the absence of God. Furthermore, given that mystical experience is acknowledged to involve experiences of absence as well as presence, it is still not clear that this would prove that such experiences are ever anything other than mystical experiences.

More importantly, all experiences of the "presence of God" are experiences, whether perceptual (or perception like) or otherwise. As such, they are necessarily mediated by epistemological and theological assumptions (Howells, 2001). Just as "God does not speak Hebrew",[26] so God does not "turn up", making himself present in some times and places when he is not present in others. Awareness of divine presence is a matter of varying experience or awareness, not variations in divine presence per se, and such experiences might be termed "mystical" whatever form they take. As Will Cather's character Father Vaillant says, in her novel *Death Comes for the Archbishop*:

> The miracles of the Church seem to me to rest not so much upon faces or voices or healing power coming suddenly near to us from afar off, but upon our perceptions being made finer, so that for a moment our eyes can see and our ears can hear what is there about us always.
>
> (Cather, 1927, p.40)

A valid or true experience of hearing the voice of God[27] is therefore not so much a matter of God "speaking" as one of attentive human listening.

I note that McGinn[28] makes an important distinction between "immediate" or "direct" consciousness of the presence of God, which he considers definitive of true mysticism, and the awareness of the divine which is characteristic of "ordinary consciousness". However, as he acknowledges, this is more about claims made by the mystics themselves concerning their experiences. They might be mistaken. Voices – like experiences of presence – might potentially be divided into immediate/direct and ordinary kinds. But would this be helpful?

McGinn acknowledges that, paradoxically, presence must include absence, and that positive language alone fails to do justice to the nature of mystical experience. However, it is not at all clear why experiences of presence/absence should be any less difficult to define with precision than voices, visions, or other perceptual (or perception-like) phenomena. That experience is a complex matter is undeniable,[29] but we cannot avoid acknowledging the inherently experiential nature of mysticism.

So – whilst I agree with McGinn that presence/absence is an important (perhaps *the* important) consideration in understanding Christian mysticism, I am not convinced that experiences of presence are any more or less helpful than voices, or other perception-like experiences, or experiences of absence, in grasping the essence of what the mystics are trying to relate. Or – to put it slightly differently – it is not clear that experiences of presence have any more or less value than experiences of voices in attempts to distil or articulate the mystical encounter with God.

Pace McGinn, I therefore propose that the *visio Dei*, whether experienced by way of a vision or voice, or a sense of presence or absence, *is* a mystical experience, and that all mystical experience may in some way or another (even if only metaphorically) be defined as an experience of the *visio Dei*. Of course, this still leaves much room for debate about exactly what might be taken to constitute the *visio Dei*. I am proposing here that the "*visio*" is only a metaphor and that it should be taken to be inclusive of a wide variety of kinds of experience, including voices and visions, and that it should not privilege sense of "presence" over other forms of experiencing.[30]

Amongst visionaries whom McGinn does not consider to be mystics, Elisabeth of Schönau (1128–1165) is an interesting example. The far larger number of visionary experiences reported by Elisabeth were concerned with saints and angels rather than with God, or God in Christ. Even where she does experience visions of the latter kind, McGinn sees the emphasis as being located elsewhere:

> Although she often talks about being in rapture (*in excessu mentis*), what she experiences in these ecstatic states is not so much direct transforming contact with God, as an entry into a heavenly world where messages are communicated to her, often in a mediated fashion by angels, messages meant to be proclaimed to the church through her writings . . . Elisabeth is a prophet, reformer, and teacher, not a mystic.[31]

For McGinn, it is the sense of the direct "transforming contact with God" that provides the unifying element amongst the varieties of Christian mysticism, and (at least as McGinn alleges) Elisabeth does not demonstrate evidence of this as the primary focus of her experiences.[32]

McGinn is surely right to look for observable evidence of transformation, either within the individual or in terms of their impact on those around them.[33] This might come in written form, in the shape of a text recognised as of enduring value for its Christian wisdom, or it might come in the shape of practical reform and way of life.[34] Some voices are associated with such evidence of transformation, and some are not, just as some experiences of a sense of divine presence are associated with such evidence and some are not. If some heavenly voices are to be determined as mystical and others not, it is arguably on this basis that there are strongest grounds for making the distinction.

Crisis and transformation

Consideration will be given here to some examples of Christian experiences of voices heard at times of crisis, transformation and change – including conversion, calling to a new vocation, and near death experiences.

Crisis

Many conversion stories are located in the context of a life crisis of some kind. For others, crisis is not the occasion of a conversion, but rather of a renewal of faith or the context for heartfelt prayer. Miller and C'de Baca (2001), for example, relate the story of a woman with a Christian background, on the verge of committing murder/suicide, who prayed "Please, help me!" in the early hours of the morning. "Suddenly it was like this angel appeared in my mind, and this voice said to me, 'Turn to me.' Just like that. I felt a presence. I didn't really see a vision. There was just a feeling of light."[35] This woman specifically states that, according to her own view, this was not a ("born-again") conversion experience – but it clearly was a crisis point at which prayer was followed by a sense of presence and a voice.

In his biography of Martin Luther King (1929–1968), Stephen Oates (1998) describes a crisis point in January 1956 when, in the course of his social activism against racial discrimination in the United States of America, King was receiving 30 to 40 hate letters and as many as 25 obscenie phone calls per day. Late one night, concerned for the safety of his family, he determined to quit the campaign.

> He put his head in his hands and bowed over the table. "Oh Lord," he prayed aloud, "I'm down here trying to do what is right. But, Lord, I must confess that I'm weak now. I'm afraid. The people are looking to me for leadership, and if I stand before them without strength and courage, they too will falter. I am at the end of my powers. I have nothing left. I can't face it alone.

He sat there, his head still bowed in his hands, tears burning his eyes. But then he felt something – a presence, a stirring in himself. And it seemed that an inner voice was speaking to him with quiet assurance: "Martin Luther, stand up for righteousness. Stand up for justice. Stand up for truth. And, lo, I will be with you, even unto the end of the world." He saw lightning flash. He heard thunder roar. It was the voice of Jesus telling him still to fight on.[36]

Again, this is not a conversion story – although it is a turning point in King's life, following which he felt stronger, more calm, and aware of a greater sense of the closeness of God. But the crisis – evoking prayer – reaches a turning point marked by a voice and a sense of divine presence.

Conversion

Edwin Starbuck's classic early study of religious conversion (Starbuck, 1901) makes relatively few references to the hearing of voices as an accompaniment of the conversion experience.[37] Contemporary research shows that voices (and visions) are not unusual accompaniments of religious conversion. Joshua Iyadurai (2015), in his study of Christian conversion experiences in India, gives a number of examples, both of visionary experiences (including out-loud voices) and "voices of God" which, in a broader sense (and usually not as out-loud voices), are received as divine communications – in the form of Bible reading, sermons, or inner reflections and thoughts. One of his subjects (Sanya), whilst studying for exams, suddenly heard a man's voice, associated with a sense of the presence of someone standing behind her, calling her by name and repeatedly commanding her to "Pray!"[38] Another subject (Sekar), for many years an alcoholic, was woken from his sleep by someone patting him on his back and saying "Sekar! Sekar! Wake up, wake up."[39]

There are numerous published biographical and autobiographical accounts of conversion experiences, mostly within the Protestant traditions. Three such experiences which include the hearing of a voice will be offered here as illustrative.[40]

Susan Atkins participated, with Charles Manson and several others, in a series of horrific murders in 1969. In her autobiography (Atkins, 1978) she describes how, on 27 September 1974, in prison, and awaiting execution, she engaged in an inner conversation with herself about whether or not she could ever be forgiven, and whether she should try to escape from prison – or kill herself. Amidst her options, she considers another possibility that has been presented to her:

I could decide to follow Jesus.

As plainly as the daylight came the words, "You have to decide."

I turned onto my side and tried to think. Very quietly, I slipped into the most solemn moment of my life. Everything was absolutely quiet and unrushed. It seemed that time stopped, and I knew one fact above all others: This was my last chance. I don't pretend to understand the theology of it, but I knew for a certainty that, at that moment, I had the opportunity to give my life to Jesus Christ and I would never have another opportunity.

The moment held still. "Am I asleep?" I thought. No. I was fully awake. I turned again onto my back.

"Behold, I stand at the door, and knock . . ." Did I hear someone say that? I don't know. But the statement was there. All else stood still.

"Okay. If you're there, come on in."

Total stillness . . . and then: "All right. I'll come in, but you must open the door."

This was incredible! I talked back to the voice. I assume I spoke in my thoughts, but I'm not certain. "What door?"

"You know what door and where it is, Susan. Just turn around and open it, and I will come in."

Suddenly, as though on a movie screen, there in my thoughts was a door. It had a handle. I took hold of it, and pulled. It opened.

The whitest, most brilliant light I had ever seen poured over me.[41]

Amidst the light, Atkins sees the figure of Jesus, who speaks to her again:

"Susan, I am really here. I'm really coming into your heart to stay. Right now you are being born again and you will live with me in heaven through all eternity, forever and ever. This is really happening. It is not a dream. You are now a child of God. You are washed clean and your sins have all been forgiven."

I was distinctly aware that I inhaled deeply and then, just as fully exhaled. There was no more guilt! It was gone. Completely gone! The bitterness, too. Instantly gone! How could this be?

For the first time in my memory I felt clean, fully clean, inside and out. In twenty-six years I had never been so happy.[42]

Although she says that she doesn't understand the theology, Atkins has clearly absorbed a lot of the evangelical language and beliefs of the Christians who have been encouraging her towards conversion. The narrative is presented within this framework – as a conversion experience – not a mystical experience. However, her account presents, in evangelical Christian terms, an apprehension of an ultimate reality a sense of timelessness, a oneness (with Jesus), and feelings of bliss and serenity – all of which are often reported features of mystical experience.[43]

Although she was not executed, Atkins was repeatedly refused parole and remained in prison for the rest of her life. She was a controversial figure and, although it is said that she became a model prisoner, there seem to have been many who questioned the sincerity of her conversion. Atkins' autobiography, like that of Margery Kempe six centuries earlier, had a readership in mind. Both women narrated an account of their lives that was intended to convey to the world their case for being understood as good Christians.

Hugh Montefiore (1920–2005), born to a Jewish family, converted to Christianity in his teens and later became Bishop of Birmingham:

> I was sixteen years old at the time, and it happened to me about 5 pm one dark wintry afternoon in 1936. I was sitting alone in my study in School House at Rugby School – all older boys had studies of their own: pillboxes, really. What happened then determined the whole future pattern of my life. I was, as I remember, indulging in a rather pleasant adolescent gloom. I suddenly became aware of a figure in white whom I saw clearly in my mind's eye. I use this expression because I am pretty sure that a photograph would have showed nothing special on it. I heard the words "Follow me". Instinctively I knew that this was Jesus, heaven knows how: I knew nothing about him. Put like that it sounds somewhat bare; in fact it was an indescribably rich event that filled me afterwards with overpowering joy. I could do no other than to follow those instructions. I found that I had become a Christian as a result of a totally unexpected and most unusual spiritual experience, although that was not how I would have put it at the time. I was aware of the living Christ, and because of that I was aware of God in a new way. People ask me why and when I decided to convert. I did not decide at all; it was decided for me.
>
> (Montefiore, 1995, p.1)[44]

A more recent example – although perhaps not strictly a "conversion" so much as a reconversion to Christianity – is interesting by virtue of the more clearly "out-loud" nature of the experience. Mike McHargue (b.1978), in his autobiography *Finding God in the Waves*, describes how, having lost his faith and become an atheist, he found himself at a Christian conference confronted with an invitation to receive the bread at a Eucharist. Deciding that taking the bread would be dishonest given his atheist convictions, he was about to walk away: "But just when I was about to turn, I heard a voice say, 'I was here when you were eight, and I'm here now'" (McHargue, 2016, p.124). A keen scientist, he reflects:

> This is the part where I should explain the science of how a sane person can hear an audible voice in a room when no one has spoken. Believe me, I've spent a long time researching it, and I would love to explain it.
>
> I can't.
>
> The closest thing I can find in the sciences are hallucinations. Maybe that's what happened.[45]

Calling and vocation

On Tuesday 10 September 1946, when aged 36 years, Mother Teresa (now known as Teresa of Calcutta) was on a train journey to Darjeeling, on her way to a retreat: "It was on this day in 1946 in the train to Darjeeling that God gave me the 'call within a call' to satiate the thirst of Jesus by serving Him in the poorest of the poor."[46] A "voice", which she began to hear on this day, and which continued until the following year addressed her as "My own spouse" or "My own little one" (p.44). "[T]he 'Voice' kept pleading, 'Come, come, carry Me into the holes of the poor. Come, be My light.'"[47]

In 1947, Teresa experienced three visions of a crowd calling out to her to save them:

> I was kneeling near Our Lady, who was facing them. – I did not see her face but I heard her say "Take care of them – they are mine. – Bring them to Jesus – carry Jesus to them. – Fear not. Teach them to say the Rosary – the family Rosary and all will be well. – Fear not – Jesus and I will be with you and your children."[48]

In her third vision, she saw the crowd covered in darkness. As she was facing the cross with Mary: "Our Lord said – 'I have asked you. They have asked you and she, My Mother has asked you. Will you refuse to do this for Me – to take care of them, to bring them to Me?'"[49] In a letter to Father Van Exem dated 19 October 1947, she wrote:

> The "voices and visions": "came unasked, and they have gone. They have not changed my life. They have helped me to be more trustful and draw closer to God. – They have increased my desire to be more and more His little child. I have obeyed you to the letter in regard of them – so I do not fear. I attach no importance to them as regard the call because my desires to immolate myself were just as strong before they came. Why they came I do not know – neither do I try to know. I am pleased to let Him do with me just as it pleaseth Him."[50]

Sister Briege McKenna (b.1946) is much less well known than Mother Teresa, but is another Roman Catholic religious for whom vocational calling has been associated with voices, both in relation to her initial religious vocation, and subsequently a call to a healing ministry:

> On Christmas Day, 1959, when I was only thirteen years old my mother died suddenly. As I cried that night, I heard a voice say, "Don't worry, I'll take care of you." I didn't really understand that it was the Lord, but I felt peace. The next morning I knew that I wanted to be a nun.
> (McKenna and Libersat, 1987, p.1)

In 1970, she experienced a sudden healing from severe rheumatoid arthritis. In June 1971, on the eve of the feast of Pentecost, she went into the convent chapel to pray:

I had been in the chapel about five minutes when suddenly this extraordinary stillness descended on the chapel – it was like a cloud, like a fog. A voice said, "Briege." I turned to look toward the door because the voice was so clear it sounded as though someone had come into the chapel. No one was there, but I was very conscious that someone was present. The voice said to me as I turned back to the tabernacle, "You have my gift of healing. Go and use it."[51]

Almost immediately she made an act of contrition "for even thinking that Jesus would speak to me", yet the following day she awoke with the words of the voice "booming in my head". Subsequently, Sister Briege has become internationally known for her healing ministry.

A Protestant example, of a rather different kind, is provided by Catherine Marshall (1951), in her biography of her husband, Peter Marshall. As a young man, Peter found himself working one summer in Bamburgh in northeast England. Catherine relates how, as he walked home one dark night across the moors, Peter heard someone call his name:

"*Peter!* . . ." There was great urgency in the voice.

For a second he listened, but there was no response, only the sound of the wind. The moor seemed completely deserted.

Thinking he must have been mistaken, he walked on a few paces. Then he heard it again, even more urgently:

"Peter! . . ."

He stopped dead still, trying to peer into that impenetrable darkness, but suddenly stumbled and fell to his knees. Putting out his hand to catch himself, he found nothing there. As he cautiously investigated, feeling around in a semicircle, he found himself to be on the very brink of an abandoned stone quarry. Just one more step would have sent him plummeting into space to certain death.

This incident made an unforgettable impression on Peter. There was never any doubt in his mind about the source of that Voice. He felt that God must have some great purpose for his life, to have intervened so specifically.[52]

In this case, the sense of calling was initially inchoate – and represented only one possible interpretation of the hearing of the Voice – rather than anything that the Voice had actually said. It was followed by other experiences (not involving voices) which were similarly interpreted.[53] Peter Marshall went on to become a Presbyterian minister, a noted preacher, and twice chaplain to the United States Senate.

Near-death experience

So-called near-death experiences (NDEs) are reported by people undergoing a near-fatal event such as a cardiac arrest, and typically include accounts of various perceptual phenomena, including out-of-body experiences, lights, and encounters with deceased relatives (Parnia et al., 2001, 2014). Although these experiences are reported by people who are thought to be unconscious, they are also sometimes associated with apparent awareness of what is said by medical staff and what is going on in the immediate environment in which resuscitation is taking place. They are reported by people from different religious traditions, but much of the research has been undertaken in the Western world, and thus has a Judeo-Christian emphasis.

The perceptual phenomena involved do not always include voices, but encounters with deceased relatives or heavenly beings do sometimes include a dialogical element. An example reported by a Christian woman who nearly drowned in a kayaking accident is illustrative. Mary Neal, in her book *To Heaven and Back*, describes as a part of her NDE a sense of "being held and comforted by Jesus",[54] and an encounter with a group of human spirits who greet her and welcome her, whose presence, she says:

> engulfed all of my senses, as though I could see, hear, feel, smell, and taste them all at once. Their brilliance was both blinding and invigorating. We did not speak, *per se*, using our mouths, but easily communicated in a very pure form. We simultaneously communicated our thoughts and emotions, and understood each other perfectly even though we did not use language.
>
> (Neal, 2014, pp.69–70)

Neal's experience has a mystical, ineffable, quality which clearly marks it out as different from voice-hearing experiences within which specific words are heard (even if not "out loud") with clarity. On the other hand, there is a dialogical, conversational, quality to it which is not dissimilar to many reports of voice hearing and, similarly, there is a marked sense of the presence of both God/Jesus, and the spiritual beings who come to meet her.

In a study of over 300 NDEs, Peter and Elizabeth Fenwick (1995) report that communication usually seems to be "intuitive" and that words are not normally involved.[55] Similarly, whilst experiences of light are common, and about a quarter of subjects reported a spiritual "presence" of some kind, few people identified specific religious figures.[56] An exception in this study was a woman who had a visionary experience of seeing Jesus, whom she twice heard speak a single word – "Come!"[57]

Mental illness

The research on AVHs in psychosis was reviewed briefly in Chapter 1. Much, but not all, of that research has been concerned with broadly Christian groups. Two particular, and contrasting, experiences of psychosis involving religious hallucinations will be considered here.

Valerie Fox (2002) provides a first person account of her experience of schizophrenia from the perspective of someone brought up within the Christian tradition. In the context of a broken relationship and separation from her children, Fox describes her experience of hearing voices:

> I was sobbing uncontrollably when I felt a presence very near to me; I believed it was Jesus. I could speak with him, and he consoled me. Then I heard the voices of the Father of Heaven and Mary, the Blessed Virgin. Jesus' voice faded for the most part, and the voices of Mary and our Father remained with me during my odyssey into the depths of schizophrenia. I had crossed the line of faith into the evil world of schizophrenia.

Fox describes a period of homelessness, abuse, and continued separation from her children during which her faith, as understood within the theatre of hallucinatory voices and delusional beliefs, provided her with much comfort.

> I started each new day with Mary and our Father. While treachery abounded all around me, my core was peaceful . . .
> Through these trials, I had my "perfect family" leading me, comforting me, and speaking quietly with me. At no time during my life did I ever know the serenity and peace I knew during this time. At the same time, I never knew such brutality, such abuse, and such poverty.

Eventually, however, Fox began to wonder why, if she was really in the care of God and the Blessed Virgin, she was living such a tortured existence and she sought admission to mental health services. Whilst not wanting to let go of her inner world, under the influence of medication it became harder to focus on the voices. Eventually, she made a conscious decision to let go of her thoughts of God and Mary and to focus on the world in which her children and her mother might be found. From this point, she dates the beginning of her healing.

Fox's spirituality and faith have clearly been transformed by this experience. She no longer goes to church, and she fears reminders and patterns of thinking that might not be good for her. Yet, she has retained her belief in God, Jesus and Mary, and says she is thankful for each day of life and for her family. Research suggests that hallucinations may be understood by those who experience them within a psychotic episode as being mystical experiences, and that their religious beliefs often help them to cope with their disorder, providing meaning and relationship to the sacred (Hanevik et al., 2017).

For others, experiences of psychosis are not of the presence of Jesus, or of the voices of God, or Mary, but of an encounter with evil. Jo Barber, for example, writes:

> One day when I was sitting in church I heard what I thought was the voice of the Devil calling me. I was petrified. It was very insistent. I do not know why I thought it was the Devil; it just was, and I just knew. He was threatening to control me and said that I did not belong to Christ. I sat there for a while paralyzed with fright, and finally left the church without speaking to anyone, in a very distressed state.
>
> (Barber, 2016, p.123)

For Barber, her initial experience of seeking help from a Christian minister was a highly negative one, as he determined that she was possessed and subjected her to an exorcism. A suicide attempt later led to a hospital admission, and an initially negative experience of mental health services ensued. Staff on the ward were impatient and unsympathetic, and medication seemed not to help.

> Looking back on it, I almost certainly had a mental illness, but with a big spiritual/religious dimension . . . It had not responded to the obvious "religious" solutions of exorcism and repeated religious conversion, and my experiences could be interpreted as hallucinations and delusions within a mental illness. However, I did have specifically religious problems in that I undoubtedly had a skewed image of God and many misunderstandings about the Christian faith and expectations of life . . . I believe I actually needed the right sort of help with my religion as well as treatment for mental illness, and neither one or the other would suffice.[58]

More positive experiences with mental health services, and later more positive experiences of church, eventually led Jo to a place of renewed spiritual well-being. She refers to her episode of illness as an experience of spiritual or religious "ill-being". Religious experiences – including voices of the Devil – are still religious experiences, even when they are negative ones. More importantly, these experiences of religious ill-being can lead eventually to a place of spiritual growth and religious well-being.

Ironically, Fox heard a voice that she believed to be God, and now no longer goes to church. Barber heard a voice that she believed to be the Devil and now does go to church again. But both have found places of renewed faith – transformed by their religious experiences in the context of mental illness.

Prayer

Prayer provides the context for the great majority of the Christian examples of hearing a voice that have been explored in Chapter 5. Since Peter went on to the roof to pray and had a vision of heaven opened, and heard a heavenly voice, many Christians have reported the experience of hearing a voice that seemed to answer their prayers.

The experience of hearing God's answering voice in prayer is not universal, and some Christians would express serious reservations about contemporary accounts of hearing God that circulate in some churches. However, it is a very widespread experience and seems to be adaptable to different traditions and theological contexts from reformed to catholic, and contemplative to charismatic. Just two examples will be taken here – from Ignatian and charismatic spiritualities.

The Ignatian spiritual exercises (discussed in historical context in Chapter 5) provide an example of a living tradition within which an experience of conversation with God as a two-way affair is explicitly encouraged. In meditation on scripture, the Christian is urged to listen for the voices of the characters in the narrative. In colloquy, the Christian talks to God, and then listens for an answer. Whilst Ignatius gives little detail concerning the nature of the experience of colloquy, Philip Endean suggests that it is a kind of "imagined conversation" (Endean, 1990, p.403). Michael Ivens writes: "As a personal prayer it has the features of conversational exchange; it is a prayer therefore not simply of speaking but of listening" (Ivens and Munitiz, 2007, p.66). Thus, the retreatant is encouraged to address questions, or conversation, to God and to "listen" for an answer, a responding or conversational inner "voice" within their prayers. As indicated in Chapter 5, these exercises in prayer are accompanied by detailed instructions for discernment which assist in a more discriminative approach to this listening component of prayer. Although this approach to prayer has its origins in the Roman Catholic tradition, it is now widely popular amongst Christians from a broad range of traditional backgrounds, including many Protestants.[59]

Within the charismatic movement, influencing both Catholic[60] and Protestant traditions, popular books with titles such as *Hearing God*,[61] *Listening to God*,[62] and *God Speaks*,[63] have remained popular for at least three to four decades. Generally speaking, this literature asserts that God speaks to Christians today through an inner voice, but some examples also describe an audible voice arising in the external world. An illustration of a voice of the former kind is described by Joyce Huggett as an example of her own early experiences of "tuning into God". She had just met with a young woman whose mother had unexpectedly collapsed and had been diagnosed as suffering from a brain tumour:

> I sensed that God was asking me to visit her in the nearby hospital. I am not claiming to have heard a voice. I did not. I am saying that an inner awareness that I shall refer to as a "voice:" spoke to me so clearly that I could not escape its implications. Indeed, it was so real that I argued with it. "But, Lord, I don't even know her. What am I supposed to say?"
>
> The voice simply replied, "You go and I'll tell you what to say when you arrive." The realisation that God wanted me to visit this sick woman would not go away. So I went.
>
> (Huggett, 1986, p.29)

In the course of exploring a practice of silent prayer, Huggett describes her further experiences of hearing this voice:

> What I heard in those times of listening was more than a voice. It was a presence. Yes. I heard the Lord call my name. But I also "heard" his tenderness. I soaked up his love. And this listening was on a level which runs deeper than mere words. Sometimes it seemed as though Jesus himself stood in front of me or beside me or above me. This encounter with him overwhelmed me.[64]

Such experiences, by nature of their subjectivity, are clearly open to misinterpretation. Many Christian writers[65] therefore offer criteria by which those that are genuinely "from God" may be distinguished from those that are not. Huggett herself offers four criteria: conformity to scripture, circumstantial support (does what the voice has said come true?), an associated attitude of humility, and a test of whether or not the voice is prompting a way of life which is honouring God.[66]

Experiences of hearing voices in prayer have only attracted serious empirical research over the last decade or so. Simon Dein and Roland Littlewood (2007), in a study of a Pentecostal church in northeast London, identified 25 individuals (out of 40 who completed questionnaires) who reported that they heard God's voice in answer to their prayers. God's voice was reported to be clearly distinguishable from respondents' own voices, associated with positive affective changes and sometimes physical changes (e.g. warmth, feeling light-headed). Informants reported an "inner sense of knowing" that the voice was divine and were commonly able to have a conversation with it. One such conversation is reported as follows, by a woman who had already spent money that she felt should have been given to the church as a "tithe":

> "Look Lord, I am just confessing that I have spent the money and I just don't know how I am going to pay it back to You". I then heard a voice that was in my head and I knew it wasn't me speaking. It basically was saying "It is a huge amount of money you owe and I said, "Yes it is". The voice continued to say "You can't pay it back, it is an unpayable debt" . . . At that moment I felt such a peace and I said "Does that mean that I don't have to pay it Lord". Then this voice said to me "What does God's word say?" I said that God's word says you give a tenth as a tithe and a voice said, "Well you know what to do then". I said "Okay" and we paid all the money but it meant that we had no money for food or bills or anything.[67]

God's voice was also reported in this study as being pragmatic, focusing on immediate and practical issues, and the need for discernment was emphasised, in order to distinguish the voice from one's own thoughts or from other voices (e.g. evil spirits). Respondents said that they would usually obey the voice, but that they had freedom not to. Fifteen out of the 25 reported that they heard God's voice out loud and in external space. This experience was often associated with bewilderment or disbelief. For most of the 15, it was a rare experience and had only happened once.

Similar findings were subsequently obtained by Dein and Cook in a study of a smaller sample drawn from a charismatic evangelical Anglican church in East London (Dein and Cook, 2015). Interviewees reported that God generally communicated with them through thoughts or mental impressions which were understood to provide direction, consolation, and empowerment in the context of the mundane affairs of their daily lives.

Tanya Luhrmann (2012), in *When God Talks Back*, reports on the findings that emerged from her study of the experiences of members of two of the Vineyard churches in the USA, the first in Chicago and then another in California.

> At the Vineyard, people speak about recognizing God's "voice". They talk about things God has "said" to them about very specific topics – where they should go to school and whether they should volunteer in day care – and newcomers are often confused by what they mean. Newcomers soon learn that God is understood to speak to congregants inside their own minds. They learn that someone who worships God at the Vineyard must develop the ability to recognise thoughts in their own mind that are not in fact their thoughts, but God's.[68]

Within these churches, Luhrmann argues:

> Hearing God's voice is a complex process. It is not a simple identification skill, like learning to spot a red-tailed hawk, nor a basic mastery task, like learning to tie your shoes. People clearly thought that an experienced Christian should be more adept than a naïve one, but they also clearly thought that distinguishing God's voice was a richly layered skill.[69]

Hearing God in the Vineyard churches, according to Luhrmann, is thus something that is learned through practice in this tradition of prayer, and she is careful to distinguish this kind of hearing the voice of God from what might more strictly be called an auditory hallucination. True AVHs, heard out loud and in external space, were not unknown in these churches, according to the accounts that Luhrmann elicited, but they were brief, startling, and rare. When such voices are heard, Luhrmann understands them as "sensory overrides". More usually, the voice is experienced as an inner voice, which is not heard out loud, is experienced much more frequently, and does not have the same startling quality.

The process that Luhrmann identifies as important, and which can lead in some cases to sensory overrides, is that of absorption. Absorption, according to Luhrmann, is "the capacity to focus in on the mind's object – what we imagine or see around us – and to allow that focus to increase while diminishing our attention to the myriad of everyday distractions that accompany the management of normal life."[70] For Luhrmann, absorption is central to spirituality: "The capacity to treat what the mind imagines as more real than the world one knows is the capacity at the heart of experience of God."[71]

Absorption is thus – according to Luhrmann – an important part of what goes on in prayer and is something that, at least in part, can be learned. It seems that some people also have more of a proclivity for absorption than others, but it is still something that can be acquired through practice. Luhrmann also found that sensory overrides (although not necessarily auditory, and not always concerned with God) are common.

Within the Vineyard churches, there are unwritten criteria for testing whether or not a voice is God's voice. Luhrmann identified four. First, the question is asked as to whether or not this is something that the person in question might have imagined themselves. If it is, then the presumption is interestingly that it is the person's own thought, and not God's voice.[72] Second, the question is posed as to whether or not it is the kind of thing that God might say, and particularly whether or not it is consistent with biblical teaching. The third question, or test, is concerned with consistency with circumstances and with the kinds of things that others are "hearing" in prayer. Finally, God's voice is said to be associated with a sense of peace.

Christian experiences of hearing voices

Christian experiences of hearing the voice of God, not to mention the voices of saints, evil spirits, or angels, are clearly diverse. However, at risk of overgeneralising, they do usually seem to be accounts of internal experience – "mental goings on" – expressed in the language of a presumed external theological reality. Sometimes we are offered nuanced and careful accounts of the internal experience, but not all Christian writers are careful to provide this. Joyce Huggett's careful acknowledgement that she is talking about an "inner awareness" that she will refer to as a "voice" – even though she is careful to say also that it is not a voice, and that this is more than a voice (more an affectively laden presence) – is unfortunately rare.

Nor are all Christians as careful as Mother Teresa to clarify that they place no weight on such experiences, because they have other reasons for believing what they do. However, traditions of criteria for testing whether or not the "voice" might be God's clearly acknowledge the widespread understanding that people do get it wrong. So, there is a system of checks for agreement between the account of inner experience and the presumed, external, theological reality. The nature of the checks tells us a lot about the theological presumptions. Evangelicals are keen to assert the importance of consistency with biblical teaching. The Ignatian rules for discernment are more focused on the subtleties and complexities of temptation to sin and experiences of suffering. They recognise the multivocal and deceptive nature of Christian experience, with the good and bad spirits vying for our attention perhaps not being too far removed from the activities of Dennett's word-demons.

Christian experiences of voices – especially of the voice of God – are not "just" experiences of voices. They often are associated with an experienced sense of presence and, even where this is not explicitly evident, they represent a mode of relationship with God. This is sometimes transacted in a once-in-a-lifetime kind of way, where crisis and transformation are marked by voices or visions as evidence of God's concerned presence and involvement in Christian lives at their lowest or highest points. In other cases, it is more of an ongoing affair of the daily round of prayer amid the mundane realities of Christian life. In either case, the voices reflect a contextual involvement of God in Christian lives. They are evidence of the presence, compassion, and involvement of God in individual human concerns.

This dynamic – of voices as transforming presence – is no less evident in mental illness than in so-called "normal" Christian religious experience. However, it is clearly more complicated here. Just as Ignatius recognised that sometimes things that seem pleasing can be a hindrance in the spiritual life, and things that are unsettling can be good for us, so in the context of mental illness voices can be deceiving. Voices from God can prove to be something that must be put aside, and the voice of the devil can draw attention to the need for positive change. In each case, the voice acts as a kind of signpost for something more important – an experience of the presence of God.

Notes

1 For further discussion and critique, see Seager (2016, especially pp.182–184).
2 Dennett (1991, p.242ff.).
3 Auditory verbal hallucinations; see Introduction.
4 I haven't found anywhere that Dennett explicitly says this – but it seems to me to be a logical possibility, given his model of consciousness.
5 Stark (2017, p.73). See also Stark (1965).
6 Alston (1991, p.35), Proudfoot (1985, p.155). Similarly, Caroline Franks Davis describes the quest as "fruitless" (1989, p.29).
7 Lash (1986, pp.154–157, 1988).
8 For example, Gabrielle Bossis (1874–1950), a Roman Catholic nurse, would appear to have had exclusively voice hearing experiences (Bossis, 2013). St Maria Faustina Kowalska (1905–1938), apart from two significant visions of Jesus, appears to have had primarily experiences of hearing the voice of Jesus/God (Drabik, 2007).
9 Swinburne (2004, pp.298–301).
10 Hick considers Paul's experience on the Damascus Road, albeit occurring two or three years later, to be essentially similar in form to that of Peter and (possibly) other witnesses to resurrection appearances of Jesus (Hick, 1993, p.24).
11 Ibid., p.25.
12 See, for example, de Menezes and Moreira-Almeida (2009), where criteria are proposed for the differential diagnosis of spiritual experiences and mental disorders

with religious content. The discussion by Franks Davis (1989, pp.210–216) is also illustrative of this trend. She, however, also perceptively observes that the distinction is suspect: "After all, it is possible that God can get through to the mentally abnormal more easily than he can to those of us who are 'properly' oriented towards mundane realities" (p.73).

13 By the same token, I may evaluate the conversion of a person from Religion A (with which I agree) to Religion B (with which I disagree) as a retrograde one. However, this does not mean that it is not a religious experience.

14 Donato (2013, pp.144–151).

15 See, for example, a helpful introduction by Julia Lamm (2013).

16 Lefebure (2013).

17 See, for example, a helpful discussion by Braud (2002).

18 Franks Davis (1989).

19 I would suggest that Origen, Gregory of Nyssa, Bernard of Clairvaux, Thérèse of Lisieux, and Thomas Merton all also fall into the category of Christian mystics who appear never to have heard voices, but I would love to hear from any reader who has evidence to the contrary.

20 Such experiences will be considered further later in this chapter.

21 Fremantle and Auden (1964), McGinn (2015, 2016).

22 Stace (1973, p.47).

23 Ibid., p.50.

24 McGinn (1991, pp.xvii–xviii).

25 Similarly, see Grace Jantzen's incisive critique of William James' understanding of mystical experience (Jantzen, 2008). Jantzen perhaps puts more emphasis on union than on presence, but her arguments follow a similar trajectory to Lash. Voices and visions, she writes, are (at best) "a help toward the ongoing project of increasing union with God" (p.313). However, union is still (according to Jantzen) an experiential matter in the broad sense, and so I think my response to her is similar to my response to McGinn. Where we all agree is in the critical importance of evidence of transforming impact of the alleged experience of God – as (for example – in Jantzen's discussion of Julian of Norwich) in the form of "contrition, compassion, and longing for God" (p.311).

26 See Chapter 3.

27 It is, of course, very difficult to say how the validity or truth of such an experience could ever – unequivocally – be established in practice. It might be easier (as discussed in Chapter 3 in the context of Hebrew prophecy) to eliminate some clearly spurious claims than to affirm beyond doubt those which plausibly may, or may not, be instances of God having spoken. The shift in emphasis that is being asserted here, however, is to move away from the question of whether or not God might be understood to have "spoken" in favour of the importance of discerning whether or not the hearer of the voice has listened well and has shown discernment and discrimination in interpreting what they have heard.

28 McGinn (1991, pp.xix–xx, 1994, p.327).

29 McGinn (1991, pp. xvii–xix).

30 I acknowledge, of course, that the medieval understanding of the *visio Dei* was one of "seeing" God. However, as McGinn explore elsewhere (McGinn, 2007), this emphasis on the visual was (and is) not unproblematic. There are biblical grounds for asserting that God cannot be seen, and those forms of vision that are accorded greater weight (as with the Augustinian typology) are those which are less perception-like and least associated with images of any kind. If an intellectual vision is image-free, an intellectual voice is presumably word-free, and it is not clear why the latter should be considered any less an experience of the *visio Dei* than the former. In any case, there is also a strong argument that the interpretation of the biblical notion of the *visio Dei* has varied significantly down

the centuries, and there would seem to be no reason to prioritise the medieval mystical understanding (Viljoen, 2012).

31 McGinn (1994, p.337).
32 There is an interesting paradox here in that, whilst affirming the transforming nature of contact with God as being important, and affirming Elisabeth as "prophet, reformer, and teacher" (thus, presumably, both transformed and transformative), Elisabeth is yet understood not to be a mystic because of the "mediated" nature of her contact with God.
33 McGinn distinguishes "mystical authors" from mystics and visionaries (McGinn, 1994, p.327). I don't find the emphasis on authorship helpful, and so am not employing that terminology. However, the principle of looking for evidence of teaching, example, and impact on others is clearly one with which I wholeheartedly agree. It is essentially similar to James' dictum "by their fruits ye shall know them" (James, 1902, p.29).
34 See, notably, Soelle (2001) for a sustained engagement with the idea that authentic mysticism is inherently transformative.
35 Miller and C'de Baca (2001, p.86).
36 Oates (1998, pp.88–89).
37 Starbuck did not specifically ask about voices or visions – but he did ask whether the conversion experience was "attended by unnatural sights, sounds or feelings" (p.23). Some examples of voices were reported. For example, one woman, reporting on her conversion at age 12 years, recorded: 'Suddenly I felt a touch as of the Divine One, and a voice said, 'Thy sins are forgiven thee; arise, go in peace'" (p.79). Another example given is clearly that of Matthew Fox (p.87; see also p.22).
38 Iyadurai (2015, p.15).
39 Ibid., p.23.
40 See also the story of Sadhu Sindar Singh, related in Chapter 5.
41 Atkins (1978, pp.229–230).
42 Ibid., p.230.
43 Franks Davis (1989).
44 Bishop Montefiore provides a separate account of the same events elsewhere, in which he states that he heard the words "Follow me" "in [his] mind's ear" (Montefiore, 2002, p.234). He also writes: "I feel sure that if anyone had been present with a tape recorder or a camcorder, nothing would have registered" (p.234). It is difficult to imagine that he would have written this if the voice had been merely a thought. (No one feels the need to clarify that a tape recorder would not have recorded their thoughts.) The voice therefore seems to have had a quality somewhere between an auditory perceptual experience and a thought – more like a voice than a thought, but less external and perceptual in its quality than the voice of another person. On the other hand, Bishop Montefiore wrote at some length on Christian visions and hallucinations (pp.213–252), and this qualification of the nature of the voice may well be simply his own clarification that he realised that the voice was a personal and subjective experience, rather than having been something that others might have heard. He goes on to say that he felt sure that his visual cortex and auditory cortex were "in some way involved". Despite this, he stops short of referring to it as an "hallucination" and says that he could not account for his vision on the basis of "any of the psychological or neurophysiological explanations on offer" (p.235).
45 McHargue (2016, p.125).
46 Kolodiejchuk (2007, p.40).
47 Ibid., p.44.
48 Ibid., p.99.
49 Ibid.

50 Ibid., pp.87–88.
51 McKenna and Libersat (1987, pp.5–6).
52 Marshall (1951, p.14).
53 Ibid., p.15.
54 Neal (2014, p.57).
55 Fenwick and Fenwick (1995, p.94).
56 Ibid., p.62.
57 Ibid.
58 Barber (2016, p.126).
59 A wide range of popular books, by authors such as Margaret Silf, have made this spiritual tradition accessible to all Christians. See, for example, Sheldrake (1991), Silf (1998, 2004).
60 Most of the examples cited here are from Protestant sources, but Briege McKenna (a Roman Catholic nun whose voices associated with calling and vocation were referred to above) also gives examples of a similar kind (McKenna and Libersat, 1987 – see, for example, pp.26, 33–34, 38, 94, 96, 101–102, 126).
61 Willard (1999). Numerous other books with similar titles can easily be found online, or in Christian bookshops.
62 Huggett (1986). This book, which has now been in print for over 30 years, has been especially influential in evangelical Christian circles in the UK. Located within the evangelical charismatic tradition, it also draws on catholic and contemplative traditions of spirituality.
63 Praying Medic (2017). This book includes chapter-length accounts of the experience by 28 different authors.
64 Huggett (1986, p.33).
65 See, for example, Williamson (2016), Praying Medic (2017, pp.59–68, 243–244).
66 Huggett (1986, p.145).
67 Dein and Littlewood (2007, p.220).
68 Luhrmann (2012, p.39).
69 Ibid., p.60.
70 Ibid., p.200.
71 Ibid., p.201.
72 This seems to be a very pessimistic view of the Christian ability to imagine what God might say!

7 Hearing the voice of God
Science and theology

Given that Christian scripture and tradition are replete with descriptions of the hearing of voices of angels, saints, demons, and of God himself, and that contemporary accounts of religious experiences involving voices are also not hard to find, what do these voices mean?

One possible answer might be to argue that such voices are meaningless. Whilst it is not always explicitly asserted, this appears to be the implicit view of the many authors who have asserted that prophets, saints and mystics, and even Jesus Christ, all heard voices because they were mentally ill.[1] A softer version of this approach might normalise the phenomenon to some degree, recognising that many people who hear voices are not diagnosed as mentally ill. Nonetheless, such voices are still to be explained on the basis of a variety of scientific models which privilege cause over meaning. The phenomenon may have meaning as a sign or symptom of some kind, but the content of the voice – what it says – remains meaningless or unimportant.

The validity of this approach is increasingly coming under pressure from voice hearers who assert that their experiences do have meaning (Woods, 2013), and in particular from the Hearing Voices Movement (Corstens et al., 2014). Moreover, the finding of meaning in what voices say is proving to be relevant to effective treatment (Dillon and Hornstein, 2013). The reductionist approach, and especially its cruder psychiatric manifestations, are thus increasingly being found unsatisfactory at best, and stigmatising at worst. In this context, spiritual and religious content of what voices say – amongst other things that they say – is again being recognised as potentially meaningful.

An approach adopted by some who affirm the importance of spirituality/ religion is to assert that some voices might be indicative of mental illness, but that others might be "genuine" spiritual/religious experiences. Thus, for example, Menezes and Moreira-Almeida (2010) have suggested criteria by which a differential diagnosis may be made between spiritual experiences and psychotic disorder.[2] This approach is problematic for a number of reasons. First, it offers a mutually exclusive choice. Either someone is psychotic, or they are having a genuine spiritual experience, but not both. It is not at all clear why this has to be the case. Why can someone not be psychotic and having a spiritual experience?[3] Second, the criteria do not relate to the content of the hallucinations or other phenomena, but only (or mainly) to the form of the psychopathology and associated signs and symptoms. They thus prioritise psychiatry over spirituality. Third, the distinction is largely one of exclusion. If mental illness is not present, then the experience seems to be accepted as spiritually "normal" in some sense. The criteria do not discriminate between good and bad, helpful or unhelpful, spiritual content.

The notion that there might be spiritual truth to be conveyed by what a voice says is potentially a big claim. On the one hand, it might be acknowledged as a kind of personal truth, meaningful to the individual whether or not God actually exists. In this case, any assertions about a spiritual realm, or theological reality, made by the voice hearer or their voices need not be accepted by another person. On the other hand, the preceding chapters of this book have sought to make clear that there are many cases within different faith traditions, and particularly within the Christian tradition, where a spiritual or theological truth conveyed by a voice has been understood as more widely meaningful. That is, other people have shared with the hearer of the voice a sense that what the voice conveyed was spiritually or theologically significant. This wider sense of asserting the spiritual or theological validity of what a voice has said is potentially problematic within a faith community, and even more so in a context of spiritual/religious plurality. Who is to judge what is a genuine spiritual/religious experience, and on what grounds?

As we have seen in earlier chapters of this book, Christian scripture and tradition offer ample scope for claiming that people have heard the voices of God, of saints and angels, and even of demons. According to the Niceno-Constantinopolitan Creed, God has "spoken by the prophets", and Pentecostal and charismatic Christians, amongst others, do not consider this to be something that ceased in a bygone age. As discussed in Chapter 6, there are plenty of contemporary examples of religious experiences involving voice hearing. There is also evidence that social stigma (high levels of which are experienced by voice hearers in general) is less amongst more religious (mainly Christian) people specifically in relation to those who report hearing the voice of God, but only as long as the reported content of the voice is positive (Phalen et al., 2018). This suggests that the possibility of hearing the voice of God is positively accepted, and perhaps even affirmed, within at least some Christian communities.

A more critical hermeneutic might dismiss much of this as pre-scientific and naïve and embark upon a programme of demythologisation.[4] However, quite apart from the fact that many ordinary Christians do not take this view, it is not at all clear in a context of increasing scientific awareness of the nature of voice hearing that voices can or should be "demythologised" at all. Voices and visions, for Bultmann, were to be understood as a part of a pre-scientific mythical world view (as discussed in Chapter 2). They are now very firmly a part of a scientific and non-mythical understanding of human experience.

Spiritual/religious meaning is not the only kind of meaning that might be identified in voices. Some voices might indeed be signs or symptoms of mental illness, not only according to professional opinion, but also according to the understanding of the person hearing the voice. Jones et al. (2003) identified six constellations of beliefs by way of which voice hearers understood their experiences, only three of which involved any element of spirituality. In this study, two out of twenty participants adopted a mental illness framework for understanding their voices. Four subjects understood their voices within a personal, psychological and biographical, framework. However, the six clusters of beliefs were not found to be entirely mutually exclusive. One subject, for example, adopted both a spiritual and a psychological framework for understanding their voices and such an approach may have much to commend it. Voices may have meaning at multiple different levels at the same time – psychologically, spiritually, biographically, and in other ways.

In the next chapter, the focus will be on a critical exploration of whether and how voices that are spiritually or theologically meaningful may be distinguished – in the Christian tradition – from those that are not. However, a prior question must first be explored. Given what is now known scientifically about voices as naturally occurring phenomena, which may or may not include spiritual/religious content, is it ever possible to understand them as being divinely inspired? This question becomes most acute when the voice is understood to be the voice of God, but it is still important when the voice is understood to be that of an angel, saint, spirit, or demon. How can the possibility of a spiritual communication be reconciled with scientifically explicable processes within the nature order – if at all? In order to address this question, we must turn first to the scientific literature. What has scientific research revealed about the nature and development of the phenomenon of hearing voices?

Varieties of voices

Experts now seem to be agreed that AVHs[5] are found in a wide range of psychiatric disorders (Kelleher and Devylder, 2017, Waters and Fernyhough, 2017)[6] and are also seen in the absence of pathology, as a manifestation of neurodiversity (Schrader, 2013). There is also general agreement that AVHs are diverse and do not represent a unitary phenomenon. However, they may be subtyped and classified on a variety of different grounds, including phenomenology, cognitive processes, neurology, causal antecedents, response to treatment, psychiatric diagnosis, and voice hearers' own attributions (McCarthy-Jones et al., 2014a). There is currently little agreement as to the best single approach to classification.[7]

In the preceding chapters, diverse examples have been given of different ways in which people have had the experience of hearing spiritual and religious voices. The heavenly voice at Jesus' baptism, the voice heard by

Francis at San Damiano, the voices heard by Margery Kempe or Joan of Arc, are all very different. Jesus, Francis, and Margery all heard the voice of God; Margery heard the voices of Jesus, God the Father, and various saints, not to mention non-verbal sounds that she took to be the Holy Spirit. Joan heard the voice of an angel and the voices of saints for whom there now appears to be no historical basis. She heard the voices – to put it bluntly – of people who never lived. For Jesus and Francis, the voices seem to have been very infrequent. For Joan and Margery, they were very common – more or less daily – experiences for much of their lives. All of this might be taken to reflect the same kind of diversity that current scientific research has shown to be in the nature of the phenomenon. However, ancient voices clearly present greater difficulties than contemporary accounts. The more scientific approach that is now adopted by historians was not the context within which any of the texts in question were written and, arguably, literary approaches to interpreting the texts have as much or more to contribute than the historical-critical method.

We simply cannot know exactly what the experiences of Jesus or Peter were, far less of Ezekiel or Moses (assuming that the latter was an historical character at all). The narratives with which we are left still situate voice hearing firmly within the Judeo-Christian tradition, but do they have any historical basis at all? Given that religious experience is inseparable from cultural and religious context, this is very significant. Jews and Christians believe in a God who is taken – according to their sacred texts – to "speak" to his people. Contemporary accounts of hearing God speak, whether derived from biographies or research studies, must to some extent reflect the expectations that this tradition creates, but this does not mean that they are the same kinds of experience as those found in the tradition.

We should therefore be wary of assuming too much common ground between contemporary and historic experiences of "hearing voices", even within the Christian tradition. It would appear that we are likely to be dealing with a wide variety of phenomena, some of which might be quite similar and others quite different. However, there is also little or no reason to believe that voice hearing as currently reported is a new experience, completely unknown to the ancient or medieval world. We might reasonably assume that people then, as now, were hearing voices but that their experience was simply understood differently – whether as a religious or mystical experience, as due to demons or magic, or in some other way. We should therefore also be wary of assuming too little common ground between contemporary and historical experiences of hearing voices. At least some of the voices recorded in scripture and other historical, mystical and theological literature may well reflect similar underlying experiences to those who report hearing voices today. We must simply remember that we do not have any direct access to those underlying experiences. We only have the texts that have been passed down to us.

The phenomenology of voice hearing

What are the voices that people hear today actually like?

In a study of the phenomenology of AVHs in 30 outpatients (Stephane et al., 2003), drawn from a larger sample with diagnoses of schizophrenia, schizoaffective disorder and psychotic depression, a cluster analysis revealed two main types of voices. The first had low linguistic complexity, were repetitive, located in outer space, but identified as one's own, and patients attempted to control them. The second type had high linguistic complexity, systematised content, were often multiple voices, were located in inner space and were attributed to others. Three important dimensions of voices were identified: linguistic complexity, attribution to self or others, and location in inner or outer space.

In a more recent and larger study, McCarthy-Jones et al. (2014b) studied the phenomenology of voices of 199 psychiatric patients (81 per cent with a diagnosis of schizophrenia). The results of the cluster analysis partly replicated those of Stephane et al. (2003) but also produced some new findings. The first cluster was described by the authors as "Constant Commanding and Commenting" and represents the typical voice-hearing experience of patients with schizophrenia. This group were seen as being similar to the first type identified by Stephane et al, and were typically repetitive. Three less common subtypes were also identified. The "Replay" type experienced voices which were identical to memories – something which Stephane et al. did not study – and which might be related to a history of traumatic abuse. An "Own Thought" type comprised first person voices which were recognised as possibly belonging to the patient's own voice/thoughts. This group included some voices/thoughts which were similar to (but not identical) with memories. Overall, 39 per cent of patients reported voices that seemed to be similar to, or identical with, memories of conversations. Finally, the "Nonverbal" type included words that did not make sense and other non-verbal sounds.

In a major UK study of 153 participants recruited by advertisement from voice hearing groups and clinical/mental health contexts, most voice hearers (81 per cent) described multiple voices, and less than half (46 per cent) reported literally auditory voices (Woods et al., 2015). Although voices were often associated with unpleasant affective states (anxiety, depression, fear), 31 per cent reported a positive emotional experience, and for 32 per cent it was a neutral emotional experience.

Importantly, voices are not "just" voices. Woods et al (2015) reported that 69 per cent of their respondents had "characterful" qualities. The voice was either identifiable as a specific, recognisable, individual (22 per cent) or at least had person-like qualities – of age, gender, emotional tone and intent. 16 per cent of voices in this study were identified as emanating from supernatural agents. Voices are generally perceived as being the voice of someone specific – an individual "agent" (Wilkinson and Bell, 2016, Leudar et al., 1997). They are thus acts of communication and many voice hearers can engage in dialogue with their voice and may form a relationship with "the voice" or, rather, the agent understood to be the source of the voice (Chin et al., 2009). These observations may have important implications both for the chronicity of the experience (Benjamin, 1989) and for potentially effective forms of therapy (Corstens et al., 2012), Deamer and Wilkinson, 2015.

Voices may also be described as a "presence". Paradoxically, some voice hearers describe awareness of this presence even when the voice is not speaking (Alderson-Day, 2016).

"Voices" may thus be more like thoughts than (out-loud) voices, but they are also more than simply voices. They are encounters – both with a characterful entity, perhaps even a personality – and also with elements of oneself, with memories and traumas of the past.

Inner speech

Voices are quite like the inner speech which characterises the waking mental life of almost all human beings. When people "think" about things, this process of thought is conscious, private, coherent, active (something we "do") and – notably for the present purpose – it is usually linguistic (Fernyhough, 2016, p.7). It is not always the case that we think in words, images also play a part and some thoughts are a bit ineffable, and a small number of people seem not to engage in inner speech at all, but to a large extent the thoughts that pass through most of our minds are rather like an inner voice. This inner speech is important. It helps to motivate us, to regulate and evaluate our behaviour, and simply to be conscious of ourselves (Fernyhough, 2016, p.11). Inner speech is often dialogical – we can have a conversation with ourselves. It is creative and reflective.[8] It also forms the basis for much mental prayer, although this is not an aspect of inner speech that has attracted much scientific research to date.

Like inner speech, voices (verbal hallucinations) frequently talk about mundane things related to the ongoing activities of the person hearing them. They influence the decisions that people make. They are dialogical, imparting information and making suggestions (Leudar et al., 1997). Of course, they are also different to inner speech in some important ways. Most patients with schizophrenia clearly distinguish their voices from their own thoughts. In particular they identify them as recognisably not their own voice, distinctly different in content, and outside their own control (Hoffman et al., 2008).[9] Other voice hearers also distinguish between their voices and their thoughts, although the distinctions are apparently not always clear-cut. In a cross-diagnostic study, including clinical and non-clinical voice hearers, Woods et al. (2015) found that 9 per cent of respondents reported that their voices were more thought like than auditory, and 37 per cent reported a mixture of auditory and thought-like qualities. Interestingly, most subjects who reported non-auditory voices still referred to them as "voices".

The voices heard by people not diagnosed with schizophrenia are, in general terms, similar to the voices of those who are so diagnosed. It is not possible to reliably distinguish the hallucinations of schizophrenia from other diagnostic groups or from non-clinical groups of voice hearers (except perhaps on the basis of age of onset). Non-clinical groups do tend to report more positive interpretations of their voices, and more positive affective concomitants, but these differences are not reliable for making a diagnosis (Honig et al., 1998, Jenner et al., 2008, Johns et al., 2014, Woods et al., 2015, Waters and Fernyhough, 2017).

This acknowledgement of the similarity of voices (AVHs) with inner speech has formed the basis for the most popular and influential theory of how voices arise. Source monitoring theory (SMT) proposes that individuals use a variety of cognitive monitoring processes in order to determine whether an experience arises from within the self of from the external world. According to the theory, AVHs are utterances of inner speech which, due to some kind of fault in the monitoring process, are wrongly attributed to external sources (Garrett and Silva, 2003). Neuroscientific research finds some support for this theory both in neuroimaging studies, which show activation of similar areas of brain cortex during AVHs and inner speech,[10] and also electromyographic studies which show subvocalisation (contractions of vocal muscles similar but smaller than those occurring during normal speech) during both inner speech and AVHs. Recently, a reduction in the length of the paracingulate sulcus – a brain region with a previously established role in reality monitoring – has been associated with an almost 20 per cent increase in likelihood of experience of hallucinations (Garrison et al., 2015). Preliminary findings also suggest the efficacy of neuromagnetic stimulation of the relevant cortical areas as a possible treatment for AVHs (Moseley et al., 2013).

Developmentally, according to the work of the psychologist Lev Vygotsky (1896–1934), children learn first to talk to others, then engage in private (but vocalised) speech with themselves, and only then learn to internalise this speech as the private inner speech that is a common feature of adult life. Initially, this inner speech is just like external speech, only silent. The fully internalised inner speech of adults, however, is also further "condensed" in such a way that it loses many of the qualities of normal speech, retaining only an abbreviated syntax which emphasises sense and meaning over verbalisation. Source monitoring errors, understood within this context, may therefore be either a failure of internalisation processes, or else a problem with re-expansion of condensed inner speech into a fully expanded inner speech. In either case, it is the appearance in the mind of the unexpectedly fully expanded inner speech which is experienced as alien (Fernyhough, 2004, Fernyhough and McCarthy-Jones, 2013).

A number of problems may be identified with SMT. For example, why are AVHs typically of the voices of others, and not one's own voice? And how can it account for hallucinations in other modalities? One variation on the theory has been to suggest that AVHs are not so much like inner speech as "imagined speech" (Gregory, 2016). The problem is still to do with source monitoring – in this case, of imagined speech, rather than inner speech – but (according to its proponents) it is because we imagine others speaking (rather than ourselves) that AVHs so typically appear as alien – the voice of another person. Arguably, this theory also has greater potential to explain hallucinations in other modalities.

Another problem with SMT is that it doesn't entirely explain how AVHs are experienced as voices, rather than thoughts. This leads on to the related question of whether and how AVHs may be distinguished from thought insertion – the experience that one's thoughts are not one's own (Humpston and Broome, 2015, Ratcliffe and Wilkinson, 2015, Wilkinson and Alderson-Day, 2015). SMT further doesn't explain the diversity and variety of different types of AVHs. These problems with SMT have recently been addressed by predictive processing and "top–down" theories (PPT).

Predictive processing theory

According to PPT, the incoming perceptual signals that the brain receives (the "bottom–up" part of the process) are potentially ambiguous and can be interpreted in a variety of possible ways (Wilkinson, 2014, Powers et al., 2016). A "bottom–up" model of how the brain processes perceptual information is thus, on its own, inadequate. Accordingly, it is proposed, the brain evaluates hypotheses as to the correct interpretation of perceptual information according to its knowledge and expectations of what the external world is like. It tries to predict what is most likely to be going on in the external world. This "top–down" influence of higher cognitive processes upon perception relies on the brain's predictions of what it expects to perceive as much (or more) than the actual perceptual input that it receives (from the bottom up). Perceptual (or perception-like) experiences can thus be generated both "top–down" – from within the brain – and "bottom–up" from incoming perceptual information. According to this model, AVHs arise due to prediction errors. For one reason or another, the brain predicts a voice when there is actually no external voice to be heard. The "top–down" influence of this prediction, and the expectation that it creates, is such as to generate a perception-like experience in the absence of any corresponding external stimulus.

PPT can be applied to a variety of potential sources for AVHs, of which inner speech is only one. For example, Wilkinson (2014) applies PPT to inner speech, memory, and hypervigilance as three different subtypes of AVHs. In each case, prediction errors result in material actually derived from internal (inner speech/memory) or external (hypervigilance) sources being interpreted and experienced as voices. PPT is therefore better able than SMT to explain the variety of kinds of AVH, and the fact that AVHs often sound more like voices than thoughts.

PPT is also concerned with how people give attention to things, and what they give attention to. In predictive processing terms, attention is a state of "high precision weighting". That is, when we give attention to things, we are more confident in what we perceive but also more likely to get it wrong. Hallucinations appear to be more likely in two scenarios (at least in psychosis): when attention is directed inwards in a quiet environment, and when it is directed outwards in a noisy environment (Wilkinson, 2014, Garwood et al., 2015).

Learning and culture

Tanya Luhrmann, an anthropologist, also considers attention to be an important factor in understanding hallucinations. She proposes that hallucinations "are shaped by explicit and implicit learning around the ways that people pay attention with their senses" (Luhrmann, 2011, p.72). Luhrmann believes that hallucinations are shaped both by culture – and particularly by local theories of mind – and by practices of mental cultivation.

In contrast to proposals that hallucinations are part of a continuous spectrum of psychotic symptoms in the population (Johns and Os, 2001), Luhrmann (2017, Luhrmann et al., 2010) distinguishes between pathological and non-pathological hallucinations. Whilst she acknowledges that the psychosis spectrum approach reflects a laudable desire to destigmatise serious mental illness, she observes that eliminating the distinction between pathological and non-pathological hallucinations has the consequence of identifying spiritual experiences as "akin to psychiatric illness".[11]

Luhrmann proposes that "it seems clear that there are, broadly speaking, three different patterns of hallucination experience that transcend culture: sensory overrides, psychosis, and the Joan of Arc pattern".[12] Sensory overrides are non-pathological, and Luhrmann employs this terminology, in part, to distinguish them from AVHs. They are typically brief, infrequent, focused on immediate (mundane) concerns, and are not distressing. Amongst a number of examples that she gives from her work with charismatic Christians is the following interview excerpt:

Congregant 1: I was walking up the lake and down the lake and I was like, should I go home now? And he [God] is like, "sit and listen."

Ethnographer: Did you hear that outside or inside your head?

Congregant 1: That's hard to tell, but in this instance it really felt like it was outside.

Ethnographer: How many times do you think you've heard his voice outside your head?

Congregant 1: Two or three.[13]

In another example, a different interviewee says:

I remember praying for a job and I interviewed and I didn't know whether I was going to take it or not. Then when I was cleaning out my room, I heard a voice say, "that's not the one." And then I said, what? I looked around, and I'm like, maybe that's someone outside. Then I realized: I clearly heard God say, "that's not the one." I have no doubt in my mind that it was God.[14]

Luhrmann understands sensory overrides as being associated with "absorption", a state not uncommonly arising in the course of spiritual practice:

Absorption is the capacity to become focused on the mind's object—what humans imagine or see around them—and to allow that focus to increase while diminishing attention to the myriad of everyday distractions that accompany the management of normal life.[15]

A proclivity for absorption is associated with sharper mental imagery, focused attention, more unusual spiritual experiences, and a predisposition to hallucinatory experiences (Glicksohn and Barrett, 2003, Luhrmann et al., 2010). Expectation is thought by Luhrmann to play an important part in predisposition to sensory overrides, and spiritual practice (or training) also makes sensory overrides more likely.[16]

The second pattern that Luhrmann identifies is that of psychosis. Hallucinations in psychosis are typically repeated and/or more extended, frequent, unpleasant, and distressing. She asserts that they are widely recognised as a feature of illness, in diverse cultures.

The third type, also non-pathological, is what Luhrmann refers to as the "Joan of Arc pattern". This pattern is much less common (according to Luhrmann) and is typified by frequent unusual sensory experiences but without the distress, associated delusions, flattening of affect, and impairment of social/cognitive functioning associated with psychosis. Historical examples proposed include Joan of Arc, Moses, and Mohammed, and contemporary examples, it is proposed, may include those reported by Romme and Escher (1989).

This classification of types of voices – as we have seen – sits alongside other typologies, at least some of which have more clearly demonstrated empirical validation, and none of which have received unanimous acclaim. However, sensory overrides would appear to be a different phenomenon, which are well documented in Luhrmann's publications, based upon her careful fieldwork, and highly relevant to groups engaged in spiritual/religious practice. It would appear unlikely that sensory overrides are represented in most phenomenological studies of clinical groups, and quite possibly also not represented in great numbers in many studies of non-clinical voice hearers. They are likely to be observed in religious groups other than Christianity (Luhrmann and Morgain, 2012, p.382) and also (less commonly) in some other spiritual but non-religious practices such as tulpamancy.

Luhrmann's category of a separate "Joan of Arc pattern" is more debatable. Joan did suffer distress as a result of her voices, and it is not at all clear that her voices were similar to those of Mohammed or other historic religious figures. Luhrmann is not alone in confidently asserting that Moses heard voices,[17] even though many critical biblical scholars have significant doubts about whether an historic figure named Moses ever lived. However, this does not commend the category as a coherent and reliably identifiable form of voice hearing.

Beyond Luhrmann's work, it is clear that the human creature does not exist in isolation, and hallucinations occur as phenomena that arise from within the interaction between biological, psychological, social, and cultural factors (Laroi et al., 2014). In particular, hallucinations conform to cultural expectations. The frequency of occurrence of hallucinations also varies between different cultural and ethnic groups. In a study of 5,196 people belonging to ethnic minorities in the UK, AVHs were reported by 1.2 per cent of white subjects, 2.8 per cent of Caribbean subjects, and 0.6 per cent of South Asian subjects (Johns et al., 2002). Rates of hallucinations in patients diagnosed with schizophrenia also vary around the world. In a study of 1,080 patients diagnosed according to DSM-IV criteria, drawn from seven countries, the one-year prevalence of auditory hallucinations varied from 66.9 per cent in Austria to 90.8 per cent in Ghana (Bauer et al., 2011).

In three samples of 20 voice-hearing subjects with a DSM-IV diagnosis of schizophrenia, drawn respectively from the USA, India, and Ghana, Luhrmann et al. found that the content of the hallucinations, and the understanding of the experience, were different in the three countries. Subjects from the USA were more likely to hear voices telling them to hurt themselves or others (n=14) and all used diagnostic language in their conversation with the researcher. Five reported hearing the voice of God. More than half of the subjects from India heard the voices of relatives (n=11), only four heard voices telling them to hurt themselves or others (n=9), and only four used the term "schizophrenia" in conversation with the researcher. Nine understood their voices as spirits or magical, and six had heard God speak audibly. In Ghana, only two subjects heard voices telling them to hurt themselves or others, only two used diagnostic labels in conversation with the researcher, and sixteen heard God speak audibly to them. Unlike subjects in the USA or India (whose experiences were largely or entirely negative), half of the subjects in Ghana reported that hearing voices was a positive experience. There is thus considerable cultural variation as to the attribution of voices, the content of what they say, and the degree of distress experienced as a result of hearing them.

Trauma

Perhaps one of the most striking findings to emerge from voice-hearing research in recent years is that of the strong association of voices with traumatic events, and especially (but not exclusively) with childhood abuse (McCarthy-Jones, 2011b, 2017). In an analysis of the 2007 Adult Psychiatric Morbidity Survey data, people raped before the age of 16 years were six times more likely to have experienced AVHs in the 12 months prior to assessment (Bentall et al., 2012).

In a study of 127 non-psychotic individuals with AVHs, 100 psychotic patients with AVHs, and 124 healthy controls, both groups with AVHs were found to have experienced significantly higher rates of childhood trauma than controls (Daalman et al., 2012). For non-psychotic individuals with AVHs, the odds ratios were 2.5 for sexual abuse and 7.3 for emotional abuse. For psychotic individuals with AVHs, the odds ratios were 3.6 and 5.7 respectively. There was no significant difference in experience of childhood trauma between the two groups experiencing AVHs.

In a study of 100 clinical cases (mostly diagnosed with schizophrenia) with an average of 18 years' experience of hearing voices, at least one adverse childhood experience was reported by 89 per cent of the sample (Corstens and Longden, 2013). In 78 per cent of subjects, the identity of the voice reflected lived experience, for example, as aspects of the self (48 per cent) or an abusive (45 per cent) or non-abusive (30 per cent) family member. In 94 per cent, voices reflected representations of experienced social-emotional conflicts.

Neurobiology

Neuroimaging studies of clinical and non-clinical subjects experiencing AVHs have demonstrated anatomical and functional alterations in brain areas associated with speech and hearing, notably in the insula and superior temporal gyri (Allen et al., 2008, 2012, Diederen et al., 2012, Palaniyappan et al., 2012, Modinos et al., 2013). Preliminary evidence suggests that there may also be alterations of cerebral blood flow in the superior temporal gyrus and related brain areas (Zhuo et al., 2017). Functional connectivity between the left and right superior temporal gyri, and between the left inferior frontal gyrus and other relevant brain regions, also seems to be important, although studies to date have variously shown disconnection and/or hyperconnectivity in different pathways (Hoffman and Hampson, 2012, Diederen et al., 2013). In particular, some studies have demonstrated disruption of the arcuate fasciculus, a tract connecting frontal and temporo-parietal language areas (De Weijer et al., 2013, Geoffroy et al., 2014). Further research is required in order to clarify the relationships between these anatomical abnormalities and the development and manifestation of AVHs (Bohlken et al., 2017).

As mentioned above, one study (Garrison et al., 2015) has demonstrated a reduction in length of the paracingulate sulcus in a group of patients with AVHs diagnosed with schizophrenia, compared with a control group with the same diagnosis but not experiencing AVHs. This brain region is known to be associated with reality monitoring, and this study therefore provides some support for source monitoring theories.

In rare cases, AVHs may be of epileptic origin. Such voices appear to be associated with damage to language related areas of the left temporal cortex and are accompanied by corresponding language deficits. The AVHs are experienced as a single voice arising in contralateral external space and are of the same gender and language as the patient (Serino et al., 2014). Whilst rare, such cases are significant in the present context given the reported association of temporal lobe epilepsy with religious experience (Dewhurst and Beard, 1970, Ogata and Miyakawa, 1998, Garcia-Santibanez and Sarva, 2015, Arzy and Schurr, 2016).

The science of hearing voices

Whilst there is much still to discover, the foregoing account demonstrates that there is also now much that is known about AVHs, or "hearing voices". The phenomenon is marked by diversity, and some forms of voice hearing – notably those referred to by Luhrmann as sensory overrides – may be particularly associated with religious practice, whereas others may be associated with various forms of psychosis. It is now clear that many people hear voices who are not diagnosed with mental disorder, but the similarities between AVHs in clinical and non-clinical groups are generally more striking than are the differences.

AVHs seem to have much in common with inner speech, and a significant proportion of them include content related to memory and biography, especially where there is a history of childhood trauma. Others may be more environmentally determined, perhaps through a process of hypervigilance, but it is clear that what we perceive – or what we think we perceive – as arising outside ourselves is influenced more than we may realise by higher level (top-down) processes of prediction and expectation from within the brain.

Voices are clearly also dependent upon learning, practice and attention. Both as a result of spiritual practice, and as a result of what they absorb from the surrounding culture, the voices that people hear, and the ways in which they experience the hearing of voices, are widely different from one country to another. Culture – including the important part played by religion – influences not only the expression of voices – what they say – but also rates of AVHs in those who are diagnosed as mentally ill in different countries, and even attributions as to what is (or is not) understood as an "hallucination".

Research also demonstrates that, at least sometimes, AVHs may arise partly or entirely as a result of biological factors – either as a form of epilepsy, in which voices are generated as a form of complex seizure – or else as a biological predisposition associated with variations upon the patterns of neural pathways connecting parts of the brain associated with processing auditory/verbal information. Human beings are complex biological organisms in interaction with their environment, and ultimately, the hearing of voices depends upon the ordered (or disordered) functioning of complex neurological pathways.

In the ancient world, a disembodied voice may have been understandable only in religious or magical terms. Today, notwithstanding the partial and sometimes contradictory nature of the research evidence, we may seem to be much closer to a situation in which such voices might be understood only in scientific terms. Is there any remaining room for understanding a disembodied voice as being the voice of God?

The voice of God as divine speech

The Christian tradition has from the beginning attested to a God who "speaks". Given that speech is a particular kind of action, the tradition has thus asserted that God acts in the world in such a way as to speak to people. Divine speech is just one kind of divine action alongside many others that are asserted in the tradition – parting the waters of the Red Sea so that the Israelites could escape Pharaoh's army, miracles of healing, the resurrection of Jesus of Nazareth, and so on. However, it is a significant one. In the first chapter of Genesis it is divine speech that brings about creation. In the prologue to the fourth gospel, Jesus is referred to as the "Word" of God which "became flesh and lived among us".[18] Divine speech is, in one sense, a metaphor for divine action in a much wider sense. In another sense it is also a very specific kind of divine action, or group of actions, alongside other acts of God.

God might be understood to speak to human beings in diverse ways – for example, through the beauty and wonder of nature, through events in human history, through the reading of a text, in moments of silence, through hearing the voice of another human being, through inner thoughts of a human mind, or – as is our primary concern here – through the hearing of a voice. Some of these putative media of divine "speech" are non-verbal, and are only verbalised (if they are verbalised at all) – in the processes of inner speech and external vocalisation – by human beings reflecting upon what they might mean. Such processes of reflection and verbalisation are quite like some of the perspectives on Hebrew prophecy explored in Chapter 3. They are human actions, concerned with finding theological meaning. This does not by any means exclude the possibility of divine action completely. Rather, it moves the putative locus (or loci) of divine action away from being an action of speech to being actions of creation or of intervention in human affairs; perhaps even actions of (non-verbal) influence upon human thoughts.

Sometimes, the "voice of God" may therefore not be an act of divine speech at all. It may even be ineffable. However, on other occasions, the voice of God may be understood in a very particular way – as in the example of Luhrmann's interviewee who heard God say "sit and listen". Importantly, in this particular example, there is an element of doubt. The interviewee actually says "And [God] was like, 'sit and listen.'" Luhrmann's attempts to clarify what this means establish that it is more like a voice outside the head than a thought inside the head – but the experience is still qualified in some way as being "like" a voice, rather than actually a voice. In other cases (as also illustrated from Luhrmann's work, above), there is no doubt. The person looks around to see who has spoken and, seeing that there is no one there, then has no doubt that it is God who has spoken. Such examples are very specific. The putative action of God in such cases is one of speech.

Clearly, Luhrmann's interviewees are sincere, and within their own theological tradition such experiences are both affirmed and expected. However, this does not mean that they need be accepted uncritically by all Christians. As Luhrmann has reported elsewhere, there is a process of discernment within the Christian congregations that she studied which seeks to test whether or not such experiences are genuine (Luhrmann, 2012, pp.62–67). Even within this tradition, it is acknowledged that people sometimes get things wrong. There is always a certain degree of possible doubt as to whether it was God or not. Equally, within this tradition, there is always the affirmation that God – sometimes – does speak to people in such specific ways. More widely, such experiences – and affirmations of them – present critical theological questions.

The possibility that God speaks and acts in the world in specific ways as a personal agent in particular circumstances is inherently problematic. Alongside narratives of divine discourse, traditional Christian theology also suggests that God is not an object of sense perception and exists without limitation.[19] If God speaks, is she just another speaker, alongside others? If God speaks, or acts, in one set of circumstances, then why not in others? Why does God not speak more often, for example, to warn people of impending disaster, or act in other ways to avert needless human suffering? A God who sometimes speaks and sometimes doesn't begins to look somewhat arbitrary. To attempt to address this question in depth would lead us well away from the topic at hand and takes us into the realm of theodicy. It will not be possible to address these questions here, but it is important to note that the idea of a God who speaks to some people raises the question of why he does not speak to others?

Divine action

Leaving aside for a moment the specific questions relating to divine speech, there are wider theological questions as to whether and how any specific divine actions within the world might be understood as possible at all. A fundamental problem is that science has proven remarkably successful in explaining how the world works. If everything works according to a natural order of cause and effect, how are we to understand God as intervening?

One possible answer to this question is to argue that God works within the natural order, without transgressing its laws, and this has been attempted in various ways. For example, Wolterstorff (1994) explores the possibility that everything was created by God in the beginning according to a plan which included all the events (including those generative of divine discourse) as a part of this natural order. God would thus not need to "intervene". However, this raises questions about the nature of human freedom, and a mind-bogglingly complicated series of consequences which God would have had to take into account. What, for example, if Augustine had not chosen to go into the garden at the particular point in time that he did,[20] and had not heard the child chanting? Supposing the child had decided to stay indoors? Supposing Augustine had never heard the story of Antony of Egypt? And so on.

Taking a more promising approach than this, but still seeking to argue that God works within the laws of nature, William Stoeger and others have built upon the Thomistic distinction between primary and secondary causes, developing a "naturalistic theism", to argue that God works within the laws of nature through a wide range of secondary causes.[21] Such an approach eliminates the problem of how God might be understood to act in the world, but it is difficult to see how – in practice – it differs from agnosticism or deism.

Another possible way of understanding divine action in a way that does not transgress the laws of nature is to invoke Austin Farrer's notion of "double agency". This complex notion is helpfully summarised by Rodger Forsman as "the type of operation in which two agents, one divine and infinite, the other creaturely and finite, do one and the same action although not as agents on the same level" (Forsman, 1990, p.139). Amongst analogies that are marshalled in an attempt to clarify this rather obscure notion, it is suggested that we might imagine a character in a novel who is both the agent of their own actions, but whose actions are also determined by the author. Or we might consider the notion of one person "changing the mind" of another. As Polkinghorne has suggested, this makes things look much more unproblematic than they really are. It also only explains how God may act in the experience of personal agents, and not in wider creation.[22]

Setting aside for a moment the possibilities for understanding God as working within the natural order, what if God does sometimes contravene this order, somehow creating exceptional circumstances which do not follow the normal "laws of nature"? In this case, we are left with acts of God as miracles, where miracles are defined as transgressions of the laws of nature. Since Hume's *An Enquiry Concerning Human Understanding* (1748), there has been much debate as to whether the evidence for the occurrence of a miracle ever can outweigh the evidence against a miracle having taken place. (Hume thought it could not.) Whilst at least some Christian theologians would want to keep open the possibility of miracles as understood in this way, it is virtually impossible to confirm scientifically whether any given allegation of a miracle (understood as a divine action transgressing the laws of nature) is true or false. For any specific case, there are almost always possible natural explanations that can neither be confirmed nor refuted.

If we do understand God as intervening, and if God is not a physical agent in the world, alongside other physical agents and causes, then how do we understand a non-material God exerting actions upon a material order? There is a problem here concerning the nature of the so-called "causal joint"[23] between God and the physical world which is very reminiscent of the mind–body problem in relation to human beings. (How can we understand our physical bodies as being acted upon in some way by our non-physical minds?)

In view of these problems, some theologians have abandoned altogether any idea that God might "act" in any specific or particular ways in this world contrary to the natural order. Famously, Maurice Wiles (1986) rejected the possibility of miracles as transgressions of the natural order, and argued that God simply did not intervene in the world at all – other than in the initial and continuous act of sustaining creation. More recently, somewhat more nuanced "non-interventionist" models of divine action have been proposed, in which the idea of a miracle as a transgression of the natural order is rejected. For example, Denis Edwards points out that God is not distant from creation, thus needing to intervene in its workings as though from outside, but rather is immanent, continuously acting in and through it. He proposes that

> divine action is present and interior to every aspect of the emergent universe and all its creatures. It works in and through the laws of nature rather than by violating, suspending, or bypassing them. God acts through created processes and entities.
>
> (Edwards, 2010, p.55)

The physical universe no longer seems as predictable or deterministic as it did in the 18th century, especially at the level of quantum mechanics. At this level, events are probabilistic rather than deterministic, and particles influence each other remotely in ways which are still not adequately understood. Initially proposed as a possible locus for divine action in 1958, by William Pollard, this is seen by Edwards (2010, p.61) as offering a possible non-interventionist mechanism for divine action, given that it is possible to imagine God influencing quantum events without any transgression of the laws of nature. However, others[24] argue that that this is still an intervention. It involves a deviation from purely random behaviour at the quantum level which, it is hypothesised, might cumulatively be capable of causing changes in events in the visible world order. Whether or not a "bottom–up" locus of divine action might operate at this level, and if so whether it could conceivably influence human history, is hotly debated.

John Polkinghorne (2005, 2009)[25] has directed attention instead to complex systems which are sensitive to infinitely small changes (chaos theory). Such systems have unpredictable outcomes, with alternative possible outcomes involving no energy difference. At this level, Polkinghorne is able to talk about divine action as involving an input of information but not energy, in such a way as might conceivably alter the course of human history. As with the proposed quantum level of divine action, this proposal has generated an ongoing debate, with no generally agreed consensus at the present time.

In a somewhat different way than Polkinghorne, Arthur Peacocke[26] has also argued that there might be a flow of information across the interface between God and the world which might provide a model for divine action. In contrast to Polkinghorne's appeal to chaos theory, Peacocke argues, on the basis of a panentheistic view of the universe as contained within God, for a "top–down" or "whole–part" influence of God on the world, analogous to the influence of the human mind upon the human body. A similar argument, confined specifically to divine influence on human beings at a mental or spiritual level, is made by Philip Clayton and Steven Knapp, leading to a participatory theory of divine–human agency in which there is an acknowledged divine–human asymmetry:

> God pre-existed the universe and initiated the processes and the specific conditions that produced all living things, including human beings. God also precedes every instance of divine interaction with each human being and, one can assume, apprehends much more in the interaction than human agents do. God is always luring, and humans are always responding, although the responses may not be conscious.
>
> (Clayton and Knapp, 2013, p.63)

These approaches assume an emergentist view of the human mind or spirit. That is, phenomena such as mind or spirit are to be understood as higher levels of complexity which "emerge" from lower levels of organ (brain), cellular, or physico-chemical composition, but are not predictable from the properties of these lower levels of structure. These models are thus forms of non-reductive physicalism.

Finally, Ian Barbour and others have developed an understanding of divine action based on the principles of process theology, developed initially by Alfred North Whitehead (1861–1947). Process theology again emphasises God's immanence within creation. More controversially it asserts a subjective, experiential, dimension, or "interiority", to all reality. Divine action is seen as operating, in a non-interventionist way, at this level, somehow enticing or attracting a decision for particular outcomes. According to its proponents, this might be understood in conventional Christian terms as the operation of the Holy Spirit, and it is further seen as compatible with current models of quantum theory. According to its detractors, it is a form of animism which runs counter to our understanding of the nature of the physical world.[27]

The voice of God as a specific divine action

The particular divine action with which we are here concerned, that God might in some sense "speak" to human beings, might be understood to occur according to any of the models of divine action that have previously been explored. For example, George Ellis (1999a, 1999b) has proposed that revelation might occur by means of divine action at the quantum level,[28] whereas Clayton and Knapp conceive of God as communicating with human beings at a mental or spiritual level. The concept of divine action as being an input of information rather than energy, as espoused by Polkinghorne and Peacocke, gets around a lot of problems and is especially appropriate to considerations of speech as a particular divine action. The human brain is a complex system – although not a completely chaotic one – and so might be amenable to the kinds of intervention to which Polkinghorne alludes. However, it is relatively easy to propose divine intervention at either the very smallest level of quantum action or the very highest level of mental or spiritual influence – both of which are very difficult to gainsay and virtually impossible to research.

Things get a little bit more complicated at the intermediate level. Given that mental events are now generally assumed always to be associated with particular brain-states, how might we understand divine action at the level of neurotransmission or brain electrical activity? There seem to be two opposing views, although these are nuanced in such a way as to make them in practice almost identical.

Fraser Watts argues simply: "Just as God's relationship to us should not be seen as purely spiritual, we should not go to the other extreme of suggesting that God somehow 'tweaks' our thought processes by controlling what goes on in our brains" (Watts, 1999, p.329). Instead, he emphasises the higher level of influence of God upon the human mind:

> What I have in mind is that people can be more or less "attuned" to God, rather as a receiver can be attuned to a transmitter, or in resonance with it. Of course, this does not exclude the notion of "action"; in physical resonance there is still a specific "input" from "outside." However, the metaphors of "resonance" or "tuning" seem to point us in helpful directions.[29]

Keith Ward, in contrast, emphasising the relationship between knowledge, mental activity, and brain-states, argues:

> God will make the divine presence known to creatures, and that will involve some change in the brain states of such embodied persons. If knowledge of God ever occurs; if as knowledge, it is partly caused by the presence of God; and if knowledge is a mental state that has, as its concomitant, some brain state; then it follows that God is part of the cause of some specific physical states in the cosmos.
>
> (Ward, 2008, p.296)

Although opposite in emphasis and starting point, affirming rather than denying that changes in brain-states may somehow immediately be "caused by the presence of God", this is not necessarily contradictory of the view espoused by Watts. Like Watts, Ward uses language of "tuning" or "resonance". He refers also to "top–down" models of causation and communication of information. In both cases, although with considerable uncertainty as to the specific mechanisms, there seems to be an acceptance that God communicates with embodied human beings.

In human minds, exchanges of information reflect particular brain-states, and brain-states are exactly what current neuroscience is interested in. Insofar as voice hearing is concerned, we know that processes of perception, attention, learning, memory, inner speech, expectancy, and prediction may all be involved. These are active processes – human actions not divine actions – with corresponding brain-states. They involve "top–down" influences upon perception which could easily be understood as very similar – at least at first glance – to Peacocke's notion of a "top–down" model of understanding divine action. They might even be understood as the component parts of Watts' metaphorical "receiver" of divine transmission, although here we have to be careful to mark the boundary between metaphor and neuroscience. All of this is firmly biological.

How, then, if at all, may we understand the voice of God as a specific divine action?

Reconciling science and theology

Amongst those Christian mystics who appear not to have heard voices, or seen visions,[30] is Thomas Merton (1915–1968). Merton, known for his writings on spirituality and prayer, became a Cistercian monk in 1941, and in 1965 became a hermit. Ironically, during the last three years of his life in solitude, he was as busy as ever with speaking engagements, writing, and a strictly governed diary of meetings with people who sought him out. Merton might be understood as something of an exception to Luhrmann's understanding of the influence of spiritual practice upon sensory experience. Few people will have spent more time in prayer than Merton, and yet (as far as we know) he never experienced a sensory override. However, that is not to say that he never heard a voice. In his journal, in an entry dated 8 June 1965, he writes:

> The voice of God is not clearly heard at every moment; and part of the "work of the cell" is attention, so that one may not miss any sound of that voice. What this means, therefore, is not only attention to inner grace but to external reality and one's self as a completely integrated part of that reality. Hence, this implies also a forgetfulness of one's self as totally apart from outer objects, standing back from outer objects; it demands an integration of one's own life in the stream of natural and human and cultural life of the moment.
>
> (Merton, 1988, p.189)

Attention was a key component of Merton's understanding of prayer (Waldron, 2007, Cook, in press), but this was an attentiveness not upon any particular object, real or imagined, so much as upon the presence of God in all things. At times, in Merton's writings, this can sound like a forgetfulness of the world, but always Merton reverts to an integrative view of the divine within all aspects of life – including the "natural and human and cultural". For Merton, prayer was attentiveness to the voice of God in all things.

Merton's view of prayer might be understood as rather similar to Watts' metaphor of people being receivers more or less "attuned" to God. God is there to be perceived at all times and in all places, but human beings may or may not be tuned in. The voice of God, according to such a model, is not a specific divine action; it is something that is present everywhere and in all places. It is not an intervention – as in an utterance of speech at a particular moment in time – but rather something that pervades all time and space. It is anchored in the mystery of God as being beyond perception, but also in the "stream of natural and human and cultural life" of each moment in time.

On the basis of such a model of understanding, hearing the voice of God is a human action of attentive listening as much as it is a divine action. However, it is still a divine action, in which human beings are invited to participate. As McKane has put it, "God does not speak Hebrew."[31] God does not speak English, either! It is in the process of active listening that human beings discern and interpret "the voice" in their own language. It is the human sympathy with divine priorities and concerns that crystallises the voice of God for any particular time or place.

Locating this view within the preceding (very brief) review of models of divine action, I would find most consistency with the participatory model of divine–human agency espoused by Clayton and Knapp (2013). This seems especially well suited to the particular action entailed in divine speech. Adopting an emergent view of human mind and spirit, it does not fall into problems of mind–body dualism. Adopting a panentheistic understanding of the relationship between the divine and the natural order, it avoids an understanding of the relationship between God and the world which overemphasises transcendence at the expense of a properly Christian understanding of God's immanence.[32] It emphasises the inextricability of the human and the divine in any particular divine–human communication:

> There is no reliable way, then, to separate the divine from the human contributions to any particular instance of divine–human interaction. That doesn't prevent one from judging, however, that one sometimes perceives the divine will more clearly than at other times, or that some persons live more fully than others in accordance with divine values (and hence with the divine "will").
>
> (Clayton and Knapp, 2013, p.63)

It also draws attention to the limits of Watts' "receiver" metaphor, and the individuality of the nature of divine–human communication:

Given the view of God we have arrived at, this divine attraction does not need to be understood as impersonal, like the force of magnetism, nor as a universal message offering the same content to all agents, as if it were a kind of divine radio broadcast. Instead, it is possible that the lure is highly differentiated, calling different individuals to different types of action or response . . . the message to each agent cannot arrive fully formed and formulated, as if each person needed only to turn on her inner receiver to know precisely what God would have her do. Instead, it is a lure that only becomes a definite message as it is interpreted and formulated by each recipient.[33]

Such a model leaves room for individuals to hear the voice of God differently, and for Merton's hearing of that voice to be no more or less valid than that of one of Luhrmann's interviewees who has experienced a sensory override. The validity, or value, of the voice must be judged on other grounds than phenomenology.

Whilst there is much to commend in Clayton and Knapp's model of divine action, it also has its limitations. For example, when it is applied to the resurrection it leads Clayton and Knapp to adopt a "personal but non-physical theory of Jesus' post-mortem presence".[34] In support of this, unconvincing and relatively superficial psychological explanations of the resurrection appearances are appealed to, drawing on Gerd Lüdemann's work, and the literature on bereavement hallucinations discussed in Chapter 4.[35] My purpose here is not to adopt or endorse their model of divine action in its entirety – or to propose it as "the answer" to the wider debate concerning the nature and possibility of special divine action. Rather, I believe that it illustrates, at least in part, a kind of model of divine action that works well in relation to the hearing of voices.

The models proposed by Pollard, Polkinghorne, and others leave open various ways in which divine action might operate within complex systems. Just as voices are diverse, there seems to be no reason to confine God to only one modus operandi. As Watts (1999) has argued, there are dangers of taking explanatory frameworks too far in either a physical or a spiritual direction. Human relationships with God are at once biopsychosocial and spiritual.

Hearing the voice of God

Far from necessitating a reductionistic denial of meaning to the experience of voice hearing, a scientific account of AVHs draws attention to the multilayered significance of the content of what voices say. Drawing in psychological, biographical, cultural, and religious themes, voices are rich with meaning, and where this is theologically or spiritually coloured there is no reason to conclude a priori that they are not divinely inspired. But – equally – it is not the case that anything that voices say should be taken uncritically. In the next chapter, we will therefore give attention to spiritual and theological frameworks for critical discernment. When – and how – might it be possible to say that one has heard the voice of God?

Notes

1 As discussed in earlier chapters of this book. See also Kauffman (2016), who acknowledges the "social utility" of hallucinations, but not the meaning of their content.
2 See discussion of this in Chapter 1.
3 See, for example, Chadwick (2007).
4 Langdon Gilkey (1961), for example, takes this approach.
5 Auditory verbal hallucinations; see Introduction.
6 For example, they are associated both with schizophrenia and borderline personality disorder (Slotema et al., 2012) and generally share similar features across diagnostic categories. AVHs may, however, be more persistent in schizophrenia than in mood disorders over the long term (Goghari et al. 2013).
7 McCarthy-Jones et al. (2014a), attempting a synthesis of different approaches, have proposed five subtypes: hypervigilance, autobiographical memory (which may be dissociative or non-dissociative), inner speech (which may be obsessional, own thought, or novel), epileptic, and deafferentation.
8 For an up-to-date and in-depth analysis of inner speech, see Fernyhough (2016). Much of what I have to say here about inner speech draws on this book, and on my conversations with its author.
9 Hoffman et al.'s (2008) study is in need of replication, and it is clearly not the case that people diagnosed with schizophrenia *always* make a clear-cut distinction of this kind. Hoffman et al. themselves had to eliminate from their study four individuals who either did not report verbal thought or else were unable to distinguish between their thoughts and hallucinations.
10 Similar brain activation is seen in both psychotic and non-psychotic individuals with AVHs (Diederen et al., 2012).
11 Luhrmann (2011, p.74).
12 Ibid., p.73.
13 Luhrmann et al. (2010, p.71). Similar examples are reported by Dein and Cook (2015) and Dein and Littlewood (2007).
14 Luhrmann et al. (2010).
15 Ibid., p.74.
16 A more extended account of sensory overrides, absorption, and spiritual practice as observed in Luhrmann's fieldwork with evangelical Christians is provided in *When God Talks Back* (Luhrmann, 2012).
17 See, for example Laroi et al. (2014, p.S214): "There is robust evidence that unusual sensory experiences have been given great importance as foundational spiritual experiences throughout the world – Moses and his burning bush, Paul on the road to Damascus, Arjuna's vision of Krishna, Buddha beneath the Bo tree."
18 John 1:14.
19 For a helpful discussion of this issue, see Forsman (1990).
20 See Chapter 5.
21 Drees (2006, pp.116–117), Edwards (2010, p.61).
22 Polkinghorne (2005, pp.15–16).
23 For a helpful discussion of this topic, see Bracken (2006).
24 See, for example, Lameter (2005).
25 See also Tracy (2006).

26 See, for example, Peacocke (2006, 2008, 2009).
27 A brief but helpful critique is provided by Polkinghorne (2005, pp.18–19).
28 See also Alston (1999, pp.188–189).
29 Watts (1999, p.343).
30 Merton did have a mystical experience in Louisville, sometimes referred to as a "vision", and also (at another time) a sense of presence of his deceased father. However, he does not appear to have experienced any auditory or visual hallucinations.
31 See Chapter 3.
32 See discussion by Cook (2013b).
33 Clayton and Knapp (2013, p.63).
34 Ibid., p.97.
35 The model of divine action that they espouse is limited entirely to the mental and spiritual realm, and hence it eschews traditional accounts of the incarnation and resurrection, taking on a modified adoptionist Christology (ibid., p.108). All of this serves to support a Christian minimalism which is alert to the concerns of theodicy and to the need to provide a rational reconciliation of science and belief. This is a radical, honest and rigorous tour de force! It is beyond the scope of the present work to engage in a full critique of it.

8 Revelatory voices

Hearing a voice is not like hearing a waterfall, touching a stone, or seeing a flower. The presence of a voice implies the presence of a speaker, and a voice heard in the absence of any visible speaker immediately invites questions. Who spoke? Where did the voice come from? What does it mean? A voice is not just a perception, not merely a hallucination; it is an act of communication. It is therefore not surprising that we have discovered that "voices" (AVHs)[1] are not just voices. They are associated with a sense of agency and, at least sometimes, if not often, a sense of presence. They are characterful. They have identities. They have meaning.

For most of human history, we might add, they have also had mystery. It is a modern innovation that has "explained" voices on the basis of mental illness or aberration, turning mystery into diagnosis and (in many cases) denying meaning to the content of what the voice says. However, this innovation has not completely removed the mystery and has not completely undermined the meaning of such experiences. There has been a resurgence of interest in the biographical meaning of what voices have to say. Many people, especially those who self-identify as spiritual or religious, find their experiences of hearing a voice deeply meaningful as a point of contact with something beyond the self. Some assert that it was God who has spoken to them. Even if the speaker is not identified as divine, a voice heard in the absence of a visible speaker, for many people, invites the possibility of a relationship with something beyond the self. It is a spiritual experience.

For Christians, such an experience inevitably invites comparison with scriptural precedents. From Genesis to Revelation,[2] the Bible offers examples of people of faith who conversed with God. Whatever historical-critical scholarship may have to say about this, for ordinary Christians, conversation with God might well appear to be normal according to a biblical model. History and tradition are similarly littered with examples of those who are recorded as having heard voices, from Antony of Egypt's combat with demons, through the familiar conversations with God had by Margery Kempe, to the voice that urged Teresa of Calcutta to serve Jesus amongst the poor.

Voices have evoked, or at least have come to be associated with, transformation of life and society. Whether or not Francis of Assisi actually heard a voice in the chapel at San Damiano, tradition has associated his radical conversion of life, and subsequent reformation of the church, with a narrative of such an experience. Teresa of Calcutta and Florence Nightingale, who each clearly did hear a voice, as evidenced by their own writings, demonstrate how voices that herald or effect a communication with God can inspire and accompany a lifetime of self-sacrifice and compassionate service to others. The voices that Joan of Arc heard urged a different kind of action, tinged with patriotic as well as religious ends, but they had no less impact on history and motivated Joan ultimately to give her life in faithfulness to what she believed they told her of God's purposes for her and for France.

Voices have also given inspiration to the writing of spiritual and theological texts of enduring value. The *Revelations of Divine Love*, by Julian of Norwich, provides an account of a visionary experience on which Julian reflected for many years, including the hearing of a voice. *Revelations* continues to be respected and reflected upon today, not only as the earliest text in the English language written by a woman, but also for its wisdom, theological insight, and beauty as a work of Christian spirituality.

Not every hearer of a voice, however, is a Julian or a Florence. Voices can also be problematic. Like Antony's demons, they may speak on behalf of evil as well as good. They may be deceptive, and it is not necessarily the case that church or society affirm the value of what the hearer of the voice reports that they have heard.

How might we know if a voice is revelatory?

The possibility still arises that some voices might be revelatory. Christian scripture, tradition, and experience all seem to affirm it. Whilst a scientific account might be taken by some to deny it, it is not clear that the scientific evidence does – or ever could – provide evidence that it is never so. Voices might be revelatory of God, or they might be revelatory by God of some truth or meaning imparted to the hearer. If the hearer passes the message on, they might then also be indirectly revelatory to others as well. This revelation might be important, and of widespread relevance, as in the case of the voice from heaven that Jesus and the crowd hear in chapter 12 of John's gospel, or the voices that Julian records in her *Revelations*. Alternatively, it might be revelatory in a much more limited sense, confined perhaps to a matter of private concern to only one particular person. In either case, how might Christians discern that this is a genuine revelation from God, rather than something else? Assuming that it is judged to be genuine, then what is the revelatory significance of the voice?

In order to pursue these questions further, it is necessary to take a brief detour to consider the nature of revelation. In fact, to do full justice to the breadth of understanding and the nature of the controversies, even confining oneself only to the Christian tradition, this detour would not be so brief.[3] As such a project would be well beyond the scope of this book, a degree of selectivity is required and attention will be devoted only to a limited number of scholars. However, it is hoped that this will at least highlight some of the salient theological issues and that future work might take the matter further.

I am clearly not primarily concerned here with what is variously referred to as general revelation, or natural theology.[4] Rather, I am concerned with special revelation, or revealed theology, and private revelation, that is instances of revelation to particular individuals, which may or may not have wider relevance to others. I am concerned with instances of revelation "of" God and "by" God. It seems to me that experiences of hearing the voice of God usually involve both of these elements to some degree and that it is not helpful here to separate them. However, the voice may not be experienced as being "God's" voice. It may be experienced as spoken by angels, saints, or spirits. Whether such voices are also experienced as associated with divine presence is a matter which might be subject to empirical research, but I am not aware that anyone has undertaken such a study. Even if they are not, they might still be understood as revelatory.

The starting point for such an inquiry might be a definition such as one proposed by Ward:

> Thus revelation in the full theistic sense occurs when God directly intends someone to know something beyond normal human cognitive capacity, and brings it about that they do know it, and they know that God has so intentionally caused it.[5]
>
> (Ward, 1994, p.16)

Applied to our exploration of the possibility that voices might be revelatory, such a definition would suggest that sometimes, when it would be impossible for someone to know something otherwise, God might literally and intentionally "speak" to someone, to bring about the requisite knowledge. Such an act of speech on God's part, Ward proposes, should also be associated with knowledge that God has caused this to happen.

Exploring "God's options" in relation to revelation of himself to human beings, Rolfe King (2008, pp.44–52) suggests that verbal communication would seem to be the optimal plan to establish divine–human interpersonal relationship. It is hard to imagine any successful revelation of God without verbal communication playing at least some part. Human beings might hear God's voice directly, or through intermediaries such as angels, or else through a more intimate inner voice. In each case, King recognises potential problems. In particular, how could anyone be sure that it was God speaking? How would they know that the voice was believable or benevolent? How would it communicate God's loving nature?

Evaluating what the voice says

Much Protestant writing about revelation takes an evidentialist approach. That is, it is concerned with whether or not there is rational justification for believing that a putative revelation is in fact something revealed by God. This seems to be the approach taken within many charismatic circles[6] when seeking to discern whether a thought or voice was actually from God. Does the evidence support that contention or not? However, it is also the basis for much scholarly philosophical and theological reflection. For example, in a widely cited work on revelation, Richard Swinburne (2007), in a discussion referring primarily to major prophetic revelations, suggests that there are four tests to be applied:

1   Is the content of the revelation the kind of thing that we would expect God to communicate to human beings? Swinburne suggests that if it is, then it will usually concern important matters that we could not easily fathom out ourselves, and that it will be true (and therefore not demonstrably false).
2   The message needs to be conveyed in such a way that God alone could have delivered it. That is, it needs to be "miraculous".
3   There needs to be an interpreting community (a church) constituted according to an original revelation.
4   The interpreting community needs to show that its interpretations of the revelation are "plausible".

Whilst Swinburne is concerned with major revelations, and many of the voices that we are concerned with would more properly be understood as conveying (putative) minor revelations, his tests are nonetheless helpful as a way into thinking about some of the issues involved. Thus, for example, a voice conveying a message which appeared to be blatantly untrue, and out of keeping with the character of God as understood by Christians, might rightly be understood as not being revelatory. Because it isn't always clear what is true, and someone must judge whether or not a voice is in keeping with the Christian understanding of God or not, there is need for an interpreting community to discern the authenticity of what is said. But Christian communities are not infallible or impartial and judgements may change. Thus, the messages conveyed by the voices heard by Joan of Arc were judged differently by different ecclesiastical courts in history. The judgements of such courts might now be interpreted as politically biased. Even today, Joan's voices are open to varying interpretation by different Christian people. And what about the genocidal voice that Samuel hears (see Chapter 3)? Few Christians (or Jews) would be likely to accept that such a voice – if heard today – was God's voice, and yet defences of such voices – as heard long ago – are surprisingly not difficult to identify (Seibert, 2016). Therefore, whilst Swinburne is right to draw attention to the need for an interpreting community, and to the importance of the plausibility of the interpretations that it offers, it is not clear that Christian communities will always – or even often – agree on what is revelatory and what is not.[7]

By definition, minor revelations will not be concerned with "important" matters in any general sense, but they might still be important to the person concerned. For example, a private revelation to a woman about her vocation, conveyed by a voice heard in response to her prayers, might be very important to her personally. But "importance" is a very subjective and ambiguous affair – as in the case of Elaine, discussed by Tanya Luhrmann (2012, p.233). Elaine heard God answer her prayers by instructing her to start a school. Even though seeming to be encouraged by this voice at the time, she subsequently ignored it and did not carry out the instructions that it gave.[8] Perhaps we might judge that this voice was therefore not revelatory? Perhaps it was, and Elaine was simply disobedient to it? Somehow, the voice was both important and not important to Elaine at the same time. There was ambiguity as to the nature of its importance at the purely personal level. Not only do Christian communities not agree on what is revelatory, but individuals may not be entirely sure or consistent about this themselves, holding at the same time both affirmative and dismissive views.

There are particular problems with Swinburne's second test, given the philosophical, theological, and scientific controversies surrounding the concept of miracle.[9] In the present context it is neither clear how miraculous voices could be distinguished from other voices, nor that any such distinction would necessarily have any correlation with revelatory content, unless revelatory content were to be defined in a circular fashion as necessarily miraculous. It is also not clear why it is necessary that for a message to be revelatory "God alone could have delivered it". If we take the voice that Jesus is reported as having heard at his baptism, for example (and just for a moment put to one side the question of whether the crowd heard it also), we can assert all kinds of scientific explanations (based on source monitoring, top–down processing, absorption, etc.) that might account for this voice. Why exactly, should the existence of any of these possible "explanations" require that the voice was not revelatory? Why could revelation not take place through precisely such psychological, social, and neurobiological processes? The test is therefore unhelpful in practice and suspect in principle.

Returning to the first, third, and fourth tests, it is already clear that they are all interconnected. The importance and/or truth of a revelation, and its consistency with the fundamental Christian understanding of the nature of God, are matters which are open to interpretation. The interpretive task which thus arises might best be referred to a Christian community, but which community? Christian communities notoriously do not always agree with each other. Furthermore, what seems "plausible" might also be open to debate.

Nicholas Wolterstorff (1994), in his book *Divine Discourse*, takes a different approach. He is fundamentally concerned with the claim that God "speaks". As a prime example of this, he takes Augustine's experience of hearing God "speak" to him through the words of a child playing.

When Augustine heard the child say, "take and read, take and read", he took this as God's command to take up and read scripture (specifically, from the epistles of St Paul, a book which he had just earlier put down). The voice (we will assume) was not an example of voice hearing in the sense with which we are primarily concerned here, as it was a voice of a human child playing. This was an ordinary perceptual experience in which one human being simply heard the voice of another – in this case, a child. However, for Augustine, it was much more than this. Through the voice of a child, and subsequently through the words of St Paul recorded in his letter to the Romans, Augustine believed that God was speaking directly to him.

Wolterstorff makes the point that Augustine had good reason to think that God might be speaking to him. Christians have a tradition of stories of God speaking to people, and Augustine had been particularly struck by the experience of Antony of Egypt, who had heard God speaking to him through the reading of the gospel in church. This was therefore a reasonable expectation in the circumstances.

Wolterstorff distinguishes between speaking and revealing. Some voices may convey revelation, but others do not. For example, in Augustine's case, Wolterstorff suggests, God's command to open the book is not itself revelatory – whereas his subsequent realisation that God was commanding him to abandon a worldly life was. A commanding voice is not necessarily, in itself, revelatory but (I would suggest) it can play a part in leading us to a point of receiving a revelation.

Wolterstorff defines revelation as that which "occurs when ignorance is dispelled – or when something is done which *would* dispel ignorance if attention and interpretative skills were adequate" (Wolterstorff, 1994, p.23). Clearly not all voices dispel ignorance.[10] Revelatory voices may therefore be distinguished by the extent to which they actually, or potentially, dispel ignorance about the speaker, or about some other person or proposition.

I cannot do justice here to Wolterstorff's full argument, but his example of an acquaintance, Virginia, who believed that God had spoken to her is helpful. Virginia did not hear an external voice, although she did describe a sense of visual "brightening" of her surroundings. She found that she suddenly knew that her pastor should leave her church. She believed further that she had to convey to the minister seven specific statements concerning this. Having delivered this message, in a state of some agitation, things did not work out as she expected and she began to have doubts. She then delivered to a church meeting a further message that she believed to be from God, and was encouraged to find this affirmed by those present. She subsequently also spoke about the experience to a priest and to a psychologist, both of whom were also affirming.

Wolterstorff points to the "uncanniness" of Virginia's quasi-mystical experience as being important. It was this that made it stand out for her, so that she had to pay attention. She therefore checked it out with others – she entertained the possibility of being wrong and took steps to assure herself that she was not wrong. Wolterstorff concludes that, in these circumstances, Virginia was "entitled" to believe that God had spoken to her. Of course, we are entitled to disagree. We don't have to believe that God did speak to her, and to a large extent Virginia has no control over what she believes. Having had the experience, having checked things out, she simply finds that she *does* believe that God has spoken to her.

I would like to propose here a category of voices as revelatory, which diverges somewhat from both Swinburne (who in any case says very little about voices) and Wolterstorff (whose purpose is different than mine). Many voice hearers report voices which are either not revelatory at all, or else which "reveal" things that might generally not be said to have spiritual or religious significance. However, some voice hearers do report voices which have either spiritual or religious significance, or both, and I would like to refer to these as "revelatory".

Perhaps some significant spiritual/religious voices are not, strictly, "revelatory"? For example, when the child Samuel, in the Hebrew narrative, hears his name being called, this is not in any narrow sense a revelation. He knows his own name and, at least initially, he misunderstands the source of the voice. Even when he is told by Eli to respond to the voice differently, which then elicits from the voice a revelatory response, he does not initially learn anything from the calling of his name for a fourth time. Despite this, I would suggest that this is a revelatory voice, in that the calling of Samuel's name is the initiation of a revelatory discourse. It gains Samuel's attention and, with the help of Eli, draws him into a realisation that God has something to reveal to him, and puts him in a place to receive this revelation.

To take a very different example, the voice of the devil, heard by Jo Barber,[11] did not tell the truth, and was deeply discouraging and distracting. Such voices are not revelatory – even though they have spiritual and religious significance. They appear intent upon increasing, rather than dispelling, ignorance. If they are in any sense "revelatory", it is a revelation of that which is not true. If Jo were to have believed the voice, then we could say that it was – at least in appearance to her – revelatory. But my proposition is that the concept of a revelatory voice should be more stringent than this because, unlike Virginia, Jo was not "entitled" to believe the voice unless she checked out the veracity of what it said, and sought advice from others who corroborated the plausibility of the revelation. In fact, this is exactly what Jo did, with different results in different churches. Jo now affirms that the voice was deceitful and not to be believed.

An evidentialist approach to revelation is therefore not without value in relation to experiences of hearing putatively revelatory voices. It has pastoral and clinical relevance and can be helpful in analysing whether and why people have good reasons for believing that the voice they have heard might be from God. However, it places the emphasis upon human powers of reason and cognition, rather than upon human receptivity to God.[12] This is not an entirely satisfactory approach for the purpose at hand, and neglects a more theological emphasis upon revelation as primarily "something that God does". Taking things from the other side, as it were, how might revelation best be understood theologically, and in particular in the light of the doctrine of the incarnation? If the truly central and unique revelation of God as understood by Christians is to be found not in the experiences of the prophets, nor in written texts, but rather in the life, death, and resurrection of the person of Jesus of Nazareth,[13] what impact might this have on our understanding of Christian experiences of hearing God's voice?

Encountering God in the voice

One of the most influential accounts of revelation offered in recent times, within which such a Christological emphasis can be found, is that provided by Joseph Ratzinger, Pope Benedict XVI.[14] Ratzinger's understanding of revelation as "God's whole speech and action with man"[15] begins and ends with God but reaches to the depths of human experience:

> it is God himself, the person of God, from whom revelation proceeds and to whom it returns, and thus revelation necessarily reaches – also with the person who receives it – into the personal centre of man, it touches him in the depth of his being, not only in his individual faculties, in his will and understanding.[16]

The divine–human encounter that revelation involves takes a dialogical form:

> Thus we can see how the idea of revelation also outlines a conception of man: man as the creature of dialogue who, in listening to the word of God, becomes contemporaneous with the presentness of God and in the fellowship of the word receives the reality which is indivisibly one with this word: fellowship with God himself.[17]

This listening (or hearing) that this dialogue entails is clearly not just about the kinds of voices that we are considering in this book. It is about hearing God through the words of scripture, and perhaps also in ways that are non-verbal. However, I do not think that hearing God's voice in a literal sense (whether internally or externally) can be excluded from the general scope of what Ratzinger is discussing.

The Christological emphasis within this understanding of revelation is set in Trinitarian context: "the movement of revelation proceeds from God (the Father), comes to us through Christ, and admits us to the fellowship of God in the Holy Spirit."[18] The Christ who is thus experienced in divine revelation is: "himself the sign and content of revelation, the great divine σημειον and μυστηριον, which alone gives power and significance to all the other signs and testimonies".[19] Revelation is, at core, Christ himself:

The actual reality which occurs in Christian revelation is nothing and no other than Christ himself. He is revelation in the proper sense: "He who has seen me, has seen the Father", Christ says in John (14:9). This means that the reception of revelation is equivalent to entering into the Christ-reality, the source of that double state of affairs which Paul alternately describes with the words "Christ in us" and "we in Christ".[20]

The comprehensive reality of revelation according to Ratzinger (and according to the documents of Vatican II upon which he is commenting here) is therefore concerned with the whole human experience of the person of Christ, "embracing what is said and what is unsaid".[21] Similarly, the work of the Holy Spirit in Christian disciples is "not a 'dictation', but 'suggestio', the remembering and understanding of the unspoken in what was once spoken".[22] For Ratzinger, revelation includes that which is mediated through scripture, but recognises revelation as being more than scripture. It goes beyond scripture both in the reality of God and in its human recipient. It has an "inner reality" which is operative in the human recipient through faith. Revelation thus "includes its recipient, without whom it does not exist".[23]

Within this understanding, tradition plays an important part in the transmission and communication of the revelation that is Christ.[24] However, this is not a backward-looking understanding of tradition as something that is merely in the past.

For to believe that Christ is the beginning certainly does not mean that everything essential now lies in the past. This impression, as though Christianity were essentially a religion of the past, for which only the past is normative and for the sake of which all time to come must be chained to something that is already gone – this notion has become more and more common because of an incorrect idea of revelation . . . If one understands revelation as a certain number of supernatural communications that took place during the time of Jesus' public life and were definitively concluded with the death of the apostles, then faith, in practical terms, can be understood only as a connection to an intellectual construct from the past.[25]

The "total nature" of tradition is "the many-layered yet one presence of the mystery of Christ throughout all the ages; it means the totality of the presence of Christ in this world".[26] The purpose of revelation thus understood is not the transmission of propositional information, not "a collection of statements",[27] but the transformation of human beings. Similarly, the revelatory work of the Holy Spirit is not the dictation of words, but "the remembering and understanding of the unspoken in what was once spoken".[28] Crucially, "*the Word* is always greater than *the words* and is never exhausted by the words. On the contrary: the words take part in the inexhaustibility of the Word".[29] Whilst Ratzinger clearly has in mind here "the words" of the past, primarily the words of scripture, his injunction has great relevance to words of revelation in present experience: "[B]ecause the Word is God, himself and all words refer to this Word, therefore revelation is never merely past but is always present and future."[30]

Ratzinger's understanding of revelation has been highly influential, not least in the contribution that that he made jointly with Karl Rahner to the document on revelation drafted at the second Vatican Council, *Dei verbum*.[31] Gerald O'Collins, a Jesuit theologian, acknowledging Ratzinger's influence,[32] asserts that revelation is primarily concerned not with "what" God reveals, but "who" he reveals. "Revelation is an experience of Someone."[33] Propositional revelation is thus a secondary (albeit not unimportant) consideration. At its core, revelation is an interpersonal encounter made possible by God's self-revelation in Christ. This interpersonal encounter does not leave the human participant untouched. It is transformative.

The Christological emphasis in Ratzinger's understanding of revelation may be seen as exclusive of non-Christian traditions. Nor will his emphasis on tradition appeal to some Protestants. However, a Christocentric approach to revelation is not only found in Roman Catholic theology. William Abraham, for example, a Methodist theologian, similarly draws attention to the uniqueness of God's revelation in Jesus of Nazareth, and suggests that this perspective necessarily requires us to understand revelation within the context of "a comprehensive vision of ourselves and our predicament".[34] Divine self-revelation is inextricably mixed up with God's plan of salvation for human beings. It is not merely a "locutionary act";[35] it invites a response on the part of the human agent. On the one hand, this affirms the dignity and significance of the human creature. On the other hand, the natural human reaction may not be one of welcome so much as fear. Human beings, living in alienation from God, do not always welcome the intrusion, and habitually adopt defence mechanisms to keep the implications of God's self-revelation at bay.

The implications of such a perspective for voice hearing in the Christian tradition are, I think, very significant. First, revelation understood primarily in terms of divine self-disclosure in the person of Christ might give cause to take more seriously instances of voices heard at key moments in the gospel accounts of the birth, life, death, and resurrection of Christ. Voices play a significant part in the theological narratives of the gospel writers. An angelic voice reveals to Mary God's purpose for her in his plan of salvation. A voice from heaven affirms the identity of Jesus at his baptism, and again at the transfiguration, as God's son. The first witnesses of the resurrection hear (as well as see) Christ speak to them. Interestingly, the single significant moment at which no voice is heard is at the crucifixion; here only the voice of Jesus himself is heard – "My God, my God, why have you forsaken me?"

Second, if Jesus heard voices, and if (as suggested in the Introduction) Jesus offers both an anthropological model of how human life should be lived, as well as a theological embodiment of divine revelation, then this might be taken to affirm voice hearing not as a primarily pathological phenomenon but as a normative aspect of Christian life and experience. In short, Jesus did not suffer AVHs diagnostic of schizophrenia but rather heard the voice of God especially clearly. We are not given reason to believe that he heard voices frequently. However, if Jesus is taken as our model of what a human life should look like when lived in close communion with God, then it would appear that – sometimes – human beings might expect to hear God speaking to them.

I realise that some might offer a dispensational argument that such phenomena ceased in post-biblical times. However, there is no evidence for this either within the biblical record or in subsequent Christian tradition. St Paul hears Jesus speaking to him on the Damascus road. St Peter hears a voice in the context of a vision that radically changes Christian attitudes to Jewish tradition. St John's apocalyptic vision includes multiple voices affirming God's revelation of himself in Christ. St Antony hears voices in the desert, and St Augustine hears a voice in the garden. St Francis hears a voice from the cross, and John Bunyan hears a voice from the sky. Teresa of Calcutta hears a voice calling her to serve Christ amongst the poor. Voices continue to play a part in the stories and traditions of the Church from earliest times until the present day.

Third, if revelation is a transformative, engaging, interpersonal encounter with God in Christ, then it cannot be simply about an experience of hearing a voice. It must also be about divine presence, and about divine and human action, consonant with God's salvific purpose. Revelatory voices will be creative, redemptive, and transformative, not merely entertaining or distracting. In discerning whether a voice is truly God's, the concern is thus not merely with rational and critical evaluation of the words heard, but with evaluating the impact of the voice in human lives and in Church and society. We might see here something of the wisdom of William James' dictum "by their fruits ye shall know them",[36] but this is about more than seeing good consequences with hindsight. Discernment as to whether or not a voice is God's becomes a matter of self-renunciation, of finding God in all things (and especially all people), and of receptivity to the transforming power of love.[37]

Fourth, and finally, voices are not just a matter of concern to some Christians who "hear voices", but rather are a part of God's self-revelation to all Christians, indeed to all human beings. They are woven into the fabric of revelation in scripture and in the tradition of the Church. This is not to say that all Christians will be voice hearers, at least not in any sense of perception-like experiences that might be labelled as AVHs. However, if experiences of the hearing of voices are woven into the fabric of the gospel narratives, and the experiences of the Church at key moments in its history, then they are an integral part of the way in which the faith has come to be communicated to us all.

None of this implies that all experiences of voice hearing are revelatory, even if they do convey spiritual or religious content. The voices that voice hearers hear are not always to be believed, any more than any other voice is always to be believed without question. However, it does affirm experiences of hearing voices as being one of the ways in which God's presence is known and in and through which his salvific purposes may be worked out. If voices (and visions) are not infallible miraculous fast-track lanes of access to knowledge of God's will and purposes, then they might still be understood as channels of communication that God does, sometimes, seem to use.

If revelation is thus understood theologically as something that God does, inviting us to participate in the reality of the incarnation, what is the corresponding theological anthropology that allows us to understand human receptivity to this divine self-disclosure? In what way might human beings be said to have a capacity to "hear" God's voice?

Spiritual hearing

God is generally understood to be beyond access of the unaided corporeal human senses. Thus Augustine, in his *Confessions*, asserts that all that is accessible to the senses is "not God", albeit the created and sensible order does communicate something of the nature of God who is beyond the reach of the senses.[38] Despite this generally agreed position, there has yet been some significant debate, in particular in regard to the vision of God, owing to divergent biblical traditions. In Exodus 33:20, Moses hears that no one may see God and live.[39] Similarly, in the New Testament, the author of the fourth gospel (John 1:18) affirms that no one has ever seen God. And yet, in Genesis 32:30 Jacob sees God "face to face", and in the beatitudes in the first gospel (Matthew 5:8), it is stated that "the pure in heart" are blessed, for they will "see God".[40] Mystical tradition also has used a rich sensory vocabulary in relation to experiences of God.[41] Encounter with that which is insensible is thus often (in scripture and tradition) spoken about in sensible terms, and it is not always clear exactly how the terminology is being employed and whether it is literal, imaginative, metaphorical, or perhaps something else.

In a seminal essay, published originally in French in 1932, Karl Rahner proposed that the idea of the "spiritual senses" provides a way in which mystics can overcome the obstacles to expressing the inexpressible.[42] Rahner dated this tradition back to Origen, but acknowledged that it had been diversely interpreted over the centuries. Rahner referred to these faculties as "partly imaginative, partly literal", and confined his use of the term only to those authors who spoke clearly of a full complement of five spiritual senses as being employed in the perception of spiritual realities. In a later and longer essay, he explored the doctrine of the spiritual senses as employed by Bonaventure and other later mystics.[43] Here, he finds that, according to Bonaventure, the primary object of the spiritual senses is God, and in particular Christ. The spiritual sense of hearing has as its object the uncreated Word (the *verbum increatum*): "Spiritual hearing grasps the 'verbum increatum', so that the soul hears its voice and highest harmony" (Rahner, 1979, p.114). In this essay, Rahner also links the doctrine of the five spiritual senses with the practice of the "application of the senses" in the Ignatian *Exercises*. Rahner's essays have provoked significant subsequent interest in the idea of the spiritual senses.

Stephen Fields (1996) contrasts Rahner's account of the spiritual senses with that provided by Hans Urs von Balthasar. Balthasar, unlike Rahner, seeks to reassert the value of corporeal sensation. He is suspicious of the apophatic dualism which he finds in the Catholic tradition, which he believes is contrary to the scriptural account of the value of sensory experience as a means of revelation, and especially to the resurrection appearances of Jesus. He therefore seeks a reformation and redemption of sensory experience by faith, such that it "allows the divine to be perceived according to the sensory forms of experience" (1996, p.227). Balthasar's understanding of the spiritual senses finds its grounding in a Christological assertion of the fundamental importance of the incarnation, within which sense and spirit are integrally united.

In contrast to this, Fields finds Rahner's account of the spiritual senses to be grounded in a philosophical account within which sensory experience is not in need of redemption by faith. Sensible forms are perceived in a dialectical relationship with a "pre-apprehension" of the infinite, and thus all sensory experience, according to this account, is implicitly religious. Faith does not redeem sensory experience, but simply develops the potential already present.

When it comes to their respective readings of Bonaventure, Rahner sees the spiritual senses as leading to a mystical union in which corporeal sensory experience is left behind and the spiritual senses are aligned with the higher powers of the soul. Balthasar understands that mystical union would involve an abandonment of corporeal sensation, and so de-emphasises this. For Balthasar, the spiritual senses, always aligned with the corporeal senses, reach their perfection in perceiving the meaning of the Word incarnate in Christ.

It may well be that Fields emphasises the contrasts between Rahner and Balthasar, at the expense of their common ground (McInroy, 2013). It is also arguable that Bonaventure is simply not precise enough, and that his writing leaves open the possibility of different understandings of the nature of the spiritual senses. He makes little explicit reference to them, and does not attempt to construct a systematic account. It is also arguable that Bonaventure is concerned more with the object of the spiritual senses than with these senses in themselves (Lanave, 2013). He is concerned more with theology than with anthropology.[44]

Other medieval mystics do give more attention to the anthropology of the spiritual senses, but the tension between the corporeal and the spiritual, and the lack of clarity about the relationship between the two, remain. Mechthild of Magdeburg, for example, in *The Flowing Light of the Godhead*, writes:

The writing in this book is seen, heard and felt in all the members of the body. I cannot, nor will not, write, unless I see with the eyes of my soul and hear with the ears of my eternal spirit and feel the power of the Holy Spirit in all the members of my body.[45]

Here and elsewhere, Mechthild demonstrates a close intertwining of spiritual and corporeal sensation. However, she also writes of tensions between body and soul, and of the dangers of diabolical deception which apply to the corporeal, but not the spiritual, senses (McGinn, 2013, pp.201–205). McGinn draws attention to a passage where she refers to three "heavens" in the soul.[46] The first is the domain of the fallen senses, and open to diabolical decepton. In the second, there is an experience of longing, and of divine love, but the soul is still "joined to her earthly senses". The third heaven is a place of seeing, and to a lesser extent hearing, God by means of what McGinn presumes to be the spiritual senses alone (2013, p.202).

Later, however, Mechthild writes of how God speaks to the soul in three places:

The Devil often speaks to the Soul in the first place. He cannot in the other two. The first place is the person's senses. This place is equally open to God, the Devil and all creatures and there they may speak as they will. The second place, where God speaks to the Soul, is in the Soul. No one other than God may enter this place. When God, however, speaks in the Soul, that happens, without any kind of awareness on the part of the Senses, in a great, powerful, swift Union of communication . . . The third place where God speaks to the Soul is in Heaven, when God transports the Soul in the delight of His will and holds her there where she may delight in His wonder.[47]

At first this might appear to be a restatement of Mechthild's earlier anthropology of three heavens in the soul, but there are significant differences. In the later passage the corporeal sense of hearing is limited to the first place alone, and the second place is the domain of the spiritual sense of hearing alone. In contrast, in the earlier passage, corporeal hearing seems to take place in both the first and second heavens.

Whilst there is thus some inconsistency, or at least lack of a completely systematic anthropology of the spiritual and corporeal senses, it is at least clear that the spiritual and the corporeal are closely intertwined. Even if Mechthild is open to deception in the first place in the soul (or in the second heaven of the soul), God does still speak to her here. The corporeal sense of hearing is thus also (at least potentially) a spiritual sense, whereas the spiritual sense of hearing may or may not have a corporeal component.

Rahner (1979, pp.81, 132) accords particular importance to the work of Augustin Poulain as having attracted fresh attention to the doctrine of the spiritual senses in the early 20th century. In a book published originally in

French in 1901, as *Les Grâces d'Oraison*,[48] Poulain adopts what he refers to as a "descriptive" approach, based upon his extensive knowledge of the Christian mystical literature. He devotes a whole chapter to the spiritual senses. Poulain proposes that in the mystic state the Christian is given an "experimental" knowledge of God's presence. He then goes on to argue that this experimental knowledge is the result of a "spiritual sensation".

Poulain is careful to make clear at the outset that the spiritual senses are to be distinguished from the imaginative senses. He later makes clear that they are not simply metaphors. He opts instead for the proposal that the spiritual senses are in close "analogy" to the physical senses, by which he wishes to assert that they have a "strong resemblance" to them. In relation to spiritual hearing, he argues that God speaks "intellectually" to the prophets and the saints. This is a matter of a "communication of thoughts", and needs neither sounds nor definite language.

In the mystic union, Poulain asserts that God makes his presence known within the soul. Apparently struggling to find the right descriptive terms he refers to "something **interior** which penetrates the soul; it is a sensation of **imbibition** (saturation), of **fusion**, of **immersion**".[49] Poulain adopts, as offering "greatest clarity", a language of "interior touch" in reference to this experience of presence, but states that it can sometimes also be experienced exteriorly. This part of the chapter is somewhat confusing, and might be taken to indicate a privileging of spiritual touch over the other senses. However, Poulain's usage of the concept of "interior touch" might also be taken to be referring more to a sense of presence that may accompany any or all of the the other spiritual senses.

Paul Gavrilyuk and Sarah Coakley (2012), like Rahner, note the diversity and imprecision of usage of the language of the spiritual senses as employed through Christian history. They do, however, make two important general observations. First, that the emphasis is often on divine action, and on the content of divine revelation, rather than on human reception (p.2). Second, they note the Aristotelian influence which often orders a hierarchy in which sight is accorded first place, and hearing second place. Sometimes the Aristotelian hierarchy is reversed. Elsewhere, the Reformation emphasis on preaching led, they conclude, to a prioritising of audition (pp.8–9). So the hierarchy may vary, but it would seem to be relatively unusual that all of the senses are treated as equal. Within these various hierarchies, audition occupies sometimes a lower, and sometimes a higher, place.

Perceiving God

In his construction of a perceptual model of the experience of God, William Alston carefully teases out the need to distinguish between sensory and non-sensory presentations of God. Mystical perceptions are taken to include both sensory and non-sensory presentations, but the latter (the main object of analysis in Alston's book) are taken to concern such things as inner voices, which are carefully distinguished by Alston from hallucinations and other perceptual experiences of externally located objects. As we have seen in the Introduction, and in Chapter 7, it is in practice difficult or impossible to make such distinctions, and hallucinations, although perceived as arising externally, may well have internal origins. Inner voices and AVHs are closely related and have much in common. Similarly, experiences of the presence of God, which Alston takes as non-sensory phenomena, are in fact perception-like, and not infrequently accompany hallucinatory experiences. Despite these limitations in Alston's analysis of the distinction between sensory and non-sensory perceptions, his later account of what it might mean to "perceive" God is in many ways helpful.

Alston distinguishes between direct and indirect awareness of God. In indirect perceptions, we perceive by virtue of perceiving something else – such as a reflection in a mirror, or an image on a TV screen. In direct perception we perceive directly. However, even most direct perceptions are actually mediated, if only by sound waves (in the case of auditory perception) and a consciousness of the experience of perception. Alston thus identifies three categories of immediacy of awareness: absolute immediacy (in which awareness is immediate and completely unmediated), mediated immediacy – also referred to as direct perception (in which awareness is mediated only through a state of consciousness), and mediate perception – also referred to as indirect perception (in which awareness is mediated through awareness of another object of perception). As Alston observes, most mystical experiences are instances of mediated immediacy, or at least may be taken to be so, explicit and precise descriptions being relatively rare. He gives an example from Poulain, in which the language is precise and explicit, as an example to make clear the distinction between mediated immediacy and mediate perception:

> In the mystic union, which is a *direct apprehension* of God, God acts immediately upon the soul in order to communicate Himself to her; and it is God, *not an image of God*, not the illusion of God, that the soul perceives and attains to.[50]

This is an example of mediated immediacy, according to Alston's typology. It is not absolute immediacy, because there is still a distinction between God and soul. The soul is conscious of a direct apprehension of God, and thus "perception" of God is mediated by this apprehension. However, it is not mediate perception either, because there is no perceptual image of God.

Alston's conceptual precision is extremely helpful, but as with many such discussions hearing is subsumed under the general heading of "perceiving God" and given little particular attention.[51] In fact, when it comes to hearing, and especially the hearing of a voice, it is hard to envisage any way in which a perceptual (or perception-like) experience of a voice alone can be understood as a direct experience of the speaker. When I hear a voice my awareness of the speaker is mediated by the voice. It is the voice that I perceive directly and not the speaker. Moreover, as discussed in Chapter 3, we may argue that "God does not speak Hebrew." A process of translation has taken place – presumably in the human brain[52] – whereby a more or less ineffable divine communication finds expression in the words of a human language, perceived as a voice. Perhaps it is for this reason that Bonaventure, Poulain, and others find touch a more immediate and direct form of spiritual sensation. To touch – or be touched – implies a much more direct contact with the Other than does the hearing of a voice.[53]

However, as discussed in Chapter 7, AVHs are rarely experienced *only* as voices. They are characterful, they are associated with a sense of agency and, often, also with a sense of presence. Much of the literature on religious and/or mystical experience fails to take into account the extent to which a sense of presence has perceptual (or perception-like) qualities and is associated with hallucinatory experiences such as AVHs. Perhaps mystical experiences of divine presence are different in some way to other experiences of a sense of presence but (to my knowledge) no distinctions have been made beyond the interpretations offered by those who have had such experiences[54] and differences in phenomenology (if there are any) have not yet been critically examined. Whilst some experiences of divine presence are not spatially located, others (such as Teresa of Avila's experience of the presence of Christ)[55] clearly are.

As Alston acknowledges, any claim to have perceived God in a sensory way is inherently problematic. Quite apart from objections to thinking about God as an "object" of perceptual experience (as exemplified in Tillich's theology of God as "ground of being"), God is immaterial. A doctrine of spiritual senses helpfully circumnavigates this difficulty, moving the focus to an uncertain locus of attention which is not physical, not imaginative, possibly metaphorical, or maybe analogous, but it is not clear that it completely avoids it and it leaves open the door to Balthasar's criticism of apophatic dualism. The "strong resemblance" that Poulain wishes to assert between the physical and the spiritual senses still feels as though it commits to a specificity of perception of God as an object among other objects. And, even if God may be perceived through the spiritual senses (however they may be understood), how is the mechanism of such a specific divine action[56] to be envisaged?

Problems with understanding voices as revelatory

If a voice is experienced and interpreted in a very literal and direct way, such that it is asserted that it has been spoken by God, then the potential for problems is particularly great. Such an assertion implies something very anthropomorphic, limiting, and specific about God. According to this model, God speaks into the human situation in rather the same way that any human speaker does. God is a speaker in the world, alongside other speakers. God, literally not visible, is paradoxically asserted to be literally audible.[57] Such an assertion usually implies an understanding of the voice as infallible and iner-rant. After all, it is understood – literally – as God's voice. However, it may also be malign, and God may be heard to say all kinds of things that Christians (or others) would not normatively accept that God would say. God is thus limited to a very anthropomorphic mode of discourse, but unlimited in what he (or she) might say. Conversely, human limitation in the experience and interpretation of what is heard remains more or less unexamined.

Such an extreme account of the experience of hearing God's voice may be relatively unusual other than in the world of psychosis. Almost all individuals and communities that acknowledge the possibility of hearing a voice that is identifiable as being in some sense divine also acknowl-edge the possibility of human error and deception. But some nonetheless tend towards this extreme. Margery Kempe's voice, for example, tells her that "those who hear you hear the voice of God"[58] and it is clear that, despite episodes in her *Book* where she sought confirmation from others of the validity of her experiences, she generally didn't doubt this. She sin-cerely believed in her voices. Samuel Williamson (2016), in *Hearing God in Conversation*, devotes a whole appendix to "Questionable and Excessive Practices", included in which is an example of a man so convinced of the truth of his prophetic message that he cannot join any church, because no church agrees with him.

Despite the problems associated with hearing such voices, there is an inherent attractiveness to a voice which makes simpler the task of knowing what God wants. As Karl Rahner writes:

> In turbulent times, the minds of men are agitated not only by the events themselves, but they also seek an interpretation of present events and a promise for the future. And if they are believers they know that the interpretation of the present and the promise of the future ultimately can be found only in God. Then they hope that this enlightening and auspicious word of God may be imparted to them as clearly and une-quivocally as possible. They seek people who claim to have perceived this special word from heaven, and they are disposed to believe in it.
>
> (Rahner, 1964, p.9)

As John of the Cross observed, voices (or visions, or other tangible sen-sory religious experiences), if allowed to become self-validating, open the Christian to possessiveness and deceit. Rather like the ring in Tolkien's novel, they can become preoccupying and all-consuming to those who bear them. It is in the nature of a voice without a speaker that questions are begged, or should be begged, about where it comes from. If such questions are not asked, and if the authenticity (let alone the moral goodness) of the voice is not questioned, pride and deception seem to lie close at hand. Such was the concern of John of the Cross about such dangers that he felt it better to ignore corporeal voices completely.

For most Christians hearing voices today, the possibility of deception is acknowledged. The problems arise in agreeing the criteria by which deception and error may be distinguished from truth. Some examples of such criteria have been discussed in Chapter 6, and vary from simply excluding a diagnosis of mental illness, through to the two sets of sophisticated rules for discernment offered in the Ignatian *Exercises*. These are essentially addressing the same problem that Moberly explores in relation to Old Testament prophecy (discussed in Chapter 3). As Moberly observes, sincerity and ecstatic accompaniment are beside the point. Ultimately, it is the moral character of the prophet and her message that counts for most. Similarly, it is the moral virtue, wisdom, and insight of what a voice says that should carry more weight than the simple fact that a voice has been heard. Such things are often more easily discriminated in retrospect. Teresa of Calcutta's life may now be said to authenticate the message of the voice that she heard as a young woman. At the time, things were less clear and her correspondence reveals that both she and her advisers found cause not to place too much weight on the simple fact of the hearing of a voice.

Other voices are problematic not because they are deceptive, but because they are blatantly abhorrent and distressing. This seems to be more especially characteristic of voices experienced as a symptom of psychosis, as in the experiences of Jo Barber, quoted in Chapter 6. Elisabeth of Schönau's initial vision, of a phantom that threatened and swore, may also have been of this kind, given that she reported significant depression and suicidal ideation at the time. However, abusive demonic voices were also a central feature of the narrative of the *Life* of Antony of Egypt, and, paradoxically, subsequent hagiography sometimes alludes to such experiences as evidence of the holiness of a saint, as in the case of Maria Maddalena de' Pazzi.[59] The abhorrence of the experience can be understood as a testing of holiness.

Hearing God's voice

There is yet a further problem, arising from the research discussed in Chapter 7. Whilst there is still much debate about the various mechanisms by which AVHs may arise, it seems increasingly clear that they arise internally. Thus "inner voices" are misattributed to external sources due to a source monitoring problem, higher mental processes generate voices as errors of predictive processing, and sensory overrides occur as a result of a state of absorption in which the subject focuses intensely upon a mental object of especial concern. In each case, the "voice" is in fact generated by the human brain. There is no need to posit the existence of any external speaker. Indeed, there is every reason not to. AVHs are perception-like, but they are not veridical perceptions of a voice emanating from the external world.

In suggesting that there is no external speaker, I am not arguing that there is no "other" whose voice is heard. However, it seems to me that the scientific evidence relocates and refocuses the discussion of what it might mean to hear God's voice.

First, the quest for a speaker is relocated. It becomes an inner quest. Where this speaker is understood to be God, then God is relocated. God is not "out there", but deeply within the machinery of our minds. To take Teresa of Avila's metaphor, the quest for God becomes a charting of the rooms of an "interior castle", rather than a journey beyond the self. It means that knowing oneself becomes an important part of coping with voices, of making sense of voices, and especially of hearing God's voice well. This process of knowing oneself might – at least in part – take the form of psychotherapy or counselling, and it is increasingly clear that psychological therapies have something effective and helpful to offer for some people who hear voices, especially where there is an association with past trauma (Romme, 2009, Thomas et al., 2014). However, the knowledge of self that psychological therapies offer, important though it is, is at best partial and incomplete.

A variety of approaches may be taken to examining the common ground, contrasts, and conflicts between the self-knowledge offered by contemporary psychological therapies and that afforded by the various traditions of Christian spirituality.[60] In exploring the approach taken by Eastern Christian spirituality, as contrasted with that taken by the depth psychotherapies, I have proposed that we might perhaps talk about the "praying cure" of the human condition offered by Christian spirituality in contrast to the "talking cure" offered by Freud and Breuer (Cook, 2011, 2012a). In the present context, I think that the contrast is less about different kinds of "cure" and more about what we look at when we look within or, perhaps more cogently, what we listen to? It is also about how we do our looking and listening. The Ignatian *Spiritual Exercises*, for example, facilitate self-knowledge primarily through prayer and meditation on scripture, rather than by an emphasis on *self*-reflection. The Quaker tradition emphasises silence as a way of giving attention to the "inner light". Alston emphasises the importance of "doxastic practices" in perceiving God.

The relationship between voices and self-knowledge might take a variety of forms. For example, in Chapter 7, attention was drawn to research which has shown that voices frequently have biographical significance. However, our concern here is with whether and how a voice might be understood to be "God's voice". A helpful approach to this particular question is provided by Teresa of Avila. In a number of places, in the *Interior Castle* and elsewhere,[61] Teresa emphasises the importance of self-knowledge.[62] However, her understanding of self-knowledge is significantly different than contemporary secular conceptions of what self-knowledge might look like. It emphasises humility and awareness of one's own sinfulness, for example. Even more importantly, it emphasises an intimate connection between self-knowledge and knowledge of God. It is not possible to know God well without knowing oneself, and it is not possible to know oneself well without knowing God, Teresa says. All of this is necessarily achieved in prayer. Within this process, self-examination plays a part, but Teresa is concerned that too much self-examination can be a bad thing.[63] It is in knowing God that one really gets to know oneself.

Teresa's experiences of hearing God's voice seem mostly (if not always) to have taken place when she was praying. To this extent, they seem to follow closely the pattern delineated in Luhrmann's research amongst charismatic evangelicals in the USA. However, in most other respects they are significantly different. Taking one example from her *Life*:

> One night while I was in prayer the Lord began to speak some words by which he made me remember how bad my life had been, and these words filled me with shame and grief. Although they were not severe, they caused consuming sorrow and pain. More improvement in self-knowledge is felt from one of these words than would be got from many days of reflection on our wretchedness, for it engraves on us an undeniable truth.[64]

Whilst the words of the voice brought Teresa shame, grief, sorrow, and pain, they were importantly different than those spoken to Jo Barber by the devil.[65] They were "not severe". Teresa experienced them as undeniably true, and as in some way giving her greater self-knowledge than her own self-examination of her failings might have done. Perhaps even more importantly, she experienced them as presaging a mystical experience which she valued all the more greatly:

> It ordinarily happens when I receive some favor from the Lord that I am first humbled within myself so that I might see more clearly how far I am from deserving favors; I think the Lord must do this. After a short while my spirit was so enraptured it seemed to me to be almost entirely out of the body – at least the spirit isn't aware that it is living in the body. I saw the most sacred humanity with more extraordinary glory than I had ever seen. It was made manifest to me through a knowledge admirable and clear that the humanity was taken into the bosom of the Father. I wouldn't know how to describe the nature of this, because, without my seeing anything, it seemed to me I was in the presence of the Divinity.[66]

This experience, largely transcending perceptual sensory experience, and apparently without words, was nonetheless a significant experience of the felt presence of God which left an enduring impression upon Teresa. She experienced such a vision three more times, and counted it the "most sublime" that the Lord had granted her. It had a purifying effect which enabled her to see priorities differently.[67] It increased both her self-knowledge and her knowledge of God, but it focused her attention primarily upon God and not upon herself.

Teresa saw God as being in the very centre of the "interior castle", in its principal chamber. Here she understood that "God and the soul hold their most secret intercourse".[68] This secret intercourse may not always take the form of a dialogue of voices, and perhaps is not even always a matter of conscious awareness, but it is at the very heart of Teresa's spirituality. God's voice is not experienced by Teresa, primarily, as something coming from outside. It is deep within.

If the scientific research relocates the source of the voice, so that we primarily hear God within us, even if the voice may sound as though it comes from without, I think that it also refocuses our understanding of the nature of the voice. "Refocusing" may not be quite the right metaphor here, being a visual one, but it helpfully draws attention to an important difference between the visible and the audible. With visual perception, I can choose to bring certain objects into focus, and thus drop others out of focus. If I want to, I can close my eyes and choose not to look.[69] With auditory perception I can try to cover my ears, but with AVHs even this won't block out the sound. The voice necessarily intrudes upon my consciousness. If there are many voices, then the cacophony may be difficult to disentangle. It's much more difficult to select just one voice amongst the others – especially if it is a quieter voice.

Despite this, it would appear that AVHs are very much concerned with what we pay attention to. Source monitoring theories essentially propose a kind of refocusing (perhaps, better, a retuning) of attention to what arises internally, thus effectively ensuring that the inner world is not neglected as a result of preoccupation with the external sensory environment. Predictive processing theories are concerned with what preoccupies us mentally – what we expect to hear. Sensory overrides[70] similarly privilege what we are giving our mental attention to, bringing it into perceptual focus. Rather like various different radio stations that we can select on a radio receiver, voices might be considered as different channels that the brain can tune into,[71] some of them being selected – and then being heard as AVHs (or VHs) – and others remaining silent. Voices that might otherwise be ignored or neglected are thus brought audibly to our attention when our brain autotunes into them. Voices that we mentally prioritise (whether consciously or unconsciously) may be turned up to a perceptual level of awareness when, through prayer or other means, we choose to give them extra attention.

The availability of multiple inner voices, and the analogy of a radio receiver tuning into different channels, both draw our attention to the importance of the interpretive response. It is not a priori clear whether any particular voice might be construed as "God's" voice or not. We need some kind of programme guide, such as that offered by Ignatius' rules for discernment of spirits, or the criteria for testing whether or not a voice is God's, as observed by Luhrmann in use in the Vineyard churches. We also need to be properly tuned in. Even the best programme guide is no good if the radio can't be tuned in and the sound is distorted.

The radio receiver analogy makes voice hearing sound much more like Alston's indirect, or mediate, kind of perception. There is no way of being sure in advance that you are tuned into the God channel. Even with hindsight, when it might be clear that what the voice said was divinely inspired, it is still not completely clear that this would qualify as being a direct perception (mediated immediacy). As discussed above, it is the message that is perceived, rather than God himself. Unless you happen to be Moses, it is more like a telephone conversation than a face-to-face meeting. In this way, perceptions of voices are different than visual or tactile perceptions. However, even if the voice itself is a mediated experience of God, the accompanying sense of presence might more clearly be identified as a direct perception. The origin of the voice deep within (even if heard externally) also has an "unmediated" aspect to it – not in Alston's sense (for the voice has perception-like otherness) – but rather in the sense that the voice is potentially, at one and the same time, both a human thought and God's voice.

Hearing God in incarnational context

God's immanent and unperceived presence within all things is not "mediated"; it is the milieu of all that exists, including human thoughts. Voices may thus – at the same time – be mediated perception of divine communication, perhaps associated with mediated perception of divine presence, and yet also evidence of an unmediated and active divine presence in human minds, operating within the complex system that is the human mind and brain. In Psalm 19 we read:

> The heavens are telling the glory of God;
> and the firmament proclaims his handiwork.
> Day to day pours forth speech,
> and night to night declares knowledge.
> There is no speech, nor are there words;
> their voice is not heard;
> yet their voice goes out through all the earth,
> and their words to the end of the world.
> (verses 1–4)

Although, strictly, it is the voice of creation that is referred to here, rather than the voice of God, the image is one of the glory of God broadcast through all creation. Voice, speech, and words all convey what is going on constantly, if we will only listen, and yet each of these metaphors must be negated as well as affirmed, for there is literally no voice, no speech, no word.

It is an interesting paradox that, although there are scriptural grounds (discussed above) for affirming both that God may not be seen, and also that God has been seen and will be seen, it nowhere seems to be clearly asserted that God may not be heard.[72] Given that visual perception usually appears first in the hierarchy of spiritual senses, this may at first appear strange. However, I think that it actually supports the position that I am outlining here. That is, hearing God is an altogether much more mediated affair than seeing or touching God. The created order mediates God's constant act of speech. On some special occasions, angelic voices convey the divine communication. Hearing the voice of God is a question of whether human minds are willing and able to "tune in" and interpret correctly what is being relayed by the Divine Locutor.

To deny that God's voice could ever be heard would be a denial of the plain statement of scripture, where again and again people are said to have heard God. On the other hand, affirming too directly that particular words are exactly as spoken by God is problematic – as illustrated by assertions of the infallibility or inerrancy of scripture, or the authority of prophetic utterance. Even if the words heard were to be infallible and inerrant, they have to be heard clearly, and they end up being interpreted by fallible and errant human beings. Communication is complex, not least when it is God who is speaking and human beings who are listening.

What I am seeking to affirm here is an incarnational approach to hearing the voice of God, modelled on Christ both as the exemplar of good human listening and as the perfect revelation of God. God communicates with human beings through the complex workings of their brains and minds. The spiritual senses and the corporeal senses cannot be completely disentangled. In particular, in relation to voices, the corporeal and the spiritual may be much more closely intertwined than traditional attempts to explicate a doctrine of the spiritual senses have generally allowed (with, perhaps, a few exceptions, such as Balthasar). God is not limited to an anthropomorphic role of being just one speaker alongside others. God's voice is woven into the fabric of all creation. However, human creatures are limited in their ability to hear well. We don't, or won't, "tune in". We misinterpret what is said. We mistake other voices (our own inner voices, or the voices of other speakers) for God's voice. We focus in on what God said to us, or to someone else, in another time and place, at the expense of hearing what God is saying to us now. Yet, despite all of these human failings, God's voice continues to be heard. Some voices are revelatory.

Notes

1 Auditory verbal hallucinations; see Introduction.
2 As explored in Chapters 3 and 4.
3 A helpful review of both Protestant and Catholic scholarship is provided by Levering (2014, pp.1–34). Ward (1994) examines the nature of revelation in Judaism, Islam, Hinduism, and Buddhism, as well as in Christianity.
4 Swinburne (2007, pp.1–2).
5 Such a definition does not, of course, require that the bringing about of knowledge by God be effected by a voice. Ward considers revelation effected in this way to be a form of "primal disclosure": "The model of 'gods speaking', even though

this is how shamans and prophets typically describe what happens, is much too literal and anthropomorphic. It fails to describe adequately the ambiguous nature of prophetic experience, the fact that most of it is erroneous and that there is no assured way of telling true from false, except with hindsight" (1994, p.89). Ward goes on to develop a fuller and more nuanced account of revelation which takes into account the influences of culture, history, and human imagination, and the cooperative part played by the human recipient.

6 For example, in the Vineyard churches, as discussed in Chapter 6.
7 This problem is perhaps mitigated, or at least takes a different shape, where there is an authoritative magisterium to which reference may be made. I am not wishing to enter here into historic or present debates between Catholic and Protestant responses to this. I recognise that different readers will have different views on the matter.
8 See also the further discussion of Luhrmann's research in Chapter 6.
9 For a helpful discussion of miracles in relation to revelation, see Sullivan and Menssen (2009).
10 Unless, perhaps, I take the view that I will virtually always be ignorant of what someone else is going to say until they actually say it. However, we are more concerned here with revelatory content of what a voice says in relation to something other than the discourse itself – for example, in relation to the speaker, or the hearer, or some other matter.
11 See Chapter 7.
12 A receptivity which, as argued in the Introduction, might be modelled upon that of Jesus in relation to God the Father.
13 For a helpful argument of the case for seeing things this way, see Abraham (2006, pp.62–65).
14 For helpful summaries, see Boeve (2008), Rowland (2008, pp.48–65).
15 Ratzinger (1966, p.35).
16 Ratzinger (1969a, p.171).
17 Ibid.
18 Ibid., p.172.
19 Ibid., p.176.
20 Ratzinger (1966, p.40)
21 Ratzinger (1969b, p.182).
22 Ibid.
23 Ratzinger (1966, p.36)
24 "the whole mystery of Christ's continuing presence is primarily the whole reality which is transmitted in tradition" (Ratzinger, 1966, p.46).
25 Ratzinger (2004, pp.81–82).
26 Ratzinger (1969b, p.184).
27 Ratzinger (2004, p.82).
28 Ratzinger (1969b, p.182).
29 Ratzinger (2004, p.82).
30 Ibid., p.83.
31 Boeve (2011).
32 O'Collins (2016, p.37).
33 Ibid., p.12.
34 Abraham (2006, p.63).
35 Ibid., p.64.
36 James (1985, p.20).
37 Identifying the central part played by Jesus in divine revelation, Ward (1994) identifies discerning principles that correspond to the traditional Christian stages of the spiritual life – the purgative, the illuminative and the unitive (pp.275–276).
38 *Confessions* 10.6.

39 This revelation is communicated to Moses by the voice of God, thus establishing an interesting distinction between hearing God and seeing God.

40 See discussion of this twin tradition in McGinn (2007), Viljoen (2012).

41 See Chapter 6.

42 See an abridged English translation of this in Rahner (1979, pp.81–103).

43 See an abridged English translation in ibid., pp.104–134.

44 In fact, there is clearly a progression within *The Soul's Journey into God* (see Cousins and Brady, 1978, for an English translation). In chapter 2, "we are led to contemplate God in all creatures which enter our minds through our bodily senses" (p.69). In chapter 4, the soul "recovers its spiritual hearing and sight" (p.89). In chapter 7, the final chapter, however, Bonaventure exhorts the reader to leave behind "senses and intellectual activities, sensible and invisible things, all nonbeing and being; and in this state of unknowing be restored, insofar as is possible, to unity with him who is above all essence and knowledge" (pp.114–115). This final, apophatic, union would seem, at least implicitly, to leave behind all sensory knowledge – whether corporeal or spiritual – before entering silence and darkness (p.116).

45 *Flowing Light*, IV.13, Andersen (2003, p.77).

46 *Flowing Light*, II.19.

47 *Flowing Light*, VI.23, Andersen (2003, p.114).

48 For an English translation, see Poulain (1950).

49 Ibid., p.91, original emphasis preserved.

50 Ibid., p.83, Alston (1991, p.23).

51 Alston's careful analysis of the epistemology of religious experience is entitled *Perceiving God* (Alston, 1991). Similarly, Gavrilyuk and Coakley's collection of essays on *The Spiritual Senses* is subtitled *Perceiving God in Western Christianity* (Gavrilyuk and Coakley, 2013).

52 We could imagine that God is also the translator, and thus the words heard (whether in Hebrew or in English) would be "spoken" by God. This view is problematic – for reasons outlined above. However, it still renders the words as an "image" of God – more like an indirect awareness of God, or at best a mediate perception of God.

53 Only when the discussion is moved firmly away from corporeal perceptual experience does this prove not to be true. Thus, when hearing is understood as one of the spiritual senses, and that which is heard as the Divine Logos, the experience begins to sound more like a direct "perception of God". However, this is not exactly the hearing of a "voice", and language here is stretched by metaphor and symbol to its limits in the face of what appears to be more or less ineffable experience.

54 Thus, for example, Teresa of Avila refers to "a feeling of the presence of God [that] would come upon [her] unexpectedly" (*Life* 10.1), and elsewhere to the presence of Christ beside her (*Life* 27.2). Shackleton, in his later accounts of his harrowing journey on foot across South Georgia with two companions, refers to a fourth presence that accompanied them (Geiger, 2010, pp.20–43).

55 As recorded in Chapter 27 of her *Life*.

56 See Chapter 7.

57 For an exploration of the arguments for the "non-dimensionality" of God in relation to mystical experience see Gellman (2001, pp.39–53).

58 Windeatt (1974, chapter 10).

59 See Chapter 5.

60 This literature is enormous, but the interested reader may wish to read, for example Hurding (1985), Jones and Butman (1991), Morea (1997), Innes (1999), Thermos (2002), Bryan (2016).

61 Notably in *Interior Castle*, 2nd Mansion, 2:9–14, and in her *Life* 13: 14–15.
62 It is interesting to note that John Calvin, in the opening sentence of his *Institutes of the Christian Religion*, sets out that he will be addressing both knowledge of God, and "knowledge of ourselves". Whilst he sees the latter as subordinate to the former, and addresses it in a more ecclesial and less interior way than Teresa, it is clear that awareness of the need for knowledge of human nature in the course of the quest for the knowledge of God is not the exclusive possession of either Catholic or Protestant writing.
63 *Interior Castle*, 2nd Mansion, 2:9.
64 *Life* 13:16. Translation by Kavanaugh and Rodriguez (1976).
65 Chapter 6.
66 *Life* 13:17. Translation by Kavanaugh and Rodriguez (1976).
67 *Life* 13:18.
68 *Interior Castle*, 1st Mansion, 1:4.
69 None of this works with visual hallucinations, of course!
70 Of course, I recognise that Luhrmann does not consider sensory overrides to be AVHs, but they are – nonetheless – voices (or visions).
71 I have borrowed the radio receiver analogy from Watts' discussion of how specific divine action might be construed in relation to the human mind (discussed in Chapter 7). As far as I am aware, no one has previously applied it to the phenomenon of AVHs.
72 The uniqueness of God's speaking with Moses is affirmed (Exodus 33:11), thus perhaps implying that God's voice is heard less directly (if at all) by others. The people also appoint Moses as their spokesperson before God, saying "let not God speak with us lest we die" (Exodus 20:19). However, I am not aware of any general statements about not hearing God which would be of a similar kind to those found in Exodus 33:20 and John 1:18 in relation to not seeing God.

Epilogue

I began, in the Introduction to this book, with an assertion of the importance of voices to our experience of ourselves as human beings. I am conscious that I have said far too little since then about silence. The focus of this book on the voices of Christian scripture, tradition, and experience should not in any way be taken to negate the importance of silence. Silence is arguably even more fundamental to our experience of ourselves as human.

As in the narrative of Elijah's experience on Mount Sinai, sometimes we hear God not in words or loud noises, but in stillness and quiet. We certainly hear our own inner voices better in silence than in the midst of busy, noisy, and distracted modern lives. The importance of the affirmation of silence echoes through Christian spirituality, finding its voice in such writers as Walter Hilton, and the author of the *Cloud of Unknowing*, and its affirmation in contemplative traditions on both sides of the Reformation divide, such as those followed, in different ways, by Carmelites and Quakers.

I argued in Chapter 8 that, although there is ambiguity about whether or not anyone can be said to "see" God, there is no ambiguity about whether or not anyone can "hear" God. It is difficult for Christians to deny that God's voice can be heard, at least sometimes, given the large number of scriptural narratives (especially as discussed in Chapters 3 and 4) within which people are said to have had exactly such an experience. It has been one of the main themes of this book to affirm that such voices are normative within Christian scripture, tradition, and experience. However, if we take seriously the concerns expressed by writers such as Hilton, and notably by John of the Cross, we may yet wish to affirm an opposite stance as an important and necessary counterbalance. There are dangers in reducing God to one voice amongst other voices, however important a voice this voice is said to be. There is a danger in too much self-confidence in one's own experience of hearing God's voice, or in certainty of one's own ability to identify or interpret God's voice correctly. Voices present temptation, as well as revelation.

I proposed in Chapter 2, drawing on the work of Ann Taves, that the hearing of voices might be understood as one of the "building blocks" of religion. I have explored this most fully in relation to Christian scripture, tradition, and experience, but I have proposed that something similar might be observed in other traditions. Whilst this acknowledges that experiences similar to what we now recognise as "voice hearing", or auditory verbal hallucinations, probably occurred in ancient times, and were then almost certainly interpreted as religious experiences, it also acknowledges the need for an historical-critical perspective. It is just too great a leap to move from such an acknowledgement to the making of assertions that Moses or Jesus were voice hearers. We simply do not have the critical firsthand accounts of their experiences that would enable us to make such bold statements. What we do have are traditions that are broadly affirmative, albeit not uncritical, of experiences of voices that appear to be revelatory of God.

One of the problems that most of us face is that there are simply too many voices. Whilst an evidentialist approach to this problem seeks to evaluate these voices, and to critically discern which ones should be attended to, it is not always possible to reach an unequivocal conclusion. One of the strengths of the Ignatian tradition is its willingness to accept the provisionality of discernment. I may think, on balance, that God wants me to be a doctor and not a priest, but in living out the one vocation rather than the other I may come to a different conclusion. In any case, neither course of action is "right" or "wrong". I may hear voices for or against each. I may be bombarded by conflicting advice from family and friends, from my spiritual director, priest, or Christian community. When I sit in the silence praying for wisdom, how can I know which inner voices reflect this wider cacophany of external voices, and which might be God's voice? The sense of consolation that Ignatius encourages us to discern, as a movement towards God, may not come as a "voice" at all, but rather as an inner conviction or peace that we cannot put into words. It may also come as a voice on both sides of the argument – speaking to me, for example, about a call to a vocation to bring healing to body, mind, and soul.

My theological argument in Chapter 8 should not be taken to suggest that revelation always comes by way of voices, although I am suggesting that it sometimes comes in exactly such a fashion. Nor should the concept of "voices" be narrowly construed. Voices take many forms. To take the influential Augustinian typology as just one example, it may be that God is more often heard more clearly through "intellectual" than through "corporeal" voices, but this is not to say that he is never heard by way of an auditory verbal hallucination. What we now know about the anatomy, physiology, and psychology of experiences of such hallucinations gives us ample scope for finding ways in which God can "speak" to us through them. The crucial questions surround our capacity and willingness to listen well.

In the Introduction I indicated that I would adopt a Christological approach to my underlying anthropological and epistemological assumptions. The Johannine account of Christ as the eternal Word, or Logos, of God provides the focal point for a Christian understanding both of the revelation to human beings by God of God's-self, and also of God's revelation to human beings of what it means to be fully human. The voice of God is, in an important sense, not a voice at all – but a person. In Jesus, according to traditional Christian theology, human receptivity to God and divine self-revelation are perfected and co-located. This receptivity and revelation are not primarily concerned with special experiences, but with the theological dynamics of redemption through death and resurrection with Christ. A Christian theology of voice hearing should, therefore, be concerned with the extent to which voices reflect this pattern. Christian voices may be judged according to the extent to which they reflect and reveal the presence of God in Christ and are transformative of those who hear them.

References

Abba, N., Chadwick, P. & Stevenson, C. (2008) Responding Mindfully to Distressing Psychosis: A Grounded Theory Analysis. *Psychotherapy Research*, 18, 77–87.

Abdelgawad, N., Chotalia, J., Parsaik, A., Pigott, T. & Allen, M. (2017) Religiosity in Acute Psychiatric Inpatients: Relationship with Demographics, Clinical Features, and Length of Stay. *Journal of Nervous and Mental Disease*, 205, 448–452.

Abraham, W. J. (2006) *Crossing the Threshold of Divine Revelation*, Grand Rapids, MI, Eerdmans.

Adams, F. (1856) *The Extant Works of Aretaeus the Cappadocian*, London, Sydenham Society.

Alderson-Day, B. (2016) The Silent Companions. *Psychologist*, 29, 272–275.

Alderson-Day, B., Bernini, M. & Fernyhough, C. (2017) Uncharted Features and Dynamics of Reading: Voices, Characters, and Crossing of Experiences. *Consciousness and Cognition*, 49, 98–109.

Aleman, A. & Larøi, F. (2009) *Hallucinations: The Science of Idiosyncratic Perception*, Washington, DC, American Psychological Association.

Ali, A. Y. (2000) *The Holy Qur'an: Translation and Commentary*, Birmingham, UK, IPCI/Islamic Vision.

Allen, C. (1975) The Schizophrenia of Joan of Arc. *History of Medicine*, 6, 4–7.

Allen, P., Laroi, F., McGuire, P. K. & Aleman, A. (2008) The Hallucinating Brain: A Review of Structural and Functional Neuroimaging Studies of Hallucinations. *Neuroscience & Biobehavioral Reviews*, 32, 175–191.

Allen, P., Modinos, G., Hubl, D., Shields, G., Cachia, A., Jardri, R. et al. (2012) Neuroimaging Auditory Hallucinations in Schizophrenia: From Neuroanatomy to Neurochemistry and Beyond. *Schizophrenia Bulletin*, 38, 695–703.

Allison, D. (2005) Explaining the Resurrection: Conflicting Convictions. *Journal for the Study of the Historical Jesus*, 3, 117–133.

Alston, W. P. (1991) *Perceiving God: The Epistemology of Religious Experience*. Ithaca, NY: Cornell University Press.

Alston, W. P. (1999) Divine Action, Human Freedom, and the Laws of Nature. In Russell, R. J., Murphy, N. & Isham, C. J. (Eds.) *Quantum Cosmology and the Laws of Nature*, 2nd ed., Vatican City, Vatican Observatory. 185–206.

Andersen, E. A. (Ed.) (2003) *Mechthild of Magdeburg: Selections from the Flowing Light of the Godhead*, Woodbridge, D. S. Brewer.

Angell, S. W. & Dandelion, P. (Eds.) (2013) *The Oxford Handbook of Quaker Studies*, Oxford, Oxford University Press.

Anklesaria, B. T. (1953) *The Holy Gâthâs of Zarathustra*, Bombay, Sabha.

Armstrong, R. J. (Ed.) (2006) *The Lady: Clare of Assisi: Early Documents*, New York, New City Press.

Armstrong, R. J., Hellmann, J. a. W. & Short, W. J. (Eds.) (1999) *Francis of Assisi. Early Documents: I – The Saint*, New York, New City Press.

Armstrong, R. J., Hellmann, J. a. W. & Short, W. J. (Eds.) (2000) *Francis of Assisi. Early Documents: II – The Founder*, New York, New City.

Arzy, S. & Schurr, R. (2016) "God Has Sent Me to You": Right Temporal Epilepsy, Left Prefrontal Psychosis. *Epilepsy & Behavior*, 60, 7–10.

Atallah, S. F., El-Dosoky, A. R., Coker, E. M., Nabil, K. M. & El-Islam, M. F. (2001) A 22-Year Retrospective Analysis of the Changing Frequency and Patterns of Religious Symptoms Among Inpatients With Psychotic Illness in Egypt. *Social Psychiatry and Psychiatric Epidemiology*, 36, 407–415.

Atkins, S. (1978) *Child of Satan, Child of God*, London, Hodder & Stoughton.

Aune, D. E. (1983) *Prophecy in Early Christianity and the Ancient Mediterranean World*, Grand Rapids, MI, Eerdmans.

Babinsky, E. L. & Lerner, R. E. (1993) *Marguerite Porete: The Mirror of Simple Souls*, New York, Paulist Press.

Bach, P. & Hayes, S. C. (2002) The Use of Acceptance and Commitment Therapy to Prevent the Rehospitalization of Psychotic Patients: A Randomized Controlled Trial. *Journal of Consulting and Clinical Psychology*, 70, 1129–1139.

Baethge, C., Baldessarini, R. J., Freudenthal, K., Streeruwitz, A., Bauer, M. & Bschor, T. (2005) Hallucinations in Bipolar Disorder: Characteristics and Comparison to Unipolar Depression and Schizophrenia. *Bipolar Disorders*, 7, 136–145.

Bahá'u'lláh (1986) *Writings of Bahá'u'lláh: A Compilation*, New Delhi, Bahá'í Publishing Trust.

Barber, J. (2016) My Story: A Spiritual Narrative. In Cook, C. C. H., Powell, A. & Sims, A. (Eds.) *Spirituality and Narrative in Psychiatric Practice: Stories of Mind and Soul*. London, Royal College of Psychiatrists Press. 121–131.

Barclay, J. M. G. (1996) The Resurrection in Contemporary New Testament Scholarship. In D'Costa, G. (Ed.) *Resurrection Reconsidered*. Oxford, Oneworld. 13–30.

Barrett, C. K. (1978) *The Gospel According to St John*, London, SPCK Publishing.

Barrett, C. K. (2002) *The Acts of the Apostles: A Shorter Commentary*, London, Continuum.

Barrett, T. R. & Etheridge, J. B. (1992) Verbal Hallucinations in Normals, I: People Who Hear "Voices". *Applied Cognitive Psychology*, 6, 379–387.

Barrett, W. P. (1931) *The Trial of Jeanne D'Arc*, London, Routledge.

Barstow, A. L. (2003) She Gets Inside Your Head: Joan of Arc and Contemporary Women's Spirituality. In Astell, A. W. & Wheeler, B. (Eds.) *Joan of Arc and Spirituality*. Basingstoke, Palgrave Macmillan. 283–293.

Bauer, S. M., Schanda, H., Karakula, H., Olajossy-Hilkesberger, L., Rudaleviciene, P., Okribelashvili, N., et al. (2011) Culture and the Prevalence of Hallucinations in Schizophrenia. *Comprehensive Psychiatry*, 52, 319–325.

Beale, G. K. (1999) *The Book of Revelation*, Grand Rapids, MI, Eerdmans.

Beavan, V., Read, J. & Cartwright, C. (2011) The Prevalence of Voice-Hearers in the General Population: A Literature Review. *Journal of Mental Health*, 20, 281–292.

Benjamin, L. S. (1989) Is Chronicity a Function of the Relationship between the Person and the Auditory Hallucination? *Schizophrenia Bulletin*, 15, 291–310.

Bentall, R. P. (2004) *Madness Explained: Psychosis and Human Nature*, London, Penguin.

Bentall, R. P., Wickham, S., Shevlin, M. & Varese, F. (2012) Do Specific Early-Life Adversities Lead to Specific Symptoms of Psychosis? A Study from the 2007 The Adult Psychiatric Morbidity Survey. *Schizophrenia Bulletin*, 38, 734–740.

Bockmuehl, M. (1990) *Revelation and Mystery in Ancient Judaism and Pauline Christianity*, Grand Rapids, MI, Eerdmans.

Boeve, L. (2008) Theological Foundations: Revelation, Tradition and Hermeneutics. In Boeve, L. & Mannion, G. (Eds.) *The Ratzinger Reader*. Edinburgh, T&T Clark. 13–50.

Boeve, L. (2011) Revelation, Scripture and Tradition: Lessons from Vatican II's Constitution Dei Verbum for Contemporary Theology. *International Journal of Systematic Theology*, 13, 416–433.

Bohlken, M. M., Hugdahl, K. & Sommer, I. E. (2017) Auditory Verbal Hallucinations: Neuroimaging and Treatment. *Psychological Medicine*, 47, 199–208.

Boisen, A. T. (1952) What Did Jesus Think of Himself? *Journal of Bible and Religion*, 20, 7–12.

Bossis, G. (2013) *He and I*, Boston, Pauline.

Bowker, J. (1999) *The Oxford Dictionary of World Religions*, Oxford, Oxford University Press.

Bracken, J. A. (2006) Contributions From Philosophical Theology and Metaphysics. In Clayton, P. & Simpson, Z. (Eds.) *The Oxford Handbook of Religion & Science*. Oxford, Oxford University Press. 345–358.

Braud, W. G. (2002) Thoughts on the Ineffability of the Mystical Experience. *International Journal for the Psychology of Religion*, 12, 141–160.

Brockington, J. L. (1996) *The Sacred Thread: Hinduism in Its Continuity and Diversity*, Edinburgh, Edinburgh University Press.

Brown, D. (1985) *The Divine Trinity*, London, Duckworth.

Brown, R. E. (1966) *The Gospel According to John: I–XII*, New York, Doubleday.

Brown, R. E. (1993) *The Birth of the Messiah: A Commentary on the Infancy Narratives in the Gospels of Matthew and Luke*, London, New York.

Brown, W. S. & Strawn, B. D. (2015) Self-Organizing Personhood: Complex Emergent Developmental Linguistic Relational Neurophysiologicalism. In Farris, J. R. & Taliaferro, C. (Eds.) *The Ashgate Research Companion to Theological Anthropology*. Farnham, Ashgate. 91–101.

Bryan, J. (2016) *Human Being*, London, SCM Press.

Buber, M. (1946) *Moses*, Oxford, East & West Library.

Bullock, J. D. (1978) The Blindness of St Paul. *Ophthalmology*, 85, 1044–1053.

Bultmann, R. (1960) *Jesus Christ and Mythology*, London, SCM Press.

Bultmann, R. (1963) *The History of the Synoptic Tradition*, Oxford, Blackwell.

Bultmann, R. (1985) *New Testament and Mythology and Other Basic Writings*, London, SCM Press.

Bunyan, J. (1666) *Grace Abounding to the Chief of Sinners*, London, George Larkin.

Caddy, E. (1988) Flight Into Freedom: The Autobiography of the Co-Founder of the Findhorn Community, Shaftesbury, Element.

Caddy, E. (1992) *God Spoke to Me*, Forres, UK, Findhorn Press.

Caird, G. B. (1985) *Saint Luke*, Harmondsworth, Penguin.

Capps, D. (2004) Beyond Schweitzer and the Psychiatrists: Jesus as Fictive Personality. In Ellens, J. H. & Rollins, W. G. (Eds.) *Psychology and the Bible: A New Way to Read Scripture*. Westport, Praeger. 89–124.

Carnley, P. (1987) *The Structure of Resurrection Belief*, Oxford, Clarendon Press.

Carroll, M. P. (1986) *The Cult of the Virgin Mary*, Princeton, NJ, Princeton University Press.

Casey, M. (2010) *Jesus of Nazareth: An Independent Historian's Account of His Life and Teaching*, London, T&T Clark.

Castelnovo, A., Cavallotti, S., Gambini, O. & D'Agostino, A. (2015) Post-Bereavement Hallucinatory Experiences: A Critical Overview of Population and Clinical Studies. *Journal of Affective Disorders*, 186, 266–274.

Catchpole, D. (2000) *Resurrection People: Studies in the Resurrection Narratives of the Gospels*, London, Darton, Longman & Todd.

Cather, W. (1927) *Death Comes for the Archbishop*, London, Virago.

Chadwick, H. (1980) *Origen: Contra Celsum*, Cambridge, Cambridge University Press.

Chadwick, P. & Birchwood, M. (1994) The Omnipotence of Voices: A Cognitive Approach to Auditory Hallucinations. *British Journal of Psychiatry*, 164, 190–201.

Chadwick, P. K. (2007) Peer-Professional First-Person Account: Schizophrenia From the Inside – Phenomenology and the Integration of Causes and Meanings. *Schizophrenia Bulletin*, 33, 166–173.

Charlesworth, J. H. (2004) Psychobiography: A New and Challenging Methodology in Jesus Research. In Ellens, J. H. & Rollins, W. G. (Eds.) *Psychology and the Bible: A New Way to Read the Scriptures*. Westport, CT, Praeger. 21–57.

Chesterman, L. P. (1994) Multi-Modal Hallucinations. *Psychopathology*, 27, 273–280.

Cheyne, J. A. (2012) Sense Presences. In Blom, J. D. & Sommer, I. E. C. (Eds.) *Hallucinations: Research and Practice*. New York, Springer. 219–234.

Childs, B. S. (1974) *Exodus*, London, SCM Press.

Chin, J. T., Hayward, M. & Drinnan, A. (2009) "Relating" to Voices: Exploring the Relevance of This Concept to People Who Hear Voices. *Psychology and Psychotherapy*, 82, 1–17.

Christensen, D. L. (2001) *Deuteronomy 1:1–21:9*, Nashville, TN, Thomas Nelson.

Churton, T. (2014) *Jerusalem: The Real Life of William Blake*, London, Watkins.

Clark, A. L. & Newman, B. (2000) *Elisabeth of Schönau: The Complete Works*, New York, Paulist Press.

Clayton, P. & Knapp, S. (2013) *The Predicament of Belief: Science, Philosophy, Faith*, Oxford, Oxford University Press.

Clines, D. J. A. (1995) Metacommentating Amos. *Journal for the Study of the Old Testament Supplement Series*, Issue 205, 76–93.

Coats, G. W. (1988) *Moses: Heroic Man, Man of God*, Sheffield, JSOT Press.

Colledge, E., Walsh, J. & Leclercq, J. (Eds.) (1977) *Julian of Norwich: Showings*, New York, Paulist Press.

Cook, C. C. H. (2004) Addiction and Spirituality. *Addiction*, 99, 539–551.

Cook, C. C. H. (2011) *The Philokalia and the Inner Life: On Passions and Prayer*, Cambridge, James Clarke.

Cook, C. C. H. (2012a) Healing, Psychotherapy, and the *Philokalia*. In Bingaman, B. & Nassif, B. (Eds.) *The Philokalia: A Classic Text of Orthodox Spirituality*. Oxford, Oxford University Press. 230–239.

Cook, C. C. H. (2012b) Keynote 4: Spirituality and Health. *Journal for the Study of Spirituality*, 12, 150–162.

Cook, C. C. H. (2012c) Psychiatry in Scripture: Sacred Texts and Psychopathology. *Psychiatrist*, 36, 225–229.

Cook, C. C. H. (2013a) The Prophet Samuel, Hypnagogic Hallucinations and the Voice of God – Psychiatry and Sacred Texts. *British Journal of Psychiatry*, 203, 380.

Cook, C. C. H. (2013b) Transcendence, Immanence and Mental Health. In Cook, C. C. H. (Ed.) *Spirituality, Theology & Mental Health*. London, SCM Press. 141–159.

Cook, C. C. H. (2015) Religious Psychopathology: The Prevalence of Religious Content of Delusions and Hallucinations in Mental Disorder. *International Journal of Social Psychiatry*, 61, 404–425.

Cook, C. C. H. (in press) Worry and Prayer: Some Reflections on the Psychology and Spirituality of Jesus's Teaching on Worry. In Manning, R. R. E. (Ed.) *Mutual Enrichment Between Psychology and Theology*. London, Routledge.

Corbin, H. (1972) *Mundus Imaginalis or the Imaginary and the Imaginal*, Ipswich, Golgonooza.

Corstens, D. & Longden, E. (2013) The Origins of Voices: Links Between Life History and Voice Hearing in a Survey of 100 Cases. *Psychosis*, 5, 270–285.

Corstens, D., Longden, E. & May, R. (2012) Talking with Voices: Exploring What Is Expressed by the Voices People Hear. *Psychosis*, 4, 95–104.

Corstens, D., Longden, E., McCarthy-Jones, S., Waddingham, R. & Thomas, N. (2014) Emerging Perspectives From the Hearing Voices Movement: Implications for Research and Practice. *Schizophrenia Bulletin*, 40 Suppl. 4, S285–S294.

Cortez, M. (2015) The Madness in Our Method: Christology as the Necessary Starting Point for Theological Anthropology. In Farris, J. R. & Taliaferro, C. (Eds.) *The Ashgate Research Companion to Theological Anthropology*. Farnham, Ashgate. 15–26.

Cottam, S., Paul, S. N., Doughty, O. J., Carpenter, L., Al-Mousawi, A., Karvounis, S. & Done, D. J. (2011) Does Religious Belief Enable Positive Interpretation of Auditory Hallucinations? A Comparison of Religoius Voice Hearers With and Without Psychosis. *Cognitive Neuropsychiatry*, 16, 403–421.

Cousins, E. & Brady, I. (1978) *Bonaventure: The Soul's Journey Into God: The Tree of Life: The Life of St Francis*, Mahwah, NJ, Paulist Press.

Craffert, P. (2009) Jesus' Resurrection in a Social-Scientific Perspective: Is There Anything New to Be Said? *Journal for the Study of the Historical Jesus*, 7, 126–151.

Craig, W. L. (1981) The Empty Tomb of Jesus. In France, R. T. & Wenham, D. (Eds.) *Gospel Perspectives: Studies of History and Tradition in the Four Gospels*. Sheffield, JSOT Press. 173–200.

Craigie, P. C. (1983) *Psalms 1–50*, Waco, TX, Word.

Cranfield, C. E. B. (1959) *The Gospel According to St Mark*, Cambridge, Cambridge University Press.

Cranfield, C. E. B. (1990) The Resurrection of Jesus Christ. *Expository Times*, 101, 167–172.

Craun, M. (2005) The Story of Margery Kempe. *Psychiatric Services*, 56, 655–656.

Crisógono de Jesús (1958) *The Life of St John of the Cross*, London, Longmans.

Critchley, M. (1979) *The Divine Banquet of the Brain*, New York, Raven Press.

Cross, F. L. & Livingstone, E. A. (1997) *The Oxford Dictionary of the Christian Church*, 3rd ed., Oxford, Oxford University Press.

Cross, F. L. & Livingstone, E. A. (2005) *The Oxford Dictionary of the Christian Church*, 3rd rev. ed., Oxford, Oxford University Press.

Cross, F. M. (1950) Notes on a Canaanite Psalm in the Old Testament. *Bulletin of the American Schools of Oriental Research*, 117, 19–21.

Crossley, J. (2005) Against the Historical Plausibility of the Empty Tomb Story and the Bodily Resurrection of Jesus: A Response to N.T. Wright. *Journal for the Study of the Historical Jesus*, 3, 171–186.

Daalman, K., Boks, M. P., Diederen, K. M., De Weijer, A. D., Blom, J. D., Kahn, R. S. & Sommer, I. E. (2011) The Same or Different? A Phenomenological Comparison of Auditory Verbal Hallucinations in Healthy and Psychotic Individuals. *Journal of Clinical Psychiatry*, 72, 320–325.

Daalman, K., Diederen, K. M., Derks, E. M., Van Lutterveld, R., Kahn, R. S. & Sommer, I. E. (2012) Childhood Trauma and Auditory Verbal Hallucinations. *Psychological Medicine*, 42, 2475–2484.

Dahood, M. (1966) *Psalms I: 1–50*, New York, Doubleday.

David, A. S. (2004) The Cognitive Neuropsychiatry of Auditory Verbal Hallucinations: An Overview. *Cognitive Neuropsychiatry*, 9, 107–123.

Davies, D. (2017) *Death, Ritual and Belief*, London, Bloomsbury.

Davies, D. J. (2003) *An Introduction to Mormonism*, Cambridge, Cambridge University Press.

Davies, D. J. (2013) Thriving Through Myth. In Cook, C. C. H. (Ed.) *Spirituality, Theology & Mental Health*. London, SCM Press. 160–177.

Davies, M. F., Griffin, M. & Vice, S. (2001) Affective Reactions to Auditory Hallucinations in Psychotic, Evangelical and Control Groups. *British Journal of Clinical Psychology*, 40, 361–370.

Davies, P. R. (2004) *Whose Bible Is It Anyway?*, Edinburgh, T&T Clark.

de Bruijn, G. (1993) Psi, Psychology and Psychiatry. In Romme, M. & Escher, S. (Eds.) *Accepting Voices*. London, Mind. 38–49.

De Menezes, A. & Moreira-Almeida, A. (2009) Differential Diagnosis Between Spiritual Experiences and Mental Disorders of Religious Content. *Revista Psiquiatria Clínica*, 36, 69–76.

De Weijer, A. D., Neggers, S. F., Diederen, K. M., Mandl, R. C., Kahn, R. S., Hulshoff Pol, H. E. & Sommer, I. E. (2013) Aberrations in the Arcuate Fasciculus Are Associated With Auditory Verbal Hallucinations in Psychotic and in Non-Psychotic Individuals. *Human Brain Mapping*, 34, 626–634.

Deamer, F. & Wilkinson, S. (2015) The Speaker Behind the Voice: Therapeutic Practice From the Perspective of Pragmatic Theory. *Frontiers in Psychology*, 6, 817.

Dein, S. (2011) Religious Experience: Perspectives and Research Paradigms. *World Cultural Psychiatry Research Review*, 6(1), 3–9.

Dein, S. & Cook, C. C. H. (2015) God Put a Thought Into My Mind: The Charismatic Christian Experience of Receiving Communications From God. *Mental Health, Religion & Culture*, 18(2), 97–113.

Dein, S. & Littlewood, R. (2007) The Voice of God. *Anthropology & Medicine*, 14, 213–228.

Dennett, D. C. (1991) *Consciousness Explained*, London, Penguin.

Dewhurst, K. & Beard, A. W. (1970) Sudden Religious Conversions in Temporal Lobe Epilepsy. *British Journal of Psychiatry*, 117, 497–507.

Diederen, K. M., Daalman, K., De Weijer, A. D., Neggers, S. F., Van Gastel, W., Blom, J. D. et al. (2012) Auditory Hallucinations Elicit Similar Brain Activation in Psychotic and Nonpsychotic Individuals. *Schizophrenia Bulletin*, 38, 1074–1082.

Diederen, K. M., Neggers, S. F., De Weijer, A. D., Van Lutterveld, R., Daalman, K., Eickhoff, S. B. et al. (2013) Aberrant Resting-State Connectivity in Non-Psychotic Individuals With Auditory Hallucinations. *Psychological Medicine*, 43, 1685–1696.

Dillon, J. & Hornstein, G. A. (2013) Hearing Voices Peer Support Groups: A Powerful Alternative for People in Distress. *Psychosis*, 5, 286–295.

Dole, G. F., Larsen, S. & Kirven, R. H. (1984) *Emanuel Swedenborg*, New York, Paulist Press.

Dominian, J. (1998) *One Like Us: A Psychological Interpretation of Jesus*, London, Darton Longman & Todd.

Donahue, D. (Ed.) (2008) *Ana De San Bartolomé: Autobiography and Other Writings*, Chicago, University of Chicago Press.

Donato, A. (2013) *Boethius' Consolation of Philosophy as a Product of Late Antiquity*, London, Bloomsbury.

Dozeman, T. B. (2016) The Pentateuch and Israelite Law. In Chapman, S. B. & Sweeney, M. A. (Eds.) *The Cambridge Companion to the Old Testament/Hebrew Bible*. Cambridge, Cambridge University Press. 187–214.

Drabik, R. J. (Ed.) (2007) *Divine Mercy in My Soul: Diary of Saint Maria Faustina Kowalska*, Stockbridge, MA, Marian Press.

Drees, W. B. (2006) Religious Naturalism and Science. In Clayton, P. & Simpson, Z. (Eds.) *The Oxford Handbook of Religion and Science*. Oxford, Oxford University Press. 108–123.

Drucker, T. (1972) Malaise of Margery Kempe. *New York State Journal of Medicine*, 72, 2911–2917.

Dundes, A. (1984) *Sacred Narrative*, Berkeley, University of California Press.

Dunn, J. D. G. (2003) *Christianity in the Making*, Grand Rapids, MI, Eerdmans.

Durham, J. I. (1987) *Exodus*, Waco, TX, Word.

Dusen, W. V. (1970) Hallucinations as the World of Spirits. *Psychedelic Review*, 11, 60–69.

Eaton, W. W., Romanoski, A., Anthony, J. C. & Nestadt, G. (1991) Screening for Psychosis in the General Population With a Self-Report Interview. *Journal of Nervous and Mental Disease*, 179, 689–693.

Edwards, D. (2010) *How God Acts: Creation, Redemption, and Special Divine Action*, Minneapolis, MN, Fortress Press.

Ellens, J. H. & Rollins, W. G. (Eds.) (2004) *Psychology and the Bible: A New Way to Read the Scriptures*, Westport, CT, Praeger.

Ellis, G. F. R. (1999a) Intimations of Transcendence: Relations of the Mind and God. In Russell, R. J., Murphy, N., Meyering, T. C. & Arbib, M. A. (Eds.) *Neuroscience and the Person: Scientific Perspectives on Divine Action*. Vatican City, Vatican Observatory. 449–474.

Ellis, G. F. R. (1999b) The Theology of the Anthropic Principle. In Russell, R. J., Murphy, N. & Isham, C. J. (Eds.) *Quantum Cosmology and the Laws of Nature*, 2nd ed. Vatican City, Vatican Observatory. 363–399.

Endean, P. (1990) The Ignatian Prayer of the Senses. *Heythrop Journal*, 31, 391–418.

Englebert, O. (1958) *Catherine Labouré and the Modern Apparitions of Our Lady*, New York, P.J. Kenedy & Sons.

Erdman, D. V. & Bloom, H. (1982) *The Complete Poetry and Prose of William Blake*, Garden City, NY, Anchor.

Esslemont, J. E. (2006) *Bahá'u'lláh and the New Era: An Introduction to the Bahá'í Faith*, Wilmette, IL, Bahá'í Publishing.

Farris, J. R. & Taliaferro, C. (Eds.) (2015) *The Ashgate Research Companion to Theological Anthropology*, Farnham, Ashgate.

Fenton, J. C. (1980) *Saint Matthew*, Harmondsworth, Penguin.

Fenwick, P. & Fenwick, E. (Eds.) (1995) *The Truth in the Light: An Investigation of Over 300 Near-Death Experiences*, London, Headline.

Fergusson, D. (1992) *Rudolf Bultmann*, London, Continuum.

Fernyhough, C. (2004) Alien Voices and Inner Dialogue: Towards a Developmental Account of Auditory Verbal Hallucinations. *New Ideas in Psychology*, 22, 49–68.

Fernyhough, C. (2016) *The Voices Within: The History and Science of How We Talk to Ourselves*, London, Profile.

Fernyhough, C. & McCarthy-Jones, S. (2013) Thinking Aloud About Mental Voices. In Macpherson, F. & Platchias, D. (Eds.) *Hallucination: Philosophy and Psychology*, Cambridge, MA, MIT Press. 87–104.

Fields, S. (1996) Balthasar and Rahner on the Spiritual Senses. *Theological Studies*, 57, 224–241.

Forsman, R. (1990) "Double Agency" and Identifying Reference to God. In Hebblethwaite, B. & Henderson, E. (Eds.) *Divine Action: Studies Inspired by the Philosophical Theology of Austin Farrer*, Edinburgh, T&T Clark. 123–142.

Fox, G. (1831) A Journal or Historical Account of the Life, Travels, Sufferings, Christian Experiences, and Labour of Love in the Work of the Ministry of That Ancient, Eminent, and Faithful Servant of Jesus Christ, George Fox. In *Works of George Fox*, vol. 1, Beaver County, PA, Marcus T. C. Gould.

Fox, V. (2002) First Person Account: A Glimpse of Schizophrenia. *Schizophrenia Bulletin*, 28, 363–365.

France, R. T. (2007) *The Gospel of Matthew*, Grand Rapids, MI, Eerdmans.

Franks Davis, C. (1989) *The Evidential Force of Religious Experience*, Oxford, Clarendon.

Freemon, F. R. (1976) A Differential Diagnosis of the Inspirational Spells of Muhammad the Prophet of Islam. *Epilepsia*, 17, 423–427.

Fremantle, A. & Auden, W. H. (Eds.) (1964) *The Protestant Mystics*, Boston, MA, Little, Brown.

Friedman, R. E. (1995) *The Disappearance of God – A Divine Mystery*, Boston, MA, Little, Brown.

Frost, J. W. (2015) Modernist and Liberal Quakers, 1887–2010. In Angell, S. W. & Dandelion, P. (Eds.) *The Oxford Handbook of Quaker Studies*. Oxford, Oxford University Press. 78–92.

Fuller, R. H. (1972) *The Formation of the Resurrection Narratives*, London, SPCK Publishing.

Garcia-Santibanez, R. & Sarva, H. (2015) Isolated Hyperreligiosity in a Patient with Temporal Lobe Epilepsy. *Case Reports in Neurological Medicine*. doi:10.1155/2015/235856

Garrett, M. & Silva, R. (2003) Auditory Hallucinations, Source Monitoring, and the Belief That "Voices" Are Real. *Schizophrenia Bulletin*, 29, 445–457.

Garrison, J. R., Fernyhough, C., McCarthy-Jones, S., Haggard, M., Australian Schizophrenia Research Bank & Simons, J. S. (2015) Paracingulate Sulcus Morphology Is Associated With Hallucinations in the Human Brain. *Nature Communications*, 6, 8956.

Garwood, L., Dodgson, G., Bruce, V. & Mccarthy-Jones, S. (2015) A Preliminary Investigation Into the Existence of a Hypervigilance Subtype of Auditory Hallucination in People With Psychosis. *Behavioural and Cognitive Psychotherapy*, 43, 52–62.

Gaster, T. H. (1946) Psalm 29. *Jewish Quarterly Review*, 37, 55–65.

Gavrilyuk, P. L. & Coakley, S. (Eds.) (2013) *The Spiritual Senses: Perceiving God in Western Christianity*, Cambridge, Cambridge University Press.

Gearing, R. E., Alonzo, D., Smolak, A., McHugh, K., Harmon, S. & Baldwin, S. (2011) Association of Religion With Delusions and Hallucinations in the Context of Schizophrenia: Implications for Engagement and Adherence. *Schizophrenia Research*, 126, 150–163.

Geiger, J. (2010) *The Third Man Factor: Surviving the Impossible*, Edinburgh, Canongate.

Gellman, J. (2001) *Mystical Experience of God: A Philosophical Enquiry*, London, Routledge.

Geoffroy, P. A., Houenou, J., Duhamel, A., Amad, A., De Weijer, A. D., Curcic-Blake, B., et al. (2014) The Arcuate Fasciculus in Auditory-Verbal Hallucinations: A Meta-Analysis of Diffusion-Tensor-Imaging Studies. *Schizophrenia Research*, 159, 234–237.

Gilkey, L. B. (1961) Cosmology, Ontology, and the Travail of Biblical Language. *Journal of Religion*, 41, 194–205.

Gilliot, C. (2006) Creation of a Fixed Text. In Mcauliffe, J. D. (Ed.) *The Cambridge Companion to the Qur'ān*. Cambridge, Cambridge University Press. 41–57.

Glicksohn, J. & Barrett, T. R. (2003) Absorption and Hallucinatory Experience. *Applied Cognitive Psychology*, 17, 833–849.

Goghari, V. M., Harrow, M., Grossman, L. S. & Rosen, C. (2013) A 20-Year Multi-Follow-Up of Hallucinations in Schizophrenia, Other Psychotic, and Mood Disorders. *Psychological Medicine*, 43, 1151–1160.

Goulder, M. (1996) The Baseless Fabric of a Vision. In D'Costa, G. (Ed.) *Resurrection Reconsidered*. Oxford, Oneworld. 48–61.

Gowler, D. B. (2010) Socio-Rhetorical Interpretation: Textures of a Text and Its Reception. *Journal for the Study of the New Testament*, 33, 191–206.

Graham, G. (2015) *The Abraham Dilemma: A Divine Delusion*, Oxford, Oxford University Press.

Gray, J. (1980) *I & II Kings*, London, SCM Press.

Green, J. B. (2008) *Body, Soul, and Human Life: The Nature of Humanity in the Bible*, Grand Rapids, MI, Baker Academic.

Gregg, R. C. (1980) *Athanasius: The Life of Antony and the Letter to Marcellinus*, Mahwah, NJ, Paulist Press.

Gregory, D. (2016) Inner Speech, Imagined Speech, and Auditory Verbal Hallucinations. *Review of Philosophy and Psychology*, 7(3), 653–673.

Griffith-Dickson, G. (2000) *Human and Divine: An Introduction to the Philosophy of Religious Experience*, London, Duckworth.

Grimby, A. (1993) Bereavement Among Elderly People: Grief Reactions, Post-Bereavement Hallucinations and Quality of Life. *Acta Psychiatrica Scandinavica*, 87, 72–80.

Guarnaccia, P. J., Guevara-Ramos, L. M., Gonzales, G., Canino, G. J. & Bird, H. (1991) Cross-Cultural Aspects of Psychotic Symptoms in Puerto Rico. *Research in Community and Mental Health*, 7, 99–110.

Gundry, R. H. (1994) *Matthew: A Commentary on His Handbook for a Mixed Church under Persecution*, Grand Rapids, MI, Eerdmans.

Habermas, G. R. (2001) Explaining Away Jesus' Resurrection: The Recent Revival of Hallucination Theories. *Christian Research Journal*, 23, 26–31, 47–49.

Habermas, G. (2005) Resurrection Research From 1975 to the Present: What Are Critical Scholars Saying? *Journal for the Study of the Historical Jesus*, 3, 135–153.

Haenchen, E. (1971) *The Acts of the Apostles*, Oxford, Blackwell.

Hagner, D. A. (1995) *Matthew 14–28*, Waco, TX, Word.

Hanegraaff, W. J. (2000) New Age Religion and Secularization. *Numen*, 47, 288–312.

Hanevik, H., Hestad, K. A., Lien, L., Joa, I., Larsen, T. K. & Danbolt, L. J. (2017) Religiousness in First-Episode Psychosis. *Archive for the Psychology of Religion*, 39, 139–164.

Hart, C., Bishop, J., Newman, B. J. & Bynum, C. W. (1990) *Hildegard of Bingen: Scivias*, New York, Paulist Press.

Hart, C. & Mommaers, P. (Eds.) (1980) *Hadewijch: The Complete Works*, Mahwah, Paulist Press.

Hasker, W. (2015) Why Emergence? In Farris, J. R. & Taliaferro, C. (Eds.) *The Ashgate Research Companion to Theological Anthropology*. Farnham, Ashgate. 151–161.

Hedrick, C. W. (1981) Paul's Conversion/Call: A Comparative Analysis of the Three Reports in Acts. *Journal of Biblical Literature*, 100, 415–432.

Heelas, P. (2008) *Spiritualities of Life*, Oxford, Blackwell.

Heery, M. W. (1989) Inner Voice Experiences: An Exploratory Study of Thirty Cases. *Journal of Transpersonal Psychology*, 21, 73–82.

Henderson, D. K. (1939) *Psychopathic States*, New York, Norton.

Henker, F. O. (1984) Joan of Arc and DSM III. *Southern Medical Journal*, 77, 1488–1490.

Heschel, A. J. (2010) *The Prophets*, Peabody, MA, Hendrickson.

Hick, J. (1993) *The Metaphor of God Incarnate*, London, SCM Press.

Hick, J. (2010) *The New Frontier of Religion and Science: Religious Experience, Neuroscience and the Transcendent*, Basingstoke, Palgrave Macmillan.

Hoffman, R. E. & Hampson, M. (2012) Functional Connectivity Studies of Patients with Auditory Verbal Hallucinations. *Frontiers in Human Neuroscience*, 6, 1–7.

Hoffman, R. E., Varanko, M., Gilmore, J. & Mishara, A. L. (2008) Experiential Features Used by Patients With Schizophrenia to Differentiate "Voices" From Ordinary Verbal Thought. *Psychological Medicine*, 38, 1167–1176.

Honig, A., Romme, M. a. J., Ensink, B. J., Escher, S. D. M. a. C., Pennings, M. H. A. & Devries, M. W. (1998) Auditory Hallucinations: A Comparison Between Patients and Nonpatients. *Journal of Nervous and Mental Disease*, 186, 646–651.

Hooker, M. D. (1991) *The Gospel According to St Mark*, London, A & C Black.

Howells, E. (2001) Mysticism and the Mystical: The Current Debate. *The Way*, Suppl. 102, 15–27.

Huggett, J. (1986) *Listening to God*, London, Hodder & Stoughton.

Humpston, C. S. & Broome, M. R. (2015) The Spectra of Soundless Voices and Audible Thoughts: Towards an Integrative Model of Auditory Verbal Hallucinations and Thought Insertion. *Review of Philosophy and Psychology*, 7(3), 611–629.

Hurding, R. F. (1985) *Roots and Shoots: A Guide to Counselling and Psychotherapy*, London, Hodder & Stoughton.

Huyssen, C. and Huyssen, L. (1992) *I Saw the Lord*, Tarrytown, NY, Fleming H. Revell.

Innes, R. (1999) *Discourses of the Self: Seeking Wholeness in Theology and Psychology*, Bern, Peter Lang.

Ireland, D. R. (2016) The Legacy of John Sung. *International Bulletin of Mission Research*, 40, 349–357.

Ivens, M. & Hughes, G. W. (Eds.) (2004) *The Spiritual Exercises of Saint Ignatius of Loyola*, Leominster, UK, Gracewing.

Ivens, M. & Munitiz, J. A. (2007) *Keeping in Touch: Posthumous Papers on Ignatian Topics*, Leominster, UK, Gracewing.

Iyadurai, J. (2015) *Transformative Religious Experience: A Phenomenological Understanding of Religious Conversion*, Eugene, OR, Pickwick.

Jackson, A. V. W. (1965) *Zoroaster: The Prophet of Ancient Iran*, New York, AMS Press.

Jackson, M. & Fulford, K. W. M. (1997) Spiritual Experience and Pychopathology. *Philosophy, Psychiatry, & Psychology*, 4, 41–65.

Jacobson, A. C. (1917) The Case of Joan of Arc: Was the Maid Insane? *Medical Times*, 45, 163–165.

James, W. (1902) *The Varieties of Religious Experience: A Study in Human Nature*, New York, Longmans, Green & Co.

James, W. (1985) *The Varieties of Religious Experience*, Harmondsworth, Penguin.

Jantzen, G. M. (2008) Mysticism and Experience. *Religious Studies*, 25, 295.

Jaynes, J. (2000) *The Origin of Consciousness in the Breakdown of the Bicameral Mind*, Boston, MA, Mariner.

Jenner, J. A., Rutten, S., Beuckens, J., Boonstra, N. & Sytema, S. (2008) Positive and Useful Auditory Vocal Hallucinations: Prevalence, Characteristics, Attributions, and Implications for Treatment. *Acta Psychiatrica Scandinavica*, 118, 238–245.

Johns, L. C., Kompus, K., Connell, M., Humpston, C., Lincoln, T. M., Longden, E. et al. (2014) Auditory Verbal Hallucinations in Persons With and Without a Need for Care. *Schizophrenia Bulletin*, 40 Suppl. 4, S255–S264.

Johns, L. C., Nazroo, J. Y., Bebbington, P. & Kuipers, E. (2002) Occurrence of Hallucinatory Experiences in a Community Sample and Ethnic Variations. *British Journal of Psychiatry*, 180, 174–178.

Johns, L. C. & Os, J. V. (2001) The Continuity of Psychotic Experiences in the General Population. *Clinical Psychology Review*, 21, 1125–1141.

Jones, N., Kelly, T. & Shattell, M. (2016) God in the Brain: Experiencing Psychosis in the Postsecular United States. *Transcultural Psychiatry*, 53, 488–505.

Jones, S., Guy, A. & Ormrod, J. A. (2003) A Q-Methodological Study of Hearing Voices: A Preliminary Exploration of Voice Hearers' Understanding of Their Experiences. *Psychology and Psychotherapy: Theory, Research and Practice*, 76, 189–209.

Jones, S. L. & Butman, R. E. (1991) *Modern Psychotherapies: A Comprehensive Christian Appraisal*, Downers Grove, IL, InterVarsity Press.

Jones, S. R. (2010) Re-Expanding the Phenomenology of Hallucinations: Lessons From Sixteenth-Century Spain. *Mental Health, Religion & Culture*, 13, 187–208.

Jung, C. G. (1983) *Memories, Dreams, Reflections*, Glasgow, Flamingo.

Kaiser, O. (1983) *Isaiah 1–12*, London, SCM Press.

Karlsson, L.-B. (2008) "More Real Than Reality": A Study of Voice Hearing. *International Journal of Social Welfare*, 17, 365–373.

Kauffman, P. R. (2016) Might Hallucinations Have Social Utility? A Proposal for Scientific Study. *Journal of Nervous and Mental Disease*, 204, 702–712.

Kaufman, G. D. (1972) *God the Problem*, Cambridge, MA, Harvard University Press.

Kavanaugh, K. & Rodriguez, O. (1976) *The Collected Works of St Teresa of Avila*, Washington, DC, Institute of Carmelite Studies.

Kavanaugh, K. & Rodriguez, O. (1991) *The Collected Works of St John of the Cross*, Washington DC, Institute of Carmelite Studies.

Kelleher, I. & Devylder, J. E. (2017) Hallucinations in Borderline Personality Disorder and Common Mental Disorders. *British Journal of Psychiatry*, 210, 230–231.

Kenney, J. P. (2013) Mysticism and Contemplation in Augustine's Confessions. In Lamm, J. A. (Ed.) *The Wiley-Blackwell Companion to Christian Mysticism*. Oxford, Wiley-Blackwell. 190–201.

Kent, G. & Wahass, S. (1996) The Content and Characteristics of Auditory Hallucinations in Saudi Arabia and the UK: A Cross-Cultural Comparison. *Acta Psychiatrica Scandinavica*, 94, 433–437.

Kent, J. A. (1999) *The Psychological Origins of the Resurrection Myth*, London, Open Gate.

Kermode, F. (1997) Introduction to the New Testament. In Alter, R. & Kermode, F. (Eds.) *The Literary Guide to the Bible*. London, Fontana. 375–386.

King, R. (2008) *Obstacles to Divine Revelation: God and the Reorientation of Human Reason*, London, Continuum.

Koch, K. (1982) *The Prophets*, vol. 1, *The Assyrian Period*, London, SCM Press.

Kolodiejchuk, B. (2007) *Mother Teresa: Come Be My Light*, London, Rider.

Kotsopoulos, S. (1986) Aretaeus the Cappadocian on Mental Illness. *Comprehensive Psychiatry*, 27, 171–179.

Krzystanek, M., Krysta1, K., Klasik, A. & Krupka-Matuszczyk, I. (2012) Religious Content of Hallucinations in Paranoid Schizophrenia. *Psychiatria Danubina*, 24, 65–69.

Kuenen, A. (1969) *The Prophets and Prophecy in Israel*, Amsterdam, Philo Press.

Kuntz, J. K. (1967) *The Self-Revelation of God*, Philadelphia, PA, Westminster Press.

Lachance, P. & Guarniari, R. (Eds.) (1993) *Angela of Foligno: Complete Works*, New York, Paulist Press.

Lame Deer, J. F. & Erdoes, R. (2009) *Lame Deer, Seeker of Visions*, New York, Simon & Schuster.

Lameter, C. (2005) *Divine Action in the Framework of Scientific Thinking*, La Grange, IL, Christianity in the 21st Century.

Lamm, J. A. (2013) A Guide to Christian Mysticism. In Lamm, J. A. (Ed.) *The Wiley-Blackwell Companion to Christian Mysticism*. Oxford, Wiley-Blackwell. 1–23.

Lanave, G. F. (2013) Bonaventure. In Gavrilyuk, P. L. & Coakley, S. (Eds.) *The Spiritual Senses: Perceiving God in Western Christianity*. Cambridge, Cambridge. 159–173.

Landsborough, D. (1987) St Paul and Temporal Lobe Epilepsy. *Journal of Neurology, Neurosurgery, and Psychiatry*, 50, 659–664.

Laroi, F., Luhrmann, T. M., Bell, V., Christian, W. A., Jr., Deshpande, S., Fernyhough, C. et al. (2014) Culture and Hallucinations: Overview and Future Directions. *Schizophrenia Bulletin*, 40 Suppl 4, S213–S220.

Laroi, F. & Van Der Linden, M. (2005) Metacognitions in Proneness Towards Hallucinations and Delusions. *Behaviour Research and Therapy*, 43, 1425–1441.

Lash, N. (1986) *Theology on the Way to Emmaus*, London, SCM Press.

Lash, N. (1988) *Easter in Ordinary*, London, SCM Press.

Laurentin, R. (1998) *Bernadette of Lourdes: A Life Based on Authenticated Documents*, London, Darton, Longman & Todd.

Lawrie, S. M. (2016) Whether "Psychosis" Is Best Conceptualized as a Continuum or in Categories Is an Empirical, Practical and Political Question. *World Psychiatry*, 15, 125–126.

Leach, J. (2007) Pastoral Theology as Attention. *Contact*, 19–32.

Lefebure, L. D. (2013) Christian Mysticism in Interreligious Perspective. In Lamm, J. A. (Ed.) *The Wiley-Blackwell Companion to Christian Mysticism*. Oxford, Wiley-Blackwell. 610–625.

Leudar, I., Thomas, P., McNally, D. & Glinski, A. (1997) What Voices Can Do With Words: Pragmatics of Verbal Hallucinations. *Psychological Medicine*, 27, 885–898.

Levering, M. (2014) *Engaging the Doctrine of Revelation: The Mediation of the Gospel Through Church and Scripture*, Grand Rapids, MI, Baker.

Licona, M. R. (2010) *The Resurrection of Jesus: A New Historiographical Approach*, *Downer's Grove*, Illinois, IVP.

Lim, A., Hoek, H. W., Deen, M. L., Blom, J. D. & Investigators, G. (2016) Prevalence and Classification of Hallucinations in Multiple Sensory Modalities in Schizophrenia Spectrum Disorders. *Schizophrenia Research*, 176, 493–499.

Lindblom, J. (1961) Theophanies in Holy Places in Hebrew Religion. *Hebrew Union College Annual*, 32, 91–106.

Lindblom, J. (1967) *Prophecy in Ancient Israel*, Oxford, Blackwell.

Lloyd, R. (1970) Cross and Psychosis: Part 1: *Faith & Freedom*, 24, 13–29.

Lloyd, R. (1971) Cross and Psychosis, Part 2: Creativeness and Envy. *Faith & Freedom*, 24, 66–87.

Lüdemann, G. (1994) *The Resurrection of Jesus*, London, SCM Press.

Luhrmann, T. M. (2011) Hallucinations and Sensory Overrides. *Annual Review of Anthropology*, 40, 71–85.

Luhrmann, T. M. (2012) *When God Talks Back*, New York, Knopf.

Luhrmann, T. M. (2017) Diversity Within the Psychotic Continuum. *Schizophrenia Bulletin*, 43, 27–31.

Luhrmann, T. M. & Morgain, R. (2012) Prayer as Inner Sense Cultivation: An Attentional Learning Theory of Spiritual Experience. *Ethos*, 40, 359–389.

Luhrmann, T. M., Nusbaum, H. & Thisted, R. (2010) The Absorption Hypothesis: Learning to Hear God in Evangelical Christianity. *American Anthropologist*, 112, 66–78.

Lukoff, D. (1985) The Diagnosis of Mystical Experiences With Psychotic Features. *Journal of Transpersonal Psychology*, 17, 155–181.

Lyall, L. T. (1965) *A Biography of John Sung: Flame for God in the Far East*, London, China Inland Mission Overseas Missionary Fellowship.

Mace, C. (2008) *Mindfulness and Mental Health*, London, Routledge.

Maggi, A. & Matter, E. A. (Eds.) (2000) *Maria Maddalena De' Pazzi: Selected Revelations*, New York, Paulist Press.

Maloney, G. A. (1975) *The Mystic of Fire and Light*, Denville, NJ, Dimension Books.

Marshall, C. (1951) *A Man Called Peter: The Story of Peter Marshall*, New York, McGraw-Hill.

Marshall, I. H. (1998) *The Gospel of Luke*, Grand Rapids, MI, Eerdmans.

Maudsley, H. (1869a) Emanuel Swedenborg. *Journal of Mental Science*, 15, 169–196.

Maudsley, H. (1869b) Emanuel Swedenborg. *Journal of Mental Science*, 15, 417–436.

McCarthy-Jones, S. (2011a) Seeing the Unseen, Hearing the Unsaid: Hallucinations, Psychology and St Thomas Aquinas. *Mental Health, Religion & Culture*, 14, 353–369.

McCarthy-Jones, S. (2011b) Voices From the Storm: A Critical Review of Quantitative Studies of Auditory Verbal Hallucinations and Childhood Sexual Abuse. *Clinical Psychology Review*, 31, 983–992.

McCarthy-Jones, S. (2012) *Hearing Voices: The Histories, Causes and Meanings of Auditory Verbal Hallucinations*, Cambridge, Cambridge University Press.

McCarthy-Jones, S. (2017) *Can't You Hear Them? The Science and Significance of Hearing Voices*, London, Jessica Kingsley.

McCarthy-Jones, S., Thomas, N., Strauss, C., Dodgson, G., Jones, N., Woods, A. et al. (2014a) Better Than Mermaids and Stray Dogs? Subtyping Auditory Verbal Hallucinations and Its Implications for Research and Practice. *Schizophrenia Bulletin*, 40 Suppl 4, S275–S284.

McCarthy-Jones, S., Trauer, T., MacKinnon, A., Sims, E., Thomas, N. & Copolov, D. L. (2014b) A New Phenomenological Survey of Auditory Hallucinations: Evidence for Subtypes and Implications for Theory and Practice. *Schizophrenia Bulletin*, 40, 231–235.

McCarthy-Jones, S., Waegeli, A. & Watkins, J. (2013) Spirituality and Hearing Voices: Considering the Relation. *Psychosis*, 5, 247–258.

McGilchrist, I. (2009) *The Master and His Emissary*, New Haven, CT, Yale University Press.

McGinn, B. (1991) *The Foundations of Mysticism: Origins to the Fifth Century*, London, SCM Press.

McGinn, B. (1994) *The Growth of Mysticism: Gregory the Great Through the 12th Century*, New York, Crossroad.

McGinn, B. (1998) *The Flowering of Mysticism: Men and Women in the New Mysticism – 1200–1350*, New York, Crossroad.

McGinn, B. (2007) *Visio Dei*: Seeing God in Medieval Theology and Mysticism. In Muessig, C. & Putter, A. (Eds.) *Envisaging Heaven in the Middle Ages*. London, Routledge. 15–33.

McGinn, B. (2012) *The Varieties of Vernacular Mysticism 1350–1550*, New York, Crossroad.

McGinn, B. (2013) Late Medieval Mystics. In Gavrilyuk, P. L. & Coakley, S. (Eds.) *The Spiritual Senses: Perceiving God in Western Christianity*. Cambridge, Cambridge University Press. 190–209.

McGinn, B. (2015) Mysticism and the Reformation: A Brief Survey. *Acta Theologica*, 35, 50–65.

McGinn, B. (2016) *Mysticism in the Reformation: 1500–1650. Part 1*, New York, Crossroad.

McGinn, B. (2017) *Mysticism in the Golden Age of Spain 1500–1650*, New York, Herder & Herder.

McHargue, M. (2016) *Finding God in the Waves: How I Lost My Faith and Found It Again Through Science*, London, Hodder & Stoughton.

McIlwain, J. T. (1984) The "Bodelye Syeknes" of Julian of Norwich. *Journal of Medieval History*, 10, 167–180.

McInroy, M. (2013) Karl Rahner and Hans Urs Von Balthasar. In Gavrilyuk, P. L. & Coakley, S. (Eds.) *The Spiritual Senses: Perceiving God in Western Christianity*. Cambridge, Cambridge University Press. 257–274.

McKane, W. (1995) *A Late Harvest: Reflections on the Old Testament*, Edinburgh, T&T Clark.

McKenna, B. & Libersat, H. (1987) *Miracles Do Happen*, Dublin, Veritas.

McKinnon, A. M. (2002) Sociological Definitions, Language Games, and the "Essence" of Religion. *Method & Theory in the Study of Religion*, 14, 61–83.

Meggitt, J. J. (2007) Psychology and the Historical Jesus. In Watts, F. (Ed.) *Jesus and Psychology*. London, Darton, Longman and Todd. 16–26.

Meier, J. P. (1994) *A Marginal Jew: Rethinking the Historical Jesus*, New York, Doubleday.

Menezes, A., Jr & Moreira-Almeida, A. (2010) Religion, Spirituality, and Psychosis. *Current Psychiatry Reports*, 12, 174–179.

Merton, T. (1988) *A Vow of Conversation*, Basingstoke, The Lamp Press.

Michaels, J. R. (1981) *Servant and Son*, Atlanta, GA, John Knox.

Miller, J. W. (1997) *Jesus at Thirty: A Psychological and Historical Portrait*, Minneapolis, MN, Fortress Press.

Miller, W. R. & C'de Baca, J. (2001) *Quantum Change*, New York, Guilford.

Millham, A. & Easton, S. (1998) Prevalence of Auditory Hallucinations in Nurses in Mental Health. *Journal of Psychiatric and Mental Health Nursing*, 5, 95–99.

Moberly, R. W. L. (2006) *Prophecy and Discernment*, Cambridge, Cambridge University Press.

Modinos, G., Costafreda, S. G., Van Tol, M. J., Mcguire, P. K., Aleman, A. & Allen, P. (2013) Neuroanatomy of Auditory Verbal Hallucinations in Schizophrenia: A Quantitative Meta-Analysis of Voxel-Based Morphometry Studies. *Cortex*, 49, 1046–1055.

Mohr, S., Borras, L., Rieben, I., Betrisey, C., Gillieron, C., Brandt, P. Y. et al. (2010) Evolution of Spirituality and Religiousness in Chronic Schizophrenia or Schizo-Affective Disorders: A 3-Years Follow-up Study. *Social Psychiatry and Psychiatric Epidemiology*, 45, 1095–1103.

Mohr, S., Brandt, P.-Y., Borras, L., Gilliéron, C. & Huguelet, P. (2006) Toward an Integration of Spirituality and Religiousness into the Psychosocial Dimension of Schizophrenia. *American Journal of Psychiatry*, 163, 1952–1959.

Mohr, S., Perroud, N., Gillieron, C., Brandt, P.-Y., Rieben, I., Borras, L. & Huguelet, P. (2011) Spirituality and Religiousness as Predictive Factors of Outcome in Schizophrenia and Schizo-Affective Disorders. *Psychiatry Research*, 186, 177–182.

Montefiore, H. (1995) *Oh God, What Next?*, London, Hodder & Stoughton.

Montefiore, H. (2002) *The Paranormal: A Bishop Investigates*, Peterborough, UK, Upfront.

Morea, P. (1997) *In Search of Personality*, London, SCM Press.

Moseley, P., Fernyhough, C. & Ellison, A. (2013) Auditory Verbal Hallucinations as Atypical Inner Speech Monitoring, and the Potential of Neurostimulation as a Treatment Option. *Neuroscience & Biobehavioral Reviews*, 37, 2794–2805.

Moulton, P. P. (Ed.) (1989) *The Journal and Major Essays of John Woolman*, Richmond, IN, Friends United Press.

Mowinckel, S. (1935) Ecstatic Experience and Rational Elaboration in Old Testament Prophecy. *Acta Orientalia*, 13, 264–291.

Mueser, K., Bellack, A. & Brady, E. (1990) Hallucinations in Schizophrenia. *Acta Psychiatrica Scandinavica*, 82, 26–29.

Murphy, H. B. M., Wittkower, E. D., Fried, J. & Ellenberger, H. (1963) A Cross-Cultural Survey of Schizophrenic Symptomatology. *International Journal of Social Psychiatry*, 9, 237–249.

Murray, E. D., Cunningham, M. G. & Price, B. H. (2012) The Role of Psychotic Disorders in Religious History Considered. *Journal of Neuropsychiatry and Clinical Neurosciences*, 24, 410–426.

Nayani, T. H. & David, A. S. (1996) The Auditory Hallucination: A Phenomenological Survey *Psychological Medicine*, 26, 177–189.

Nayler, J. (1716) *A Collection of Sundry Books, Epistles and Papers Written by James Nayler, Some of Which Were Never before Printed, with and Impartial Relation of the Most Remarkable Transactions Relating to His Life*, London, J. Sowle.

Ndetei, D. M. & Singh, A. (1983) Hallucinations in Kenyan Schizophrenics. *Acta Psychiatrica Scandinavica*, 67, 144–147.

Ndetei, D. M. & Vadher, A. (1984) A Comparative Cross-Cultural Study of the Frequencies of Hallucination in Schizophrenia. *Acta Psychiatrica Scandinavica*, 70, 545–549.

Neal, M. C. (2014) *To Heaven and Back: A Doctor's Extraordinary Account of Her Death, Heaven, Angels, and Life Again*, Colorado Springs, Waterbrook Press.

Neihardt, J. G. & Deloria, V. (1979) *Black Elk Speaks*, Lincoln, University of Nebraska Press.

Nickalls, J. L. (Ed.) (1975) *Journal of George Fox*, London, Religious Society of Friends.

Nielsen, T. (2007) Felt Presence: Paranoid Delusion or Hallucinatory Social Imagery? *Consciousness and Cognition*, 16, 975–983, discussion 984–991.

Nigosian, S. (2015) *The Middle Eastern Founders of Religion: Moses, Jesus, Muhammad, Zoroaster, and Bahá'u'lláh*, Eastbourne, UK, Sussex Academic Press.

Nineham, D. E. (1963) *Saint Mark*, London, Penguin.

Nissinen, M. (2000) Spoken, Written, Quoted, and Invented: Orality and Writtenness in Ancient Near Eastern Prophecy. In Ben Zvi, E. & Floyd, M. H. (Eds.) *Writings and Speech in Israelite and Ancient near Eastern Prophecy*. Atlanta, GA, Society of Biblical Literature. 235–271.

Oates, S. B. (1998) *Let the Trumpet Sound: A Life of Martin Luther King*, Edinburgh, Payback.

Obbink, H. T. (1939) The Forms of Prophetism. *Hebrew Union College Annual*, 14, 23–28.

O'Collins, G. (2011) The Resurrection and Bereavement Experiences. *Irish Theological Quarterly*, 76, 224–237.

O'Collins, G. (2016) *Revelation: Towards a Christian Interpretation of God's Self-Revelation in Jesus Christ*, Oxford, Oxford University Press.

O'Connell, J. (2009) Jesus' Resurrection and Collective Hallucinations. *Tyndale Bulletin*, 60, 69–105.

Ogata, A. & Miyakawa, T. (1998) Religious Experiences in Epileptic Patients with a Focus on Ictus-Related Episodes. *Psychiatry and Clinical Neurosciences*, 52(3), 321–325.

Ohayon, M. M. (2000) Prevalence of Hallucinations and Their Pathological Associations in the General Population. *Psychiatry Research*, 97, 153–164.

Os, B. V. (2011) *Psychological Analyses and the Historical Jesus: New Ways to Explore Christian Origins*, London, T&T Clark.

Palaniyappan, L., Balain, V., Radua, J. & Liddle, P. F. (2012) Structural Correlates of Auditory Hallucinations in Schizophrenia: A Meta-Analysis. *Schizophrenia Research*, 137, 169–173.

Palmer, G. E. H., Sherrard, P. & Ware, K. (Eds.) (1984) *The Philokalia: The Complete Text Compiled by St Nikodimos of the Holy Mountain and St Makarios of Corinth*, vol. 3, London, Faber & Faber.

Palmer, G. E. H., Sherrard, P. & Ware, K. (1995) *The Philokalia. The Complete Text Compiled by St Nikodimos of the Holy Mountain and St Makarios of Corinth*, vol. 4, London, Faber & Faber.

Palmer, M. E. (Ed.) (1996) *On Giving the Spiritual Exercises: The Early Jesuit Manuscript Directories and the Official Directory of 1599*, St Louis, MO, Institute of Jesuit Sources.

Parnas, J. & Henriksen, M. G. (2016) Epistemological Error and the Illusion of Phenomenological Continuity. *World Psychiatry*, 15, 126–127.

Parnia, S., Spearpoint, K., De Vos, G., Fenwick, P., Goldberg, D., Yang, J. et al. (2014) Aware-Awareness During Resuscitation – A Prospective Study. *Resuscitation*, 85, 1799–1805.

Parnia, S., Waller, D. G., Yeates, R. & Fenwick, P. (2001) A Qualitative and Quantitative Study of the Incidence, Features and Aetiology of Near Death Experiences in Cardiac Arrest Survivors. *Resuscitation*, 48, 149–156.

Parrinder, G. (1974) *The World's Living Religions*, London, Pan.

Peacocke, A. (2006) Emergence, Mind, and Divine Action: The Hierarchy of the Sciences in Relation to the Human Mind–Brain–Body. In Clayton, P. & Davies, P. (Eds.) *The Re-Emergence of Emergence: The Emergentist Hypothesis from Science to Religion*. Oxford, Oxford University Press. 257–278.

Peacocke, A. (2008) Some Reflections on "Scientific Perspectives on Divine Action". In Russell, R. J., Murphy, N. & Stoeger, W. R. (Eds.) *Scientific Perspectives on Divine Action: Twenty Years of Challenge and Progress*. Vatican City, Vatican Observatory. 201–223.

Peacocke, A. (2009) The Sound of Sheer Silence: How Does God Communicate With Humanity? In Shults, F. L., Murphy, N. & Russell, R. J. (Eds.) *Philosophy, Science and Divine Action*. Leiden, Brill. 53–95.

Peoples, G. A. (2015) The Mortal God: Materialism and Christology. In Farris, J. R. & Taliaferro, C. (Eds.) *The Ashgate Research Companion to Theological Anthropology*. Farnham, Ashgate. 331–343.

Phalen, P. L., Warman, D. M., Martin, J. M. & Lysaker, P. H. (2018) The Stigma of Voice-Hearing Experiences: Religiousness and Voice-Hearing Contents Matter. *Stigma and Health*, 3(1), 77–84.

Pine-Coffin, R. S. (1961) *Saint Augustine: Confessions*, Harmondsworth, Penguin.

Plantinga, A. (2015) *Knowledge and Christian Belief*, Grand Rapids, MI, Eerdmans.

Platts, D. E. (Ed.) (1999) *Divinely Ordinary Divinely Human: Celebrating the Life and Work of Eileen Caddy*, Forres, UK, Findhorn Press.

Polkinghorne, J. (2005) *Science and Providence: God's Interaction with the World*, Philadelphia, PA, Templeton.

Polkinghorne, J. (2009) The Metaphysics of Divine Action. In Shults, F. L., Murphy, N. & Russell, R. J. (Eds.) *Philosophy, Science and Divine Action*. Leiden, Brill. 97–109.

Porteous, N. (1979) *Daniel*, London, SCM Press.

Porter, J. R. (1981) Ancient Israel. In Loewe, M. & Blacker, C. (Eds.) *Divination and Oracles*. London, George Allen & Unwin. 191–214.

Posey, T. B. & Losch, M. E. (1983) Auditory Hallucinations of Hearing Voices in 375 Normal Subjects. *Imagination, Cognition and Personality*, 3, 99–113.

Poulain, A. (1950) *The Graces of Interior Prayer: A Treatise on Mystical Theology*, London, Routledge & Kegan Paul.

Powers, A. R., Kelley, M. & Corlett, P. R. (2016) Hallucinations as Top-Down Effects on Perception. *Biological Psychiatry: Cognitive Neuroscience and Neuroimaging*, 1(5), 393–400.

Praying Medic (Ed.) (2017) *God Speaks: Perspectives on Hearing God's Voice*, Gilbert, AZ, Inkity Press.

Proudfoot, W. (1985) *Religious Experience*, Berkeley, University of California Press.

Rahner, K. (1964) *Visions and Prophecies*, New York, Herder & Herder.

Rahner, K. (1979) *Experience of the Spirit, Source of Theology*, London, Darton, Longman and Todd.

Ratcliffe, M. & Wilkinson, S. (2015) Thought Insertion Clarified. *Journal of Consciousness Studies*, 22, 246–249.

Ratzinger, J. (1966) Revelation and Tradition. In Rahner, K. & Ratzinger, J. (Eds.) *Revelation and Tradition*. London, Burns & Oates. 26–49.

Ratzinger, J. (1969a) Revelation Itself. In Vorgrimler, H. (Ed.) *Commentary on the Documents of Vatican II*. London, Burns & Oates. 170–180.

Ratzinger, J. (1969b) The Transmission of Divine Revelation. In Vorgrimler, H. (Ed.) *Commentary on the Documents of Vatican II*. London, Burns & Oates. 181–198.

Ratzinger, J. (1987) *Principles of Catholic Theology: Building Stones for a Fundamental Theology*, San Francisco, Ignatius Press.

Ratzinger, J. (2004) *On the Way to Jesus Christ*, San Francisco, Ignatius Press.

Reed, P. & Clarke, N. (2014) Effect of Religious Context on the Content of Visual Hallucinations in Individuals High in Religiosity. *Psychiatry Research*, 215, 594–598.

Rees, D. (2010) *Pointers to Eternity*, Talybont, UK, Y Lolfa Cyf.

Rees, W. D. (1971) The Hallucinations of Widowhood. *British Medical Journal*, 4, 37–41.

Rieben, I., Mohr, S., Borras, L., Gillieron, C., Brandt, P.-Y., Perroud, N. & Huguelet, P. (2013) A Thematic Analysis of Delusion With Religious Contents in Schizophrenia. *Journal of Nervous and Mental Disease*, 201, 665–673.

Robinson, D. N. (2015) Theological Anthropology and the Brain Sciences. In Farris, J. R. & Taliaferro, C. (Eds.) *The Ashgate Research Companion to Theological Anthropology*, Farnham, Ashgate. 73–79.

Robinson, J. a. T. (1972) Discussion of "Cross and Psychosis": Was Jesus Mad? *Faith & Freedom*, 25, 58–65.

Robinson, T. H. (1953) *Prophecy and the Prophets in Ancient Israel*, London, Duckworth.

Rojcewicz, S. J. & Rojcewicz, R. (1997) The "Human" Voices in Hallucinations. *Journal of Phenomenological Psychiatry*, 28, 1–41.

Rollins, W. G. (1999) *Soul and Psyche*, Minneapolis, Fortress Press.

Romme, M. (2009) Psychotherapy with Hearing Voices. In Romme, M., Escher, S., Dillon, J., Corstens, D. & Morris, M. (Eds.) *Living With Voices: 50 Stories of Recovery*. Ross-on-Wye, PCCS Books. 86–94.

Romme, M. A. J. & Escher, A. D. M. A. C. (1989) Hearing Voices. *Schizophrenia Bulletin*, 15, 209–216.

Romme, M., Escher, S., Dillon, J., Corstens, D. & Morris, M. (2009) *Living With Voices: 50 Stories of Recovery*, Ross on Wye, PCCS Books.

Roof, W. C. (1999) *Spiritual Marketplace: Baby Boomers and the Remaking of American Religion*, Princeton, NJ, Princeton University Press.

Rowe, B. (2016) Voices Become Gods. In Kuijsten, M. (Ed.) *Gods, Voices and the Bicameral Mind*. Henderson, NV, Julian Jaynes Society. 54–77.

Rowland, C. (1982) *The Open Heaven: A Study of Apocalyptic in Judaism and Early Christianity*, London, SPCK Publishing.

Rowland, C. (1993) *Revelation*, London, Epworth.

Rowland, T. (2008) *Ratzinger's Faith*, Oxford, Oxford University Press.

Ruiz, F., Roascio, G., Salvatico, G., Rodríguez, J. V., Egido, T., San Román J. B. et al. (1991) *God Speaks in the Night: The Life, Times and Teaching of St John of the Cross*, Washington, DC, ICS Publications.

Sarbin, T. R. & Juhasz, J. B. (1967) The Historical Background of the Concept of Hallucination. *Journal of the History of the Behavioral Sciences*, 3, 339–358.

Sato, Y. & Berrios, G. E. (2003) Extracampine Hallucinations. *The Lancet*, 361, 1479–1480.

Saver, J. L. & Rabin, J. (1997) The Neural Substrates of Religious Experience. *Journal of Neuropsychiatry and Clinical Neurosciences*, 9, 498–510.

Sawyer, J. F. A. (1993) *Prophecy and the Biblical Prophets*, Oxford, Oxford University Press.

Schrader, S. R. (2013) Illuminating the Heterogeneity of Voices in a Multiple Perspectives Research Paradigm. *Psychosis*, 5, 216–225.

Schreiber, M. (2013) *Hearing the Voice of God: In Search of Prophecy*, Lanham, MD, Jason Aronso.

Schwab, M. E. (1977) A Study of Reported Hallucinations in a Southeastern County. *Mental Health & Society*, 4, 344–354.

Schweitzer, A. (1948) *The Psychiatric Study of Jesus: Exposition and Criticism*, Boston, Beacon.

Scott, B. J. (1997) Inner Spiritual Voices or Auditory Hallucinations? *Journal of Religion & Health*, 36, 53–63.

Seager, W. (2016) *Theories of Consciousness: An Introduction and Assessment*, London, Routledge.

Seibert, E. A. (2016) Recent Research on Divine Violence in the Old Testament (With Special Attention to Christian Theological Perspectives). *Currents in Biblical Research*, 15, 8–40.

Serino, A., Heydrich, L., Kurian, M., Spinelli, L., Seeck, M. & Blanke, O. (2014) Auditory Verbal Hallucinations of Epileptic Origin. *Epilepsy & Behavior*, 31, 181–186.

Shantz, C. (2009) *Paul in Ecstasy: The Neurobiology of the Apostle's Life and Thought*, Cambridge, Cambridge University Press.

Sheldrake, P. (Ed.) (1991) *The Way of Ignatius Loyola: Contemporary Approaches to the Spiritual Exercises*, London, SPCK Publishing.

Sherley-Price, L. (1988) *The Ladder of Perfection*, London, Penguin.

Siddle, R., Haddock, G., Tarrier, N. & Faragher, E. B. (2002) Religious Delusions in Patients Admitted to Hospital With Schizophrenia. *Social Psychiatry and Psychiatric Epidemiology*, 37, 130–138.

Silf, M. (1998) *Landmarks: An Ignatian Journey*, London, Darton, Longman & Todd.

Silf, M. (2004) *Companions of Christ: Ignatian Spirituality for Everyday Living*, Norwich, UK, Canterbury Press.

Sims, A. C. P. (2010) Religion and Psychopathology: Psychosis and Depression. In Verhagen, P. J., Van Praag, H. M., López-Ibor, J. J., Cox, J. L. & Moussaouri, D. (Eds.) *Religion and Psychiatry: Beyond Boundaries*. Chichester, Wiley-Blackwell. 253–269.

Singh, S. S. (1922) *At the Master's Feet*, Madras, India, Christian Literature Society for India.

Skodlar, B., Dernovsek, M. Z. & Kocmur, M. (2008) Psychopathology of Schizophrenia in Ljubljana (Slovenia) from 1881 to 2000: Changes in the Content of Delusions in Schizophrenia Patients Related to Various Sociopolitical, Technical and Scientific Changes. *International Journal of Social Psychiatry*, 54, 101–111.

Slade, P. D. & Bentall, R. P. (1988) *Sensory Deception: A Scientific Analysis of Hallucination*, London, Croom Helm.

Slotema, C. W., Daalman, K., Blom, J. D., Diederen, K. M., Hoek, H. W. & Sommer, I. E. (2012) Auditory Verbal Hallucinations in Patients With Borderline Personality Disorder Are Similar to Those in Schizophrenia. *Psychological Medicine*, 42, 1873–1878.

Smith, D. B. (2007) *Muses, Madmen and Prophets: Rethinking the History, Science and Meaning of Auditory Hallucinations*, New York, Penguin.

Soelle, D. (2001) *The Silent Cry: Mysticism and Resistance*, Minneapolis, MN, Fortress Press.

Spencer, C. D. (2015) Quakers in Theological Context. In Angell, S. W. & Dandelion, P. (Eds.) *The Oxford Handbook of Quaker Studies*. Oxford, Oxford University Press. 141–157.

Stace, W. T. (1973) *Mysticism and Philosophy*, London, Macmillan.

Stanghellini, G., Langer, Á. I., Ambrosini, A. & Cangas, A. J. (2012) Quality of Hallucinatory Experiences: Differences Between a Clinical and a Non-Clinical Sample. *World Psychiatry*, 11, 110–113.

Starbuck, E. D. (1901) *The Psychology of Religion: An Empirical Study of the Growth of Religious Consciousness*, London, Walter Scott.

Stark, R. (1965) A Taxonomy of Religious Experience. *Journal for the Scientific Study of Religion*, 5, 97–116.

Stark, R. (2017) *Why God? Explaining Religious Phenomena*, West Conshohocken, PA, Templeton.

Steenhuis, L. A., Bartels-Velthuis, A. A., Jenner, J. A., Aleman, A., Bruggeman, R., Nauta, M. H. & Pijnenborg, G. H. (2016) Religiosity in Young Adolescents With Auditory Vocal Hallucinations. *Psychiatry Research*, 236, 158–164.

Stephane, M., Thuras, P., Nasrallah, H. & Georgopoulos, A. P. (2003) The Internal Structure of the Phenomenology of Auditory Verbal Hallucinations. *Schizophrenia Research*, 61, 185–193.

Stewart, C. (2013) Benedictine Monasticism and Mysticism. In Lamm, J. A. (Ed.) *The Wiley-Blackwell Companion to Christian Mysticism*. Oxford, Wiley-Blackwell. 216–234.

Stompe, T., Bauer, S., Karakula, H., Rudaleviciene, P., Okribilashvili, N., Chaudhry, H. R. et al. (2007) Paranoid-Hallucinatory Syndromes in Schizophrenia: Results of the International Study on Psychotic Symptoms. *World Cultural Psychiatry Research Review*, 63–68.

Stompe, T., Karakula, H., Rudalevičiene, P., Okribelashvili, N., Chaudhry, H. R., Idemudia, E. E. & Gscheider, S. (2006) The Pathoplastic Effect of Culture on Psychotic Symptoms in Schizophrenia. *World Cultural Psychiatry Research Review*, July/Oct, 157–163.

Strauss, D. F. (1865) *A New Life of Jesus*, London, Williams & Norgate.

Strauss, D. F. (1973) *The Life of Jesus Critically Examined*, London, SCM Press.

Strauss, J. S. (1969) Hallucinations and Delusions as Points on Continua Function. *Archives of General Psychiatry*, 21, 581–586.

Streeter, B. H. & Appasamy, A. J. (1926) *The Sadhu: A Study in Mysticism and Practical Religion*, London, Macmillan.

Suhail, K. & Cochrane, R. (2002) Effect of Culture and Environment on the Phenomenology of Delusions and Hallucinations. *International Journal of Social Psychiatry*, 48, 126–138.

Suhail, K. & Ghauri, S. (2010) Phenomenology of Delusions and Hallucinations in Schizophrenia by Religious Convictions. *Mental Health, Religion & Culture*, 13, 245–259.

Sullivan, T. D. & Menssen, S. (2009) Revelation and Miracles. In Taliaferro, C. & Meister, C. (Eds.) *The Cambridge Companion to Christian Philosophical Theology*. Cambridge, Cambridge. 201–215.

Sutcliffe, S. J. & Gilhus, I. S. (2013) Introduction: "All Mixed up" – Thinking About Religion in Relation to New Age Spiritualities. In Sutcliffe, S. J. & Gilhus, I. S. (Eds.) *New Age Spirituality: Rethinking Religion*. Durham, UK, Acumen Publishing. 1–16.

Sweeney, M. A. (2016) The Latter Prophets and Prophecy. *The Cambridge Companion to the Hebrew Bible/Old Testament*. Cambridge, Cambridge University Press. 233–252.

Sweet, J. (1990) *Revelation*, London, SCM Press.

Swinburne, R. (2004) *The Existence of God*, Oxford, Oxford University Press.

Swinburne, R. (2007) *Revelation: From Metaphor to Analogy*, Oxford, Oxford University Press.

Tandon, R. (2016) Conceptualizing Psychotic Disorders: Don't Throw the Baby out With the Bathwater. *World Psychiatry*, 15, 133–134.

Taves, A. (2011) Special Things as Building Blocks of Religions. In Orsi, R. A. (Ed.) *Special Things as Building Blocks of Religions*. Cambridge, Cambridge University Press. 58–83.

Taves, A. & Asprem, E. (2017) Experience as Event: Event Cognition and the Study of (Religious) Experiences. *Religion, Brain & Behavior*, 7, 43–62.

Taylor, C. (1989) *Sources of the Self: The Making of the Modern Identity*, Cambridge, Cambridge University Press.

Taylor, J. H. (Ed.) (1982) *St Augustine: The Literal Meaning of Genesis*, vol. 2, *Books 7–12*, New York, Newman.

Taylor, T. (2003) *Bernadette of Lourdes: Her Life, Death and Visions*, London, Burns & Oates.

Thalbourne, M. A. & Delin, P. S. (1994) A Common Thread Underlying Belief in the Paranormal, Creative Personality, Mystical Experience and Psychopathology. *Journal of Parapsychology*, 58, 3–38.

Thermos, V. (2002) *In Search of the Person: "True" and "False" Self According to Donald Winnicott and St. Gregory Palamas*, Montreal, Alexander Press.

Thomas, N., Hayward, M., Peters, E., Van Der Gaag, M., Bentall, R. P., Jenner, J. et al. (2014) Psychological Therapies for Auditory Hallucinations (Voices): Current Status and Key Directions for Future Research. *Schizophrenia Bulletin*, 40 Suppl 4, S202–S212.

Thomas, S. (2004) *Voices: Divinity or Insanity?* Tigard, OR, Purple Pixie.

Tien, A. Y. (1991) Distributions of Hallucinations in the Population. *Social Psychiatry and Psychiatric Epidemiology*, 26, 287–292.

Tracy, T. F. (2006) Theologies of Divine Action. In Clayton, P. & Simpson, Z. (Eds.) *The Oxford Handbook of Religion and Science*. Oxford, Oxford University Press. 596–611.

Tucker, G. M. (1978) Prophetic Speech. *Interpretation*, 32, 31–45.

Turner, G. (2017) *That Other Voice: In Search of a God Who Speaks*, London, Darton, Longman & Todd.

Van Os, J., Linscott, R. J., Myin-Germeys, I., Delespaul, P. & Krabbendam, L. (2009) A Systematic Review and Meta-Analysis of the Psychosis Continuum: Evidence for a Psychosis Proneness–Persistence–Impairment Model of Psychotic Disorder. *Psychological Medicine*, 39, 179–195.

Van Os, J. & Reininghaus, U. (2016) Psychosis as a Transdiagnostic and Extended Phenotype in the General Population. *World Psychiatry*, 15, 118–124.

Vanhoozer, K. J. (2010) *Remythologizing Theology*, Cambridge, Cambridge University Press.

Verdoux, H., Maurice-Tison, S., Gay, B., Os, J. V., Salamon, R. & Bourgeois, M. L. (1998) A Survey of Delusional Ideation in Primary-Care Patients. *Psychological Medicine*, 28, 127–134.

Viljoen, F. P. (2012) Interpreting the *Visio Dei* in Matthew 5:8. *HTS Teologiese Studies/Theological Studies*, 68(1), 1–7.

Visala, A. (2015) Theological Anthropology and the Cognitive Sciences. In Farris, J. R. & Taliaferro, C. (Eds.) *The Ashgate Research Companion to Theological Anthropology*. Farnham, Ashgate. 57–71.

Wahass, S. & Kent, G. (1997) Coping With Auditory Hallucinations: A Cross-Cultural Comparison between Western (British) and Non-Western (Saudi-Arabian) Patients. *Journal of Nervous and Mental Disease*, 185, 664–668.

Waldron, R. (2007) *Thomas Merton: Master of Attention*, London, Darton, Longman & Todd.

Walsh, C. (2007) *The Cult of St Katherine of Alexandria in Early Medieval Europe*, Aldershot, UK, Ashgate.

Ward, B. (2003) *The Desert Fathers: Sayings of the Early Christian Monks*, London, Penguin.

Ward, K. (1994) *Religion and Revelation*, Oxford, Oxford University Press.

Ward, K. (2007) *Divine Action: Examining God's Role in an Open and Emergent Universe*, Philadelphia, PA, Templeton.

Ward, K. (2008) Divine Action in an Emergent Cosmos. In Russell, R. J., Murphy, N. & Stoeger, W. R. (Eds.) *Scientific Perspectives on Divine Action: Twenty Years of Challenge and Progress*. Vatican City, Vatican Observatory. 285–298.

Waters, F. & Fernyhough, C. (2017) Hallucinations: A Systematic Review of Points of Similarity and Difference across Diagnostic Classes. *Schizophrenia Bulletin*, 43, 32–43.

Watkins, J. (2008) *Hearing Voices: A Common Human Experience*, South Yarra, Melbourne, VIC, Michelle Anderson.

Watkins, M. (2000) *Invisible Guests: The Development of Imaginal Dialogues*, Putnam, CT, Spring Publications.

Watts, F. (1999) Cognitive Neuroscience and Religious Consciousness. In Russell, R. J., Murphy, N., Meyering, T. C. & Arbib, M. A. (Eds.) *Neuroscience and the Person: Scientific Perspectives on Divine Action*. Vatican City, Vatican Observatory. 327–346.

Watts, F. (Ed.) (2007) *Jesus and Psychology*, Philadelphia, PA, Templeton.

Watts, J. D. W. (2005) *Isaiah 1–33*, Nashville, TN, Thomas Nelson.

Westermann, C. (1961) *The Praise of God in the Psalms*, Richmond, VA, John Knox.

Westermann, C. (1967) *Basic Forms of Prophetic Speech*, London, Lutterworth.

Wiebe, P. H. (1997) *Visions of Jesus: Direct Encounters From the New Testament to Today*, New York, Oxford University Press.

Wieseltier, L. (1987) Leviticus. In Rosenberg, D. (Ed.) *Congregation: Contemporary Writers Read the Jewish Bible*. San Diego, Harcourt Brace Jovanovich. 27–38.

Wiethaus, U. (Ed.) (2002) *Agnes Blannbekin, Viennese Beguine: Life and Revelations*, Cambridge, D. S. Brewer.

Wiles, M. (1986) *God's Action in the World: The Bampton Lectures for 1986*, London, SCM Press.

Wilkinson, S. (2014) Accounting for the Phenomenology and Varieties of Auditory Verbal Hallucination Within a Predictive Processing Framework. *Consciousness and Cognition*, 30, 142–155.

Wilkinson, S. & Alderson-Day, B. (2015) Voices and Thoughts in Psychosis: An Introduction. *Review of Philosophy and Psychology*.

Wilkinson, S. & Bell, V. (2016) The Representation of Agents in Auditory Verbal Hallucinations. *Mind & Language*, 31, 104–126.

Willard, D. (1999) *Hearing God: Building an Intimate Relationship with the Creator*, London, Fount.

Williamson, S. C. (2016) *Hearing God in Conversation: How to Recognise His Voice Everywhere*, Grand Rapids, MI, Kregel.

Wilson, R. R. (1979) Prophecy and Ecstasy: A Reexamination. *Journal of Biblical Literature*, 98, 321–337.

Wilson, R. R. (1980) *Prophecy and Society in Ancient Israel*, Philadelphia, PA, Fortress Press.

Windeatt, B. A. (Ed.) (1994) *The Book of Margery Kempe*, London, Penguin.

Winkworth, M., Marnau, M. & Bouyer, L. (1993) *Gertrude of Helfta: The Herald of Divine Love*, New York, Paulist Press.

Wolterstorff, N. (1994) *Divine Discourse: Philosophical Reflections on the Claim That God Speaks*, Cambridge, Cambridge University Press.

Wood, L. J. (1979) *The Prophets of Israel*, Grand Rapids, MI, Baker Book House.

Woods, A. (2013) The Voice Hearer. *Journal of Mental Health*, 22, 263–270.

Woods, A., Jones, N., Alderson-Day, B., Callard, F. & Fernyhough, C. (2015) Experiences of Hearing Voices: Analysis of a Novel Phenomenological Survey. *Lancet Psychiatry*, 2(4), 323–331.

Woods, A., Jones, N., Bernini, M., Callard, F., Alderson-Day, B., Badcock, J. C. et al. (2014) Interdisciplinary Approaches to the Phenomenology of Auditory Verbal Hallucinations. *Schizophrenia Bulletin*, 40 (Suppl 4), S246–S254.

Wright, N. T. (2003) *The Resurrection of the Son of God*, London, SPCK Publishing.

Wynn, M. (2017) Tradition. In Abraham, W. J. & Aquino, F. D. (Eds.) *The Epistemology of Theology*. Oxford, Oxford University Press. 126–140.

Yip, K.-S. (2003) Traditional Chinese Religious Beliefs and Supersitions in Delusions and Hallucinations of Chinese Schizophrenic Patients. *International Journal of Social Psychiatry*, 49, 97–111.

Zhuo, C., Zhu, J., Qin, W., Qu, H., Ma, X. & Yu, C. (2017) Cerebral Blood Flow Alterations Specific to Auditory Verbal Hallucinations in Schizophrenia. *British Journal of Psychiatry*, 210, 209–215.

Zucker, D. J. (1994) *Israel's Prophets*, New York, Paulist Press.

Index

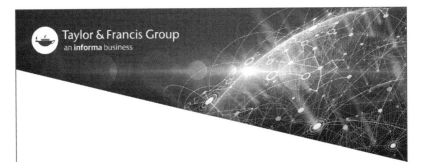

Printed in Great Britain
by Amazon